The
Complete
Peter
Cushing

The
Complete
Peter
Cushing

DAVID MILLER

Reynolds & Hearn Ltd
London

For Stuart

First published as *The Peter Cushing Companion* by
Reynolds & Hearn Ltd
61a Priory Road
Kew Gardens
Richmond
Surrey TW9 3DH

© David Miller 2000, 2002, 2005

ISBN 1-903111-93-5

Designed by Peri Godbold

Printed and bound in Great Britain by Biddles Ltd, King's Lynn, Norfolk

Acknowledgments

My special thanks to:
Veronica Carlson, for graciously providing the foreword.

The BBC Written Archive Centre, Caversham, and particularly to Neil Somerville, whose enthusiasm was so inspiring; Graham Skeggs for information about Peter's Hammer work; Marcus Hearn, David O'Leary and Richard Reynolds for their unswerving support and dedication to the project; Ingrid Pitt and Tony Rudlin, who started the ball rolling; Jonathan Rigby, Mark Gatiss and Jan Vincent-Rudzki who provided constant friendship and inspiration.

Peter Nicholson for his glorious collection of photographs.

For their generous hospitality in granting interviews and supplying photographs: Joan Craft, Richard R Greenough, Terence and Gina Morgan, Michael and Ann Redington, Donald Tosh and Derek Whitehurst.

For sharing their memories of Peter: Roy Ward Baker, James Bernard, Joyce and Bernard Broughton, William Franklyn, John Fraser, Shelagh Fraser, Eunice Gayson, Michael Gough, Bryan Hands, Hugh Harlow, Alice Krige, Christopher Lee, Francis Matthews, Andrée Melly, Caroline Munro, Oscar Quitak, Andrew Ray, Helen Ryan, Jimmy Sangster, Prunella Scales, Ian Scoones, Peter Graham Scott, Barbara Shelley and Madeline Smith.

Also thanks to: Brian Murphy, Leslie Schofield, The British Film Institute, The Mander and Mitchenson Theatre Collection, the estate of Roy Plomley, Andrew Pixley, Colin Cutler, Donald Fearney, Simon Flynn for the picture on page 169, David Howe, Stephen Payne, Simon Scott, Stuart Targett, Wayne Kinsey, Mike Hodges for providing interviews with Eugenio Martin, Paul Naschy and Francisco R Gordillo, Adam Jezard for interviews with Roy Ward Baker and Andrew Keir and John Walter Skinner for information about the Connaught Theatre, Worthing.

Brian Holland for his sterling work as editor of *The Cushing Courier* and organiser of The Peter Cushing Association and for his kindness in swiftly supplying various films. To Christopher Gullo, for continuing Brian's work with the Peter Cushing Museum website.

Finally, thanks to Mum and Dad, Ian and Graham Miller, Claudia Andrei, Lee Binding, Josephine Botting, Michael Fillis, Richard Flowers, Ian Garrard, Derek and Michelle Handley, Julian Knott, Daniel Milford-Cottam, Mark A Miller, Alex Wilcock and all the staff of Visual Imagination.

Cover images: The Kobal Collection
Frontispiece: 1955 portrait by Count Zichy

Contents

Foreword

'I am here to talk about Peter Cushing.' My opening statement at a convention in Washington in 1999 brought the house down. Such cheering, whistling and prolonged applause! I am delighted to introduce this fine book, and honoured to once more say that 'I am here to talk about Peter Cushing.'

My first meeting with Peter was fleeting, during Hammer's presentation of the Queen's Award To Industry in 1968. Less than a year later we were reunited when I was cast as Anna in *Frankenstein Must Be Destroyed*.

Any nervousness I may have felt about joining the long-established partnership Peter shared with director Terence Fisher was dispelled when Peter greeted me with a slight bow and kissed the back of my hand.

The filming of my character's death scene says much about Peter's meticulous approach to his craft. 'I've been giving this a lot of thought,' he told Terry Fisher. 'Anna will hopefully still be holding the scalpel with which she inflicted a mortal wound on Brandt. I could simply take her hand, turn it towards her heart and embrace her.' Terry, eager to commit my dramatic demise to film, thought the idea was wonderful. Thus it was.

Shortly before filming ended, Hammer's managing director Jimmy Carreras rushed onto the set, clutching a copy of the script. 'There's not enough sex in this movie!' he exclaimed, thrusting some pages at Terry before abruptly leaving the sound stage. The pages detailed a new scene in which Frankenstein raped Anna. Terry reasoned with Jimmy, explaining that there were only five days' filming left. Peter said it was totally out of character for Frankenstein, and all I could think of was how the scene would affect the continuity of my performance. My reactions to Frankenstein would have been totally different were I aware that the scene was in the script from the outset.

Peter took me out for a lovely meal, though the spectre of the imminent scene loomed large. 'We simply *have* to talk about it,' he said. 'I know that Terry will go along with whatever we work out. You must trust me Veronica.' He placed his hand over mine and gave it a gentle squeeze.

We tried our best to perform the scene 'tastefully', and afterwards Peter found it impossible to hide his distress. 'I'm so sorry darling,' he said as he embraced

me. 'Just remember it isn't me.' There was such compassion in Peter, and I loved him for that.

Peter introduced me to his beloved wife Helen at the première of *Frankenstein Must Be Destroyed*. She was so gracious and complimentary, and as we ascended a broad staircase together I noticed she had difficulty breathing. I realised then that she was frail, but I had no idea how ill she really was. By the time I worked with Peter again she had passed away.

My next film with Peter was *The Ghoul*, which was directed by Freddie Francis in 1974. I played a character called Daphne and Peter played Doctor Lawrence. The loss of Helen had changed Peter so much – always thin, he was now almost skeletal in appearance. He had become a very solitary man, and retired to his dressing-room at every available opportunity. The mischievous twinkle in his eyes had gone. To me, it seemed a part of Peter had died along with Helen. I grieved for him.

The filming of one scene in particular is extremely difficult for me to recount. Daphne asks a question to which Doctor Lawrence replies 'My wife is dead...' The tone of utter finality and loss in his voice was absolute. At this point Doctor Lawrence picked up a photograph of his late wife – in actual fact Peter had insisted on using a picture of Helen. This scene was shot about seven times, and each time Peter uttered that awful sentence he became more broken. Finally, tears streaming uncontrollably down his face, he swiftly walked off the set. Freddie Francis simply turned and looked at the floor amid a horrible silence.

In later years I kept up a correspondence with Peter thanks to his long-time friend and secretary Joyce Broughton. When Peter's health was rapidly declining, I dreaded the inevitable phone call from Joyce to tell me that Peter had passed away. 'Sir wanted me to be the one to tell you when this happened,' she said. 'You were one of his favourite people.' I will always be grateful for the kindness she showed me when she herself was heartbroken. We both agreed that he had joined Helen at last.

I don't want to believe that Peter is dead, and I know that I don't have to believe it – this remarkable chronicle of his career, along with the ongoing appreciation of his thousands of fans around the world, will help ensure that he remains alive and well in our hearts.

Veronica Carlson
Florida, May 2000

Introduction

One of the few sadnesses in my happy association with *Shivers* magazine was that I became editor six weeks after Peter Cushing died. A few months earlier, I bemoaned, and I could have interviewed him myself. Now all I could do was pay tribute, and my first opportunity to feature Cushing on the cover of *Shivers* was to commemorate the first anniversary of his death. But I immediately became aware of the esteem in which Peter Cushing was held all over the world, and the great sense of loss that was felt not just by horror fans, but by anyone who had experienced his work. True, the horror genre had lost a champion, but England had lost one of its finest actors, and a gentleman to boot.

He was always my favourite film actor. His name stood for a particular kind of sincerity, nobility and gentleness. I recall the Cushing performances that I have enjoyed over and over again. His awestruck stare at the Yeti in the conclusion of *The Abominable Snowman*; his swashbuckling confrontation with Christopher Lee's Dracula, who is reduced to ashes in a shaft of sunlight; the insane glint in his eyes as Baron Frankenstein when he determines to bring life to the dead. He could play dotty professors and bank managers and junkmen with a finesse that other actors would find hard to match if playing Hamlet.

I was aware of several excellent books devoted to Cushing's film work, but these were published in America and dealt only briefly with his stage and television careers. I felt a patriotic urge to celebrate Cushing from a British point of view, having grown up with my parents' stories of ENSA and air-raids and the production of *Nineteen Eighty-Four* that emptied the pubs and caused all that fuss in the papers.

As I explored his work, I discovered that Cushing had no less than five careers, each one smartly after the other. He progressed from small English repertory theatres to star in Hollywood films, then returned to the stage in London to join the court of theatre's royalty – Sir Laurence Olivier and Vivien Leigh. He followed this by becoming one of the first television stars, then returned to film and became a worldwide star in Hammer's Gothic fantasies. To each of these disciplines he gave nothing but his best, and each step on the ladder informed and enriched the next. It was fascinating to see how each success led to another.

Cushing's very welcome autobiography in 1986 (and its companion volume *Past Forgetting* in 1988) are testaments to the secret of his success – his wife Helen, whom he first met outside the stage door of the Theatre Royal Drury Lane, and who became his constant companion, his encouragement, his strength. 'My belovèd Helen,' he said, pinching a line from Shakespeare, 'shone like a good deed in a naughty world.' When she died in 1971, Cushing said that his life, as he knew and loved it, ended.

In compiling this book, I have endeavoured to speak to people who have not been interviewed before and to use contemporary correspondence that has not been published before. I have been delighted to meet close friends who knew Peter and Helen at the happiest points of their lives, particularly Joan Craft, the ENSA stage manager who introduced them, and Michael and Ann Redington, who used to share trips to rugby matches and evenings enjoying the latest board-games brought back from New York.

My intention with this book is to convey something of the times in which Cushing lived and worked, to show the breadth of his talents and his appeal. I hope that despite the constant and sincere affirmations of his saintliness, I have shown that he was no pushover, and could more than stand his ground when necessary. Here you will find some choice reminders of some classic Cushing moments, and I am sure that while there are new fans for his work, Peter Cushing will never be forgotten.

Chapter One

Little Horror

Peter Wilton Cushing was born on the morning of Monday 26 May 1913, at 'Normandy', Godstone Road, Kenley, Surrey, to George Edward and Nellie Maria Cushing. George was a quantity surveyor and Nellie was the daughter of a carpet merchant. Little Peter had an elder brother, David, three years his senior.

It seems Nellie Cushing had wanted a girl. 'Wanting "one of each" she had mitigated any disappointment in my arrival by dressing me in girls' frocks,' Cushing explained, 'allowing my hair to grow in long curls, tied with pink ribbon.' Eventually, 'father exerted his gentle authority' and the boy was more appropriately attired. By Peter's own admission, the Cushings were 'by no means a rich family. I should think very middle class with just enough to get by. No ... more than "just enough", because tax wasn't a problem in those days. Looking back we always had what was to me a very nice house, and always a very nice garden.'[1]

The family moved to Dulwich during the 1914-18 war and among Cushing's earliest memories was the sight of the Zeppelins overhead. After the war, the family moved back to Surrey, to Purley near Croydon, living near the station and then subsequently at the top of Downs Court Road.

Although there were no theatrical connections in his immediate family, Cushing's lineage included several figures who were involved with the stage. The career of Cushing's paternal grandfather, Henry William Cushing, was checkered, but he was listed (among other things) as 'Actor (Tragedian)', in such exalted company as Forbes Robertson, William Terris and Ellen Terry. His step-uncle, Wilton Herriot, after whom Cushing was given his middle name, wrote and performed his own music hall sketches. There was also the flamboyant Aunt Maude, who trod the boards in South Africa, and the mysterious Uncle Bertie, who was 'banished' to Australia in 1901 – for no reason Cushing could discover, save that he reportedly had an 'artistic temperament'.

Even as a child Cushing had a formidable imagination – from the age of five he drew strip-cartoons, and would earn money from his long-suffering relations by taking them for make-believe bus rides, with David as the driver, or giving Punch and Judy shows. 'Uncle

George Gatenby suggested that we not charge an entrance fee, but make a collection as the audience left. We collected what was to us a nice lot of money and my share was about three shillings – which meant something in 1917! It enabled us to indulge in our favourite comic, the *Gem*, and several bags of bullseyes.'[2]

Young Peter's great difficulty with words troubled him all his life. This made school a trial and his academic advancement minimal. 'Ever since I can remember, I have seen things in terms of shapes and movement,' he said in 1955. 'I have always found it easier to draw, paint or mime something than to present it in words.'[3] His fractured spelling became a sort of trademark, and one that he would use to entertain friends, although his later work 'improving' threadbare scripts was legendary and highly effective.

Cushing suffered pneumonia for three successive years in infancy, the third time developing double-pneumonia which in the 1920s was generally fatal. He survived, but this encouraged his mother to cosset him all the more. Despite his close friendship with his brother, Cushing became a rather solitary child, often creating elaborate imaginary scenarios. From a young age he was enchanted by the cinema, and an early hero was the cowboy Tom Mix. 'Returning from the "Picture House" I would re-enact some tales of derring-do which I had just witnessed, using the back garden as a prairie,' he wrote. 'We had a long garden that sloped down from a railway and I would rush along this embankment, fall down and terrify people. I just came crashing down on bruised knees and cut elbows, but I enjoyed every minute of it. I remember hanging myself once, after having seen Tom Mix being hanged in a film. So I hanged myself from my mother's washing line but fortunately she didn't see me. I suppose it's all to do with imagination and trying to copy what one's hero did.'[4] This boundless enthusiasm for play-acting translated directly into Cushing's later work, when it was his mixture of wide-eyed delight (whether for adventures or horrors) mixed with almost reckless physical force that distinguished his performances.

Cushing took his code of honour from the pages of the *Popular*, a weekly comic which featured the escapades of schoolboy Tom Merry – 'true-blue, eye-on-the-ball, no cribbing and no smoking.'[5] He tried to stick to Merry's tenets of honesty and decency all his life – except for the last one, and he only started smoking when he needed to smoke a pipe for a role on stage. In early years he had an insatiable appetite, but he later took to eating in moderation and became a strict vegetarian. After a trip to the Christmas pantomime, he fell in love with Peter Pan, but as he was quick to point out, the 'boy who never grew up' was, in this case, played by a girl. Sex education was rather more rudimentary in those days. When young Peter was invited to a mixed bathing party, Nellie's advice was 'If you see anything you haven't seen before, dear, throw your hat at it.' David filled in the gaps for his little brother, whom he called 'Brighteyes', by taking him off to a nearby farm for a practical demonstration. Still Peter was not convinced. '"But they're animals," I protested. The wise one spoke: "And so Brighteyes," he said profoundly, "are we."'[6]

'The rod was always spared in our home,' Cushing attested, but his mother nevertheless had a particularly chilling method of punishing her little ones. Her tactics were to sing the first few bars from 'Love Will Find A Way', a song made famous by José Collins in the musical *The Maid of the Mountains*, adding her own lyrics. She would sing 'I'm going away, away, away, across the ocean blue...' and then pretend to be dead. This quite terrified the young boy, who loved his mother dearly. 'Don't sing that song mother,' he would cry, 'it's a

A 1940s publicity still of the aspiring film star

horrid song!' The experience left him, he admitted, with a morbid and unreasonable fear of death. Sensible brother David said that if she did it again, he was to pinch her to prove she was play-acting. Cushing couldn't bring himself to do this, but when next his mother tried the trick, he went at her with a slice of bread and marmalade, slapping it in her face. 'The cure was effective immediately,' he reported, 'and Mother's resurrection permanent.'[7] Even so, he could not bear to listen to the song ever again. This terrible fear of death was allied with another fear of the dark – instilled in him by his father who once punished him by locking his son in the cellar. Cushing was later able to overcome this particular fear by taking long moonlit walks.

At 11, he was sent to a boarding school at Shoreham-by-Sea in Sussex. He lasted one miserable term before he was returned to the family bosom. He was then sent to Purley County Secondary School, which was within a few hundred yards of the Cushing home. 'By the time I was 16, I stood six feet tall and weighed 12 stone 5lb.' As a reaction to his mother's early attempts at transvestitism, he insisted on wearing short trousers in all weathers to show off his scarred knees. 'I even refused to have my rugby injuries bandaged,'[8] he said. The athletic pursuits served him well in later life, however, when he admitted he was rarely in a film where he didn't have to fall or get knocked down.

Cushing's favourite teacher at Purley was Mr D J Davies, the physics master. 'He needed no gift of insight to conclude that I was no budding Einstein,' said Cushing. 'In fact, had he not been the producer of the school plays, I'm sure he would have had me banned from the physics classes on the grounds that I was mentally deficient.' But Davies encouraged Cushing's acting, and cast him as the lead in many of his school productions, which included Sheridan's *The Rivals*. 'I think it was Mr Davies more than anyone else,' said Cushing, 'who encouraged me to take up acting professionally.' Davies also let Cushing paint the scenery, which got him out of lessons and enabled him to practice his slapstick in front of the other children. In the evenings, as well as taking part in school plays, Cushing studied painting and drawing under Mr Percy Rendell at the Croydon College of Art. He would continue these art classes for four years, long after he had left school.

George Cushing was eager that his sons should make a living for themselves. He set David up in an apprenticeship at a farm in Pulborough and then bought a smallholding for him in Norwood Hill. But as for Peter... 'Just consider my qualifications for the harsh world of commerce and big business – top marks in art, nil for everything else; capped for Rugger, medals for athletics and swimming; played the lead in nearly all the school productions; the ability to fall down a cliff without breaking my neck and, just for good measure, an appetite like several horses.'[9] Cushing senior would not accede to his son's request to go into the theatre, and, 'by pulling a few strings' ultimately secured a position for his younger son with the local council.

Chapter Two

The Madman of Purley

In the summer of 1933, at a salary of one pound ten shillings a week, Cushing started work in the drawing office of the surveyor's department at Coulsdon and Purley Urban District Council. 'The plans I drew up were architect's nightmares,' he remembered. 'One had a garage on the front of the house, leading on to the kerb; another highly decorative chimneys placed in impossible positions. Yet another showed a semi-detached house with a bathroom extending into the adjoining house. It was said of my plans that any resemblance to a real building was entirely coincidental.'

Despite his grand title of surveyor's assistant, Cushing found himself as little more than a glorified office-boy. He remained in this lowly position for nearly three years by going to the most extravagant lengths to avoid doing any work. He knew he was destined for the theatre, and this job was merely a distraction.

Cushing's duties included street-numbering and collecting the money from public conveniences. Whenever he was let out of the office, he endeavoured to make the job last as long as possible, then nipped off home if he thought he could get away with it. In the office, he was put in charge of the numbering machine, and even here he found a chance for unscheduled (and unwanted) performance. He would hand-stamp his papers to the rhythms of popular tunes and invite his co-workers to guess what the tunes were. 'Inviting everyone to stand, I always ended these recitals with a spirited rendition of the National Anthem.'[1]

Work with Cushing in those days may have been a noisy experience, but it was surely never a boring one. He was a member of the National Association of Local Government Officers (number 16851) and was featured in the programme for the Council's ninth annual dinner. This booklet contained ditties and cartoons of NALGO members – 'Twenty personalities libelled in Caricature and Verse' – and under a startlingly accurate profile of young Mr P Cushing it read: 'We're very fond of Peter/He has some charming habits/His brother is a poacher/Who sends us fine fresh rabbits.' This seems rather more libellous towards Cushing's brother, who was actually a trainee farmer – it's difficult to think of Cushing, who thought that fishing was unkind to the *worm* as well as the fish, bringing dead rabbits into the office.

Although several years beyond school, he was able to continue appearing in the school plays thanks to the good offices of his friend and former teacher Mr Davies, and he also appeared in local amateur productions, including W S Gilbert's *Pygmalion and Galatea* (for which he shaved his legs). Despite such theatrical distractions, Cushing was becoming increasingly depressed – as he would at several points throughout his career. So, at the age of only 23, he decided to end it all. He took a bank holiday excursion to Exmouth and made his way along the cliff path to Straight Point, 'on the look-out for a good spot to drop off into oblivion.'[2]

It was a glorious day, however, and he was stopped in his tracks by the majesty of the view and the splendour of the surrounding coastline. While taking in the glory of the Devon countryside, his eye was caught by the antics of a little bird, a wheatear, which deflected him from his more sinister purpose. Cushing followed the bird and ended up in Budleigh Salterton, where he enjoyed a cream tea and decided that 'Life was good'. He left his bus fare to Exmouth as a tip for the waitress and walked back to the station.

From an advert in a discarded newspaper on the home-bound train, he learned that there were acting scholarships on offer at the Guildhall School of Music and Drama, so he went along for an interview. He was duly presented to Allan Aynesworth, a terrifying thespian of the old school. As Cushing wrote later, this was a trying experience.

'He rose to his feet as I was ushered in ... and asked, "Well laddie, and what can I do for you?"

My reply sounded something like "I wanna go on the styge."

Aynesworth glared. "This isn't an audition," he snapped. "Speak in your normal voice."

"But this *is* me normal voice. I wanna go on the stage!"

The elderly gentleman uttered a cry like a wounded stag, clasped his hands to his ears and boomed "Take him away! His voice offends me!"'[3]

'I didn't know what a dreadful accent I had until I got rid of it,'[4] Cushing said. He was sent away with a list of phrases with which to improve his speech. He called on James Cairns-James, of the original D'Oyly

Carte Opera Company, who offered advice and assistance. Cushing was then able to marry his vocal exercises with his love of the countryside. 'To improve my diction and practice voice projection, I used to go for long walks over the nearby downs, bawling such lines as: "How now brown cow? The moon in June is full of beauty." I became known as "the Madman of Purley".' Later in his career, whenever possible, Cushing went on long walks to learn his lines. 'I was also given a device to fit between the teeth,' he said later. 'It was a piece of wood with a notch at each end. I put it between my teeth and talked. It really made your lips and your tongue work!'[5]

Mr. P. CUSHING.

We're very fond of Peter,
He has some charming habits,
His brother is a poacher
Who sends us fine fresh rabbits.

An affectionate caricature of Cushing from the NALGO programme

In 1935, Cushing was finally accepted for evening classes at the Guildhall School. 'Never did a more ardent and punctual pupil attend those classes,' he said. 'So different from the slacker at those other schools!' He attended the classes twice a week, travelling up to town on the train and, at the end of the year, he took part in performances of *The Red Umbrella* and George Kelly's *The Torch-Bearers*. These he proudly placed on his CV, along with a photograph which, he said 'made me look like a glassy-eyed juvenile delinquent in the last stages of degeneracy.'[6]

Meanwhile the day-job in the surveyor's office was not going at all well. 'My chief at the surveying office caught me playing darts with the sharp-pointed surveyor's instruments. "Young man," he said, "as a surveyor you give one of the worst performances I've seen. I'm sure you could do better on the stage."'

Cushing redoubled his efforts to find work in a repertory company and the focus of his first letter-writing campaign (there would be several more) was Bill Fraser, manager of the Connaught Theatre at Worthing in Sussex. Scottish-born Fraser became famous in the 1950s and 60s as Snudge in the popular TV comedy *The Army Game*, but as the 28-year-old actor-manager of Worthing Rep, he was using the rather more fearsome moniker of W Simson Fraser, and had a formidable reputation. Cushing wrote to him every few weeks asking for a job and eventually, he received a curt request to come down to Worthing.

'When I walked into Bill Fraser's office, he barked: "Who are you?" "I'm Peter Cushing," I revealed, and waited expectantly. "Look, Mr Cushing," said Fraser

wearily, "I only wanted to see you to tell you this: Please, *please*, stop writing to me for jobs."'[7]

Cushing was 'utterly shattered' by this rebuttal. The sensitive 23-year-old was reduced to tears. But Fraser must have appreciated Cushing's feelings, since he had left a banking job himself at 24 to turn to a career in the theatre. All he could offer was a position as an assistant stage manager at 15 shillings a week, and a walk-on role as one of the creditors in J B Priestley's play *Cornelius*. But to Cushing, it was nothing less than his passport to a new life.

Apart from stage appearances, the ASM's duties included looking after three lots of props at the same time. He had to return the last week's props to whoever they had been borrowed from, marshal those for the current play and find the props for next week's production. To distinguish them, they were marked green, red and blue. Cushing spent the whole day at the theatre, from 8.00 am to midnight, and his digs – bed and breakfast – cost all of his 15 shillings a week. To get by, he made the best of a huge breakfast and, like some scavenging creature, ate what he could find at the theatre. At least all the food on the stage

SOUVENIR OF THE 9th ANNUAL DINNER

TWENTY PERSONALITIES LIBELLED IN CARICATURE BY VERSE BY

was real, supplied by various local companies in return for a mention in the programme. 'I made a point of scanning advance scripts for eating scenes,' Cushing remembered. 'North-country plays were popular with me; they often featured a high-tea. Whatever its dramatic merits, I did not care for St John Ervine's *Anthony and Anna*. The chief character, an American invalid suffering from indigestion, had to be fed on charcoal biscuits and no other food was supplied for the play. By the end of the week I felt I could portray the invalid with more conviction than the leading actor.'[8]

Cushing began to see his name appearing in the cast-lists more frequently. He played the role of Johnson in *It Pays to Advertise* for the week commencing 15 June 1936, Mr Tooke in *Bees on the Boatdeck* by J B Priestley from 29 June, and the police surgeon in *The Man at Six* from 20 July. All these productions were produced and directed by Bill Fraser.

After several weeks, Peter Coleman, who would later run the Palmers Green Intimate Theatre in North London, came to Worthing from Southampton as a guest producer and leading player, relieving Bill Fraser, who went on holiday. Coleman would oversee

Cushing's roles as the expressman in *Potash and Perlmutter* (from 3 August), Boano in *Aloma* (from 17 August) and Kingsford in *The Midshipmaid* (from 24 August).

When Coleman returned to the rather more affluent Grand Theatre in Southampton, he took Cushing with him as an ASM, where he stayed for the next nine months. The salary was higher and the parts were bigger, although if they were not, Cushing did everything in his power to make them so. 'For the small but important role of John Fairweather in *Lean Harvest*, the script described the character as "slightly merry". I staggered onto the stage with balloons tied to the ends of my tie and bottles of gin sticking out of my pockets. So much the "drunk" was I that no one understood a word I said.'[9]

Possibly Cushing's earliest professional appearance as a villain was at Southampton, playing King Rat in *Dick Whittington* at Christmas 1936. To liven things up, he worked out an acrobatic routine which 'nearly killed the actor playing the cat.' Soon he was playing juvenile leads at two pounds a week, which was then a generous salary for repertory actors. There were character parts, requiring considerable ingenuity with greasepaint and putty to transform the dashing, rugby-playing juvenile into an elderly traveller (for *Winter Sunshine*) or a Chinese servant (in *Lady Precious Stream*).

Also in the Southampton company was Doreen Lawrence, later the wife of film star Jack Hawkins. She was living locally with her parents, and on discovering the disgracefully damp state of Cushing's digs, invited him to stay with her until alternative accommodation could be found. The stage manager, Bill Johnson, was another great friend, and one who would appear later in Cushing's story.

Armed with new confidence and a year's worth of acting experience, Cushing scanned the pages of the actors' newspaper *The Stage* for likely new positions. He subsequently left Peter Coleman to join the William Brookfield Players in Rochdale, where he appeared, among other roles, as an army officer in *Marigold*. He later travelled with the company to Scarborough and there were week-long 'special' engagements at Burnley and several other northern theatres.

In 1937, the pinnacle of achievement in repertory was to join Harry Hanson's 'Court Players', a team (in fact, several teams) of actors who toured the country

Cushing in his repertory days (1937)

with scaled-down versions of West End hits. To his delight, Cushing was invited to join the Court Players at the Theatre Royal Nottingham. A fellow traveller on the train up to Nottingham was actor Peter Gray, who recounted his first meeting with Cushing in the foreword to *Past Forgetting*.

Gray had just, in his own words, been 'jilted' and was sitting in a railway carriage like Greta Garbo, wanting to be alone. 'Suddenly ... rumble, crash! The door was flung back and a substantial hunk of masculine brawn ... beamed happily back at me. "Mind if I join you?" I felt like saying "Of course I mind, *fathead*, can't you see I'm on the rack of unrequited love?" But how could I?... My resistance began to crumble, eroded by the torrent of bonhomie from my companion and his disarming candour.'

By the time they got to Nottingham, Cushing had persuaded Gray to join him in the search for digs, and they ended up at 6 Hampden Street, ten minutes from the Theatre Royal, under the watchful eye of Mrs Robinson (full board, fires in all rooms, 30 shillings a week). 'We had to supply our own clothes for the weekly plays,' Gray recalled, 'but a made-to-measure dinner jacket (of superlative cloth and pure silk facings) cost only three pounds ten shillings at Montague Burton's. Tails were seven pounds.'[10]

Touring brought Cushing and the Players nearer to London (the Penge Empire) in a piece with the alarming title of *The Greeks Had a Word for It*. This ran for a week at the end of March 1938 and the following week Cushing joined in a performance of *Fresh Fields* by Ivor Novello. Back at the Theatre Royal Nottingham at the end of May, Cushing played Mr Lilywhite in *This Money Business* by Cyril Campion.

Cushing had an abiding love for the movies and was entranced by the stars of Hollywood. With a little money saved, he decided that he wanted to fulfil a long-held ambition and seek work in America. But he didn't have enough money for the fare, so asked his father for assistance. Father agreed, and paid for the trip, but only bought a one-way ticket – Cushing would have to 'work his passage home'. Most of the Christmas period was taken up with preparations for the trip, and in the third week of January 1939 he set off.

When he returned to England, he would have become, in the meantime, a movie actor and a Broadway star. But by then, the world would be at war.

Chapter Three

Hooray For Hollywood

Thoughts of war were a long way from Cushing's mind when, on Wednesday 18 January 1939, he set sail for America on the *SS Champlain* out of Southampton. He was 25 years old. After an uneventful voyage, he arrived in New York at the beginning of February and booked in for a week at the YMCA. From there, he attempted to contact the East Coast representatives of the Hollywood film studios, and received the expected polite dismissals. Only one person thought he could help – a Columbia executive who gloried in the name of Larney Goodkind. He was true to his name, for he had a contact with Edward Small Productions in Hollywood and, not without a word of friendly warning, agreed to provide Cushing with a letter of introduction.

Also in New York at the time was English actor Robert Morley, who was starring on Broadway as Oscar Wilde. Although Cushing had not met the actor before, he went backstage to ask for advice. Morley told him that he was not alone in wanting to be a Hollywood star, but at least the weather was going to be nice, so he should be sure to take his swimming things. While in New York, Cushing splashed out on a ticket to a Broadway show – in 'the Gods' – seeing Franchot Tone and Sylvia Sidney in *The Gentle People*. It was his first experience of Hollywood stars in the flesh.

The next leg of the journey to Hollywood was to be made by rail, crossing 12 states in five days. Cushing boarded the *Challenger* at Grand Central station on 6 February and arrived in Los Angeles five days later in the pouring rain. During the journey he befriended a trio of college students who entertained the passengers with barber-shop songs. As Cushing couldn't sing or play the ukulele, he was elected treasurer and entrusted with passing round the hat.

'After the stuffiness of New York and the days of being cooped up on the train,' Cushing wrote, 'the crisp Californian air and the scent of the orange groves quite went to my head. I began to feel like a film star before I had even set foot in the studio.'[1] He duly checked into the Hollywood branch of the YMCA, where his 'Britishness' won over the desk clerk, who took his watch and $16 as security for a room. Then it was off to follow up Mr Goodkind's lead, at the offices of Edward Small Productions.

Edward Small was a onetime actor and agent who had subsequently become an independent producer. He was about to start a film with the English director James Whale. So, in a weird presentiment of his later career, Cushing's first job in the movies was with Whale, the director of the 1931 version of *Frankenstein* for Universal Studios. There would not be another straight retelling of Mary Shelley's story until Cushing's went into production in 1956.

By 1939, through a combination of studio politics, homophobia and his own disillusionment, James Whale had fallen from grace since his glory days at Universal, and was in the ignominious position of being a director-for-hire. In 1938, Small had signed a five-picture deal with United Artists and wanted Whale to direct his most expensive production, a swashbuckling adaptation of Alexandre Dumas' *The Man in the Iron Mask*. Filming commenced at the General Services studios in Hollywood in the last week of February 1939 with Louis Hayward playing the dual role of the tyrannical Louis XIV of France and his good twin brother Philippe. A double was required to stand in for Louis Hayward whenever he was acting opposite himself, then the two Haywards would be spliced together and the double removed. In one stroke, Cushing became the King of France. After little more than a couple of weeks, he was acting opposite a Hollywood lead for a princely $75 per week.

'Apart from easing my immediate financial anxiety,' he wrote later, 'here was a Heaven-sent opportunity for someone who had never set foot in a film studio before to observe and learn how such old hands as Joseph Schildkraut and the rest of the distinguished cast set about the method of acting in this very technical medium, so different from giving a live performance in the theatre. Furthermore, I would be able to see the daily rushes and correct the many faults I was bound to commit, and so gradually improve. 'I dislike the word "technique" but that was where I learned the technique of screen acting.'[2]

Best of all, Cushing was in a position to refine his performance before the camera, knowing that it was destined for the cutting-room floor. As compensation for all his hard work, and to at least ensure that his

Stan Laurel and Oliver Hardy, with Wilfred Lucas (the Dean), look down at the floored students (Cushing, as Jones, first left) in *A Chump at Oxford* (1939)

face was seen on the screen, albeit briefly, Cushing was offered the part of the king's messenger (or 'Second Officer' as it is presented in the film's credits). His single line is delivered on horseback, he looks young but not completely terrified. His voice is perhaps lighter than expected but unmistakeable.

This 'new' role involved much ferocious swordplay, so Cushing had to convince James Whale that he had been fencing since childhood. He had never fenced in his life, but by sheer bare-faced honesty he got on the good side of the film's fencing master, Fred Cavens, who taught him enough to pass muster in the fight scenes, where, significantly, Cushing is on the side of the baddies.

The script for the film, by George Bruce, was massively overlong. Edward Small disliked and distrusted directors and Whale saw his control of the film slipping away during endless on-set rewrites. Whale did everything he could to antagonise Small, even sitting under the camera puffing on a cigar, letting the smoke drift into shot. Inevitably, Whale was fired.

The resulting production is fast-moving and enjoyable, with at least a few of Whale's trademark touches, like Hayward's effete, 'sissified' delivery as the wicked King and the grotesque close-ups of the iron mask in which the King tortures his brother. For Peter Cushing, however, making the film was the making of his career. In his personal life, he made friends easily. Louis Hayward found fellow Englishman Whale aloof

and difficult to get on with, but this was clearly not the case with Hayward's English stand-in. Cushing was a frequent visitor to Hayward's home, a villa on the Brentwood heights, and was 'adopted' by Hayward's London-born wife, Ida Lupino. Cushing even tagged along to watch the location filming of Lupino's film *High Sierra*, where her co-star Humphrey Bogart entertained them by shooting coins in mid-air. Lupino, a practical joker, started a story about her 'adopted son' coming to stay. A puzzled columnist followed up the story 'Ida Lupino is always talking about her adopted son who lives in. People are always surprised when they meet him, because he is 6ft 2in Peter Cushing, the RKO actor.' Ida, then 23, gave Cushing a photo signed 'To my son, love always, Mother.'[3]

Although *The Man in the Iron Mask* was by no means a runaway success, it performed respectably against the big films of the year, which included some of cinema's most beloved and enduring classics – *The Wizard of Oz*, *Stagecoach* and *Gone With the Wind*.

On completing his first Hollywood picture, Cushing was once again a free agent, although with his finances now healthier than they had been for some time. In Schwab's Drug Store, a favourite hang-out for actors between engagements, he learned that Hal Roach Studios required English actors for the new Laurel and Hardy picture, *A Chump at Oxford*. Cushing went along, was accepted, and was with the legendary comedy duo for one week.

In this film, street sweepers Stan and Ollie decide that they should get some education to bring themselves out of the gutter. When the pair accidentally foil a bank robbery, they are rewarded with a trip to Oxford. They arrive in a hansom cab, wearing Eton collars, much to the amusement of a group of students. Among them is Cushing, who gets noticeably more lines than his fellows, presumably because he had an authentic English accent, and he looks every inch the star in his pencil moustache, waved hair and rakish mortar board.

'I think they're entitled to the royal initiation, don't you?' pipes Cushing. The initiation involves getting the chumps lost in a maze, and then putting them to bed in the dean's lodgings – a cue for much business with a soda siphon. Cushing gets to play some very energetic slapstick and later wears a huge fake moustache, like Monsewer Eddie Gray from The Crazy Gang. When the students march on the Americans in a bloodthirsty posse, they are one by one flung out of the window by Stan and land in the pond. Cushing remembered that this sequence was filmed in the evening, and that Laurel and Hardy ensured that those actors who got wet were looked after with dry towels and hot drinks. Cushing was lucky to appear in one of Laurel and Hardy's finest comedies, which contains some priceless bits of comic business. Cushing adored comedy – and comedians – all through his life, and doubtless learned a lot from this experience.

After *A Chump at Oxford*, Cushing found himself involved in his longest and most rewarding Hollywood film role, opposite Carole Lombard in *Vigil in the Night*, adapted from A J Cronin's novel. The director, George Stevens, had recently finished the rousing *Gunga Din* with Cary Grant, Victor McLaglen and Douglas Fairbanks Jnr, and would later make Hollywood history twice over with *Shane* in 1952 and *Giant* in 1956. *Vigil in the Night* details the struggles of a young nurse, Anne Lee (Lombard), who takes the blame and loses her job after a fatal mistake made by her sister Lucy (Anne Shirley), also a nurse. Anne joins the staff of an impoverished country hospital, where she finds love with Doctor Prescott (Brian Aherne) but has to deal with a smallpox epidemic. Cushing was asked to play Joe Shand, boyfriend to the selfish Lucy.

The dialogue director for *Vigil* was Robert Coote, whom Cushing had met at a celebrity cricket match with David Niven, C Aubrey Smith and Boris Karloff. 'They were looking,' said Cushing 'for someone who could speak with a modified Lancashire accent that would be understood by American audiences.'[4] Cushing's 'modified Lancashire' sounds a little outlandish and it would surface again, with further modifications, in *From Beyond the Grave*.

Soon after shooting began in July 1939, Carole Lombard was hospitalised with acute appendicitis,

and the production was stopped. In the six-week hiatus, Cushing was reportedly offered two other 'substantial' film roles, which, chiefly out of loyalty to Lombard, he declined. He was also reportedly screen tested for *Tom Brown's Schooldays*, directed by Robert Stevenson at RKO.

Cushing was able, however, to accept an offer from Ida Lupino to join her in a stage production of Frank Vosper's *Love from a Stranger* at Palm Springs. The year before, Cushing had appeared in the play with the Court Players at Nottingham. This time, however, he was playing the lead, Bruce Lovell.

Cushing's Hollywood career was, by any standards, going very well, until the turn of world events all but stopped it in its tracks. On 3 September 1939, Britain declared war on Germany. At first, Cushing did not believe the headlines, 'but this "sensation" was the real thing.' He later admitted that, like many, when Neville Chamberlain had declared 'peace in our time', he'd believed him and 'got on with the job in hand.'[5] Full of patriotic fervour, Cushing immediately tried to enlist, regardless of his contract. He was classified 4C, however, due to torn ligaments in his knee from an old rugby injury and a perforated ear-drum. He failed the medical. 'They are not in need of cannon fodder yet!'[6] Cushing was cheerfully informed by the MO.

Filming on *Vigil in the Night* re-commenced at the end of September, finishing on 30 November, and throughout the shooting Cushing still regarded the Hollywood 'goddesses' as sacrosanct. 'Before starting my first scene with Miss Lombard, I whispered to the director "Am I allowed to touch her?" He looked at me in astonishment and said "You can do what you like with her, as long as you cause no bodily harm."'[7] RKO reported that George Stevens was so impressed with Cushing's early work on the film that he gave him a specially-written confrontation scene with Lombard and Aherne near the conclusion, in which Joe blames Anne for Lucy's death in the smallpox outbreak. 'More than one male star has hit his stride with just-such high-keyed histrionics,' noted the pressbook. And the scene did indeed make an impression. 'Peter Cushing dominates two dramatic scenes,' reported the *New York Daily News* when the film opened in May 1940. 'His acting has the same forceful quality that distinguishes Spencer Tracy's performances.'

After these several successful engagements, and by thriftily continuing to reside at the YMCA, Cushing was able to purchase a car by instalments. An infection in his heel, however, spread upwards and there was a risk that he would lose the leg. A more acceptable treatment was found but it still required several weeks of painful and costly attention. His leg was saved but the car, alas, had to go. Cushing kept busy with several projects, including *Laddie* with Tim Holt and Virginia Gilmore, *The Howards of Virginia* with Cary Grant (so forgettable that he did not even mention it on subsequent CVs) and *Women in War* with Patric Knowles. Many of these were small roles, requiring little more than a few days' work, although the money was very useful.

Perhaps the most bizarre subjects that Cushing worked on in Hollywood were three short films in the *Passing Parade* series, produced by John Nesbitt. These were 10-minute MGM support features, without dialogue but with a voice-over from Nesbitt, illustrating curious events and scenes from history.

In *The Woman in the House*, Cushing plays a character who leaves his fiancée (Ann Richards) to go off to the Boer War. When he dies of malaria, she becomes a recluse and doesn't leave the house for 40 years. In *Dreams*, directed by Felix E Feist, Cushing is seen in fitful sleep – in his dream, his feet are chained to a railway line and a train is bearing down on him. The narration explains that the dream represents the dreamer's desire to escape from the circumstances of his life, but he is held back by devotion to a loved one. Cushing gives a very affecting impression of inescapable dread in this brief scene.

Cushing's most memorable *Passing Parade* role was in *Your Hidden Master*. This related an event from the early life of Robert Clive when, in a fit of despair, he tried to take his own life. But when Clive brought a revolver to his head, the gun would not fire. A second attempt and again, nothing. The third time, Clive aimed at a pitcher of water and the gun fired. He took this as an omen and gave up the attempt. Cushing's compelling portrayal of the young Clive, influenced no doubt by the actor's own self-destructive feelings before the start of his stage career, led to talk at MGM of grooming him for stardom. However, as the war continued to rage in Europe, and horrifying news came through of the London Blitz, Cushing's thoughts turned more and more to returning home.

Towards the end of 1940, James Whale was booked to direct a new film for Columbia. *They Dare Not Love*, a story of Nazi persecution in Austria, starred George Brent and Martha Scott. Although the film was intended to revive Whale's failing career, his fee was only $30,000, and the production, which began on New Year's Day 1941, was an uncomfortable one. The director disliked the script ('curiously naïve romantic propaganda'[8] the reviews called it) and did not get on with either his leading man or the raucous Columbia producer Harry Cohn. Eventually, three weeks later, he was asked to leave and the remainder of the film was shot by Charles 'King' Vidor. Whale would never work as a film director again. Cushing's role was Sub-Lieutenant Blacker, who leads a raid at the end of the film to rescue Brent and Scott. If Cushing did indeed leave Hollywood on 18 January 1941, as he states in his autobiography, then he left *They Dare Not Love* before even Whale, and probably knew nothing of the director's dismissal.

One of the first things Cushing saw on returning to New York City was a banner outside a hospital urging him to 'Give Blood For Britain'. ('I thought "That's all I've got at the moment!"') He went in, donated a pint of blood, came out, and fell flat on his face. He was carried inside again, had two pints of blood pumped *back in* and was hospitalised for a fortnight with nervous exhaustion. 'My first war effort,' he bemoaned, 'could hardly be called a success.'[9] A number of colourful but tedious jobs followed in rapid succession. He worked for NBC radio, in a serial called *The Grandpa Family*, and played Tom Prior in a radio production called *Outward Bound*, as well as participating in several radio commercials.

After a disastrous morning as a car-park attendant (he was too timid to smash the cars into position) he found himself briefly cast as an assistant to a fey and slightly boss-eyed illusionist. Cushing quickly learned the secrets of the trade, such as various coded signals and different ways to hold the cards, but the engagement only lasted three weeks and he was faced with the uncomfortable prospect of sleeping in a flophouse.

Help came via a chance meeting in Greenwich Village with Canadian actor John Ireland, who recognised Cushing from his film appearances. This led to the two actors pooling their resources and Ireland told his new friend that as social security payments had been deducted from his previous salaries he was entitled to $18 unemployment benefit per week. This kept them going until the pair, and Ireland's wife Elaine, found employment in the American equivalent of a repertory company, a summer stock troupe at the Green Mansions camp near Warrensburg, New York State. Although there were no wages, all expenses were paid by the company and there was a bonus of $100 at the conclusion of the four-month contract. They began in May 1941 and worked through a varied bill, including a production of *Macbeth* presented in modern dress, in which Cushing played Banquo and the Doctor.

Other productions at Warrensburg included an Irish one-act comedy *Pound on Demand*, in which Cushing played an Irish policeman, and this was presented with the short Noël Coward play *Fumed Oak*, with Cushing in the lead as Henry Gow. There followed *The Ghost Train* by Arnold Ridley, *The Petrified Forest* by Robert E Sherwood (Cushing's role of Alan Squire was played in London by Owen Nares) *Biography* by S N Behrman and *Night Must Fall*. The troupe were accommodated in spacious log cabins near a lake, among the pine trees of upstate New York, and after four invigorating months, Cushing was eventually able to put $25 into his savings for his return to England.

The Warrensburg shows had been attended by various talent scouts and, as a result of their attentions, Cushing was invited back to New York to take part in a show on Broadway. He had planned to

Joan Carroll as Little Sister and Mary Forbes as Mrs Pryor with the young Cushing as Robert in *Laddie* (1940)

make his way over the Adirondack mountains to Canada, the better to secure a passage home, but fate (briefly) had other ideas. Although he was also offered a part by Gilbert Miller in a play called *RAF*, Cushing joined the cast of the Theatre Associates production of *The Seventh Trumpet* by Charles Rann Kennedy at the Mansfield Theater on Broadway. He played Police Constable Percival, a London 'Bobby' wounded in the Blitz, in what he called 'a mystical war play. It mystified the audiences, the critics and the cast.'[10]

Although this experience enabled Cushing to say, in future years, that he had in fact played on Broadway, it was hardly the most auspicious run in theatre history. The play opened on 21 November and closed on the 29th. Nine days later, world events took a further tragic turn, as the USA declared war on Japan. It now became imperative that Cushing return to England as soon as possible. He redoubled his efforts to raise the fare home and was advised to go to Canada where a working passage would be more easily secured. He eventually left New York in February, sent on his way with donations from friends and colleagues that included a significant sum from Rita Heyworth.

On 8 February 1942 Cushing arrived in Montreal and immediately made his way to the YMCA. His

various jobs in Canada were no less varied than they had been in New York, his first being as a cinema usher, in a pill-box hat and an ill-fitting uniform. He found work with a local studio who were filming inserts and special effects shots for the film *49th Parallel*. The film was being made in England, directed by Michael Powell, and starring Laurence Olivier and Eric Portman (both of whom Cushing would work with later in his career). Cushing's job for the art department was to manufacture miniature flags depicting the Japanese rising sun and the Nazi swastika. However, his handiwork was discovered by a cleaner in his bedroom at the YMCA and Cushing was arrested as a fifth columnist. A telephone call to the film studio soon set matters right, and the Mounties who apprehended him at least provided some reference for his next job, which was portraying Captain Roberts of the Royal Canadian Mounted Police in the Canadian Ministry Film *We All Help*.

The remuneration from these various activities meant that Cushing finally had enough money to sail for England. He joined the crew of the Merchant Navy ship *Tilpala* and left for England on Sunday 15 March 1942.

He was on his way home.

Chapter Four

Take Me Back To Dear Old Blighty

'I sat in a barrel high up on the mast, my feet in 12 inches of rain water. I was up there for six hours. By the end of the watch my legs had frozen and I could not get down. Two men were sent up to rescue me,' Cushing recounted mournfully. 'My second attempt to help win the war was no more successful than my fiasco as a blood donor. When he heard I was an actor, the Captain muttered some uncomplimentary expletive and put me in charge of the ship's cat for the rest of my service at sea.'[1]

On Friday 27 March 1942, the *Tilpala* neared a severely bomb-damaged Liverpool. It was more than three years since Cushing had seen England, and he remembered how his heart fell at the sight of the wrecked ships in the Mersey. He boarded a train and headed for his brother David's poultry farm at Norwood Hill, near Reigate, where his parents were also staying. His sudden appearance was completely unexpected, and Cushing remembers that his mother took one look at her returned 'prodigal' and fainted quite away. Three days later, Cushing was once again turned down for active service, and headed for the Drury Lane offices of the Entertainment National Services Association – ENSA, which the services quickly took to mean 'Every Night Something Awful'.

In charge of the ENSA drama department was actor Henry Oscar (who would appear with Cushing in *The Brides of Dracula* as the peppery schoolmaster, Herr Lang). Cushing recalled that Oscar had been searching everywhere for 'a presentable young man with talent', but they were all in the services, or playing leads in the West End. Suddenly, he seemed to have found an actor exempt from service, fresh from Broadway, *insisting* that he work for ENSA. When asked whether he could learn the part in three days, Cushing said 'Yes, of course.' 'For just a few moments,' Oscar remembered, 'I thought he was an escaped lunatic.'[2]

Cushing was placed in a company touring with Noël Coward's *Private Lives*, the Master's brittle comedy of a divorced couple who meet up in a French Riviera hotel where they are on honeymoon with their respective new partners. Cushing was to take over the lead, Elyot Chase, a part Coward had written for himself and played to enormous acclaim in the première run in 1930. Sonia Dresdel was cast as the female lead, Amanda Prynne, the part originally played by Gertrude Lawrence. Miss Dresdel, born Lois Obee in 1909, ultimately made a reputation playing villainous women. Humphrey Morton and Yvonne Hills played the other partners – 'the skittles' as Coward referred to them – originally played by Laurence Olivier and Adrienne Allen.

Members of the ENSA touring parties were paid a comfortable £10 a week, although anything up to £3 was given over for accommodation (generally hostels) and ration-books were surrendered. Joan Craft, who was stage manager for the tour, went on to be one of the first female television producers at the BBC and still remembers the ENSA days with great affection. 'We toured Army, Navy and Air Force camps all over England. It was all planned by Drury Lane, so virtually all one had to do was to get into a coach in London and get driven off. We rarely knew where we were going, or where we were when we got there.'

The first engagements were in the relative comfort of the fully equipped garrison theatres, but as time went by, and the locations became more isolated, the company had to take with them a wooden framework which was fitted-up on site and hung with black drapes to form a stage. 'We had a carpenter with us who would help,' Craft recalls, 'and the soldiers would lend a hand – but they didn't really know what to do. We intended to enjoy it, though. Because we had the day free, there was always something to see, and Peter would find something new wherever we went. The show pottered along quite happily. I think it did some good because we ended up in some places that were terribly isolated – it couldn't have been drearier. Not that I'd say the boys really *liked* it, to be honest, but it was a night's entertainment.'

As for what brought Cushing home, Craft is under no doubt. 'It was his patriotism that brought him back to England. I think that if he had stayed in America he could have been a very good light British actor abroad, another David Niven-type. He was on a cloud when he was in London. He could hardly believe he was back. He went around wide-eyed. It nearly made you weep, the enthusiasm in him when he got back to London.'

Craft and Cushing became good friends. 'He had the most extraordinary laugh,' she says. 'We were at the theatre in London, the two of us, I can't remember what we were seeing, but there was this line 'I never knew anyone who took sleeping together so literally' and it happened we were sharing a bed in London at that time. There was suddenly this great booming '*Ah-Ha-Ha!!!*' Everyone turned around and it was him. It made me laugh like mad or blush like mad, I can't remember which. He was like a very young person, a child, really, in his absolute astonishment at life.'

Sonia Dresdel had been working solidly with ENSA for more than a year. She left the company in May 1942 and the part of Amanda was recast. The new actress was called Helen Beck. 'Peter was cuckoo about her,' says Craft, 'in the sweetest way.'[3]

Cushing met his future wife for the first time outside the stage door of the Theatre Royal, Drury Lane.

'At the stage door,' Helen remembered, 'I saw a man with an old suitcase listing to starboard and a grubby ancient mackintosh, wearing a *very* old grey velvet hat. It was Peter. He swept the hat off and greeted me as if I were royalty – he seemed unconscious of his appearance. I thought: 'This is the strangest individual I've ever met – but the most attractive!'[4]

'I had never met him, yet I knew, deep in my deepest heart, we had been together before. Tall and lean, a pale, almost haggard face, with astonishingly large, blue eyes, a jacket beyond description and repair, spotless white shirt badly frayed at cuffs and collar, a pair of once dark blue corduroy trousers, most of the nap long since worn away through constant wear, down-at-heel shoes of grey suede. Later, I was to discover the soles were as worn down as the heels, and had holes as large as half-crowns in their centres, also woollen stockings that have never known the comfort of a darning needle. He walked with a slight limp, using an ash walking-stick, the ferrule now a mere useless ring of metal around its tip, on his back a huge and obviously heavy kit-bag, such as sailors use.' (The stick, which went with Cushing everywhere, was christened 'Elyot'.) 'There was an aura about this "beloved vagabond". His hands told me he was either a musician or an artist – they reminded me of those drawn by Albrecht Dürer – and when he bent over one of mine to kiss it, a faint and quite delightful waft of tobacco and lavender water hung upon the air. I knew I would love him for the rest of my days – and beyond.'[5]

'Can you think of a more romantic place to meet?'[6] Cushing said later. They were waiting for the coach to take them to their next port of call at Colchester. They sat together on the coach to run through their lines. 'Helen was word-perfect and soon we began to

One of Peter's favourite pictures of Helen, taken during a holiday on the Norfolk Broads

talk of other things...'[7] Helen had much in common with Cushing, including a love for classical music and literature. She also adored whodunnits and Jimmy 'Schnozzle' Durante.

'I wouldn't have said that they fell in love straight away,' says Craft, 'but they got on terribly well in the beginning. Peter wasn't tremendously mature, in fact he never was, there was always a naïveté about him. Helen worshipped him, I think, it was that sort of score. He was terribly fond of her, but she was just smitten by him.'[8]

Violet Helen Beck was born on 8 February 1905 in St Petersburg. Her father, Ernest Beck, was a Lancashire industrialist, proprietor of the James Beck Spinning Company, at the time the largest firm of cotton spinners in Russia. The mills had been handed down for generations by his family, who, though British, had helped to pioneer the textile industry there. In Russia, Ernest Beck married a Nordic beauty of Swedish-Polish parentage (Helen's mother). The Becks lived in luxury until the 1917 Revolution, when, almost penniless, they escaped to Britain with 12-year-old Helen, who was already set on being an actress.

'When I was four,' Helen told the *TV Mirror* in October 1955, 'I spoke fluent French, German, Russian and English, English the worst of all. When I finished school in Switzerland my English was so bad that something had to be done about it. So my father sent me to Kate Rorke, the teacher of voice production who trained so many of our actors and actresses, and there I learned to speak properly. That's how I went into the theatre.'[9]

Helen worked for André Charlot and C B Cochran, who put on popular revues filled with beautiful young ladies. She was selected from 500 girls for a part in a Cochran revue staged in America and at the age of 21 while in Hollywood she appeared with Eric Fawcett – then an actor, later a television producer – in Raoul Walsh's silent film *What Price Glory?* Later she switched to the stage and toured the United States.

Returning to England, Helen became the English tutor to Yvette la Brousse, who was soon to marry the Aga Khan. Helen declined a permanent job with her in Egypt, opting to stay with her parents in England. She was a secretary to comedian Sonnie Hale and his then-wife, the musical star Jessie Matthews, and went on to join several repertory companies. Helen's previous marriage, to Kenton Redgrave, had been 'disastrous' and she rarely spoke of it.

Actor Michael Redington and his wife Ann became friends with the Cushings in the late 1940s. 'Helen didn't make any demands for herself,' Ann recalls. 'which was bad, really, because I think you have to make demands as a woman. But they were very, very happy together. Helen never really spoke about her previous marriage, because it was so awful. She was very, very unhappy. She had a child, which she lost, and the man deserted her. I think it coloured her whole idea of marriage. So I think, in a way, Peter made up for the child as well as being her husband.'[11]

'Even then, Helen wasn't very well,' says Joan Craft. 'She wasn't very strong. She was very ill towards the end of the run, in Canterbury.'[12] Helen suffered a haemorrhage while staying at Bridge in Kent, and Cushing himself was later diagnosed with congestion of the lung while in Taunton, Somerset. Helen kept him warm and nursed him back to health, a difficult task with the war-time rationing of food and fuel. Soon, it became clear that the ENSA tour had exhausted them both and they were invalided out. Free from one lot of responsibilities, Cushing assumed another. He proposed to Helen.

'After nearly a year of fighting on the stage,' says Cushing, 'we decided to try it at home.'[13] Peter Wilton Cushing and Violet Helen Beck were married on 10 April 1943 at Marylebone Register Office. Helen's parents were the witnesses, Cushing having decided not to tell his own parents, in case of objections. 'I married Helen for money,' he later admitted. 'She had £30 and I had £23 and ten shillings.'[14] After a short holiday in Sussex, the couple took lodgings at 18 Bellingham Mansions, Pitt Street, Kensington, not far from Helen's parents.

Following his de-mob from ENSA, Cushing was taken on by agent Al Parker. Albert Parker was an ebullient New Yorker, who had been a writer, actor and director in silent films including John Barrymore's *Sherlock Holmes* in 1922. Finding work difficult to come by when the talkies arrived, Parker came to England, where he directed short films until 1938 when he became a full time agent. In May, Parker secured for Cushing not one but two roles in an optimistically extravagant production of *War and Peace*, directed by Julius Gellner. Cushing played Captain Ramballe and Alexander I, Emperor of Russia. With him in the cast were Barry Morse, Peter Illing, Paulette Preney, Frederick Valk and Henry Oscar again.

War and Peace was a mammoth 32-scene production that lasted nearly four hours. The scenery consisted of a series of raised levels and staircases, and the backdrops were projected slides – a revolution in the theatre then. 'Hardly any canvas has been needed,' reported *Illustrated* magazine in a large colour feature announcing the London presentation, 'a valuable saving in these days of fabric scarcity. The backdrop may be ... a palace garden, a clouded sky, Moscow roofs, a bleak plain or a snow-clad forest, by the simple swift means of a coloured lantern slide, which gives a brighter and more sharply defined background than the scenic painter could achieve.'[15] This was all well and good, but as Cushing recalled, the slides frequently got muddled, were placed in upside down and sometimes didn't appear at all. 'After cavorting around and about in Moscow,' he said, 'to the music of Tchaikovsky, Glinka, Mozart and Rameau, we were transported swiftly to Borodino, where a mighty battle ensued.'[16] Special records were made for the battle of Borodino; the prologue and epilogue of a Moscow Anti-Aircraft battery in 1941 included actual air-raid recordings. Apparently it was sometimes difficult to differentiate between the war onstage and the one going on outside.

Nevertheless, this was one of the most involved pieces to be staged in war-time London, and it received a hefty charge of publicity. In one photograph of the company sitting in the stalls of the Phoenix Theatre, Cushing can be spotted, heavily bandaged as Captain Ramballe, somewhat the worse for wear and looking for all the world like he had just retreated from Moscow himself.

War and Peace opened at the Grand Theatre Blackpool in June; at the Palace Theatre Manchester in July; and at London's Phoenix Theatre in the Charing Cross Road in August. Reviews praised its scope and ambition. 'Mr Valk's Kutuzov and Mr Illing's Napoleon are notable rivals in vocal power ... and make the artillery seem but a faint accompaniment to their choleric explosions.'[17] Unfortunately, despite expectations, the play lasted just 20 performances (6 – 21 August 1943). As the play closed, there was a rumour that producer Tom Arnold had *intended* the play to be a flop, so that a legitimate loss could be shown on the income tax returns. 'If that was what Tom wanted,' Cushing said 'that sure was what he got!'[18]

Cushing's next engagement didn't even get to a first performance. Bernard Miles was to star and the director was a refugee from Hitler's purge of the Jews. Cushing's part was a civil engineer. He realised the project was doomed when the director asked 'Doz zis mean you are polite viz zer machines?' The rehearsals limped on for a few days before the whole thing was quietly laid to rest. Al Parker looked for alternative work for Cushing, and in securing a part for him in a radio play, so began a relationship for the actor that would last for 50 years and lead to some of his greatest successes. In September 1943, Peter Cushing went to work for the BBC.

Since the Blitz, the BBC had decided it was unsafe to broadcast plays from London, so Cushing's first radio role, in *Mendelssohn*, was broadcast from the Bedford Corn Exchange on 8 September. The programme was an hour-long musical biography featuring the BBC Orchestra and Chorus conducted by Sir Adrian Boult. Cushing's fee was ten guineas, plus two nights' subsistence at 20 shillings a night, and a third class return from London to Bedford. There was nothing third class about the cast, however – Basil G Langton played Mendelssohn and Peggy Ashcroft his sister Fanny, with Patricia Wynne and Austin Trevor as Queen Victoria and Prince Albert. The supporting cast included comedy actor Deryck Guyler and Carleton Hobbs, who in the 1950s and 60s would achieve fame with a 17-year run as radio's most popular Sherlock Holmes. Cushing listed his character as 'Paul' although it was not given in the *Radio Times*, and he referred to the production as *Memoirs of Mendelssohn*.

Throughout his career, Cushing's letter-writing was prodigious. Letters of thanks, praise, inquiry, suggestion, correction and criticism. After *every* broadcast on radio, and later on television – more often than not the very same night – he would write a letter of appreciation to the producer. The following, to Stephen Potter, producer of *Mendelssohn*, is typical of many that followed, although this letter contained a reference to a heartening turn in world events. 'May I express my appreciation for your courtesy and thought in arranging for me to play in the Mendelssohn programme this week. Coupled with the Italian Armistice, it was a most happy experience!'

On 29 September, Peter and Helen moved to Airlie Gardens in Kensington. For £3 a week, they rented the garden flat in a cul-de-sac backing onto the tennis courts. Property in that location is now highly valued, but the Cushings found their home easily because of the general evacuation of London due to the bombing. They had little furniture, and even less money, so Helen decorated the flat with furniture made of wooden crates and boxes found on bomb sites.

The end of 1943 saw the beginning of another long association for Cushing, and one that would help him greatly in times of dire financial straits. He took part in a performance at the 'Q' Theatre, situated near Kew Bridge at Richmond. The tiny independent theatre was run by Jack and Beattie De Leon and was a starting ground for a great array of actors and actresses. Dirk Bogarde, Vivien Leigh, Joan Collins, Anthony Quayle and Margaret Lockwood all trod the boards for the first time at the 'Q'. John Schlesinger, Richard Attenborough, Flora Robson and Michael Hordern all appeared there too.

Cushing's first play at the 'Q' was *The Morning Star* by Emlyn Williams, which ran from 16 November, with Charles Hickman as producer. The fee was a single ten-guinea payment for a fortnight's rehearsal and a week-long run of nine shows. Cushing played Cliff Parrilow, and this was the first time, of many, that he would share the bill with the character actress and comedienne Irene Handl.

The 'Q' programmes are crammed with gems of incidental detail. 'This theatre is disinfected throughout with Jeyes' Fluid.' 'Smoking is permitted, "Abdullas" for choice.' The seat prices range from 7/6 to 3/6, or, if you were 'skint', the pit stalls at 2/6. Although the conditions, particularly in war-time, could be spartan, the love and dedication of the De Leons shone like a beacon. 'There will always be a warm place in my heart,' Cushing wrote later, 'for the dear old "Q".'[19]

Cushing then returned to the BBC for two more radio broadcasts, *Destination Unknown*, recorded on 11 November at Bedford College for producer V C Clinton-Baddely (the fee in this case only seven-and-a-half guineas) and *The Lay of Horatius* on 16 December 1943 for producer John Burrell (for only six guineas). Burrell was on the board of the Old Vic and later directed Olivier's *Richard III*, which Cushing would appear in during the Old Vic tour of Australasia.

On 14 December 1943, Cushing had had a meeting with producer Sydney Attwood at the BBC. 'Since my return from the USA I have often felt a stranger in my own land,' he wrote to Attwood the following day. 'My visit to you yesterday made me feel as if I had never been away and was urgently needed here! Thank you for this encouragement and the courteous reception which I most warmly appreciated.' To further his cause he enclosed a list of the 'dialects and foreign languages' in which he was proficient. 'French, Welsh and German', were only 'accents'. The dialects were 'West Country, Lancashire, Cockney, Irish and Scotch'.

As the war continued to rage, Cushing, assisted and supported by his wife, began to see his career as an actor flourish, but there were still surprises and hardships to come.

Chapter Five

French Without Tears

After Christmas, Cushing was back at the 'Q' for *The Dark Potential* by Joan Morgan. This was a domestic melodrama involving the descent into madness of Olivia Russell, who is prevented from controlling the lives of her son and daughter and tries to poison her husband. The action takes place in the Russells' house near the Crystal Palace, and involves the burning down of the palace on 30 November 1936. For this play, Cushing was reunited with his old ENSA sparring partner Sonia Dresdel, who played Olivia; Peter Copley was the husband and Renée Asherson played the daughter, Fenella, while Cushing played Valentine Christie.

The Dark Potential transferred to the Comedy Theatre with the new title *This Was A Woman* but Cushing declined to join the new production. It ran for more than a year in London and was made into a film in 1948, with Sonia Dresdel and many of the London cast, and it is interesting to speculate what might have happened if Cushing had gone with the play to the West End.

However, during the brief 'Q' run Helen had fallen seriously ill and was admitted to the Samaritan Free Hospital for Women in the Marylebone Road. Cushing was reluctant to leave her alone while she convalesced. In his autobiography, Cushing related simply that 'Helen had to undergo major surgery for a hysterectomy and a lifeless foetus was discovered within her womb.'[1]

After Christmas little was forthcoming from the BBC, so Cushing returned to the 'Q'. He appeared in a play every month or so, beginning with *The Fifth Column* by Ernest Hemingway on 27 March 1944. Next, on 7 May was *The Crime of Margaret Foley*, a play set in Dublin written by actors Percy Robinson and Terence de Marney. Cushing played a character called Kevin Ormond, with Judy Kelly in the title role plus George Merritt, Percy Robinson himself and Ian Fleming (no relation to the James Bond writer). 'The Week's "Q" Thought' given on the programme, shows a hardening of attitudes to the ongoing conflict. 'You are just as safe inside a theatre as anywhere else – why not forget for a little while that you are not as safe anywhere as in peacetime.' Cushing's next 'Q' play was a drama with a German setting, *Watch on the Rhine*, in mid-June (Helen was tutor on the German accent) and he followed this with another turn as Elyot in *Private Lives*.

Cushing tried the BBC for work again, asking Sydney Attwood if there was anything suitable for which he would be considered. 'I do hope you are keeping well,' he wrote 'and are ready for the peace, which I feel is not so far off now, don't you?'

With the autumn came a return to the West End, this time as Private Charles, a Free Frenchman, in a new play called *Happy Few* at the Cambridge Theatre. Once again, Helen taught him the correct inflection for each line. *Happy Few* was written by a 26-year-old Canadian officer who went under the *nom-de-plume* of Paul Anthony – apparently even director William Mollison (who had previously specialised in musical comedies) did not know the writer's real name. The play was set at El Alamein in the nine days leading up to the Eighth Army advance in October 1942, and was described by Beverley Baxter in the *Evening Standard*: '*Happy Few* is simply the story of a young captain with a dozen men who held a hill in the desert. A stretcher-bearer mysteriously joins the beleaguered little garrison. His hands are bandaged because they have been wounded. When the cook's eyes are injured, these wounded hands bandage the poor fellow's eyes. Two days later, these same hands remove the bandages, slowly, tenderly, while all the soldiers stand by to find out if the cook is blinded. When the bandages are removed, the stretcher-bearer says "Open your eyes slowly. Have courage. You will see." And when the cook cries pitifully that he can see, I am sorry for anyone in the theatre whose tears were dry. Yes, it is the Christ theme, *The Servant in the House*, *The Passing of the Third Floor Back*.'[2] So this was nothing less than a theatrical parable and it must have struck a chord for Cushing, a man with strong religious convictions.

The cast included popular Cockney character actor Wally Patch, Tony Quinn, Derek Blomfield and John Slater. The play opened on 10 October 1944 and though very well reviewed, only ran for a fortnight. During this short run, however, Cushing was seen by Elsie Beyer, general manager with the well-known and influential theatre management company H M

Tennent Ltd. Tennent's were producing Terence Rattigan's comedy *While the Sun Shines* at the Globe Theatre. The play had been running since 1943 and concerned the misadventures of an American soldier, Lieutenant Wiseman, and a Free Frenchman, Lieutenant Colbert, who attempt to woo the eligible Lady Elizabeth Randall away from her intended husband, the Earl of Harpenden. On 12 January 1944 the *Tatler and Bystander* had written 'a Rattigan play is fast becoming a good reason in itself to go to the theatre and in this comedy-cum-farce playgoers will not be disappointed. The slenderness of the plot is cunningly concealed amidst situations amusingly conceived and outrageously dispelled, so much so that the plot itself becomes of secondary importance.'

The play's director was Anthony Asquith, who had directed the film of Rattigan's *French Without Tears* in 1939, and the thriller *Cottage to Let* in 1941. He would go on to direct the film of *While The Sun Shines* in 1946. The original cast included Michael Wilding as the Earl, Hugh McDermott as Wiseman and Eugene Deckers as Colbert. Deckers had to take a break after an 18-month run, and Cushing, with his recent experience playing a Frenchman, was just the man to take over. He joined the production at the end of 1944.

Practical joker Michael Wilding kept the cast amused with his antics during the long run, and became a good friend to the Cushings. So too did veteran actor Ronald Squire, who played The Duke of Ayr and Sterling (the Earl's father) in the original run, and who rejoined the production when it went on tour in March. The cast were in Bolton when the end of the war in Europe was announced on 8 May 1945, and Squire was responsible for organising the V E Day celebrations. He had joked that he would see that 'Cushing was well-placed' and as the tour reached its last week, met up with an old friend, Edith Evans, who was about to direct a production of Sheridan's *The Rivals* with William Armstrong. Squire suggested Cushing for the role of Faulkland and Evans accepted readily.

The Rivals was a celebratory production to re-open the Criterion Theatre, which had been occupied by the BBC during the war. Before coming to London, how-ever, there was a brief tour of the North. In the role of Jack Absolute for this prepatory run was Terence Morgan, who shared a dressing room with Cushing and who would work with him again several times in the future. 'I was totally wrong for Jack Absolute,' Morgan recalls. 'I was far too young, so I didn't get to London. Edith had a bizarre way of directing. It was something to do with the movement of stillness. So she stood stock still in the middle of the stage and everyone had to move around her. She didn't really direct at all. Tyrone Guthrie did most of it.'[3] Cushing remembered William Armstrong complaining that co-directing with theatrical *grande dame* Evans was somewhat trying – 'he couldn't see any-

A contemporary cartoon for Edith Evans' production of *The Rivals* (1945)

thing going on "from under Edith's thumb" so Guthrie was also enlisted to act as arbitrator. We always knew our performances were below par if Guthrie popped his head around the dressing-room door and said "Loved your hat, dear."'[4]

The London production starred Anthony Quayle, whose Jack Absolute was described as 'fresh, hearty, and as likeable as a games master in one of our best public schools.' Edith Evans played Mrs Malaprop, with able support from Morland Graham, Pauline Jameson and Reginald Beckwith. Sheridan's Faulkland is a jealous and temperamental beau, forever finding fault with his love Julia, although she is faithful and tolerates his difficult nature. This was Cushing's most prominent role so far, and he received considerable acclaim in the first-night reviews. 'Peter Cushing conspires to make that dreary creature Faulkland both comic and sympathetic', said W A Darlington in the *Post* of 26 September. The *Times* praised 'A Faulkland in Peter Cushing who cleverly contrives to relieve that part of the tedium which the doubts and hesitation of the melancholy lover so often arouse.'[5] 'Peter Cushing raves most ardently as Faulkland...'[6] raved the *Tatler and Bystander*.

Although it was generally felt that the whole show, except for Evans, lacked comic gusto, it ran through Christmas and clocked up 166 performances. Oliver

Messel's costumes and settings were lavish, bringing a touch of glamour to a war-weary London starved of spectacle. The scenery featured a backdrop depicting 18th-century Bath, Edith Evans looked like a galleon in full sail, while Cushing, in his buckled boots, powdered wig and bicorn hat looked very like Captain Pearson, the character he would play in *John Paul Jones* more than ten years later. Also in the cast was Michael Gough, who would later join Cushing in Hammer's *Dracula*. Cushing and Gough shared a dressing room on tour, and in Liverpool their dresser won the pools and went on a spree. 'From the first interval,' Gough remembers 'the pub next door was dispensing free drinks until closing time.' When the play moved to Newcastle, Cushing ensured that the dresser had a forwarding address, in case the lucky man's largesse had exceeded his actual winnings. As Gough recalls, 'Peter said "If he's only won a few bob, how is he going to pay the pub's bill? I dare say we could help, couldn't we?" Peter would help anyone.'[7]

On 22 January 1946, the cast of *The Rivals* were invited to the broadcast of a radio play by the producer David Chandler. Cushing wrote to apologise for his booming laugh. 'It was so kind of you to let my wife and I come to the show last night, and to put up with my noise. But I really did enjoy the show and I'm afraid that was my way of showing it.' There was also discussion about another project. 'I shall be awfully glad to see the script of Frank Richards', if it's no bother to you to look one up.' Chandler replied 'I have now procured a copy of the Richards script from the files. Would you come round one morning or afternoon to read it? Incidentally, I see George Orwell is bringing out a collection of his essays shortly, including the article he wrote for *Horizon* on Richards. Combined with Richards' own ingenious piece, it ought to keep you amused for days!'

'When the run of *The Rivals* ended,' wrote Cushing, 'so began an 18-month period of unemployment. The rent for the flat had risen, ten per cent of all earnings went to my agent and I was now just inside the income tax bracket. Soon I was heavily in debt.'[8] There is an indication that at one point Cushing fell foul of Hugh 'Binkie' Beaumont, the powerful managing director of H M Tennent, who reputedly held unofficial auditions at his house in Lord North Street reclining in pastel pyjamas on black silk bedsheets. While claims are exaggerated of a 'gay mafia' operating in the London theatre during the war, there were undeniably a large number of homosexual directors, writers and actors, including Noël Coward, Terence Rattigan, John Gielgud, Emlyn Williams and Michael Benthall, with whom the heterosexual, somewhat unsophisticated Cushing had little in common. His idea of a good evening in was to knock over battalions of lead soldiers with a pop-gun, a world away from the social whirl of the theatrical cocktail party.

In addition to this, there was another hurdle. Cushing admitted that he was 'the world's worst at auditions, not once getting the part I had read for at those … humiliating sessions.'[9] Times may have been extremely hard, but as far as acting roles were concerned, when *The Rivals* finished on 16 February 1946, the next year-and-a-half was not completely barren. Although not particularly lucrative, there were several more fortnight-long engagements at the 'Q', including the role of Doctor Dorn in Chekhov's *The Seagull* and the Coward triple-bill *Tonight at 8.30*. This trio of short plays saw Cushing in three parts (Chris Faber in *The Astonished Heart*, Karl Sandys in *We Were Dancing* and Henry Gow in *Fumed Oak*) and sharing the bill with Joan Greenwood, who had already appeared in several films, and would achieve lasting fame in the Ealing comedies *Kind Hearts and Coronets* and *The Man in the White Suit*.

There was more radio work and Cushing's first serial for the BBC, a 12-part adaptation of Anthony Trollope's novel *Orley Farm*. Cushing received ten guineas – equivalent to a fortnight at the 'Q' – for each of his four half-hour episodes as Mr Round, Junior. The Rounds, father and son, were a somewhat disreputable pair of solicitors; Round Senior was played by Leo Sheffield, and the cast included Arnold Ridley (who wrote *The Ghost Train* and achieved a kind of immortality as Private Godfrey in *Dad's Army*), Barbara Lott, Roderick Lovell and Philip Wade. It was produced by Howard Rose and adapted by H Oldfield Box. The programme was recorded for a weekly repeat and discs were produced for overseas transcription services. There is therefore a chance that these recordings may still exist in a sound archive or a private collection.

At this time, there were only two radio channels, the Home Service and the Forces' programme. Radio was the principal form of entertainment for the nation, and doggedly cheered the population along with *Music While You Work* and *Wot, No Gloom?* (Home), *The RAF March Past* and Eric Barker in *Merry-Go-Round* (Forces). On 11 December Cushing was back at the Home Service for the *Wednesday Matinee*, *A Fourth for Bridge* with Raf de la Torre. The producer was Hugh Stewart, to whom Cushing wrote the following day. 'Thank you for the kind and helpful way you guided me through our little "piece" yesterday afternoon. Normally, I'm so nervous that my knees knock together like castanets and my voice gets higher and higher with fright! But thanks to your diplomatic guidance and encouragement, I felt comparatively cosy. So much I enjoyed the last few days that I wish they were not over!' It seems that Cushing must have provided some impromptu 'sound effects' for the play, as he adds the PS 'I can also "do" a chicken and a motor horn!'

Interspersed with Cushing's BBC work was the title role in another 'Q' production, *The Curious Dr Robson* by J Lee Thompson (26 November – 1 December 1946). The play was a contemporary whodunnit, set in Robson's house in the Devon village of Clevely, involving such characters as a local seamstress and the village schoolmistress.

As a favour to Peter Gray around this time, Cushing joined the cast of his repertory production of *The Rivals* at the Theatre Royal, Windsor, once again playing Faulkland, and was ribbed mercilessly when he tried to incorporate a bit of stage business he had used 'when we did it in London.' Determined to give Helen a spectacular Christmas present, Cushing purloined a square of silk from one of Helen's mother's old ball gowns which was due to be made into dusters. He secured it on a pastry-board and painted it with characters from Dickens, then left it on Helen's pillow on Christmas morning.

Cushing's next play at the 'Q' was one of his most interesting roles in this period – and is the third significant Priestley play that he cannot quite remember in the 1988 documentary *A One-Way Ticket to Hollywood*. It was *They Came to a City*, Priestley's 'fable for our times'. This experimental, allegorical fantasy presents nine disparate characters, including a bank clerk, a charlady, a waitress and a railway-worker, who find themselves one morning at the gates of a city. The doors of the city open and the group enter – some gladly, some fearfully, some out of curiosity. The second half of the play, which takes place the following evening, shows the return of the explorers, who describe their experiences in the city during the day. Cushing played the role of the heroic stoker Joe Dinmore, a role that was played by John Clements in the original West End production in 1943 and in the Ealing film of the play in 1944.

Once again, the Priestley magic was to work for Cushing. Helen wore her hand-painted scarf to the first night of *They Came to a City* at the 'Q' where it caught the eye of actress Roberta Huby, who was playing the waitress in the play. She asked to borrow it to show to a friend of hers who was a textile manufacturer in the North of England. Though reluctant to part with it, Helen knew that the contact would prove useful. And so it did.

In his autobiography, Cushing protects the identity of the bluff Macclesfield factory-owner who diddled the insurance to build a new wing for his factory, but posterity owes him a great debt for keeping the Cushings from ruin. For the next ten months, Cushing was employed to design scarves on a freelance basis, eventually securing a similar contract from 'Sammy' scarves, a firm who supplied Marks and Spencer.

Helen was still troubled with a persistent cough and was taking in sewing to bring in a little more money. Cushing remembers it was a gruelling period. 'I used to look through my cuttings books, trying to reassure myself that I was destined to be an actor. I had been acting for 11 years. I had soon reached the goal of repertory actors – Harry Hanson's Court Players, at 24, I had played second lead to Carole Lombard in Hollywood. I had a role on Broadway, then, roles in London's West End. Even when the play was bad the critics had singled me out for praise. So where had I gone wrong? Later I realised nothing was wrong. I believe those 18 months of disillusionment, depression, and frustration were put into my life to widen my emotions.'[10]

During this period, there were two more radio plays for the BBC. *The Face of Theresa* was broadcast on 25 January 1947 from the Langham Hotel, produced by Hugh Stewart, and Cushing received ten guineas for playing Blane. The *Radio Theatre* production *It Speaks for Itself* came from Broadcasting House on 1 May 1947 for producer Peter Watts.

When Cushing repeated his West End performance as Colbert in *While the Sun Shines* at the 'Q', he was seen by Anthony Bushell, who was then preparing the film version of *Hamlet* with Laurence Olivier. In the autumn of 1946, Cushing had auditioned for Olivier for a production of the American play *Born Yesterday* by Garson Kanin, but had turned down the role of Paul Verrall because he did not think he would be able to

Cushing as Osric in *Hamlet* (1947)

carry off an American accent. Bushell was impressed enough with Cushing's French accent to decide that he should play Osric, 'that sinister Beau Brummell of the Danish Court.'

Olivier's first film as director was *Henry V* in 1944. He was awarded a special Oscar and won enormous acclaim at home for producing so rousing a piece of patriotic pageantry. On New Year's Day 1947, Olivier had received word that he had financial backing to realise a long-held ambition to produce a film of *Hamlet*, which he would star in and also direct. He then spent the first months of the year developing the abstract look for the sets with designer Roger Furse (Olivier wanted 'a hell of a lot of smoke and emptiness all over the place'[11]) planning the script and the technical considerations. Reginald Beck, Helen's brother, who had edited *Henry V*, was associate producer. Unlike the Technicolor tapestry of *Henry V*, *Hamlet* was to be filmed in black-and-white using deep-focus photography, enabling the viewer to take in whole tableaux as on a theatre stage, rather

Osric holds the dying Laertes (Terence Morgan) in *Hamlet* (1947)

than being drawn to part of the screen by the focus of the camera. Banks of powerful lights were necessary, which made the sets uncomfortably hot, especially for players in heavy costumes and armour.

Filming began at the D&P studios at Denham in early May, on a closed set. This was partly a trick to increase press anticipation, partly to keep the filming on schedule. Because Olivier was already committed to leading the Old Vic company – including his second wife, Vivien Leigh – on a tour of Australia in January 1948, their time was strictly limited, and after a while tempers began to fray.

'When the production started, Larry was a kind, considerate, patient director,' Cushing said. 'But as time went by he became more and more autocratic. At first it was "let's try it this way" or "what do you think about going from here to here instead of from there to there?" But towards the end it was "do it this way, do it that way, and don't argue, goddamit!" We all started calling him Willie behind his back, after the stories we'd heard about William Wyler. But I must say, the directorial method he settled on got great results. Whoever said *Hamlet* couldn't be done on film was made to eat his words by Larry.'[12] During filming it was announced, in the Queen's birthday honours list, that Olivier was to be knighted 'in recognition of his services to England'.

Terence Morgan, who played Laertes, was involved with the film from the earliest screen tests – there were 23 screen tests for Ophelia alone. Morgan also helped with the preliminary special effects work for the ghost, which involved being filmed with a lit electric bulb in his mouth. It was Olivier's intention to play Hamlet and the ghost, the ghost being seen in negative in the same shot. Unfortunately, this proved beyond the limits of the technology of the time. Nevertheless, the ghost's materialisations, accompanied by a monstrous, distorted heartbeat, are exceptionally eerie, as good as any horror film. As the ghost informs us, this is a tale of 'murder most foul...'

In fact there are several presentiments of things to come. The creeping shots through the corridors of Elsinore prefigure Terence Fisher's camerawork for several sinister prowls around Castle Dracula and when Hamlet goes to face the spectre of his father, Olivier grimly carries his sword hilt-upwards, making the shape of a cross, with the same glint of defiance in his eyes that Cushing would adopt for Van Helsing. There is madness, murder, a ghost – and Jean Simmons' Ophelia drifting through the whole looking like nothing so much as a vampire's bride. 'If *Hamlet* had been a Hammer film,' Cushing quipped later, 'they'd say "This is disgusting! Dreadful! All these deaths. Think of the bodies littering the floor!"'[13]

Osric makes his entrance flouncing into the scene with letters from Hamlet, waving his hat, and holding his nose ostentatiously as he ejects the Sea Captain (Niall MacGinnis). His costume is glorious, and the little details like the tiny moustache, beard and ear-ring add an exotic touch to this strange figure. Despite Osric's prancing gait, Cushing still has a noticeable limp, but he nevertheless manages a rather spectacular comic pratfall while trying to bow going down a flight of steps backwards. Cushing gives Osric a tight-lipped, 'plummy' delivery, and the character is clearly a figure of fun, intended to provide a little light relief from the grief and the gore, but he is obviously not without influence in the court. In the great procession before the duel, he takes the Queen's arm with a deferential nod to the King and, for all his dandified foolishness, the 'water-fly' is a conspirator in Hamlet's murder by giving Laertes the poisoned sword.

Cushing's only problem with *Hamlet* came after the filming was finished. He recalled that he suffered an abscess in his soft palette and treatment required the removal of 'three perfectly good front teeth'. The dental work was paid for by his agent, Al Parker, but when Cushing joined Olivier for post-synching on the film, he was conscious of his new false teeth and could not project properly. Olivier moved nearer to Cushing and instructed him 'Drown me. It will be a glorious death.'

While filming was still underway, however, and Cushing was sitting in the make-up room with his hair in rollers (for Osric's flowing locks) Olivier came to him with a proposition. Would he join the company for the Australasian tour? Cushing's first thoughts were for Helen – he couldn't bear the thought of leaving her for ten months. Olivier's solution was simple. 'There were enough separations during the war. Helen must come with us...!'[14]

Chapter Six

Down And Under And Back Again

The programme for the Old Vic tour of Australasia was to comprise three plays: Richard Brinsley Sheridan's *The School for Scandal*, Shakespeare's *Richard III* and Thornton Wilder's 'History of the World in Comic Strip', *The Skin of Our Teeth*, which had been a great success for Vivien Leigh at the Phoenix Theatre in 1945. Olivier's performance as Richard III – 'that bottled spider ... foul bunch-back'd toad' – first seen at the Old Vic in 1944 was already legendary.

The company rehearsed for two months in Donald Wolfit's scenery repository near Holloway Women's Prison. The store was a huge, high building, cluttered with old furnishings and uncomfortably damp. George Relph, one of the senior actors on the tour – and who suffered more than most – said it was damp 'with the tears of all the actors who were never paid.'[1] Vivien Leigh suffered from the damp atmosphere too, and – worse for the Cushings – no one was paid for the entire rehearsal period. Things improved once on board ship. Junior members of the cast, including Cushing, Terence Morgan and Michael Redington, were paid half-wages at £15 per week. Helen, along with Georgina Jumel (Morgan's wife), received £6 per week.

The *SS Corinthic*, a 15,000-ton refrigerated cargo ship which carried 100 first-class passengers, set sail from Liverpool on 14 February. Daily rehearsals for *The School for Scandal*, in which Cushing was to play the dashing if shallow Sir Joseph Surface, took place in the dining saloon, generally in the mornings. For the rest of the time the company were able to relax and play deck tennis, housey-housey or swim in the canvas swimming pool constructed near the mast. In the evening, they played 'The Game' – a kind of charades. Michael Redington elaborates: 'The players would be given bits of paper with names on and then they'd have to impersonate people. Peter was brilliant at it, as you can understand. He used to do a terrific impersonation of Sid Field – and Olivier would encourage him. Eventually the passengers used to gather to watch and we asked them to join in. Of course, the passengers were hopeless, so, very kindly, Peter and the others did these wonderful impressions of the passengers making fools of themselves.'

At the end of February, the ship docked off Cape Town and the company enjoyed their second trip abroad. Table Mountain was unfortunately wreathed in low cloud but – 'the next best thing' wrote Cushing – there was a chance to see Ivor Novello in *Perchance to Dream*, which he was touring around South Africa. After the show, Novello, who at 55 was still regarded as something of a matinée idol, invited the company to supper.

In the early morning of 14 March, the *Corinthic* docked at Fremantle and the passengers were able to disembark after being checked over by the ship's doctor. The first show of *The School for Scandal* was to be performed on the following Saturday, so rehearsals commenced almost immediately, punctuated only by various official receptions. The actors flagged in the stifling humidity of a 100-degree late-summer heatwave, but the prospect of seeing the Old Vic company had already sold out the first night at the 2280-seat Capitol Theatre in Perth. However, the theatre was designed as a cinema, the acoustics were very poor, the actors' voices were drowned out by the air-conditioning unit and there were only two dressing-rooms.

Lady Teazle (Vivien Leigh), Charles Surface (Terence Morgan), Sir Peter Teazle (Laurence Olivier) and Sir Joseph Surface (Cushing) in *The School for Scandal*, as represented by 'Tom Titt' in the *Tatler*

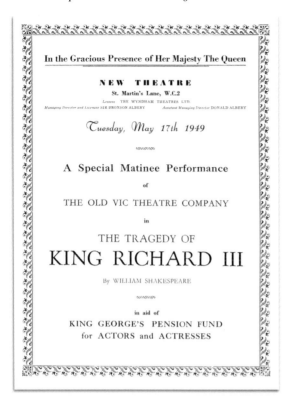

In the Gracious Presence of Her Majesty The Queen

NEW THEATRE
St. Martin's Lane, W.C.2
Lessees THE WYNDHAM THEATRES LTD.
Managing Director and Licensee SIR BRONSON ALBERY   *Assistant Managing Director* DONALD ALBERY

Tuesday, May 17th 1949

A Special Matinee Performance

of

THE OLD VIC THEATRE COMPANY

in

THE TRAGEDY OF

KING RICHARD III

By WILLIAM SHAKESPEARE

in aid of

KING GEORGE'S PENSION FUND
for ACTORS and ACTRESSES

By Royal Appointment…

Unused to live performances, the Australians were generally disinclined to react and the show was initially a depressing exercise for the players. The first scene passed in silence until Cushing made his entrance as Joseph Surface, seized the initiative and played for all he was worth. Everyone followed suit. Olivier wrote 'We were bashing over Sheridan's trifle like *Hellzapoppin*' with everything we knew or had.'[2] Whatever the performances were like, the reviews were rapturous, and after Olivier and Leigh, Cushing led those who received the highest praise. There was praise too for Cecil Beaton's black-and-white toy-theatre sets, accented with gloriously coloured costumes.

Wednesday of the second week saw an invitation to Sir Laurence and the company from the Reelers – members of the Australian film industry. It was a dour – and teetotal – experience, but on the coach home Cushing entertained all with an impersonation of the Reelers' MC.

The School for Scandal was the only play performed in Perth, while *Richard III* was rehearsed during the day. After the final performance at the Capitol Theatre, there was a beach party, and at midnight the company boarded two Skymaster aeroplanes to cross the Nullabor plain to Adelaide.

In *Richard III*, Cushing played the doomed Duke of Clarence – 'false, fleeting, perjured Clarence' – who is drowned in a vat of Malmsey. After Clarence's death, Cushing came back on to play Cardinal Bourchier, the Archbishop of Canterbury. 'It was the scene with the princes in the Tower,' remembers Michael Redington, 'and Peter played that very naughtily. Laurence Olivier used to go up to the princes and they'd say "What's that Uncle?" pointing to his sword. He'd say "Wouldst thou have my weapon?" and nudge the Cardinal. Then Peter would then make this rather outraged expression, and cross himself very quickly. And every night, it got more and more outraged. Pip Barnard and I were holding a canopy, and we got the giggles. And the more we got the giggles, the more this canopy shook. Olivier always had his back to us so we were all right. Except for one night, when he turned around and saw this canopy shaking about. We got in the most terrible trouble, and it was all Peter's fault.'[3]

On the second day in Adelaide, 10 April, after two shows of *Richard III* to ecstatic reviews, the Oliviers gave a party to celebrate the Cushings' fifth wedding anniversary, with oysters and champagne in abundance and dancing until 3.45 am. Olivier was meanwhile preoccupied with setting and lighting *The Skin of Our Teeth*, which he variously called 'the Picasso of our repertoire' the 'Salvador Dali' or the 'Henry Moore'. (The *Sydney Tribune* called it 'a play for morons and lunatics'.) Cushing played several small parts, including a hunchback. 'Peter had a cushion that he tied on his back,' Michael Redington recalls. 'On the thing was written 'P Cushion'. Someone had said "Who's this for?" and someone else said "P Cushing" and that was that.'[4] *The Skin of Our Teeth* was presented in a vaudeville style with the characters deliberately two-dimensional. Though the play baffled many Australians, it was generally well received.

One of the chief delights for the Cushings was the chance to enjoy the local fauna. He wrote 'Our favourite without doubt was the duck-billed platypus, a quite adorable creature. Helen thought it looked like an animated rubber hot-water bottle wearing a fur coat.'[5] Other delights included the brush turkeys, fabulously coloured birds of paradise and parakeets.

The company left Adelaide on 18 April and travelled to Melbourne for an eight-week engagement at the Princess Theatre. Melbourne was cold, in both weather and attitude, and the company were succumbing to fatigue. Olivier's local talent-scouting included an audition for Keith Michell, who subsequently came to England to study at the Old Vic School (and in 1963 would play a memorable Mark Antony to Cushing's Cassius in *The Spread of the Eagle*). Helen Keller, the deaf and blind scholar, visited a performance of *Richard III* and had the play relayed to her by her companion Polly Thomson. This would also have a connection with Cushing's later career.

The day before the Melbourne season ended on 12 June, the Oliviers and some members of the cast, including Cushing, attended the Australian première of *Hamlet*. Then the company was off to Tasmania, travelling to Hobart in a two-engined Dakota. En route, one of the engines caught fire, and the plane was forced to land in Launceston, Northern Tasmania, where it missed the runway and had to be towed back onto the tarmac by tractor.

The tiny Theatre Royal in Hobart was welcoming, but bitterly cold. One of the most famous moments of *The School for Scandal* is the 'screen scene' – in which Lady Teazle is discovered hiding from her husband Sir Peter – and in one Tasmanian performance of the play Cushing remembered catching sight of Leigh behind the screen, huddled in a mink coat by an electric fire.

Plans to open in Sydney were delayed by a cast holiday until 29 June, when *The School for Scandal* opened at the Tivoli Theatre. They stayed in Sydney for an eight-week run, during which time Cushing was invited to take part in two radio broadcasts for NBC Australia. He played the title role in a production of *Beau Brummell* as well as taking part as a guest in the popular panel game *Twenty Questions*.

Critics wrote in admiration of Olivier's synthesis of eighteenth century theatre with film techniques and, once again, Cushing's performance as Joseph Surface came in for particular praise. Oliver carried on as Richard III despite tearing a cartilage in his knee – he used a crutch, which became an integral part of the character.

On 9 July, Olivier received a blow from the chairman of the Old Vic governors, who effectively stated that he was being given the sack as a director. It was the start of the process that would lead to the creation of Britain's National Theatre, Olivier's dream project, and one that he would see to fruition in a purpose-built complex on London's South Bank. However, at this time, communication between Australia and the homeland was excruciatingly slow, so the business had to wait until the company's return. In the meantime there was a performance of *The Skin of Our Teeth* for the Australian Prime Minister Ben Chifley on 19 July.

There was also a cricket match organised between the company and the staff of the Tivoli. Michael Redington remembers Cushing's contribution. 'I was captain of the cricket team, and Peter was in the team, even though he would hold the bat the wrong way round. He was game for anything, but he would have been the first to admit he wasn't the best cricket player in the world.'[6] The company won by ten wickets.

Preparations were already underway for the company's return to Britain, when a season at the

Cushing (far right) as Clarence in Olivier's *Richard III*

New Theatre in St Martin's Lane would comprise *The School For Scandal*, *Richard III* and Jean Anouilh's *Antigone*, which John Burrell would direct. The Anouilh replaced *The Skin of Our Teeth* which had already had a successful London run. There was a final fortnight in Brisbane with *The School for Scandal*, and another cricket match (a draw, this time) before a flight to Auckland for the last leg of the tour in New Zealand.

New Zealand made a refreshing change from Australia – it resembled England somewhat and alleviated the company's homesickness a little. More than 33,000 people attended the 17 performances at the St James Theatre in Auckland and there were similar crowds at the St James Theatre in Christchurch and His Majesty's Theatre in Dunedin. In one of the final performances in Wellington, Olivier's knee locked and he was booked into hospital for an operation to remove the damaged cartilage. He made a swift recovery, but because of his leg in plaster, had to be taken on board the *Corinthic* in a tarpaulin sling along with the luggage. (A photograph exists of Olivier being hoisted between Cushing and scenic artist Roger Ramsdell.)

The return journey for the near-exhausted company began on 16 October 1948 and rehearsals began on board for the season at the West End. A little less than a month later, the company were back in England and were installed in the New Theatre.

Antigone was considered too short to provide a substantial night's entertainment at the New Theatre, so it was preceded by Chekhov's one-act comedy *The Proposal*. Cushing was given the lead in this three-hander – the role of the hypochondriac Ivan Vasilyevitch Lomov. 'The normal running time was about half-an-hour,' wrote Cushing 'but Sir Laurence suggested we performed it in the fashion of a speeded-up Keystone Kops car chase. Once we got into our stride it was all over and done with in 19 minutes flat. It took me another 19 to recover.'[7]

The Proposal was performed in front of a painted cloth with the actors in heavy make-up looking and acting like marionettes. Michael Redington recalls the performance: 'Physical business was Peter's forte,' he says. 'Because all the furniture was painted on the backcloth, Peter had to "sit" in mid-air on a painted seat. Then there was a point in the script when he had to do a big double-take. He'd done it in rehearsals and we'd all fallen about – Olivier said that I'd be better off out in front because I was laughing so much. So on the first night, Peter did a somersault – right over. It was the most amazing thing. He said "Well, I'd been thinking about it, so I just thought I'd do it."'[8]

Kenneth J Hurren in *What's On in London* was not impressed. '*The Proposal*, a brief farce by Anton Chekhov, was performed by three minor members of the cast got up to look like circus clowns. The play seems to have no distinction and I found the break-neck speed of the production both ludicrous and tedious. Several of my neighbours were laughing quite immoderately; myself, I've had more fun with Abbott and Costello.'[9]

However, in the *Old Vic Yearbook* for 1949, Ivor Brown wrote 'Sir Laurence directed, at lightning speed and with a genuine gusto for the broadest comedy, Chekhov's farcical comedy *The Proposal*. Possibly Chekhov might not have recognised his own little piece by the time the energetic players, well led by Peter Cushing, had done with it. But I'm sure he would have laughed freely at the lively antics of the players. We are too ready to regard the Tsarist Russians as only sweetly sad. Sir Laurence demonstrated their scope for robust absurdity.'[10]

Cushing had now been working without a break since before *Hamlet*. The Australasian tour, the added strain of 'carrying' *The Proposal* as well as roles in *Richard III* and *The School for Scandal* stretched his nerves to the limit, and when the run at the New Theatre finished, he was physically and emotionally spent. During the rehearsals for his next job, Cushing suffered a nervous breakdown.

Following Olivier's dismissal as director of the Old Vic, he took on the managership of the St James' Theatre in King Street, between Pall Mall and Piccadilly. The first play to be produced was *The Damascus Blade* by Bridget Boland, about the French Resistance during World War II and starring Peter Finch and John Mills. Olivier offered Cushing the now familiar part of a Free Frenchman. During a rehearsal, Cushing repeatedly failed to understand a simple cue and broke down in tears. He was unable to work for six months. In a typical act of generosity, Olivier kept Cushing under contract – and paid – during this period of illness, no doubt as repayment to Peter and Helen for two years of hard work and devoted service. This was something of an ill omen for *The Damascus Blade*, which was cancelled before it even reached London.

During the breakdown, Cushing would lock himself in the lavatory for hours on end, fretting that he had forgotten something. 'Come on out, you silly old Bloggs,' said Helen by way of encouragement. 'It's no good trying to remember things you haven't forgotten yet!'[11] They started writing notes to each other in a kind of nonsensical phonetic language. Helen's pet name for Peter, 'Bois' (pronounced 'boys') would inspire a series of characters and stories, which Cushing eventually published as *The Bois Saga* with his own illustrations.

1950 saw a happy event for Michael and Ann Redington: they were married and Cushing played a leading part. 'He kept prompting me,' says Redington. 'Things like "When are you going to marry m'daughter?" He drew me a card with an outraged father waving a shotgun. Ann's parents weren't very happy about her marrying an actor, so we asked Peter to give Ann away at the altar. He said "Is it a speaking part?" and Ann said "Well, when you're asked 'Who gives this woman to be married to this man?' you have to say 'I do'." So, when the time came, with every ounce of the actor's command and projection, he said "*I do!*" at the top of his voice, and everybody in the church looked at him.'[12]

By September 1950, Cushing was strong enough to return to work and joined the cast of a musical adaptation of Molière's *La Malade Imaginaire*. 'It was called *The Gay Invalid*,' Cushing ruminated. 'I felt like one!'[13]

The Gay Invalid at the Garrick was dubbed 'Molière without Tears' by the *Tatler*. Cushing's part was once again that of an ardent young soldier, this time pressing his suit to Daphne Slater as the daughter of the crotchety hypochondriac Crank (played by veteran actor A E Matthews). The huge set was hinged to depict the inside and outside of a house in Paris – 'The adapter's intentions are chiefly spectacular,' continued the *Tatler*. 'Inside, Crank sits among his thousands of medicine bottles, without a Commedia Dell'Arte troupe cavort in the snow. It is indeed a very theatrical evening, with nothing much omitted, except perhaps the finer points of Molière's comedy.'

The performance saw the much-trumpeted return to the London stage of the Polish-born star Elisabeth Bergner, who had appeared in musical comedy in the 1930s. In the part of the quack medico Professor Purge was no less than Tod Slaughter, whose blood-and-thunder melodramas on stage and screen (*Sweeney Todd*, *Maria Marten*, etc) had made him a British horror star and as such a direct precursor to Cushing. There was later a direct coincidence of subjects – Slaughter's 1948 film *The Greed of William Hart* was a version of the Burke and Hare story written by John Giling – in 1959, Cushing starred in Gilling's remake, *The Flesh and the Fiends*.

After an out-of-London tour taking in the Manchester Opera House and the Malvern Festival

Heartwell (Micheal Shepley), Crank (A E Matthews), Toinette (Elisabeth Bergner), Professor Purge (Tod Slaughter), Angelica (Daphne Slater), Valentine (Cushing) and Harlequin (Walter Gore) in *The Gay Invalid* (1951)

Theatre, *The Gay Invalid* ran in London for two months at the beginning of 1951, concluding on 24 March.

Meanwhile, plans were afoot for the Festival of Britain, a government-sponsored jamboree to help Britain out of its post-war doldrums with an exhibition and funfair on the South Bank next to the newly-built Festival Hall.

At the St James' Theatre, Sir Laurence Olivier was preparing a festival season which would feature Vivien Leigh as Cleopatra in both Shaw's *Caesar and Cleopatra* and Shakespeare's *Antony and Cleopatra*. Olivier's chief intention was to display his wife's versatility in presenting two aspects of Cleopatra's life – as a teenager bewitching Caesar and as the ruthless politician, the 'serpent of old Nile' who seduced Mark Antony. The two plays were directed by Michael Benthall, who was using the season to give *his* partner, the celebrated ballet dancer Robert Helpmann, an opportunity to move into acting as his dancing career was reaching its end. Helpmann's performance as Apollodorus almost overshadowed Olivier and Leigh.

Olivier was aware that Cushing was still in some-what fragile health and offered him two small roles – Alexas Diomedes in the Shakespeare and the dandyish Bel Affris in the prologue to the Shaw play. In *Caesar and Cleopatra* Wilfrid Hyde-White played Brittanus, a doleful Briton whom Caesar has employed as his secretary. When Hyde-White left to honour another commitment, Cushing was invited to take over. According to Audrey Cruddas' costume designs, Britannus was decked out in long ringlets and a short blue tunic. 'Larry gave these one-word directions,' says Michael Redington. 'For Brittanus he said "He's a scout-master" and that was that. Peter took that, and that was how he did it.' Brittanus is a comic character, full of his own importance and easily outraged. 'Is it true that when Caesar caught you on that island you were painted all over blue?' asks Cleopatra.

There were plenty of old colleagues in the Festival Season cast – including Niall MacGinnis, from *Hamlet*, Dan Cunningham from the Old Vic tour, Thomas Heathcote – and Henry Oscar again. Cushing befriended the actor Esmond Knight, who was almost blind but who nevertheless could negotiate Roger Furse's revolving set without hazard. A strong female contingent included Maxine Audley, Elspeth March and a young Jill Bennett while Desmond Llewelyn, who later became Q in the James Bond films, had a walk-on role as a Roman soldier.

During the rigorous schedule of daily performances at the St James', the Cushings relaxed at home by listening to the radio. On 10 July 1951, Cushing wrote to David Davis, producer of *Children's Hour*. 'I just wanted to thank you so *very* much and to congratulate you, if I may, for the charming *Jennifer's Journeys* programmes on the *Children's Hour*. They epitomise the very spirit of England and a feeling of love for this dear country of ours comes shining through to the listener! I hope we shall hear more.'

By the beginning of October, the St James' season was drawing to a close, and there was a blow for the Cushings – Peter was not to be included in the cast for the Broadway run of the plays. Wilfrid Hyde-White was returning as Brittanus, and the other parts would be recast. Perhaps Olivier, in his wisdom, realised that Cushing could do better than these minor roles, and that staying in London would advance his career further. Helen suspected that Larry had been nobbled. 'You have been unaware of jealousy in high places,' she told her husband. 'But I have heard and seen things going on behind your back ... You received an ovation every time you played Lomov and stopped the show as Britannus. That is why you were not asked to repeat your performance on Broadway. Larry was not the instigator of this injustice – we have good reason to be grateful to him – but there are others at court whose influence is very strong. Wilfrid is excellent, but he is older than you and well-established. You are a 'new boy' and represent a threat. They cannot stand that kind of competition.'[15] Among the new players who went to New York were Donald Pleasence, Patrick Troughton, Harry Andrews and Alec McCowen.

Determining that her man should 'become independent', Helen began a letter-writing campaign to a number of radio producers, many of whom Cushing had worked with before. Among the targets were Archie Campbell, Douglas Cleverdon, Val Gielgud, Peter Watts, Martyn Webster and Ayrton Whittaker. Cushing was careful to point out that at the time of writing he was still under contract to Laurence Olivier Productions Limited.

Hugh Stewart, a member of the Old Vic company who joined the Australasian tour, returned to his BBC job as a radio producer and supervised the broadcast excerpts from *Antony and Cleopatra* on 13 August. Cushing had worked with Stewart in 1947 and again in 1949 on *The Alien Corn* while he was still suffering the nervous breakdown.

'I hope there is a possibility of working with you again,' Cushing wrote to Stewart on 9 October, putting a rather more positive spin on his position. 'Having finished the season at the St James's I have decided not to go to America. It would give me tremendous pleasure to resume what was for me a most happy association and experience!' Stewart replied immediately. 'It was very nice to hear from you again, and I am glad to take this opportunity of

telling you how much I enjoyed your performances in both plays at the St James'. I wish I had known a few weeks ago that you would be free now, as I should certainly have been able to offer you a part in my forthcoming serial *Quentin Durward*. However, I hope something will come along soon!'

On 8 November, the letter-writing campaign to television producers began in earnest. During the 1950s, the BBC used the term 'producer' to cover the role of director also. The targets included Ian Acton, Alan Bromly, Pamela Brown, Naomi Capon, Harold Clayton, Cleland Finn, Joy Harrington and Vivian Milroy. Many gave positive but non-committal replies.

Helen used one of her contacts too, and wrote a personal letter to BBC producer Eric Fawcett, with whom she had worked in silent pictures in Hollywood. The letter, on Helen's own notepaper with a monogram of an 'H' in two diamonds, says much about the circumstances of the Cushings at the time, Helen's relationship with Peter, and their situation in late 1951.

'My dear Eric,' she wrote, 'shades of America in 1926! I was then a new and rather horrid beginner. The years have made me see sense enough to give up the whole idea. Anyway, since I have married Peter Cushing I haven't had much of a chance to do much else except join all the other housewives in their daily procession of toil. The last time we met was when you were accidentally ushered into my room at the Samaritan Hospital during the war. You looked most taken aback, as well you might! I am really writing now because Peter wants so much to meet you. He is not going to America with Laurence Olivier (to whom he is under contract) because they both feel it is wiser for Peter to carry on in Britain. He was in the USA for five years [sic] and wants to do a greater variety of work at home before he goes back. Wise – don't you think? Anyway, I enclose some data about Peter, which you will perhaps contemplate at leisure. And let us know if and when it would be convenient to see you? I am so very glad you are doing such fine and interesting work, Eric. It is always such a pleasure to see as the years go by that the people you knew are doing well. With every kind wish for all the very best, sincerely yours, Helen Cushing. PS: In the Dark Ages I was Vi Beck, don't let it worry you if you have forgotten!'

Fawcett would indeed remember his old association with Miss Beck, and agreed to meet Peter shortly afterwards. Although they would not work together until 1954, Fawcett would produce one of Cushing's award-winning television sucesses, the light comedy *Tovarich*. In his autobiography, Cushing states that a script came by 'return of post' and this seems to be no exaggeration. They did not waste time in television production in 1951, and when offered an actor of Cushing's talent there was even less reason to delay.

Chapter Seven

The Pride of Alexandra Palace

BBC Television in 1951 bore little resemblance to the multi-million pound business that exists today. In charge was a talented combination of ex-actors (the producers) and ex-servicemen (the upper management) who existed in a kind of bewildered tolerance of each other. Almost all television was broadcast from the London Television Station at Alexandra Palace, although the BBC had by now acquired Gainsborough's Lime Grove film studios, where Hitchcock had made *The Lady Vanishes* in 1938. Programmes were broadcast from late afternoon until 10 or 11 at night, sometimes with breaks of as much as an hour between shows.

All productions were live, that is, broadcast from the studios as they were performed, with little provision for covering mistakes beyond blacking out the screen and the deathless announcement 'normal service will be resumed as soon as possible'. Recordings were not made at this time because of an agreement with the actors' union Equity, who perceived danger to its members' livelihoods if the BBC stockpiled old performances. This same restriction extended to on-screen music, which in many cases was played live off-set by a small orchestra. Provision was made to record some programmes 'for use in a national emergency' but it was generally considered that the quality of telefilming was not acceptable for rebroadcast at this time.

Television plays were generally rehearsed for three weeks beforehand in various drill halls and boys' clubs ('which stank of plimsolls, stale perspiration and attar of cats'[1], Cushing wrote) followed by a day's camera rehearsal in studio, to practise the camera moves before transmission.

The principal drama of the week was the Sunday night play. This was repeated on Thursday night, which involved an entire remount of the production – assembling sets, cast and crew all over again, and performing the whole again. This was occasionally a risky business. ('Disaster could strike in many forms,' says writer Nigel Kneale of those times. 'Your leading man could fall sick or drop dead. It's remarkable that more didn't do so.'[2]) If the first performance was a success, there was the responsibility of matching its quality in the repeat. If it had been a failure, the repeat was a dispiriting rerun of the whole embarrassing exercise.

Helen's belief in Peter's reputation was proved absolutely correct. Assistant head of drama Michael Barry wrote back 'Although I am not at the moment producing, I shall use my good offices to bring you to the attention of the producers in television. I greatly admired your crisp and brilliantly-coloured performance as Bel Affris.'

On 12 November, just four days after the letter-writing campaign began, Cushing was called to the BBC's rehearsal room at the Inns of Court, Drury Lane, to begin work on J B Priestley's *Eden End* with producer Harold Clayton. There were the usual three weeks of rehearsals for *Eden End*, and Cushing's fee was 40 guineas. (35 guineas basic, plus an extra five for the repeat performance.) Clayton told him that he had seen him on stage in various disguises in the past nine years and 'wanted to see what Peter Cushing really looked like.'

The work of J B Priestley had already proved a good omen for Cushing, after his first professional stage appearance in *Cornelius* at Worthing and the scarf-painting job precipitated by *They Came To A City*.

Eden End concerns the family of Doctor Kirby, in the Yorkshire village of Eden End. Kirby's daughter Lilian (played by Rachel Gurney) discontentedly keeps house for her father, while in love with the local gentleman farmer. The elder daughter, Stella (Helen Shingler), arrives back at the house, separated from her drunken actor husband Charles Appleby (Cushing). Stella has the chance of a new life with her old admirer, the gentleman farmer, but then Lilian brings Charles up to Eden End ... So convincing was Cushing's performance as the inebriated Appleby that his wife suspected him of being a secret tippler.

The technical restrictions were arduous and the performance, in the BBC's cupboard-like studios at Alexandra Palace, was very taxing for a newcomer. Cushing was overcome with nerves. To ensure he could cover for missed lines, he learned the *entire* script. A scene where he had to lean jauntily on a piano almost ended in disaster when the stagehands started to pull it away. Cushing, not knowing that the set furniture often had to be moved around to accommodate the huge, unwieldy cameras, clung grimly on to the piano until he was frantically signalled to let go.

With no audience reaction to gauge, Cushing felt the production was a wretched failure. He went home, still in his make-up – 'with my clothes sticking to me.'[3] The Cushings did not have a television set and Helen had watched the play with friends. When she returned, she did her best to reassure her husband that success was now guaranteed, but Cushing was far from convinced. A phone call from the BBC the next morning, however, brought a request from producer Fred O'Donovan for Cushing to play the juvenile lead in his forthcoming Christmas Day production of Priestley's *When We Are Married*.

This production forced the Cushings to give up their Christmas dinner at home, since the play was rehearsed in studio during the day of the 25 December. Cushing's fee was higher for this job, however, at 40 guineas for only one performance. And after a solid month's work for the BBC, the next job was just as soon coming.

Eden End and *When We Are Married* were successful enough, but it was the next performance that set the seal on Cushing's television popularity. Campbell Logan, an imperious but kindly Scot, was another former actor-turned producer. On 2 January 1952, he asked Cushing to play the lead in a six-part dramatisation of Jane Austen's *Pride and Prejudice*. This classic story tells of the unlikely romance between the spirited, independent Elizabeth Bennet and the noble Mr Darcy, who is described in Logan's notes as a 'fine tall person, with handsome features, a noble mien, haughty, reserved, but fastidious. His manners, though well-bred, are not inviting...' Daphne Slater, who had starred as Cushing's paramour in *The Gay Invalid*, played Elizabeth Bennet, with Ann Baskett, newly graduated from RADA, as her sister Jane.

The third sister, Lydia Bennet, was played by 'a newcomer to television from the Bristol Old Vic' – Prunella Scales. 'It was shot live, of course, at Alexandra Palace,' she remembers. 'There was no audience, but I remember rushing round the back of the set for quick changes, trying not to trip over the lighting and camera cables. Peter was charming and benevolent, and smashing in the part.'

Also in the cast was Lockwood West, who became Miss Scales' future father-in-law. 'He played Mr Collins in the production and gave a very splendid and flamboyant performance. I knew he frequently worked for H M Tennent in the West End so I thought to myself, very privately, "This is probably what is known as an 'old queen'. They are very powerful in the theatre, and I must be very respectful to him!" I subsequently met my future husband in another Campbell Logan production, *She Died Young* (subtitled by the cast "None Too Soon") and on being introduced to Timothy by Campbell – "This is Timothy, Prunella, Harry Lockwood West's son" – I realised my mistake!'[4]

A budget of £3,222 was allocated for six episodes, which were shown on Saturday nights at 8.15.

Rehearsals were held each day from 10.30 to 6.00 at the Mansergh Woodall Boys' Club, 23 Hill Road, St John's Wood, beginning on 14 January. The period for all furniture and props was specified as 1795, with a great many 'dainties' in evidence ('a dainty chair' 'a dainty bowl of fruit', etc) except in the case of Lydia, who was to be furnished with 'a remarkably ugly bonnet'. One 'short-handled quizzing glass' was provided for Darcy.

On 2 February, an unforeseen circumstance threatened the whole production for the most mundane of reasons. All British citizens of voting age, apart from convicts, the insane and peers of the realm are called upon by random selection to serve on a jury. Peter Cushing was duly summoned to the Old Bailey on Tuesday 26 February. This would have been four days before the fifth episode of *Pride and Prejudice*. There was no question of recasting, and the serial could not reasonably be held up. It seems that this was something of a new occurrence for both the BBC and the courts of criminal justice. Rather ferocious letters thundered back and forth between the Old Bailey and Alexandra Palace. 'This sort of thing was easier to get round on the radio,' protested one BBC sage. Eventually Cushing had to go to the Old Bailey in person on 26 February and explain himself and, finally, he was excused.

The *Radio Times* noted that Cushing, as Darcy 'looked surprisingly at ease in the costume of the period.'[5] and Lt-Colonel A B Knight wrote to Campbell Logan on 8 March to say 'I have never had so much pleasure from one of my great-great-Aunt Jane's romances before!'

As *Pride and Prejudice* drew to a close, Cushing wrote to Michael Barry wondering if it would be possible for him to play Stanhope in 'a tele vision [sic] production of *Journey's End*' – if the war theme was acceptable for popular entertainment. Barry returned 'There is a ridiculous situation at present with regard to *Journey's End* by which a television production of this English play is prevented by the American film copyright held by MGM. When it is up, we shall do it again, and I would like to think you'd be in it. Darcy is a most distinguished performance, full of thought and style. Don't be depressed by the unending difficulties and breakdowns!'

Cushing replied to Barry 'So glad you are pleased with Mr Darcy and to know that something comes across apart from prostrating nerves! I was interested and a little melancholy to read of what you say about *Journey's End. They* seem to have *everything*, don't they?'

Meanwhile, the strain of television production was manifesting itself physically with Cushing. 'The symptoms, in my case, were acute pains across the eyes, forcing me to close them for a few seconds every so often.'[6] He sought treatment, and the Cushings' doctor prescribed a new tranquiliser that had just come

---

onto the market. 'After my next TV appearance,' he wrote, 'the doctor rang to ask if they had helped. "Not really," Helen replied.

"How many did he take?"

"Five."

There was a pause. "And is he still *alive*?" The pills were "purple hearts", one being considered potent enough to stun a fully-grown elephant for 24 hours, apart from the danger of turning me into a raving drug addict.'[7]

The last part of *Pride and Prejudice* was broadcast on 6 March, and by the end of the month, Cushing was back in the rehearsal rooms for a play called *Bird in Hand*. This project marked the first time Cushing worked in the Lime Grove studios, which would become a home-from-home in the next two years; it was also the first time he worked directly with Michael Barry, who produced the play with Dennis Vance. Barry and Cushing were well on the way to becoming firm friends. After *Bird in Hand*, Cushing wrote to Vance: 'I really enjoyed working with you and was much less nervous than usual.' Vance replied: 'How anyone with your ability could feel nervous, I can't understand. Let's repeat the dose as soon as possible.'

Cushing's television success raised his profile significantly and he was engaged for a short scene in John Huston's lavish, gorgeously coloured production of *Moulin Rouge*, which was filmed in England and France starring Jose Ferrer on his knees as the artist Henri De Toulouse-Lautrec.

'His manners, though well-bred, are not inviting.' Mr Darcy greets Elizabeth Bennet (Daphne Slater) in the BBC's 1951 serial adaptation of *Pride and Prejudice*

Cushing's segment seems to have been filmed around the end of April. About two-thirds of the way through the film, Cushing appears at a racecourse, beautifully attired in a grey suit and top hat, as Marcel De La Voisier, whose wife Myriamme has left him for Lautrec. Cushing is only there to provide a kind of stock 'handsome man' – a paragon next to whom the deformed Lautrec has only his wits and his talent. The role of cuckolded husband is one that he would essay many times – 'I suppose he'd got that sort of face,'[8] Joan Craft suggests. Lautrec is unimpressed with his vanquished rival 'He is as handsome a man as his horse is a horse,' he states, before presenting De La Voisier with a drawing of the horse, Magnifique. The film does at least record, briefly, the French accent which Cushing had used as a stock-in-trade for several years, but Cushing's appearance is hardly remarkable. The cast for *Moulin Rouge* included, in the role of Georges Seurat, and with a somewhat better French accent, a young hopeful called Christopher Lee.

On 5 June, 1952, Cushing wrote to Vance asking about the possibility of a part if he was casting a new serial. 'Helen has had to go into hospital, but she is getting along fine now.' 'In the one I am doing there is no Cushing part,' Vance replied 'though I should truly love there to be. I look at every script that comes my way with an eye for finding a juicy part for you.'

Helen had ruptured herself badly moving heavy furniture, causing a hernia with complications. She was taken to St George's Hospital for an operation and Cushing visited her every day. The doctor recommended some sea air and a neighbour offered them

Marcel de la Voisier meets his ex-lover Myriamme (Suzanne Flon) and Henri de Toulouse-Lautrec (José Ferrer) in *Moulin Rouge* (1952)

the use of a cottage in Polzeath, Cornwall. Even with the recent TV work, Cushing's finances were so low that, seeing no alternative, he was forced to ask his father for assistance. This was the deadening day when Cushing senior told his son he was 'nearly 40 – and a failure'. Their holiday on the Cornish Riviera brought Helen back to reasonable health, but Cushing had not told his agent that he was leaving, and may have missed out on several television roles in the meantime. Irene Sutcliffe, a good friend of the Cushings, overheard Robert Helpmann saying that he'd been trying to get in touch with Peter for some time as he had a role for him in the new play he was about to direct. Cushing returned from Cornwall immediately, and was invited to join the cast of *The Wedding Ring*.

This was Helpmann's first play as a director, and was produced by his partner Michael Benthall who had produced the Cleopatra plays at the St James'. *The Wedding Ring* was set in a marriage bureau, and starred two formidable actresses, Adrienne Allen (who had appeared with Coward in the original run of *Private Lives*) and Irene Brown. Also in the cast were Gladys Henson, 'Q' veterans Irene Handl and Shelagh Fraser and a young actor called Patrick Macnee.

Shelagh Fraser, who had also worked with Peter at the 'Q', remembers *The Wedding Ring* well. 'We went on what was called a "Number One" tour, then we were supposed to be coming to London. The play was written by Simon Waddell and his then-boyfriend Kieran Tunney, who I remember was not such a good

writer and a bit of a trouble-maker. We opened in Manchester and, without telling any of us, Tunney went to the Midland Hotel and sought out Noël Coward, who was staying there. He did a bit of a sob story and got him to come to the dress rehearsal of this light comedy in the barn which is the Manchester Opera House. Adrienne, Irene and Gladys Henson were old friends of Coward's and when they found out, the balloon went up. Tunney went from dressing room to dressing room, stirring trouble and eventually the women, who knew each other well, were scarcely speaking.'[9]

'Noël Coward said it was the worst play he'd ever seen,' Patrick Macnee says. Macnee, however, made friends with Cushing. 'From Manchester,' he remembers, 'he would walk up into the hills outside Cheshire and paint.'[10]

'We went to Cardiff with *The Wedding Ring*,' recalls Shelagh Fraser. 'Adrienne gave a big party in a local restaurant for everyone. Peter was very broke at the time and living in digs, but he didn't suck up to the two stars, like some did. Adrienne, alas, was a terrible snob and left Peter out of the party. At another time, Adrienne, who loved games, insisted we all played the one where everyone has a label pinned on their backs and they have to guess who they are. Adrienne prided herself on being best at all these things but couldn't guess what Peter had pinned on her. It was "The Iron Butterfly"! Her isolation of him had really backfired.'[11]

Helpmann's encouragement to his suffering actors was 'speed, speed, speed.' 'But,' Cushing wrote dolefully, '*The Wedding Ring* needed something more subtle than speed to attract the customers.'[12] 'There was so much trouble and intrigue...' remembers Shelagh Fraser, 'we never did get to London!' The play is not mentioned in Helpmann's biography – overshadowed, no doubt, by his later worldwide successes directing the likes of Katherine Hepburn and Robert Donat. Cushing's chief reminiscences about the tour concerned a theatrical landlady and his enforced separation from Helen.

Back in London, Cushing was immediately clasped back to the bosom of the BBC for what was to be an unbroken run of 12 productions in as many months. The first of these plays, *If This Be Error*, for director Stephen Harrison, went out on 11 November after the usual two-week rehearsal period. Cushing was reunited with Shelagh Fraser who remembers particularly the 'cut-out' keys, which would cut the sound from the studio so that a live prompt could be given. The cast also included Gillian Lind, the veteran comedy actor Frank Allenby and Dandy Nicholls, the immortal Else from *Til Death Us Do Part*.

Cushing's next role was in the French play *Asmodée*, a complex, allegorical chamber piece. He played the sinister tutor Blaise Lebel, who exerts an almost hypnotic influence over the household of the young widow Marcelle de Barthas and her daughter. His plans are thwarted by the arrival of a guileless young Englishman who represents 'Asmodée' – a devil who is reputed to take the roofs off houses and cause havoc among their occupants. For the part of Lebel, producer Harold Clayton suggested that Cushing fill in the sides of his distinctive widow's peak to emphasise the character's vanity. It made a subtle and sinister change to the shape of his face. 'Thank you for your most tremendous help and the trust you put in me,' Cushing wrote back to Clayton. 'And for the brilliant idea of the hair-line! I think it was that that put the proper seal on old Blaisie!'

Shortly after Christmas, Cushing played the Spanish Lord Henriques in the first episode of a children's drama serial that held distinct hints of things to come. *The Silver Swan* was written by C E Webber and produced by Rex Tucker, and involved a young girl who travelled through time with the aid of a magical violin. More than ten years later, Webber and Tucker would help create another children's series with a time-travel theme – *Doctor Who*.

On 16 January, Cushing began rehearsals at the Jewish Lads' Club, Hanway Place, for the play *Number Three*, once again with producer Stephen Harrison. The cast included many popular television names – Ursula Howells, Jack Watling, Raymond Huntley, Terence Alexander and Jack Howarth, who would become the legendary Albert Tatlock in *Coronation Street*. The play was set in an isolated nuclear research centre where the brilliant Professor Brander (Huntley) is attempting to develop a limitless source of cheap electricity. The scientists are all but ignored by the government, until it is discovered that the process could also produce a weapon more powerful than a hydrogen bomb, whereupon the centre is immediately Top Secret and Top Priority. While Brander celebrates what he considers a scientific and patriotic triumph, his assistants realise that they have now created a means to save the world, or annihilate it.

The role of Simpson, the myopic minister in *Number Three*, was the part that secured Cushing the services of a new agent, John Redway. He would remain as Cushing's agent and a good friend until his death. *Number Three* was also Cushing's first involvement with the work of BBC staff writer Nigel Kneale who, with George F Kerr, adapted Charles Irving's play for television. Later in the year, television would terrify the nation for the first time with the transmission of Kneale's serial *The Quatermass Experiment*.

Asmodée was performed again on 17 February 1953. After this, Cushing wrote to Harold Clayton, 'I think the second Blaisie wasn't up to the standard of the first – hope that's just me!' Clayton's wife, the documentary producer Caryl Doncaster, approached Cushing with a view to doing a project with her but he was now fully booked for the foreseeable future, and had to decline. He was about to embark on another serial, *Epitaph for a Spy*, a six-part mystery for Saturday nights based on a novel by Eric Ambler.

Giles Cooper, who adapted the story for television, set the scene in the *Radio Times*: '*Epitaph for a Spy* addresses one of the author's favourite themes; the intrusion of espionage and other evil into the lives of ordinary harmless men – that spies seldom wear cloaks and carry daggers but... they quite often wear bathing-dresses and carry pictures of their children.' Cooper described Cushing's character of Josef Vadassy as 'the most inoffensive man alive. He is a keen photographer and a conscientious teacher – not in the least the kind of man *to whom things happen*. When they *do* happen to him, Ambler sees to it that we feel that we ourselves would behave in much the same way Vadassy does.'[13]

Epitaph for a Spy was set in the Hotel de la Réserve in the Riviera town of St Gatien in 1937. Vadassy, a teacher of languages, is stateless – a Hungarian by birth, but because of the 1920 Peace Treaty, a Yugoslav by law. He is suspected of photographing a coastal defence installation but Beghin, of French Naval Intelligence, cannot believe in so incompetent a spy. Knowing that the enemy agent must be in the Hotel, Beghin forces Vadassy to investigate his fellow guests at the Réserve. But the real spy knows that he is being spied upon, and Vadassy the hunter is also the hunted...

Stephen Harrison was once again in charge for the weekly broadcasts from Alexandra Palace. The cast included Ferdy Mayne, Raf de la Torre, Philip Leaver and John Vere. Cushing's fee for each half-hour episode was a substantial 30 guineas. Meanwhile, he was having to cope with the new sensation of being a national celebrity, and he relates this demonstration of public affection in his autobiography. 'Visiting the city one day to call on my solicitor, I stopped opposite the bank ... awaiting the chance to nip across the tarmac. Emulating *In Town Tonight*, a constable on point duty stopped the mighty roar of London's traffic from all directions and beckoned me gravely to the other side. When I reached it, he winked "Can't have you run over Mr Cushing, the wife'll never forgive me if she don't see what happens in the last episode of your serial!"'[14]

On 10 April 1953 Cushing wrote to producer John Irving about his upcoming role as Henry Robbins in the *Wednesday Theatre* production of Max Beerbohm's satire *A Social Success*. 'So glad you liked *Moulin Rouge* and that you spotted me! I think the moustache idea for Henry is an excellent one. I'll try to grow it as I *can't bear* that glue!'

The transmission of *A Social Success* on 29 April was followed by a highly enjoyable assignment for Cushing in *Rookery Nook*, undoubtedly the most popular of Ben Travers' famous Whitehall farces, presented by the BBC from the stage of the Scala Theatre, Kingsway on 23 May. *Rookery Nook* was produced by Lionel Harris and the cast included David Kossoff and Lally Bowers. Further down the cast was a young actress called Beryl Bainbridge, who later achieved great success as a novelist.

William Johnson, who as a stage manager had worked with Cushing in his repertory days in Southampton, went on to become the manager of a department store, Z Dudley Ltd in High St, Kingsland E8. Cushing's model tithe barn, which he began constructing as a kind of occupational therapy during the war was publicly exhibited for the first time at his store in May of that year and Johnson wrote to the BBC encouraging them to show it on television.

'You will doubtless know of Peter Cushing, whose recent performances in Television drama have met with such favourable comment. I am rather proud to say that we are very old friends and what you will not know is that he is also an extremely gifted artist in other fields. His natural modesty has been, and still is, his own worst enemy, and it is only because I am a businessman rather than an artist that I have managed at last to obtain his permission to borrow and exhibit in my store a model which took him three years to create. It is being officially opened to public exhibition tomorrow – but already it has caused real amazement. The model is of an Elizabethan Tithe Barn, which is finished in antique furniture and adapted for use as a modern Elizabethan home. To describe it and do it justice defeats me! The scale is half-an-inch to the foot, and the detail is simply wonderful. It is hand painted and the ingredients are chiefly plain white paper and seccotine. The lighting is beautiful. I am showing it, at Peter's request, to raise funds for the SSAFFA (Soldiers, Sailors and Air Forces Families' Association) while I have it here and later I hope to have it shown elsewhere in London.' Unfortunately, it is not recorded whether the BBC took up Johnson's offer or not.

1953 was a historic year for British television. Although pioneering viewers tuned their pre-war TV sets to watch the Coronation procession of King George VI in 1937, it was with coverage of the coronation of Queen Elizabeth II on 2 June 1953 that television established itself as the eyes of the people. Televising the Coronation for western Europe forged a TV link between Britain and the continent, with both social and political importance for the future. To match the unprecedented spectacle of the ground-breaking outside broadcast, Michael Barry marked Coronation week with an expensive studio production of his play *The Passionate Pilgrim*, based on Charles Terrot's novel about the women who accompanied Florence Nightingale to the Crimea. Peter and Helen enthusiastically attended the performance at Lime Grove. 'My dear Michael,' Cushing wrote later, 'Helen and I would like to express our appreciation of your splendid production and offer our congratulations. It was a most moving production with such glorious shots! Apart from Marion Pryor, of course, also excellent were Anthony Nicholls and Willoughby Gray. Such real human beings!'

Cushing's next performance for the BBC, in *The Road*, was the first of three French plays that he would take part in during the next two months. This adaptation of Jean Jacques Bernard's *Nationale Six* starred Wilfrid Lawson, Josephine Griffin and Bryan Forbes, and concerned a young artist (Cushing) and his father who unexpectedly find happiness in the simple rural home of an old man and his daughter. In their autobiographies, both Cushing and Christopher Lee relate anecdotes about Wilfrid Lawson – as a teenage flier he crashed in the trenches during the First World War. He almost drank himself to death to stay alive, and he continued this regimen for the rest of his life. He was an almost uncontrollable but often brilliant character actor, and can be seen on fine form as a fey, pixie-like bookseller in Cushing's 1960 film *The Naked Edge*.

In Marcelle-Mauret's play *Anastasia* Cushing found himself embroiled in post-Russian-revolutionary capers, doubtless spurred by Helen's historical connection with the time. The play took as its central conceit the legend that the Tsar's youngest daughter, Anastasia, was not killed by the Bolsheviks and was somehow smuggled out of the country. A criminal syndicate comprising the disreputable émigré Prince Bounine and his discredited fellow-exiles, the former banker Chernov and the drug-addict Petrovsky (Cushing) claims that she has been found, and raises money among Russian refugees in Berlin, ostensibly for her aid and succour. The fund draws in the money, and the scheme works well until the subscribers become impatient to see their long-lost Princess.

Co-producing *Anastasia* with Michael Barry was John Counsell, who produced the play in Windsor, brought it to the BBC and later took it to the St James' Theatre where it was produced by Laurence Olivier. The television version was broadcast on 12 July 1953 and the stage production opened in August. Many of the BBC cast, including Helen Haye, Mary Kerridge (Counsell's wife) and Anthony Ireland repeated their roles on stage, and while Cushing did not, he attended the first night in the company of Margaret Lockwood, Herbert Wilcox, Robert Helpmann, Olivier, Vivien Leigh and Orson Welles. *Anastasia* is preserved in the BBC archive, making this the earliest surviving example of Cushing's television work.

Chapter Eight

Busy Days and Black Knights

Somerset Maugham's adaptation of *The Noble Spaniard*, a French farce by Grenet-Dancourt, was broadcast on 4 August for producer Stuart Latham. It was set in a villa in Boulogne in 1850 where, wrote James Doran in the *Radio Times*, 'into a party of English tenants arrives a Spanish nobleman, hot in the pursuit of love.' Cushing, of course, played the noble spaniard of the title, the Duke of Hermanos. 'The object of his desire is a beautiful English widow whom he has worshipped at a distance for three long weeks – and he will be kept at a distance no longer. The impetuosity of his wooing bundles the English holidaymakers into a series of ingeniously contrived misunderstandings – most of them matrimonial. The action, in all its improbabilities, is hustled smartly along at the point of a rapier rather than at the end of a cudgel.'[1]

The misadventures of a society artist – with a sideline in jewel robbery – and his wily 'fence' formed the basis of the comic drama *Portrait by Peko* by Philip Walker-Taylor, which was transmitted on 23 August 1953. Patrick Barr played Peko, with Irene Handl as the wealthy Mrs Hassall, Ursula Howells as Peko's girlfriend and Cushing as Seppi Fredericks – described simply in the BBC casting documents as 'a crook'. That the *Radio Times* described Fredericks as 'rather a work of art in his own right'[2] gives a clue to his ultimate fate – he is sealed up inside Peko's latest statue. Cushing can be seen in the *Radio Times* during rehearsals for *Peko*, wearing an expression of puppy-dog innocence and his palms raised in a 'would-I-lie-to-you?' gesture of supplication.

Irene Handl brought her tiny dog to appear in one scene – the producer Lionel Harris stated firmly that the animal's well-being was to be *entirely* the actress's responsibility. The production was budgeted at £989, with the actors' fees taking up just over £600. With the rest, designer Richard Greenough had to create an artist's studio, a town square and a number of special props, including three unfinished portraits and the statue itself, which was supposed to have Cushing's face (although it was specified that this would not require a head-cast to be taken of the actor). The sets held no terror for Greenough who, on the night before *Peko*'s transmission, had been required to reproduce Westminster Abbey in Alexandra Palace

and fill it with malignant alien vegetation for the concluding instalment of *The Quatermass Experiment*.

Portrait by Peko was chosen to be performed at the Dusseldorf Television Festival, from where it would be broadcast by Nordwestdeutscher Rundfunk on 31 August. The Dutch Television Service, Nederlandse Televisie Stichting Hilversum, also relayed the broadcast. All artists had to ensure that their passports were in order to travel to Germany on the 29th – there were two days' rehearsals before the evening performance. Helen Cushing accompanied her husband on the trip, paying her own expenses throughout – the itinerary listed her as 'Mrs Peter Cushion'.

Richard R Greenough's sets for *Portrait by Peko*. Cushing's character, Seppi Fredericks, was sealed up inside the statue. The artist's studio set was the scene of a near disaster at the Dusseldorf TV Festival

The villainous Sir Palamides shows his true colours in a last-reel duel with *The Black Knight*

appear in the role of Charles Price in *The Guilty Party* on 13 September, but his contract was cancelled when he was offered a role in the film *The Black Knight*. Charles Price was eventually played by Ferdy Mayne.

Cushing worked on *The Black Knight* from early September to late November, travelling to Wales and Spain and finishing up at Pinewood Studios for three weeks. No film can be all bad with a cast that includes André Morell, Harry Andrews, Patrick Troughton and Anthony Bushell but *The Black Knight* is, at best, cheerful, childish nonsense. It was directed by Tay Garnett, who had made *A Connecticut Yankee in King Arthur's Court* in 1949 and must have liked Camelot, since this film is set there, too, although he has a quaintly skewed idea of England and the English. The film was produced by Albert R 'Cubby' Broccoli, who later co-produced the James Bond series, and starred Alan Ladd, who was contracted to a series of British films of which this was the last. Despite a heart-warming jaunt to locations in Spain, Ladd was weary of the British drizzle and anxious to return to America. The exteriors were shot in Castilla le Nueva, which while it provided some substantial granite castles for backdrops, ensures that the Stonehenge sequences look more like plains in Spain than in Salisbury.

Cushing is in his element as Sir Palamides, acting out on a grand scale the sort of *Boy's Own* adventures that had previously been confined to his living-room floor. Palamides moves through the film like a silver snake – a villain's villain, in dusky make-up with dubious foreign inflections (he talks a lot about 'Sarry-cens' and 'Cammy-lot') and sporting a collection of rather alarming hats. At one point, for reasons too complicated to go into, we have Cushing (from Kenley) playing a Saracen, disguised as a Viking. Not politically correct, certainly, but surely no more ludicrous than Alan Ladd in King Arthur's Court – 'Lemme speak, sire,' he squawks, bursting in on the Knights of Camelot 'You gotta listen to me!'

Cushing looks magnificent throughout, his blue eyes glittering in the dark make-up, his face framed by a dark wig, black beard and earrings. He revels in some faintly camp one-liners and sarcastic put-downs, and though the film is little more than a pantomime in glorious Technicolor, Cushing is never less than convincing. "There is a saying in my country," he

A copy of Greenough's set was made by the NWDR designer Herr Joksch in the Europe Hall in Dusseldorf, although the special props, including the infamous statue were transported to Germany. The production was mounted on ground level with the public looking in on the production from a circular gallery halfway up the sides of the walls. The rapt audience was witness to a narrowly avoided disaster when a working Bunsen burner on Peko's bench accidentally set light to some rags. Cushing was able to douse the flames with a jug of water and stop the gas pipe with his foot, while the attentive floor manager, John Jacobs (who had been taken along because he spoke German and was able to act as interpreter), crawled in to turn off the tap to the gas cylinder.

Silent footage of Cushing with Ursula Howells, Patrick Barr, Hilda Fenemore and Michael Barry at the Dusseldorf exhibition, from a 2 September news item entitled *British Television on View*, is preserved in the BBC archive.

After returning from Dusseldorf with Helen in September, Cushing did not take part in any more BBC plays until after Christmas. He was intended to

spits at Ladd, "when a puppy yelps at his master it is time to clip his tail!"

If 1953 was a defining year for British television, 1954 was a defining year for Cushing, culminating in his most acclaimed television performance. In January, however, Cushing was at work rehearsing *Tovarich*, Jacques Deval's comedy about an exiled Russian Prince and his wife who are forced into domestic service. The play co-starred film actress Ann Todd, whom Cushing nicknamed 'Annoushka' throughout rehearsals. She had agreed to take part in the play 'only if she could act opposite Peter Cushing'. Miss Todd, whose film appearances included *The Seventh Veil* (1945) and *The Paradine Case* (1948) was married at the time to the film director David Lean, and her inclusion in a television production was a coup for the BBC. The play was directed by Eric Fawcett, to whom Helen had written at the outset of Cushing's television career.

Barney Keelan explained the plot of *Tovarich* in the *Radio Times*: 'Her Imperial Highness the Grand Duchess Tatiana Petrovna and her husband, Prince Mikail, living the hard life common among Russian exiles, are reduced to a little mild shoplifting in the Paris markets. The Prince has a fortune in the bank, but his promise to the late Tsar, for whom he holds it in trust, forbids him to spend it on the grocer's bills. "Life," as he says, "is very, very sad and very, very beautiful." When the Grand Duchess and the Prince decide that, in their extremity, work is the only solution, life also becomes very, very amusing, and particularly so when the royal couple is played by Ann Todd, the film-star, and Peter Cushing, a television star in his own right.'[3]

Stars Ann Todd and Cushing appeared on the cover of the *Radio Times* in the BBC's *Tovarich*

Ann Todd and Cushing in *Tovarich*

Peter Cushing, in costume as Beau Brummell, is joined by studio manager Barry Lupino and Helen in the Lime Grove canteen

Daphne Slater, Walter Fitzgerald, producer Campbell Logan and Cushing in rehearsals for *Beau Brummell* (February 1954)

Worth winning Best Television Actress. He was concerned, however, given the preparation for *Anastasia*, that he would not be able to do justice to the presentation ceremony on 30 January, which had previously involved the recipients performing an extract from a play. He wrote to Michael Barry, who had been unwell, on 31 December. 'I'm thrilled at having won the Television Award but ... having won the honour by virtue of the standard of the work, I would not like even ten minutes to be below that standard. A telefilm would not be the same thing to both the live and viewing audience on that night. Irene Worth is inclined to agree with me, and we think it better just to have a two-minute spot each with a prepared speech of thanks, etc, to give the audience a chance to see their "choices" as themselves for a change, and not in character. (I'm told they prefer this anyway.) Please don't think that I'm being uncooperative, but I am truly thinking what would be best for all concerned. *Tovarich* and Irene's play at the Haymarket wouldn't allow us any time at all to work on anything as we would *want* to. Helen joins me in sending you all good wishes for 1954, and an appeal again for you to consider your own health – for all our sakes.' The awards ceremony went out on the evening of Friday 29 January, the day after the second performance of *Tovarich*.

Cushing had played the lead in a sponsored radio broadcast of *Beau Brummell* in Australia, and it was good practice, he said, for his subsequent appearance on television as George Bryan Brummell, the celebrated dandy and favourite of the Prince Regent, who for 20 years imposed his dress, manners and wit upon the fashionable world. 'Men copied his stylish extravagances, women longed for his favour and all were, in turn, delighted and wounded by his tongue,' wrote Barney Keelan in the *Radio Times*. 'But the pace was hot, and before his inevitable downfall, this play suggests, two people at least saw beyond the brittle frivolity of his character. Brummell's chivalry towards the unfashionable Georgiana and the man who loved her may have been quixotic, but did it not disclose a melancholy yearning for another mode of life? Here, at any rate, is the suggestion, blended with scintillating glimpses of an age devoted to cultivating the highest of high life. In Regency days, above all, the style was the man – and the man was Beau Brummell. In this production, style is in the safe-keeping of Peter

The exiles become butler and parlour-maid in the household of a banker, M Dupont. Their presence changes the lives, not only of Dupont and his wife but also of the two young members of the family (who learn such Imperial pastimes as osculation – kissing – and fencing), and the play climaxes with a riotous dinner party. 'Russians may be red or white, nice or nasty,' concluded Keelan, 'but they are seldom predictable...'[4] Clive Morton played the blustering Charles Dupont and Richard Marner, best known for his bumbling German colonel in *'Allo 'Allo!* played Commissar Gorotchenko. Michael Newell, later known as a film director as Mike Newell (*Dance with a Stranger* and *Four Weddings and a Funeral*) played the Dupont son, Georges.

Cushing had won the *Daily Mail* Readers' Award for Best Television Actor of the Year 1953, with Irene

Cushing as Brummell and Daphne Slater as the humble girl who makes him hesitate at the height of his triumph. These two players have already shown viewers their skill in presenting another aspect of the period in *Pride and Prejudice*.'[5]

The action took place in 1816 in London and Brighton, with a cast that included Ferdy Mayne, Peter Copley, Walter Fitzgerald, Prunella Scales (again) and David Peel, who in 1960 would star as the vampire Baron Meinster opposite Cushing in *The Brides of Dracula*. Campbell Logan was the producer, and Cushing's fee was 65 guineas – the first rise in salary he'd had in more than eighteen months. John Paddy Carstairs, guest TV critic for the London *Evening Standard* said that Cushing's 'impeccable diction' as Brummell 'would enthral American viewers.'[6] Carstairs, a film producer and director, was the brother of Anthony Nelson Keys, who would produce some of Hammer's greatest successes. Perhaps the seeds were being sown even then. A clear sign of Cushing's growing celebrity can be gleaned from a letter in January 1954 to the *TV Mirror,* the first magazine solely dedicated to television, which suggested a production of *Lorna Doone* bringing together two TV favourites – Petula Clark as Lorna and Peter Cushing as Carver Doone.

Cushing's participation in the popular radio programme *A Book at Bedtime* in 1954 was an epic in miniature. First of all, Helen sent a choice of books to Patrick Harvey, the producer, with Peter stipulating 'No American accents for me please!' Together they decided upon *Natural Causes* by Henry Cecil, to be read in 15 15-minute instalments, Monday to Friday for three weeks.

But first, there was the small matter of the book itself. 'Would you please let us have it back?' entreated the producer's secretary, on dispatching a reading copy. 'We've had to borrow it from the *Times* Library.' Harvey also outlined the *Book at Bedtime* 'ritual', which is endearingly quaint even by BBC standards. Pre-recording was not uncommon on radio at this time, but the instalments were still broadcast live at 10.45pm each night. Cushing received seven guineas for each instalment, and had to all but turn the lights out when he'd finished. As Harvey told him in the '*Book at Bedtime* ritual' – 'Report to the Duty Officer about 10.45 pm and then go to studio 3C. If you can remember, would you please write on the top of your script the time you come off the air? By deducting 16 or so seconds for the opening announcement, we have a timing for the programme as broadcast. Please don't bother about this if it's going to worry you. After transmission, kindly take your script, and the studio manager's, if it is lying around, back to the Duty Officer who will supply you with a drink if you want one.'

The series was a success, and Harvey duly forwarded a letter of congratulation with a letter from an enthusiastic listener. Cushing returned his usual hearty reply. 'My dear Patrick, how jolly nice that you were satisfied with our mutual effort on *A Book at Bedtime*! I must say I felt a complete fool when I first kicked off, but you were so helpful and co-operative that if I succeeded at all it was because of the sympathetic and tactful guidance you gave me. I must say that nobody was more surprised than I at the reaction to the bibulous solicitor and his associates (I didn't know I had it in me!) I hope that we may one day repeat our double act.'

Cushing took part in two more radio broadcasts in rapid succession, narrating *The Bride in the Bath* on *Morning Story* on 2 March 1954 and playing the Marquess of Quex in *The Gay Lord Quex* by Arthur Wing Pinero. ('In 1900, Lord Quex, a genial rake, has become engaged to a "typical creamy English girl" but at a country house-party he becomes embarrassingly involved with the Duchess of Strood.') This was recorded on 31 March, and broadcast on the Home Service on 5 April (after *The Goon Show*!) The producer was Archie Campbell and the 'special' fee was 18 guineas. As a further indication of Cushing's success, in April 1954, the *TV Mirror* began a serialised autobiography of 'TV's popular star', which ran for five weeks under the title of 'The Peter Cushing Story'. Cushing's story was actually related to Robert Hirst, who later published it along with similarly 'autobiographical' pieces on Terry-Thomas and Arthur Askey, under the title *Three Men and a Gimmick* for the World's Work press.

Cushing was narrator again on a 20-minute TV programme called *May Day* which went out on 1 May from Lime Grove – 'Television recalls some of the customs and ceremonies which are traditional on the first day of May.' 'Thank you for your patience and trust,' Cushing wrote to producer Paul Johnstone 'over what I found an extraordinary ordeal until transmission. Any show of temperament please put down to my not having enough time for "conning" the lines.' As well as the turn as narrator, Cushing suddenly found himself in demand as a 'celebrity guest'. He was on 'expenses only' however, when he appeared on the magic show *Men of Mystery* ('A programme in which an attempt is made to deceive you') on 14 May, with TV magicians David Nixon, David Berglas and 'Chandu'. 'Be at the studio at 9.15,' specified Angela Heathcote, secretary to producer Bill Ward, 'in evening dress (dinner jacket). I am asking the accounts department to forward a cheque for ten guineas to cover all your expenses in connection with this appearance.'

Men of Mystery was recorded while Cushing was beginning rehearsals for a tour of the play *The Soldier and The Lady* by Ian Stuart Black. This new piece was directed by Sam Wanamaker, the American actor and producer who devoted the latter part of his life to the construction of a replica of Shakespeare's Globe Theatre on London's South Bank. Wanamaker was trained in Stanislavsky and the new vogue of 'method' acting, with emphasis on the inner motivation of a character. This had little in common with Cushing's repertory and television training, which had taught meticulous precision simply by the volume of work. Cushing apparently found some difficulty in adapting to Wanamaker's approach, but nevertheless his performance was exemplary, and the play seems to have been a happy, if short-lived, experience for the director and star.

Cushing as 'the soldier' played opposite Richard Attenborough's wife, Sheila Sim as 'the Lady', the tour beginning at the Wimbledon Theatre on 31 May, taking in Eastbourne's Devonshire Park Theatre at the end of June and finishing the run in Southsea. Cushing remembered that during rehearsals, Wanamaker would direct the action while doing handstands on a cane chair placed perilously close to the edge of the stage. While finishing the run, Cushing was able to extol the virtues of a subject close to his heart when he appeared on a *Woman's Hour* segment entitled *Woman, Lovely Woman*, dealing with fashion in the 1930s and 40s.

On 13 June 1954, Cushing wrote to Michael Barry: 'Forgive me taking up your precious time, but I wonder if you have any suggestions for a play I could do soon on Television? *The Soldier and The Lady*, in which I'm now touring, I don't think will come to town, and at present we only have two positive dates, a week in each.'

A fortnight later, however, he was under contract for a film, and so had to decline Royston Morley's offer of a starring role in a new production of *Peer Gynt*. He was, however, able to appear in the panel game *Down You Go!* with Kenneth Horne, Patricia Cutts and Elizabeth Gray (who had featured in *Lord Quex*) on 29 July 1954. The show was presented by Ernest Maxim from the Television Theatre, Shepherd's Bush, and on Maxim's request Helen supplied some photographs of her husband, apologising that they were not 'full length' as he had specified. After his appearance on *Down You Go!* Maxim asked Cushing to appear on the show again immediately, but Cushing sadly had to decline. 'My film commitments will prevent me from appearing for some time.'

The film was *The End of the Affair*, based on Graham Greene's complex novel and directed by Edward Dmytryk, who had made several highly regarded *film noir* thrillers, including *Murder My Sweet* and *Crossfire* and came to England because of the anti-Communist blacklisting in America.

The film was produced by David Lewis, the longtime lover of James Whale. Whether Lewis remembered the handsome stand-in for Louis Hayward or not, this was certainly an important part for Cushing to land, opposite Hollywood star Van Johnson and Deborah

Kerr. Greene's book was an examination of his own faith and, although it was not known at the time, was a *roman-à-clef* for the novelist's own adulterous affair with Catharine Walston. The film is shot through with a tone of pessimism and disappointment, and in the end all but collapses under a cartload of Catholic guilt.

There's a rather flamboyant piano score too, much given to melodramatic bashing on the keyboard at particularly emotional moments. Johnson is woefully miscast – he does his usual flat turn and seems not to understand the material. Greene, who vetoed Gregory Peck for the lead was appalled at the choice of Johnson and noted that the actor chewed gum during the love scenes when not in shot. Cushing however, achieves a kind of brilliance with his portrayal of the wronged husband, a man with 'a mind as neatly creased as his trousers' and it is sobering to think that but for *Nineteen Eighty-Four* he might have carried on playing this kind of repressed individual for as long as it was needed.

The plot of *The End of the Affair* is fragmented, and told in a series of flashbacks. During the Second World War, American Miles Bendrix (Johnson) is writing a book on the British civil service when he meets Henry Miles, who works in service pensions. Miles presents Bendrix to his devoted wife Sarah (Deborah Kerr) – and soon Bendrix and Sarah are having an affair. (Although what they actually *do* is left terribly vague.) After an air-raid, Sarah suddenly becomes cold to Bendrix and returns to Miles. The rest of the film reveals the reasons for her sudden change of heart.

Though stuffy and pompous, Miles is genuinely in love with Sarah. As time passes and her behaviour remains erratic, he considers employing a private detective to investigate her, but ultimately cannot. 'They always say, don't they, that the husband is the last to know...'

Miles is equally unable to answer his wife's questions about her faith. When she asks her husband if he prays, he is at a loss. 'I was *taught to*. In church, whenever I go ... Really, this isn't the sort of thing to go into over a cup of tea!' Towards the end of the film, Miles is a man on the point of despair and Cushing's performance is deeply affecting. 'I know I'm dull for you, Sarah ... frightfully dull...' he sobs. 'But I couldn't start again. It's too late, do you see?' As Sarah succumbs to a fatal fever, Cushing descends the stairs with a blank expression, unable to comprehend. It is another meticulous and disciplined performance, and Deborah Kerr is a graceful and generous co-star.

After nearly three months at Shepperton Studios, it was back to the Jewish Lads' Club for rehearsals for *The Face of Love* from 17 September to 3 October. This was a contemporary retelling of the story of Helen of Troy featuring Cushing as Mardian. It was transmitted on 5 October from Lime Grove. The producer was Alvin Rakoff, a young Canadian whose work Cushing admired.

Henry Miles helps his wife Sarah (Deborah Kerr), who has been caught in a rainstorm, in Edward Dmytryk's *The End of the Affair* (1954)

Cushing's fee for *The Face of Love* was 74 guineas. After this, there was a sudden, considerable leap in salary – his wages almost doubled. There was a general increase in BBC artists' fees, but Cushing's growing standing as a film actor must have given John Redway extra clout. Part of the reason for the rise in wages was the imminent arrival of a new independent television station, as outlined in the government's bill in the summer of 1954. The BBC's biggest drama of the year, its adaptation of George Orwell's *Nineteen Eighty-Four*, was well into pre-production, and Cushing was to star. Before that, however, he had to make a trip to Bavaria to appear in the film *Magic Fire*.

'Republic's Top 1954 Picture – Life of Wagner,' trumpeted the *Daily Cinema*. 'William Dieterle will produce and direct. Production in Technicolor starts in Germany on September 11th. As the launching stage of Republic's major production this year, *Magic Fire*, the story of Richard Wagner's life and loves, contracts have been signed with Yvonne De Carlo, Rhonda Fleming and Rita Gam for the three feminine leads. This, one of Republic's most ambitious productions, is based on the recently published biography by Bertita Harding.'[7]

The film is slow and heavy-handed, albeit with spectacular reconstructions of scenes from Wagner's operas involving giants, valkyries and such. Alan Badel plays the composer who is given to much melodramatic suffering at the harpsichord and whose work is hampered by his roving eye and fierce political convictions. Yvonne De Carlo plays Wagner's first wife Minna but is encumbered by a series of elaborate costumes that make her look like Bo-Peep. Cushing appears in the middle of the film as Wagner's friend and sponsor Otto Wesendonk, but the friendship sours when Wagner runs off with Wesendonk's wife Mathilde (Valentina Cortese). Cushing's brief appearance is chiefly interesting for showing him in an outfit like the one he will famously wear as Frankenstein, with waved hair, a frock-coat and side-whiskers. Filming took place in Bavaria in October 1954, and Helen was able to accompany her husband to Munich for an enjoyable holiday. With *Magic Fire*, Cushing consolidated his position as an attractive and reliable supporting player, but with his next project, he would earn himself a very different reputation…

Chapter Nine

Nineteen Eighty-Four
And All That

The BBC's adaptation of George Orwell's *Nineteen Eighty-Four* was produced by Rudolph Cartier and broadcast on 12 December 1954. It was British television's first masterpiece.

The production had been first mooted after Cartier's success as producer of *The Quatermass Experiment*, and he was keen to take on the project having first read Orwell's novel in serial form in 1950. Cartier was born in Vienna in 1904 and had worked at the UFA film studios in Berlin, leaving Germany when Hitler came to power in 1933. After the war, Cartier was invited by Michael Barry to join the BBC as a staff director and Cartier, with his usual uncompromising candour, told Barry exactly what he thought of the BBC's drama output. He knew that the way forward was not merely to restage popular stage successes, but to develop new writing specifically for the television medium.

By February 1954 dramatist Hugh Falkus was working on an adaptation with George Orwell's widow, Sonia Blair. A 60-minute TV version of the book had been produced by CBS in America in 1953, but it was, according to Barry, 'restrained to the point of being dull.' There were delays with the project until May. Mrs Blair had sold the film rights to an American company, who granted the rights back to the BBC on the condition that they produced the play within the year. The programme, with a new script by Nigel Kneale, was finally scheduled for December, allowing for a lengthy pre-production period. It was budgeted at £3000, making it the most expensive BBC production to this date. An original costing of £2500 was rejected by Cartier, who eventually used 22 sets in two studios at Lime Grove, 60 actors, a small orchestra and more pre-filmed inserts than had been used for a television drama up to that time.

However, even the BBC's staff were worried at the strength of the material they were being asked to work with. In September 1954 Barry Learoyd, the designer assigned to *Nineteen Eighty-Four*, wrote to Michael Barry. 'This really is no business of mine, but I'm working on *Nineteen Eighty-Four* and I feel so strongly about it that I wonder if others will not do the same. Every time I refer to the script I feel it should not be put on ... I hope you will excuse this

interference.' Cartier was more concerned that the sets were looking shoddy, and demanded that Learoyd be given more money to rectify matters. Jack Kine and Bernard Wilkie of the fledgling visual effects department were set to work on the special props – including the all-seeing telescreens – and a large model of the dried-up River Thames overshadowed by the Ministry of Truth.

Cushing was cast as hero Winston Smith and joined the production for the filming of the location sequences on 10 November. The first filming sessions were at Studio B, Alexandra Palace, and in the adjacent parkland on 10 and 11 November, and the remainder of pre-filming took place at Lime Grove from the 18th – 20th. Rehearsals were then held at the Mary Ward Settlement, Tavistock Place, from 22 November, and at 60 Paddington Street from 29 November. Studio rehearsals were held at Lime Grove on 11 and 12 December. Cushing was paid 150 guineas, his highest fee yet for a BBC project.

Nineteen Eighty-Four presents a vision of life in Britain in the future where a totalitarian regime has been established. Fronted by the image of 'Big Brother', the government uses surveillance devices – telescreens – to monitor the daily lives of the population, who are divided into three castes – the privileged Inner Party, the Outer Party and the uneducated 'Proles' who are fed computer-written pornography, music and drugs to keep them in a state of placid ignorance.

Winston Smith is an Outer Party worker whose job is to censor archived news reports to conform with the current party line. He keeps a diary in which he secretly questions the omnipotence of Big Brother, and he commits the ultimate crime when he falls in love with a girl called Julia (Yvonne Mitchell). They enjoy a forbidden courtship in the Prole sector, knowing that this is an unforgivable crime and that they can never win but, as Winston says, 'Some kinds of failure are better than others.'

Ultimately there can be no escape. At the Ministry of Love, Inner Party member O'Brien (André Morell) subjects Winston to a barrage of electric shocks, then to the horror of Room 101. 'By itself, pain is not always enough,' he explains. 'What happens in Room

In the Chestnut Tree café, Syme (Donald Pleasence) confesses to Winston Smith that he has committed 'thoughtcrime'. From *Nineteen Eighty-Four* (1954)

101 is the worst thing in the world. It can be death by burning, burial alive, or something quite trivial, not even fatal.' In Winston's case, the worst thing in the world is rats. O'Brien presents a mask, attached by a tube to a cage of rats. 'The mask ... fits over the head, leaving no exit. When the plastic door is raised up, the rats will shoot out like bullets. It was a common punishment in Imperial China...' in the climactic scene of the play, Winston breaks. 'Do it to Julia! I don't care what you to her. Do it to Julia! Not me!' The play concludes with Smith a broken man. Cushing's face fills the screen: 'I love Big Brother. I love Big Brother.'

Although Kneale effectively transformed Orwell's journalistic fable into a compelling play, and Cartier created, with documentary clarity, a nightmarish vision of a ruined, downtrodden London, it was Cushing's performance that gave the production its heart. Without him as 'the guardian of the human spirit' there would surely not have been the huge public outcry that resulted. People were responding to the sight of *Peter Cushing* being tortured – so convincing was the performance. Cushing gave everything to the role – even sacrificing his vanity (such as it was) by removing his false front teeth to show the brutality of Winston's ordeal.

Detail is the key here. On several occasions, with Cushing's face in extreme close-up, he is acting solely with his wide pale eyes. 'He said that to blink was too much on television,'[1] Joan Craft recalls. 'He served

Winston Smith and Mrs Parsons (Hilda Fenemore) with the Parsons children (Keith Davis and Pamela Grant)

Julia (Yvonne Mitchell) and Winston unwisely share a toast with O'Brien (André Morell) in *Nineteen Eighty-Four* (1954)

the close screen very well.' Smith bears the horror of 1984 with a weary determination, the traditional bulldog spirit, but distaste and resignation at the grime and the stench, the lack of razor-blades and the revolting 'regulation' stew. It must have had arrowing resonances to those who had lived through the privations of the war – meat rationing had only just been suspended in the summer of 1954.

As well as acting, Cartier also required Cushing to *sing*. 'He said "Zere is a sentimental sonk for ze Proles vich I vish you to sink,"' Cushing remembered, imitating Cartier's Viennese tones. 'So I sunk.'[2] Cushing is heard, off-screen, warbling 'It was Only a Hopeless Fancy' – the synthetic song created for the Proles ('The sentimental ones are issued sparingly,' murmurs O'Brien, 'so they're always popular'). He also sings the version of 'Underneath the Spreading Chestnut Tree' which is played in the café.

Cushing always worked well with a strong cast and the support here is exceptional. Yvonne Mitchell was voted Top TV Actress of 1953, and brings beauty and spirit to Julia. It is easy to believe that Winston and Julia are in love. In two intense scenes, Donald Pleasence presents Syme, who is translating the English dictionary into the insidious, economical 'newspeak' with an almost puritanical zeal. But it is André Morell's O'Brien, with whom Cushing shares the last act, who is the most terrifying representation of the regime. In Morell's hands, O'Brien's interrogation scenes are uneasily like seduction. 'My poor friend,' he whispers, 'you are almost well. It is not enough to *obey* Big Brother. You now know ... who it is you must love.'

The second performance of the play was recorded

by the BBC, and despite Cushing's insistence that it wasn't a patch on the first performance, it still makes for uncomfortable viewing. The haunting black-and-white photography owes more to European filmmaking than Hollywood, hardly surprising given Cartier's UFA background. Nothing like it had been seen on television before. The most disturbing alternative on the BBC in 1954 was indomitable quiz-show walrus Gilbert Harding hectoring the contestants on *What's My Line?*

'We don't give figures,' said a BBC spokesman, 'but a very considerable number have complained.' And indeed they had. 'Thank God for Wilfred Pickles and *The Grove Family*!' sighed D Hunt of Leicester. 'For weeks on Sundays we have to watch dismal, immoral and sadistically highbrow plays. The persons responsible for putting on *Nineteen Eighty-Four* are sadists and readers of horror comics.'

'I have a screen television,' wrote Lt Col J B Leicester-Warren, principal of Tabley House School for Boys 'and I had some very senior boys in to watch *Nineteen Eighty-Four*. This kind of play is the antithesis of anything Christian.' 'Unspeakably putrid. I hope you will not again pollute the air with similar muck!' said Mrs Pearl Lee of Colnbrook. 'If that is what the world is going to be like, we might as well put our heads in the gas ovens now.'

On the evening of 15 December there was a televised debate on *Nineteen Eighty-Four* with Cartier and Malcolm Muggeridge. There were questions in the House of Commons about whether such plays were appropriate for a Sunday and a suggestion that the scheduled repeat on Thursday 16th should not go ahead as planned. This repeat was to be a live broadcast of a second performance and the potential risks to personnel and equipment were taken very seriously indeed. On 15 December, even the unflappable Cartier requested extra security at Studios D and E, Lime Grove, for the next day in case anyone broke in to interfere with the transmissions or tamper with equipment.

Alison McLeod in the *Daily Worker* wrote, 'Orwell imagined that talk of "Communist immorality" might sound rather attractive, so sex ... was forbidden and we were edified by the sight of Peter Cushing and Yvonne Mitchell defiantly taking a roll in the hay for freedom. The final scene, which showed a Socialist torture machine looking like something out of the Festival of Britain ... bore out the BBC's warning that the play was not suitable for children or old people. They might have added "or anyone in between".'[3]

'People were asking me all yesterday,' wrote Cushing in the *Daily Express*, 14 December, 'why I agreed to play the part of Winston Smith. Well, to be frank, it was a job of work. But it was also more than that. People have complained that there is no hope in the play. That was Orwell's point. "Don't let totalitarianism happen," he said, "because if it happens, hope will die and love will die." Some of the critics have likened *1984* to a horror comic. In the play, Orwell shows a factory producing horror comics to debase the minds of the people. If his play is a horror comic, then it is a horror comic to expose what horror comics can do. I do not in the least blame or criticise the people who took offence at the play. I do not like whisky, but I do like tea. This does not mean that I wish to stop people drinking whisky, so long as they do not want to stop me drinking tea. I was reminded in rehearsing *1984* of *Gulliver's Travels*, which Dean Swift wrote as a vicious tirade against governmental abuses. I do not suggest that *1984* will ever become a book for children – but it must be remembered that George Orwell, too, was campaigning against the possibility of gross abuse of power.' Yvonne Mitchell also took up the cause: 'All of us who took part in this TV play were convinced of its importance and were proud to take part in it.'[4]

Not all the comments on *Nineteen Eighty-Four* were hostile. 'Thank Goodness Big Brother Could Not Strangle the BBC' cheered the *Daily Sketch*. 'I estimate that the BBC received about 1,000 calls,' said a reporter in the *Evening News*. 'out of a viewing audience of possibly nine million, this can hardly be regarded as damning evidence of disapproval. It is good to see the BBC doing something adventurous and sticking to its guns.'[5]

Michael Barry met Princess Margaret, who told him that she and her mother had watched on Sunday. 'In her view' he reported, 'it was one of the best productions she had ever seen on television.' Another of the BBC heads, D K Wolfe-Murray, was

presented to the Duke of Edinburgh on 15 December, and spent some time talking with him. 'He expressed his admiration for the play and message contained in Cartier's production. He also stated that the Queen herself was of the same opinion. He did not in any way charge me to be his messenger, but I have taken upon myself to inform R C and his three leading actors.'

Without doubt the most succinct and moving communication on the subject was a telegram to the BBC from H Stollery of Ipswich after the first broadcast which said simply: 'Please repeat *Nineteen Eighty-Four*. No doubt some have forgotten Belsen.'

While the furore over *Nineteen Eighty-Four* raged, Cushing was already preparing for his next play, again with a script by Nigel Kneale, again directed by Cartier and with Barry Learoyd again as designer. The play was called *The Creature*, and concerned the fabled Himalayan creature known as the Abominable Snowman. Cartier was leading an expedition to the

The intrepid botanist Doctor John Rollason embarks on a quest for the Abominable Snowman in Rudolph Cartier's production of *The Creature* (1955)

Jungfraujoch in the Bernese Oberland in Switzerland for location filming in the first week of the New Year, and there was some concern about possible hazard to the BBC's popular star. But Cushing wasn't going to be left behind, as he told Michael Barry. 'If it is for any reason other than a financial one that you didn't want me to risk doing the film work abroad I couldn't be more willing or eager to go on location for *The Creature*. I'm never keen on the idea of a double being used as I like to know what I'm doing in a play *all* the time. However, I appreciate your thoughts as to my well-being.' Cushing was allowed to participate in the overseas filming, and there was additional shooting at Lime Grove on 10 January. (When Hammer remade *The Creature* as *The Abominable Snowman* two years later, Cushing repeated his role but was *not* taken on location.)

Cushing played botanist John Rollason, who joins explorer Tom Friend on an expedition to find the legendary 'yeti' in the high peaks of Tibet. They are accompanied by a trapper, Brosset, and a young man called McPhee who sighted yeti footprints on a previous climb. When one of the man-like creatures is captured and killed, the explorers experience various kinds of telepathic assault, and all but Rollason are ultimately destroyed by their own fears.

The legend of the yeti in other hands would be no more than an excuse for a man in a fur suit to run amok. Kneale's script is his usual rich mix of mysticism and scientific hypothesis, brimming with atmosphere and imagination. The use of characters is economical and they are familiar Kneale types – the noble scientist, the venal hunter, the 'sensitive' loner. The script addresses Kneale's beloved themes of mind-control and ancient intelligence, as well as the idea that humanity, speeding headlong to his own destruction, will only continue to argue while greater powers wait in the wings. The writer's ability to create a whole civilisation in a handful of words is ably displayed in the Lama's speeches about 'those who will succeed man'.

In an interview in *Sight and Sound* magazine in 1959, Kneale recalled the transmission of *The Creature* for less than auspicious reasons. 'The play ... had what was intended as a tense, penultimate scene in a Himalayan ice cave at 22,000 feet. Two heavily-clad characters were acting hard on transmission when a figure appeared outside the cave. It wore a dust-coat and was busily sweeping up the eternal snows. A booby, it turned out, who was in a hurry to get home and thought he would clear up early. In those days plays were repeated live a few days later, so at the second transmission he was firmly warned. To make sure, the cave was rendered booby-proof with a black sky-cloth and a large stack of boxes. But, with a waywardness that had something wonderful in it, he managed to appear again.'[6]

Stanley Baker appeared as Friend, Simon Lack played McPhee and Eric Pohlmann played Brosset. Kneale's character names McNee and Shelley had been changed to McPhee and Brosset shortly before transmission, but were changed back for the film script. As well as Cushing, Arnold Marle (the Lama) and Wolfe Morris (Nima Kusang) would repeat their roles in the film. The play was transmitted on 30 January and 3 February from Studio D, Lime Grove.

The *Times*, which headed its review 'Quest Play on Television' on 31 January was singularly unimpressed and, with regard to the script, frankly unfair. 'The play in performance hovered always on the margin of the ludicrous, and alas, often overstepped it. Every conceivable effect of atmosphere – vast snowscapes, fiercely howling wind, foreboding music, night flares shining in the mountains, a whole monastery full of masked monks with Arnold Marle effective as the cropped, goggle-eyed lama – was put into Mr Rudolph Cartier's production to help the piece along, but nothing could raise it from the banal level of its dialogue and narrative. The main trouble presumably lies in the subject ... Mr Kneale's yeti in his big animal mask never became any more of a reality than the team of explorers with the attitudes and ideas of schoolboys who set out to catch him. For once even that good television actor Mr Peter Cushing, playing their leader, seemed dull.'[7]

The Independent Television Authority was established on 30 July 1954, and would create Britain's first commercial television network within 18 months. The opposition to independent television was vociferous and splenetic – some saw it as nothing less than the end of civilisation. As soon as the Independent Television Bill was passed, the BBC's immediate concern was that their stars would defect to 'the other side' and so began hurried negotiations to sign exclusive contracts with their most popular stars. Cushing was offered a contract on 24 December guaranteeing him eight plays in three years, at a fee of £1000 per annum. Cushing in turn had to guarantee a minimum of two performances per year. He could only appear on BBC television, but the contract could be suspended for 'a good part' on stage or in a film. Cushing's agent, John Redway, was part of the MCA Agency at 139 Piccadilly. As Cushing's film appearances were increasing but his television roles were also requiring a considerable amount of attention it was decided that Kenneth Cleveland, another MCA agent, would handle television work while Redway concentrated on the films. Cleveland could, however, drive a hard bargain and in the course of the next two years would give the BBC some cause for exasperation. Nevertheless, he was able to secure, to Cushing's advantage, a BBC contract for six plays in two years for a total sum of £1800. Little did MCA or the BBC suspect how Cushing's career would take off in the next two years, or how difficult it would be for him to complete the required six plays.

'BBC Sign Up Star of "1984"' wrote the *Observer* on 6 February 1955. 'The BBC have signed up Mr Peter Cushing, star of the televised production of "1984", Miss Anne Crawford, the stage and screen actress, and Miss Gillian Lutyens to appear exclusively in BBC television programmes for the next two years. These are the first of a series of contracts which are intended to give the BBC exclusive rights to the services of actors and actresses.'[8]

This news was a little premature. Cleveland was hammering the BBC's various draft contracts into shape and Cushing was not actually signed to the BBC over a sixpenny stamp until 17 March 1955. His first play under contract, however, was *The Moment of Truth*, which began rehearsals on 14 February.

The Moment of Truth was written for the stage by Peter Ustinov, based on the fate of Marshal Petain. It was a broad modern interpretation of *King Lear*, set in an imaginary country with Ustinov as the aged Field Marshal, an annoyed and intractable character who commands respect only by his reputation. Suddenly the Field Marshal finds himself called upon to deal with a new crisis – an atomic war –which he is completely unable to comprehend. Cushing played the Prime Minister, 'an apostle of surrender' as Ustinov wrote in the *Radio Times*. 'He is no villain in the accepted sense of the word; on the contrary he is a Prime Minister of crystalline perception, a man who, in his own words "Will save millions of lives; they will thank me by killing me" ... and who claims to be a better patriot than the ambitious general who wishes to continue the war of attrition.'[9] Also in the cast were Jeanette Sterke as the Marshal's daughter, Ian Colin as the General, and Hugh Griffith as the compassionate photographer, the everyman figure looking on at the conflict of love, duty, devotion, and honour. This was the third play in a row for Cushing directed by Rudolph Cartier, and was it broadcast on 6 and 10 March. In January, Michael Barry had written 'the quality of telerecording is improving so rapidly that it is now more than probable that we shall be making full use of telerecording facilities within the next three

General Memnon bids 'a bitter farewell' to his wife Barsine (Claire Bloom) in Robert Rossen's *Alexander the Great* (1955)

months.' Significantly, *The Moment of Truth* was the last play of Cushing's to have a performed repeat.

The rehearsal period for this heavyweight piece was leavened by the series of lunatic correspondences passed between Ustinov and Cushing which were reproduced in *Past Forgetting*. So involved were these notes, loaded with puns, caricatures and 'faked' newspaper cuttings that it is surprising they got any rehearsing done at all. Ustinov's notes to Cushing are masterpieces of abstract wit, Cushing's replies by comparison are more naïve, with his usual deliberately fractured spellings, as in *The Bois Saga*. On 8 March, between performances of *The Moment of Truth*, Alvin Rakoff suggested 'a Mexican play' (*The Legend of Pepito*) for broadcast on 5 June. Cushing declined.

In mid-March, shortly after signing his BBC contract, Cushing flew with Helen to Spain for his most ambitious film project yet – *Alexander the Great*. This

Barsine (Claire Bloom) with powerful rivals Memnon and Alexander (Richard Burton) in *Alexander the Great* (1955)

was an epic feature from United Artists, in Cinemascope, directed by Robert Rossen at the Sevilla Studios in Madrid. 30-year-old Richard Burton played the 22-year-old Alexander with an all-star cast including Fredric March, Harry Andrews, Stanley Baker and Claire Bloom while Cushing played Memnon, the Athenian general who opposed Alexander at the Battle of Granicus. In his long black wig and saturnine beard, Cushing cuts a far more heroic figure than poor Richard Burton, who with his peroxide blonde curls looks like nothing so much as an elderly cherub.

Memnon is employed by the Persians (in charge, a blacked-up Harry Andrews) to use his military skills against Alexander. 'My Lords of Persia listen well!' proclaims Cushing, an index finger stabbing the sky, 'Alexander is like a hungry lion on the scent of blood. He needs a fight, a kill, and he needs it quickly...' The Persians will not agree to Memnon's scorched-earth policy, so he returns to his wife Barsine (Claire Bloom), knowing that a straight fight with Alexander will mean certain death. But Barsine has already fallen in love with Alexander. 'This is a bitter farewell...' murmurs Memnon. Cushing's goodbye scene with Claire Bloom is superb and the actors seem to have a genuine rapport.

The staging of the Battle of Granicus is duly massive, with swarms of teeming actors and Cushing in leather armour leading the attack on horseback. Memnon loses his horse and quickly loses his life, but his death-scene is peculiarly shot and strangely anti-climactic, victim of the director's fondness for (often messy) montage. 'Not a scene is held for a second longer than its worth,' huffed Alexander Walker. 'Greatness is pictured in constant dissolve.' As befits an epic, Cushing's performance throughout has a perfectly-pitched theatricality, but the emotion there is brilliantly controlled. Among some very high-powered actors his is quite possibly the finest performance in the film.

While in Spain, Cushing continued an active correspondence with the BBC, considering new roles and reading scripts. On 14 April 1955, he wrote to Michael Barry on specially embossed *Alexander the Great* notepaper, from the Castellana Hilton. 'Dear Michael, I am more than enthusiastic about *The Sun and I*, an enchanting play! I would dearly love to play Charles, and have written in detail to John Redway about it and my time here, which at the moment is highly pro-longed [sic]. I do hope some mutually convenient arrangement could be made to enable me to do the play. My only fear is that it might be somewhat episodic – might it be cut down to an hour-and-a-half? Michael Redington would be ideal as 'David' and I do hope you will bring your good offices to help this young and deserving actor. One cannot help but see Peggy Ashcroft as the wife and Kathleen Harrison as the maid! Do you agree?'

Filming for *Alexander the Great* was indeed prolonged, much to the fury of several cast members – Richard Burton in particular was losing faith with the project. On 29 April Michael Barry made the decision to proceed with *The Sun and I* without Cushing. The play concerned the disappointed life of headmaster Charles Cartwright, a 'big fish in a small pond'. It was directed by Campbell Logan and broadcast on 29 May 1955, starring David Markham (who had appeared with Cushing in *Pride and Prejudice*) as Cartwright and Pauline Jameson as his wife.

Cushing wrote back to Barry on 13 May. 'I am so sorry to miss *The Sun and I* and wish you all success with it. This film is taking much longer than was at first anticipated but we hope to be home early in June. I'm not sure of my future dates yet, and I would like a week or so free when I return (to recover! and deal with the accumulated mail, etc), but I would like to do *The Browning Version* very much sometime this year, if it will fit into the scheme of things to come!'

Chapter Ten

Richard II, Irving Nil

Terence Rattigan's short play *The Browning Version* was fitted into the scheme of things almost immediately. The play was rehearsed the following month from 25 June to 11 July. Rattigan was consulted about the casting and replied by telegram 'Agree Peter Cushing if Eric Portman impossible.' Portman had originated the role on stage.

The Browning Version presents an hour in the life of a severe public school master, Andrew Crocker-Harris – 'the Crock' as he is nicknamed by his pupils. He is retiring due to a weak heart, he has failed to get the headmastership he once coveted, he has failed to earn the love of his pupils and has singularly failed to keep the love of his wife, Millie, who is having an affair with another master, Frank Hunter.

'Crocker-Harris is the old type of schoolmaster,' wrote Peter Currie in the *Radio Times,* 'a classicist in a world that has no time for the classics. And now, forced into premature retirement, he needs all he can muster of the stoic spirit. Yet in the heart of such a man there is more rejoicing over one pupil who responds more than all the rest and appropriately it is

Millie Crocker-Harris (Joyce Heron) displays her contempt for her passionless husband Andrew in the BBC's adaptation of Terence Rattigan's *The Browning Version* (1955)

Peter with Helen (and the Jaguar) on holiday in Norfolk, summer 1955

one of the boys who brings some comfort to Crocker-Harris.'[1]

At the end of the play, Crocker-Harris is given a present by his pupil Taplow – a translation of the *Agamemnon* by Robert Browning, inscribed with the quotation 'God from afar looks graciously upon the gentle master.' Because of Taplow's kindness, and because of his wife's vain attempt to spoil the gesture, Crocker-Harris is able finally to take control of his life.

The play was transmitted from Lime Grove on 12 July and the producer was Campbell Logan. Joyce Heron co-starred as Millie Crocker-Harris and Michael Gwynn was her lover, Frank Hunter. (In 1958, Gwynn would play the unfortunate victim of one of Cushing's experiments in *The Revenge of Frankenstein*.)

In the role of John Taplow was Andrew Ray, the wide-eyed child star of Ealing's *The Mudlark* (1950) and *The Yellow Balloon* (1952). 'I remember well appearing with Peter in *The Browning Version*,' says Ray. 'I was only 14 at the time but I remember what a lovely gentle man he was and what a fine actor. He was wonderful as Crocker-Harris and I have often thought since that if he had not taken the Hammer road to horror he would have had a very distinguished career in other areas of theatre. This is not to decry those movies, but in a way his talents were wasted in them, I feel.'[2]

With a profitable blockbuster under his belt and a critical success on television, the Cushings had reason to celebrate in the summer of 1955. They went to stay with Michael and Ann Redington near Cromer, where Redington was running a small repertory theatre for a summer season. With the money from *Alexander*, Cushing had been able to purchase his dream car – a

powder-blue Jaguar, which was pressed into 'active service' rather sooner than anticipated, as Redington recalls. 'Peter went all the way to Coventry to get this Jaguar, and the rules then were that you could only go at 30 miles per hour with a new car. Helen knew all about our theatre and said "We'd love to come up and stay with you, have a lovely holiday, Peter can do his paintings." So Peter and Helen stayed in a flat in our digs. It was a very simple town hall theatre, not much more than a village hall, and we didn't have any lights, so I asked Peter if he would go to Covent Garden and pick some up. So there he was, in this brand new Jaguar, driving all the way up to Cromer loaded down with my lights. He adored it. He enjoyed being in the countryside, and near to Edward Seago, who lived there, and he had the whole of East Anglia to paint. He was very happy and very relaxed.

'He used to encourage me, because I was running this theatre on my own, and I was only 28. One play we were doing was one of the Whitehall farces, and there were asterisks all over the script. It said "This is for the benefit of amateur performers. An asterisk indicates where the main laughs come." You couldn't see anything remotely funny near any of these asterisks, so I said to Peter please come to the first night, and help us with the laughs. Darling Peter, I shall never forget as long as I live, the curtains drew apart very, very slowly and he laughed. That started the whole thing off and it was terrific.'

Soon after independent television began transmission on 22 September, Redington became an ITV producer. 'I did the religious programmes, probably because no-one wanted to do them. One thing I wanted to do, as a religious programme, was an interview with the Devil. A sort of *Face to Face* thing, with Peter as the Devil. Christopher Hollis wrote a brilliant script, but in the end we couldn't do it. I think there were some raised eyebrows at the idea.'[3]

By 17 August, discussions were well underway for Cushing to star in a production on the life of the actor Henry Irving. Michael Barry sent a draft script by Christopher Hassall and also suggested 'something that might appeal and work in not too arduously. I am currently completing an adaptation of *The Scarlet Pimpernel* – I dare not tell you how drastically, because the old piece certainly requires it. Nothing would make me happier than to have you with me playing Chauvelin, which I believe you would relish without having to become involved in too much thoughtful work – boot and spur fun.'

Considering that *Irving* was to be broadcast only four days after *The Scarlet Pimpernel*, it is extremely odd that Barry should encourage Cushing to work on the two plays in parallel. Despite his love of 'boot and spur fun' Cushing declined *The Scarlet Pimpernel*, which went ahead on 18 September 1955 with Tony Britton as Sir Percy Blakeney and Douglas Wilmer as Citizen Chauvelin. Wilmer, a popular actor of imperious bearing, would inherit several 'Cushing parts' and in 1965 would become an extremely popular *Sherlock Holmes* for the BBC.

At the beginning of September 1955, Cushing finally rejected *Irving*. Even Michael Redington, who was with him at the time, can offer little by way of explanation. 'He just didn't want to do it. It was about real people and I just don't think Peter thought it was very true. I know Helen read a lot of the scripts, and she was generally spot on. But I don't know why he didn't want to do *Irving*. Maybe he thought it was too big.'[4]

On 8 September, Michael Barry wrote to Cushing in some bewilderment. 'Thank you for your letter. In it you say that you thank me for understanding but in this case I do not. I find myself deeply concerned ... and a frank and personal letter appears to me to be the only course. You speak of your rejection of *Irving* in the terms that we mutually understand when discussing this or that play. I submit that this project has never been regarded in that light. From the inception of the programme, in discussions with you early this year, the intention has been to pay tribute. This was clearly understood and I made it the key to all my conversations both within and without the Corporation. The intention was supported by a sense of professional dedication. I deliberately use these words and avoid "obligation" or "moral", but it has seemed to me that the responsibility spread deeply across our profession with an importance that does not begin to exist on the occasion of a normal BBC television play. It was for this reason that we selected with care the work. Skill and affection has been directed towards this project during the past months. A contemporary poet and dramatist of standing has completed a script to the considerable satisfaction of Laurence Irving and myself, backed on this occasion by the unanimous approval of the small group whose critical opinion are used to support me when my script decisions are made ... My own work as a writer ... makes me reluctant to allow criticism to pass completely unchallenged. You Peter have expressed a contrary opinion, although you have yet to give, as far as I am concerned, one valid reason. In the normal course of events, once I am convinced that a respected actor has formed an opinion personal to his art ... I am satisfied. On this occasion, and in the light of the wider background I have tried to remind you of, I am by no means satisfied that the decision is not too puny for the Peter Cushing I know as a professional colleague.'

However, Cushing was still under contract to the BBC so work went on to find another suitable TV role. Meanwhile, he took part in three radio plays – *Wife For Sale*, the navy comedy *Seagulls Over Sorrento* (Cushing's personal choice, which was presented in a season called *Stars In Their Choices*) and *Escape Me Never*.

In *Wife For Sale*, Cushing was once again called upon to sing. Producer Charles LeFaux had been expecting to get a double for the singing, but it suddenly became necessary to pre-record the song as classical guitarist Julian Bream was only available on one day, 9 September. Cushing wrote to LeFaux on 31 August: 'Please don't imagine that I regard myself as a singer, I am anything but! However, I have done a little in similar parts (including the "prole-ified" song in *Nineteen Eighty-Four* – the budget wouldn't "go" to a professional singer) and I like to do everything that is humanly possible *myself* to the building of a character. I know that you will have patience with me at the recording of this (and I hope Julian

Peter and Helen in front of their digs during the idyllic summer of 1955. Another of Michael and Ann Redington's holiday snaps from Cromer

King Richard is comforted by his young wife Anne (Jeanette Sterke)
in *Richard of Bordeaux* (1955)

into transcription discs. The recording of *Seagulls* on 30 November 1955 was obviously trying for Cushing. He wrote to LeFaux: 'Thank you so much for all your great help on *S.O.S.* – what an apt abbreviation! I do hope it was really alright. I had so many doubts afterwards!'

The end of 1955 saw him receiving the Guild of Television Producers and Directors Best Performance Award for *Nineteen Eighty-Four*.

After the radio plays, Cusing was straight into rehearsals on 5 December for *Richard of Bordeaux*. This was to be broadcast on 29 December from Lime Grove. The producer was Victor Menzies.

The *Radio Times* wrote: 'Produced at the New Theatre in 1935, *Richard of Bordeaux* was a historic play in more than the obvious sense. It made John Gielgud, already a fine actor, into a star recognised by an enormous public. What dramatist in England would have had the courage to take Shakespeare's hero and a good many of Shakespeare's subsidiary characters, re-shuffle them, afford them everyday, even casual contemporary speech, and make them into a smash hit? Charm is the play's keynote. It has a light, tragi-comic elegance, a light wit, a light melancholy. Richard is a magically charming, brilliant, many-faceted character – the role is a rewarding one for an actor of variety, pyrotechnical expertise, dazzle and the sort of magic that can enslave an audience. Where chronicle plays are often tedious, involved, and emotionally dead, *Richard of Bordeaux* presents historical events and personages in a graceful and contemporary manner. Romantically rosy, no doubt, but persuasive. London was completely bewitched; the play's last line (and Gielgud's delivery of it) became part of theatrical history: "How Robert would have laughed!" The play is a marvellous context for star performance, and it is fitting that the leading parts tonight should be played by two who largely owe their fame to television – the lean-featured Peter Cushing, and pretty, dark-eyed Jeannette Sterke.'[5] *Richard of Bordeaux* was written by the novelist Josephine Tey (*Brat Farrar*, *The Franchise Affair*) who was born Elizabeth MacKintosh in Scotland and wrote plays during the 1930s under the pseudonym Gordon Daviot.

In the early part of the production, Cushing's attempts to present the lovestruck, petulant young Richard are hampered by his high-pitched, flowery

Bream will too!)' Cushing duly recorded the song on the 9th and the rest of *Wife For Sale* on 12 September 1955. His fee was 28 guineas.

At the end of October, another television role was offered – the lead in the BBC's prestigious Christmas production of *Richard of Bordeaux*. Cushing liked the part and was keen that Alvin Rakoff direct but Rakoff turned it down. The director wrote to Cushing, telling him this was 'the sort of thing other people can do so much better than I!' Cushing was quick to argue the contrary. 'Alvin, dear fellow,' he wrote on 7 November. 'I saw yer *Makepeace* last night! It doesn't matter what the play is like as long as you are producing it. Congratulations and ONWARDS to further glories. (Pity about *Richard*!)'

Rakoff's '*Makepeace*' was the *Sunday Night Theatre* production of *The New Executive* broadcast on 6 November 1955. This was the last in a cycle of four plays, collectively entitled *The Makepeace Saga*, chronicling the life of an industrial family in the North of England.

Escape Me Never was rehearsed on 23 and 24 November, and recorded on the 25th. *Seagulls Over Sorrento* was rehearsed and recorded the following week for a fee of 40 guineas. Both plays were made

delivery, although it is a stretch to expect *any* 42-year-old to play a teenager convincingly. Jeanette Sterke's oo-la-la French accent – ''Ees silly tender 'art betrayed 'im', etc – doesn't help. The chief delights are Richard's bullying uncles – Joseph O'Conor's roaring, bearlike Gloucester ('as tactful as an angry wasp') and George Woodbridge's grumbling Earl of Arundel. With a deft touch, the ever-reliable Robin Bailey plays Richard's brother, the poetically-inclined Earl of Oxford, who is 'searching for a rhyme having failed to find reason.' As Richard matures, so Cushing's performance becomes more assured. The young King is forced to realise that 'to become an expert in murder cannot be so difficult...' Cushing revels in a moment of cutting wit, as Richard tells his enemies 'The only persons I trust are 2,000 archers, paid regularly every Friday.'

The last scenes are touching, as we see Richard, worn down by battle and saddened by the death of Anne, facing exile. 'I should have learned from the archbishop how to do an evil thing gracefully' he sighs. His voice cracks in disbelief as he reads the charges against him: 'Insufficient and useless ... unworthy to rule ... Tyranny. Have I been a tyrant?

At least no tyrant has shed less blood.' He is imprisoned, but still finds time to worry about his worn-out shoes. 'Could I start a new fashion – shoes with no toes? To lose one's kingdom is humbling, but to be *down at heel* is utter humiliation.'

The play is obviously several notches down technically from *Nineteen Eighty-Four*, with clumsy camera moves, threadbare scenery and ponderous, irrelevant filmed inserts, making Cartier's achievement of a whole year before all the more incredible.

Nevertheless the *Daily Telegraph* praised the 'fluent and successful' production. 'The revival of ... *Richard of Bordeaux* on BBC television last night revealed that the play has lost little of its power ... In this study of Richard II mastering his early defects of character, only to succumb in the end to over-confidence, there is perhaps little depth, but much lightness, fluency and grace. As the King, Peter Cushing gave as usual, an intelligent, carefully thought-out performance, yet a romantic quality in the character, an aspect of which Gielgud made much, escaped him.'[6] A telerecording of *Richard of Bordeaux* is preserved in the National Film Archive.

Jeanette Sterke as Anne of Bohemia with Cushing as the young King Richard in the BBC's *Richard of Bordeaux* (1955)

In the first few months of 1956, Cushing took a rest after the hectic schedule of 1955, and in April was again released from his BBC contract to take part in the West End production of *The Silver Whistle* by Robert McEnroe at the Duchess Theatre. Cushing played Oliver Erwenter, a tramp-like confidence trickster who inveigles his way into an old people's home but ultimately changes the lives of the residents for the better. The part of Erwenter had originally been played on Broadway by Jose Ferrer, and Cushing described it as being something like the character played by Robert Preston in *The Music Man*. The production was supervised by Lee Marvin's brother Mark, and starred, in a presentiment of Cushing's career-changing film of later in the year, 77-year-old Ernest Thesiger. In 1935, Thesiger had played the waspish Doctor Pretorius in James Whale's *Bride of Frankenstein*. Other character players involved in *The Silver Whistle* included Robin Bailey (from *Richard of Bordeaux*), Alfie Bass, Peter Vaughn, Olga Lindo and Mary Merrall.

The play was not, however, destined for a lengthy run. It closed on 12 May after some exceptionally bad notices and only twelve performances. 'It was a very good performance from Peter,' wrote Kenneth Cleveland. 'A pity the critics were not of the same opinion!' The dismayed cast learned shortly afterwards that Mark Marvin had returned to New York and commited suicide.

Later in May, Cushing was invited onto the popular *House* magazine programme to talk about his collection of toy soldiers. The armies were to be brought into the studio – 'the producer to arrange insurance cover and transport'. The producer was Josephine Douglas, who wrote to thank Cushing for agreeing to give up his Whit Sunday to come into the studio. Cushing replied that he was nervous about giving an impromptu talk. This was duly sorted out and Cushing wrote to Douglas again. 'I'm very pleased that Larry Forrester is giving me my words. I am no good at making them up and become quite asinine unless they are written for me.' Jo Douglas, who was also an actress, would eventually go into feature film production and was the producer of Hammer's *Dracula A.D. 1972*.

Cushing's next role was in the film *Time Without Pity*, directed by Joseph Losey. American director Losey fled Hollywood in 1952 during the Cold War witch-hunts initiated by Senator Joseph McCarthy, by which all those suspected of Communist allegiances, particularly those in the entertainment industry, were blacklisted and prevented from working. (*The End of the Affair*'s director Edward Dmytryk had come to England for the same reason.) Losey was allowed to live and work in England, and directed two films under the alias Joseph Walton. His first credit under his own name on a British film was the 1955 Hammer short *A Man on the Beach*.

Time Without Pity was produced by Leon Clore for his own company Harlequin Films and was backed by distributor Eros to the tune of £100,000. The film was based on Emlyn Williams' play *Someone Waiting*, which Losey and Clore rewrote significantly. Three months of filming began in June 1956 at British National Studios, Elstree, although Cushing was only required between 25 June and 28 July at a fee of £150 per day. The BBC contract was suspended during shooting, the Corporation's bookings manager Holland Bennett noting sternly to Kenneth Cleveland: 'I have given you a good deal of latitude over the interpretation of this contract.'

Cushing was part of a distinguished British cast, including Michael Redgrave (who was on a fee of £5000 for the film) Leo McKern and 'Dear Annoushka' – Ann Todd. Redgrave played alcoholic author David Graham, who is forced to conduct his own frantic investigation when his son is accused of murder and sentenced to death. The film was scarcely noticed in England upon its opening in March 1957 (largely because Losey fell out with his backers, who then refused to promote it) but it apparently caused great excitement among cinephiles when it was released in France three years later.

Losey encouraged some strong performances from his cast – Redgrave's harrowing portrait of a desperate, tragic father, Leo McKern's barnstorming turn as a bullying car magnate – but Cushing has little to work with as lawyer Jeremy Clayton, who is something of an automaton. 'Stop thinking like a lawyer,' wails Graham. 'Tell me what you believe as a *man*!' When Clayton meets Graham at the opening of the film, Cushing clearly shows that the lawyer is upset at conveying the devastating news. When Redgrave says 'I couldn't come sooner' Cushing's mute nod conveys everything the lawyer already knows about Graham's alcoholism. Losey presents a portrait of fifties' London as only an outsider could paint, at once modern and stiflingly old-fashioned, but the film conveys a real sense of rising panic and the genuinely terrifying threat of the death penalty. Critic Foster Hirsch stated that the film tried to be 'too many things at once – a chase thriller, a psychological study of dominance, a statement against capital punishment – without having the force or clarity to treat any of its themes in depth.'[7]

Cushing's filming on *Time Without Pity* overran into the rehearsal period for his next BBC project, the popular suburban mystery *Home at Seven*, in which he played David Preston. Four years earlier, in 1952, Ralph Richardson had directed and starred in a film version of the play, which had been a great success on the London stage. The BBC rehearsals were scheduled from 25 July to 11 August, and *Home at Seven* was broadcast on 12 August 1956 from Lime Grove, produced by Stephen Harrison. 'David Preston works in a London bank,' explained Elwyn Jones in the *Radio Times*. 'He is a senior official and hopes to become manager of the branch in Eastbourne. Meanwhile he lives in Bromley, Kent with his wife Janet. It is an ordinary humdrum existence. David and Janet are devoted to each other and have grown to respect each other's susceptibilities. There are not many of these, except that Janet does not really approve of alcohol and is anxious not to have strong drink in the house. David, on the other hand, likes his glass of sherry in the evening, and contrives to have it without offending Janet. Against this conventional, even dull background, R C Sherriff's unexpected drama is played out. David always arrives home at seven. And in his mind tonight is the same as any other night. As the town hall clock begins to strike seven, he puts his latch-key in the door, hangs up his coat and drops his umbrella into the hall-stand. "It's been just an ordinary day, dear," he says "just like any other Monday." The catch is that it *isn't* Monday...'[8]

In the role of Janet Preston was Helen Shingler, who had played Cushing's screen wife before, in his first television play *Eden End*. Shingler's kindness to the desperately nervous beginner on that occasion was never forgotten. Cushing was also delighted to be in a play by RC Sherriff, author of his beloved *Journey's End*.

Aware that Rudolph Cartier was preparing *Cyrano De Bergerac*, Cushing sent him a casting suggestion for the female lead and finished with a nod to *Nineteen Eighty-Four*. 'To Rudy re: *Cyrano*. Virginia McKenna as Roxanne? Helen joins me in sending you love and the cry "Down with Goldstein!"' McKenna was a co-winner with Cushing of the *Daily Mail* Television Award for 1955. On 17 July, Cushing provisionally agreed to appearing in *Dark Victory* for the BBC on 18 November.

On 7 August, Cleveland wrote to the BBC stating that *Home at Seven* was Cushing's fifth play under contract and *Dark Victory* would be the sixth, thereby concluding the contract. He told the BBC that Cushing had been offered a 'very nice part in a TV film series in about two or three weeks' time.' The series was *The Adventures of Sir Lancelot*, produced by Dallas Bower for Sapphire Films. With William Russell playing Lancelot, it is likely Cushing was being sought to play King Arthur or Merlin.

The BBC were not pleased at all. Norman Rutherford wrote in the strongest terms to Holland Bennett: 'I feel that Cushing is now such a nuisance that the goodwill of Kenneth Cleveland we could claim by granting this request is more valuable than

Peter and Helen Cushing arrive at the Savoy for the Guild of Television Producers and Directors Awards. Cushing received the Best Actor Award for *Nineteen Eighty-Four*

anything we or our audience will gain by sticking to protocol.' On 9 August, Bennett wrote, with clenched teeth, to Cleveland. 'We have no objections to Cushing doing a series of television films provided you confirm he will be able to do *Dark Victory*.'

On 10 August, Cushing turned down *Dark Victory*. There was no reason given for this decision, and it was a play that Cushing seemed keen to do. (By the transmission date of 18 November, however, Cushing would be under contract to Hammer Film Productions.)

On 23 September, *Henry Irving* finally surfaced, a year later than Michael Barry had originally intended. Cushing was interested in appearing in *Uncle Vanya* but this went no further. The assistant head of bookings noted of Cushing: 'I gather that this artist has not been particularly helpful over the different parts you have suggested his playing under his long-term contract.' Barry responded immediately that 'this is not the time to drop a valuable property.' The BBC asked Cushing to suggest a play and he nominated the Victorian melodrama *Gaslight*. Before that, however, came *The Curse of Frankenstein*.

Chapter Eleven

Enter Baron Frankenstein

It is understood that Hammer had tried to engage Cushing before 1956, although not in which film he was to have starred. What is likely is that they would have been considering *The Creature* as a subject after its transmission in January 1955 – having already completed the film of *The Quatermass Xperiment* (as Hammer renamed the television serial) at the end of 1954. Producer Anthony Hinds attests that he and Hammer managing director James Carreras pursued Cushing, believing that a popular television name would bring audiences back into the cinema.

Cushing saw the trade advertisements for a new colour version of *Frankenstein*, recalled the 'marvellous' film starring Boris Karloff and Colin Clive and, feeling that it could be a potential hit, asked John Redway to put his name forward. The timing of events here was providential – Cushing's preferred vehicles, the 'well-made' plays of Coward and Rattigan, were facing extinction in the West End following the arrival of John Osborne's anti-establishment tirade *Look Back in Anger*, first staged at London's Royal Court Theatre in May 1956. The Angry Young Man and the 'Kitchen Sink' drama were suddenly the rage and Cushing, like many actors of his generation, could not see himself in work of that style. As it was, in one move he established a new career for himself, and was given a rather different type of angry young man to play.

Cushing was invited to a screening of the newly-completed Hammer film *X the Unknown*, Jimmy Sangster's *Quatermass*-inspired story of a sentient radioactive slime that menaces a remote army base. Cushing enjoyed the film and was sold on Frankenstein. His contract with Hammer was signed on 26 October and reported in the *Kinematograph Weekly* edition of 8 November.

The Curse of Frankenstein began filming at Hammer's Bray Studios on 19 November 1956 with director Terence Fisher. Cushing's fee, at £1,400, was equivalent to more than a year's pay at the BBC. He was contracted at £100 per day for 14 shooting days in the original schedule, but shooting over-ran by three weeks and details of Cushing's final fee are not recorded. Cushing's contract gave the title of the film as simply *Frankenstein*.

To preclude the legal intervention of Universal, who held copyright in the image of Karloff's flat-headed Creature, screenwriters Jimmy Sangster and (the uncredited) Anthony Hinds had to develop a completely new script from Shelley's story. They cut it down to the basic concepts and a minimum of characters, placing it in a Victorian chocolate-box *milieu* of frock-coats and crinolines. Baron Frankenstein became a Byronic figure, to which Cushing was ideally suited.

Awaiting the guillotine in his prison cell, Frankenstein tells his story to a priest: of how, after years of research, he and his former tutor Paul Krempe had developed a means of bringing life to a dead body. Frankenstein then determined to build a perfect Creature, and went about acquiring materials from charnel houses. He murdered the elderly Professor Bernstein so that the Creature could possess 'the matured brain of a genius' but the brain was damaged, and when the Creature was brought to life, its first and only instinct was to kill...

Such is the economy of storytelling that we are scarcely ten minutes into the film before the grown-up Baron is up to his grisly business in his attic laboratory with Paul (played by Robert Urquhart) looking on. In keeping with his intention that the story was to be presented like a fairy-tale, Fisher leads us through an almost magical array of vividly-coloured liquids, humming machinery and the spinning vanes of the generator. With total control, Cushing conducts a symphony of sparks and flashes, adjusting a retort here, flicking a lever there, his eyes darting from one piece of equipment to the next. Fisher used close-ups judiciously and rarely fills the screen with the Baron's face, except just after Frankenstein and Paul complete their first experiment to resurrect a dead puppy. Frankenstein listens for the dog's heartbeat and Cushing's expression of wonder is accentuated by a triumphal key-change in James Bernard's thrilling score. The great attraction of the Baron's character is his complete delight in his own work. Cushing's charm ensures that the viewer *wants* Frankenstein to succeed, however dreadful his intent. 'Neither wicked nor insane,' says Paul of his former pupil. 'Just so dedicated that he can't see the terrible consequences that could result.' Later Frankenstein

Paul Krempe (Robert Urquhart) watches as Frankenstein revives a dog in *The Curse of Frankenstein* (1956)

shows off a stolen pair of hands with a guileless little smile, like a schoolboy with a prize conker, and sings happily to himself as he pops a pair of eyes into a jar.

Despite criticisms of excessive gore and gristle, Sangster and Hinds' script elucidates more grisly details than we actually see. 'Half the head's eaten away' grimaces Paul of the newly acquired corpse they bring back to the laboratory. Fisher deftly catches the glint of light on a knife and Urquhart's look of suspicion and revulsion as Frankenstein cuts off the head, then idly wipes his bloodied hand on his lapel.

Throughout the film, the Baron is rarely off the screen for more than a few moments, and when he is not delivering his lines Cushing shows us that Frankenstein is listening and thinking, his mind working each new situation to his advantage. When his cousin Elizabeth (Hazel Court) arrives, engaged to marry him under a childhood arrangement, Frankenstein uses her as a housekeeper – while carrying on an affair with the maid Justine (Valerie Gaunt). Then, when he needs a bargaining tool to ensure Paul's co-operation, he threatens to involve Elizabeth. The jealous Justine announces that she is

pregnant, and the Baron throws her to his newly re-born Creature without compunction.

The Creature itself is only on screen for about ten minutes and unconscious for half of those. But its first appearance is a moment of true horror that shows Terence Fisher's ability to deliver a really potent scare when he wanted to. In the role of the creature was 34-year-old Christopher Lee and, after attempting to strangle Cushing to death in their first scene together, went on to be a lifelong friend.

Lee was another client of John Redway – the agent was asked simply to suggest tall actors to play the Creature. Lee was chosen, and then endured an arduous series of make-up tests before a suitable image for the monster was found. For Lee, working on the film was a happy and rewarding experience, not least because of his chief co-star. 'From the first time we met at Bray, Peter Cushing and I were friends,' Lee admits. 'I soon found Peter was the great perfectionist who learned not only his own lines but everybody else's, but withal had a gentle humour which made it quite impossible for anybody to be pompous in his company.'[1]

Derek Whitehurst was working at Bray on a television series with Errol Flynn when he was asked to be first assistant director on *The Curse of Frankenstein*. 'There was nothing at Bray then. There was just the house and one tiny stage. We shot *The Curse of Frankenstein* in the winter, which was bitterly cold. There was no central heating! I don't think Peter knew what he was in for – that this was the start of a career in that sort of thing. Seeing him do anything vicious onscreen was always such a shock, because there was nothing vicious about him at all. He was very charming and very gentle. Helen wasn't around at Hammer in the early days, he didn't need it. But Peter used to flirt deliciously. It meant nothing of course, but it was a delight to see. Just this charming, gentlemanly, courteous flirting. And Peter was very athletic. There was lots of swagger and thrust, and those little sets at Bray couldn't really stand up to it when he was really belting around. But it was *precisely* controlled. He should have done the show with Errol Flynn because Peter was once of the original swashbucklers.

'Nobody got very much money – I think Chris Lee got £500. I was 22 or 23 and as an assistant director I was getting £25 a week. At the beginning there were conferences at the Hammer offices in Wardour Street, and everybody used to throw ideas in. Even a lowly junior like me could throw in suggestions. I said Frankenstein should have a Gladstone bag and they kept that in. Peter would come up with lots of suggestions about his wardrobe. At the start of the film, he would always have his props ready. Certainly on the first *Frankenstein* he was very particular about the whole set up, his fob watch, the magnifying glass, the boots and the cane.

'The prison entrance was shot in the main house, where the reception at Bray is now. They just clad it and painted it. You can see the fire-buckets. Next to the house was this little white building, and that was the stage. It was crammed with Frankenstein's workshop – all the machinery – you could hardly

Peter Cushing as Frankenstein with Hazel Court as his betrothed Elizabeth in *The Curse of Frankenstein* (1956)

move. Everything was jammed in there, and the camera. In one of the first scenes we did with Peter we had a little puppy for the Baron to try out his machinery. Peter was standing at the table and the puppy was given anaesthetic to keep it still. The owner said it was alright just to give it a whiff, but somebody overdid it and it died. It was very sad, Peter was terribly upset. It could never happen now, and it shouldn't have happened then. Every time I go to that stage I think of that poor dog.

'We filmed the scene when the monster has just killed the blind man and it was on the river's edge at Bray on a freezing cold miserable day. Chris was staggering about, and Peter shoots him in eye. Peter does it brilliantly and Chris does it brilliantly, and nature adds the most wonderful touch. As the creature falls, there is just a gust of wind and all the leaves billow around. Chris got the blood behind his contact lens and they had to spend forever washing his eye. Jack Asher photographed it in Eastmancolor, and it looked gorgeous. I think Peter appreciated Jack very much – there was a great affinity between them as technicians. And of course, Peter hit it off with Chris immediately. They were enormously fond of each other.'[2]

Lee would join Cushing in impromptu musical numbers, Victorian patter songs and snatches from grand opera. It could sometimes be a bizarre experience, as Whitehurst recalls. 'One day at the viewing of the rushes, just to entertain us, Peter got up – I suppose he was in costume – with Chris, who had the whole horror thing on, and they did a little dance, a macabre little two-step, in front of the screen.' Lee would also do impersonations. Searching the Bray pantry for something he could eat without ruining his make-up, Lee imitated the exasperated splutter of Sylvester the Cat – 'Bird theed! I'll *thtarve*!!' The phrase, and Lee's delivery of it, would never fail to reduce Cushing to helpless fits of laughter.

For a film now regarded as one of the most influential fantasy/horror films ever made, contemporary reviews in Britain were generally unkind. When the film opened on 2 May 1957, the *Observer* placed it 'among the half dozen most repulsive films I have encountered in 10,000 miles of film reviewing.'[4] 'The most revolting exhibition I can remember seeing on the screen!'[5] frothed R D Smith in the *Tribune*. And so it continued. Cushing, very wisely, took no notice, and his faith in the project was borne out in a couple of weeks by the spectacular box-office returns. The American reviews were subsequently much kinder, many singling Cushing out for particular praise. 'Cushing enacts the role of ... Frankenstein without overacting,' wrote Jim O'Connor in the *New York Journal* on 7 August. 'You could almost hear the nerves snapping in the audience!'[6]

'The Americans just could not believe that such a quality film could be made for that amount of money in that amount of time,' said Cushing. 'They just *would* not and *could* not believe it. It just took off. It went all over the world, especially in America where they were bonkers about it, then everywhere else. Japan loved it. Adored it. That put the seal on my international "fame".'[7]

Cushing's last days of shooting on *The Curse of Frankenstein* – which wrapped on 3 January – overlapped with the start of rehearsals for the BBC's *Gaslight* on 27 December. Old-fashioned plays were still a successful staple on television. Patrick Hamilton's celebrated thriller, in which a Victorian villain, Manningham, attempts to drive his wife mad, had already been made into a film twice – in Britain in 1940 with Anton Walbrook and Diana Wynyard, and in Hollywood in 1944 with Charles Boyer and Ingrid Bergman. In this version, produced by Stephen Harrison and broadcast on 13 January 1957 from Lime Grove, Mary Morris starred as Bella Manningham with Billie Whitelaw as Nancy the maid and Mervyn Johns as Sergeant Rough. In the *Radio Times* article accompanying *Gaslight*, it was announced that Cushing's next role for the BBC would be as Cyrano De Bergerac.

There was fierce criticism for Cushing's performance as Manningham from the *Daily Telegraph* on 14 January 1957. 'On BBC television last night the 20-year-old *Gaslight* must have made a

gripping entertainment for those unfamiliar with the play. For viewers already acquainted with it, interest lay in comparing present with past performances, and both Mary Morris and Mervyn Johns were well up to the standard of their predecessors. On the other hand, the usually reliable Peter Cushing as the sadistic adventurer trying to drive his wife into insanity showed an unfortunate tendency to overact and gave what could almost be described as a "sneery" interpretation.'[8]

There was an engineering fault at the start of *Gaslight* and Michael Barry wrote, in an internal memo, 'the fault ... has been investigated at the very highest level. I have dropped a note to Peter to reassure him that performances and production have spoken for themselves.' But after a lengthy pre-transmission wrangle with Kenneth Cleveland over Cushing's billing in the *Radio Times*, Barry had suspicions that a rift was growing between the BBC and 'their' star.

On 17 January, Cushing wrote back to Barry. 'I was delighted ... that you enjoyed the performance of

The villainous Mr Manningham with Mervyn Johns as Sergeant Rough in Stephen Harrison's production of *Gaslight* (1957)

'Act in the name of mankind and act humbly...' Arnold Marle as the Lama offers advice to John Rollason while Helen Rollason (Maureen Connell) and Peter Fox (Richard Wattis) look on in *The Abominable Snowman* (1957)

Gaslight. It means so much to be told because, at the end of a play and its rehearsals one has an awful feeling of let-down and is never quite sure how it's come across. I was a little distressed that you should think that there was any idea of a rift – this has never occurred to me! Naturally there are things that crop up, from the business angle, that have to be gone into. But I'm sure this happens in the best-respected families. One – of course – is the *Radio Times'* attitude to billing, eh? And I understand that steps are being taken to make this a little more co-operative.' He concluded 'It would be lovely to have dinner with you, dear Michael, but may I defer the pleasure for a little while? I'm starting work on the film of *The Abominable Snowman* on Monday week, with the usual costume fittings prior to this and preparing for *Cyrano De Bergerac* (fencing lessons, nose fittings etc). So as we are all ready for the filming sequences as soon as I finish *A.S.*, it's a pretty tight schedule. I look forward enormously to doing this play with Rudy (with not a few quakings inwardly too!)'

The Abominable Snowman, Hammer's version of *The Creature*, began filming at Bray Studios on 28 January. For his latest Hammer film, Val Guest once again found himself working from a Nigel Kneale storyline. Guest streamlined the script of *The Creature* to simplify some of the relationships and concepts. Cushing's character of John Rollason was given a wife, also called Helen. There was also now some gentle comic relief from Richard Wattis as Rollason's exasperated assistant Peter Fox. Arnold Marle repeated his role as the Lama from *The Creature*, giving a memorably weird performance. 'Act in the name of mankind and act humbly,' the Lama warns Rollason as he seeks the yeti. 'For man is near to forfeiting his right to lead the world.'

The Abominable Snowman is a beautiful and unjustly neglected film, a priceless record of Kneale's atmospheric play. Arthur Grant's crisp black-and-white photography lends an appropriate majesty to the snowy peaks; Humphrey Searle's score complements this with an epic theme and the subtler strains of gongs and cymbals. Several moments, like the yeti reaching into the explorers' tent and the phantom radio messages are genuinely chilling.

Cushing's sensitive and relaxed performance is the centre of the film and he clearly enjoys the chance to return to the part away from the rigours of live television. Rollason is a gentle and inquiring character, with a childlike wonder for the new sights and experiences of Tibet. He is appropriately heroic whether facing the self-serving philosophies of Friend and his hunters, or facing the unknown. 'Suppose they're not some pitiable remnant,' Rollason theorises as they begin to learn the true nature of the yeti. 'Suppose we're the savages. *Homo Vastens*. Man the Destroyer!'

'Peter Cushing was a perfectionist,' Kneale remembers. 'He would always challenge something. He'd say "I don't believe this. Why am I doing this?" And he would want an answer. He would then play to the answer he got and convince you it was possible that he was facing the monster and that there was a monster there to be faced.'[9]

Rollason's ultimate encounter with the yeti is breathtakingly moving in its simplicity. After the final avalanche and the sequence in which Rollason calls after Friend (almost a dry run for the conclusion of Kneale's *Quatermass and the Pit*) he retreats back into the cave and is suddenly aware of other figures – huge, humanoid shapes. Cushing barely moves. With a subtle inclination of the head and an almost imperceptible widening of the eyes, he expresses an overwhelming sense of awe.

Forrest Tucker recalled that Cushing was even concerned about details like the contents of his prop kit-bag, and whether smoking at high altitudes was actually possible. 'I'd say "Pete, I'm going to ******* smoke a cigarette at nine thousand feet and I'll find a way to get the bastard lit, now you watch me."' But Tucker had to concur that Cushing's mania for research was a valuable asset to a production. 'He can save you thousands of dollars because of what he's gonna do himself. It was an experience for me to watch an actor work that hard in other areas of making a film.'[10]

Val Guest was full of praise for Cushing too, particularly for his mastery of props. 'We rehearsed the scene where he gets the yeti tooth. We went into the take and Peter brought out the file and the tape measure ... we got it in the first take because I knew we'd not last through another one without collapsing. The take is in the film and that was the first any of us knew he had he props with him. We used to call him Peter "props" Cushing.'[11]

Cushing did oppose Guest for one shot, however. In the final scene on the mountainside, Rollason is discovered standing motionless in the snow. Guest wanted Cushing to keep his eyes open for the shot – even though an aeroplane propeller was being used to blow the fake snow onto the set. Cushing said if Guest wanted him to keep his eyes open he should come in and try it for himself. Guest quickly changed his mind.

Based on Guest's location footage, and on an extremely limited budget, Bernard Robinson created superb snowscapes at Pinewood Studios and a magnificent exterior courtyard for the monastery – the English winter adding an extra detail of making the actors' breaths hang on the air. Jock May's sound plays an important part, suggesting everything from the howling Himalayan winds to the rumbles of the avalanches and the mournful moans of the yeti. Make-up artist Phil Leakey, who had transformed Christopher Lee into Frankenstein's Creature, mimicked Peter Cushing's high forehead and aquiline nose to create the wise face of the barely-glimpsed yeti, played by the Irish actor John Rae. Filming on *The Abominable Snowman* was completed by 5 March.

Meanwhile, back at the BBC, *Cyrano De Bergerac* seemed doomed. At the eleventh hour, it was discovered that the copyright had not been cleared and the production was called off. Kenneth Cleveland wrote to the BBC that as Cushing had prepared for the role and had already learned the lines, this abandoned production should be regarded as his final production under contract. Cleveland's agenda was clear – he wanted Cushing released from his BBC contract as soon as possible.

Michael Barry stood his ground in a letter to Cleveland dated 11 March. 'So far as any claim for exclusivity was concerned, Peter's contract should be regarded as being at an end, and he is now free in that respect. On the other hand, the inability to produce *Cyrano De Bergerac* on 7 April should not put us in the position of writing off the last payment for a production under his contract.' Barry offered two immediate replacements *The Public Prosector* and *Eden End*, both of which Cushing declined. 'Your letter,' Barry continued to Cleveland, 'suggests that you wish to interpret the contract strictly without this give-and-take so commonly required in a contract of this kind. I can well understand Peter's disappointment about *Cyrano* but this is shared between us. You and I have a responsibility to the actor in this case. It may well be asking too much for Peter, busy with a film, to make spontaneous suggestions. The idea of *White Cargo*, mentioned between us on the phone and the ideas separately put by him to Cartier seem to me backward-looking suggestions of subjects laden with repertory dust. Should we not be looking forward, and, if we are unable to find something quite new, at least find a vehicle in which his special talents can be shown at their best?'

'I have never been able to decide,' harrumphed an exasperated G M Turnell of the BBC's Long-Term Contracts Department in a letter to Barry on 19 March. 'whether Cleveland's habitual misconstruction

The camera closes in on David McCallum as troubled teenager Johnny, watched by Father Laidlaw, in *Violent Playground* (1957)

Rough' – an aggravating piece of sub-Rock-Around-the-Clockery.

There are strong, if passionless performances from Stanley Baker and Ann Heywood, and David McCallum, at 24, is too old to play the teenage tearaway Johnny. Only Clifford Evans stands out as a gentle, progressive headmaster. Appearing as Baker's copper sidekick is John Slater, who won the Best TV Actor award for 1952, the year before Cushing. With his rather more weatherbeaten features, however, he was subsequently offered few leading roles in film. As Father Laidlaw, Cushing gives a rather severe, tight-lipped performance. His face is pinched and stern, his hair oiled down, his delivery strangely monotonous. Laidlaw never seems at ease, never makes decisions and speaks almost in riddles, drawing conclusions from Baker and McCallum. Even the priest's heroic stand in the final reel, climbing a ladder to talk down the machine-gun wielding Johnny, is an empty gesture as the ladder is pushed over and Laidlaw falls to the ground.

The film is obviously struggling for a message but with strands involving teenage crime, broken families, religion and youth policing in the script, nothing comes across clearly. The *Times* found *Violent Playground* a fudge. 'A film which sets out with such self-avowed high purposes degenerates into something dishonest because the issues are avoided. The ineffectual priest, to whose platitudes not even Peter Cushing can give weight, has no reality.'[12] On 9 March 1958, when the film was on release, Cushing, Baker and McCallum recorded a special excerpt from *Violent Playground* for the radio programme *Follow the Stars*.

On 4 September, Cushing wrote to producer Hal Burton about his production of *Time and the Conways* transmitted on 25 August – 'How *good* Gwen Watford was!' Burton subsequently offered Cushing the role of John Robinson in his planned production of *The Night of the Tigers*, but Cushing had to decline, although he enjoyed reading the play – 'It is excellently written, isn't it?'

Cushing signed a contract for *Dracula* on 9 October 1957. John Redway saw that Cushing's contractual fee was now £2,500. With that kind of wage being offered for six weeks' work, it was hardly surprising that the BBC were made to bide their time – Cushing was fast becoming a very bankable star. Hammer were clearly aware of this, and eager not to lose him, so Cushing was contracted for two Hammer films on the same date – *Dracula* and the sequel to *The Curse of Frankenstein*.

of contracts is due to stupidity or to his rather clumsy attempts to put one over on us. Obviously we want to find some way of having our sixth performance from Cushing without additional payment.'

Cushing and Barry subsequently had a quiet meeting over a meal and matters were calmed down considerably. Barry offered Cushing a play called *The Lover*, to be produced by Johnny Jacobs, but Cushing was not keen. 'The mid-thirties obsession with "sex in the raw",' he wrote, 'seems oddly naïve and a little shocking because its naïvety is no longer important.'

From July, however, he was working with director Basil Dearden on the film *Violent Playground*. The production was undoubtedly intended to address 'modern' themes, but set in the world of rock-and-roll and troubled teenagers, it now seems marooned on the wrong side of Beatlemania. For a picture set (and in part filmed) in Liverpool, there is a conspicuous lack of scouse accents in the swarm of headscarved women clucking disapprovingly on the periphery. The film lurches from one sensational piece of melodrama to the next, like a whole year of soap opera condensed into 90 minutes, a po-faced British copy of *The Blackboard Jungle* scored with a song called 'Play

Chapter Twelve

A Feast for the Horror-Gobblers

Dracula was well underway as the box-office takings of *The Curse of Frankenstein* continued to roll in. The new film had a budget of £82,000, but most of the elements of cast and crew that had made the first colour Hammer horror a success were unchanged. With Christopher Lee as Dracula, Cushing was cast as Van Helsing but was initially unsure how to play the part. 'In the book, Van Helsing was a little old gentleman who almost literally speaks double-Dutch. When I was cast I said to Tony Hinds "oughtn't we to get a little double-Dutchman?" and he said "No, I think the thing to do is to play him as you" – so it became one of my parts. It was always a fascinating character to play.'[1]

Anthony Hinds was wise enough to realise that Cushing's impeccable English was wooing the overseas audiences and there was no need to encumber him with a foreign accent. Peter Cushing they wanted and Peter Cushing they got, notably 'above the title' in *Dracula*.

Jimmy Sangster, who had pruned *Frankenstein* so effectively, cuts Stoker's sea voyages and European treks down to a couple of border-crossing gallops in a coach. Terence Fisher again creates a realistic environment that never once leads us to question that there *are* such things as vampires. To speed the plot further, Van Helsing and his associate Jonathan Harker (played by John Van Eyssen) are fully conversant with vampire lore from the off, and seem, by implication, to belong to a larger band of vampire hunters. So Harker, rather than Stoker's virginal innocent, goes into Castle Dracula on a kind of commando raid – unsuccessfully, as it turns out. Although Harker is able to stake the Count's vampire bride, the first game goes to Dracula.

Castle Dracula itself is sombre and magnificent, featured in the film's title sequence to the accompaniment of James Bernard's forbidding score which uses the rhythm of the word

'Dra-cu-la' like a fanfare. Hammer had constructed a new soundstage at Bray using money from a co-production deal with Columbia Pictures. This gave designer Bernard Robinson enough room to create his exquisite, finely-detailed interiors – including the great hall with its candy-twist columns and animal skins decorating the walls, the 'apartments', the grand staircase and the library.

As Dracula, Christopher Lee came out from behind the creature make-up and immediately proved his magnetic screen presence. Peter Cushing matched it – presenting a man of Van Helsing's force opposite a creature like Dracula reinforces both characters. We are given an indication of Van Helsing's mettle before he is even seen, when he enters the inn at Klausenberg. Fisher keeps Van Helsing's back to camera – in his fur coat and Homburg hat he looks rather like an old-style actor-manager – and we see the apprehensive reactions of the villagers. Then we hear the voice, see the face and are instantly reassured. As with Frankenstein, Cushing makes Van

The Count (Christopher Lee) recoils from Van Helsing's crossed candlesticks in the legendary climax of *Dracula* (1957)

Van Helsing warns Mina Holmwood (Melissa Stribling) of the mortal danger to her sister Lucy in *Dracula* (1957)

Helsing a living character. He runs his hand through his hair and rubs his neck when he's tired, he looks around while he's kept waiting, he blows into his hands when he's cold.

At Castle Dracula, Van Helsing finds Jonathan Harker in the crypt, transformed into a vampire. Cushing buries his head in his hand, then grimly takes up Harker's discarded stake and mallet. Later Van Helsing visits Arthur Holmwood (Michael Gough) and his wife Mina (Melissa Stribling) to break the news of Harker's death. Holmwood's sister Lucy was Harker's fiancée and Arthur is upset at Van Helsing's apparent indifference. Cushing leaves them with a gentlemanly click of the heels to Mina.

However, Van Helsing is very concerned indeed. Back in his study, he listens to his notes on vampires research on a phonograph. Cushing enjoys the business with the setting of the machine and his dictation of the 'rules' of vampirism is completely bewitching. Again, it is a question of economy – we are effectively informed of all the technicalities of what is to follow. 'Certain basic facts established. One: Light. The vampire, allergic to light, never ventures forth in the daytime. Sunlight fatal – repeat – *fatal*. Would destroy them. Two: Garlic. Vampires repelled by odour of garlic. Three: The crucifix, symbolising the power of good over evil. The power of the crucifix in these cases is two-fold. It protects the normal human being, but reveals the vampire, or victim of this vile contagion when in advanced stages. Established that victims consciously detest being dominated by vampirism, but are unable to relinquish the practice, similar to addiction to drugs. Ultimately death results from loss of blood, but unlike normal death, no peace manifests itself for they enter into the fearful state of the *un-dead*.' All the elements come together. Cushing knows enough about screen acting to bring his eyes to the camera as he finishes his dictation. 'Since the death of Jonathan Harker, Count Dracula, the propagator of this unspeakable evil, has disappeared. He must be found, and destroyed!' On Van Helsing's last line, Fisher cuts suddenly to a startling close-up of Dracula, who has come to prey on Lucy.

Mina Holmwood summons Van Helsing, telling him Lucy is very sick. Cushing borrowed much from his theatre training, particularly the dynamic physical style of Olivier, and here uses a trick of distractedly looking out of shot and then turning suddenly to emphasise a particular line – so he spins round, eyes widened as Mina says 'Our family doctor says it's *anaemia*' and would repeat this 'turn', to varying degrees, in many of his films. When Van Helsing discovers a vampire bite on Lucy's neck, Cushing gives an affecting expression of revulsion. 'I cannot impress upon you strongly enough how important it is that you obey my instructions,' he orders. 'Do exactly as I say, and we may be able to save her,' – Cushing holds up his forefinger for emphasis, as he did in *Frankenstein* – this too would become a signatory gesture. 'If you don't, she will die!'

But Van Helsing's advice is not heeded, and Lucy dies. Van Helsing leaves Harker's diary with Mina by way of explanation. As well as furious activity, Cushing could also use stillness to great advantage, as seen when he delivers his condolences to the Holmwoods. But the greater horror for Lucy is yet to come.

Later, in the Holmwood crypt – a setting with moonlight and bare twigs like some fairy-tale illustration – the vampirised Lucy leads the housekeeper's daughter Tanya (Janina Faye) down into the dark. Arthur is there, waiting for her. 'Dear brother...' she croons. 'Come, let me kiss you...' As she advances, Cushing leaps out with a silver crucifix held up in grim determination – the cross brands Lucy's forehead and she flees. Van Helsing takes the little girl to one side and wraps her in his coat protectively. The line is clearly improvised by Cushing. 'You look like a teddy bear now,' he says, giving her a crucifix. 'Will you wear this pretty thing – there? Isn't that lovely?'

Lucy is finally laid to rest with a stake through the heart. Van Helsing asks for Holmwood's help in tracing Dracula. 'The study of these creatures has been my life's work,' he tells him, tapping his cigarette onto the cigarette-case in a little echo of the staking. Van Helsing and Holmwood discover where the coffin has gone, but Mina is already under Dracula's spell. Terence Fisher instructed Melissa Stribling to 'imagine that you have had one whale of a sexual night, *the one* of your sexual experience. Give me that in your face.'[2] And so she did, while Phil Leakey's make-up for the ravished Mina – blusher, a touch more red lipstick – speaks of a new voluptuousness.

Van Helsing gives Mina a crucifix for protection but it instantly burns her hand. Cushing prises her hand open and looks grave. Holmwood and Van Helsing decide to keep watch outside the house, but Dracula foils them and attacks Mina again. Stribling's expressions are wonderfully ambiguous – she is almost biting her lip like a schoolgirl with a crush. Later, Mina is discovered on the bed, unconscious. Van Helsing immediately performs a transfusion, and Cushing has clearly studied the correct procedure – although he does manage to hook his arm into one of the tubes at one point.

Mina had forbidden the servants to go into the cellar – this is Dracula's hiding-place. Van Helsing goes down to the cellar and puts a crucifix in the coffin he finds there. But Dracula is close behind him – almost on top of him. Cushing leaps over the banisters and smacks the hysterical housekeeper Gerda around the face. But Mina is gone – taken by Dracula.

Cushing drives the gig for the chase after Dracula. The vampire could hide in the castle vaults for years. They would lose him there – and Mina. Van Helsing pursues Dracula through the castle, accompanied by Bernard's insistent chase theme. Dracula catches Van Helsing and tries to throttle him, Van Helsing tricks Dracula by playing dead. Then, in the nick of time, he leaps up. The vampire and vampire-hunter stand off like tigers. Then Van Helsing makes his final move...

The script dictated that Van Helsing should brandish a crucifix and force Dracula into a shaft of sunlight. Errol Flynn fan Cushing wanted a bit more for his finale. He was all for jumping off a balcony or swinging on a chandelier, but he explained, 'dear Terry wouldn't let me, in case I was injured.' Although a stuntman was used for the jump, it was Cushing's own suggestion that he pelt down the table and rip down the curtains. However, he was bothered by the appearance of yet another crucifix. 'Van Helsing was like a salesman for the things,' he said. 'They were practically coming out of his ears. He gives one to Mina, one to the little girl, he was throwing them in coffins, and so on. At the end he was supposed to pull out *another* one.'[3] Cushing came up with a clever solution. 'I remembered seeing a film years ago called *Berkeley Square*, in which Leslie Howard was thought of as the devil by this frightened little man who grabbed two candelabra to make the sign of the cross with them. I remembered that this had impressed me enormously. Originally the candelabra we used were the type with four candles on each base. You could tell what I was doing, but it didn't look like a cross. So they were changed to the ones I used in the film.'[4] For screenwriter Stephen Volk, who wrote the script for Ken Russell's *Gothic* (1986), this final image of light defeating darkness was 'the 20th century equivalent of a stained glass window, in the dark of a movie theatre.'[5]

As Dracula decays, Van Helsing's haunted expression conveys a mixture of exhaustion, revulsion, sadness and relief. Cushing later explained his own feelings about the shot: 'I was reading a book that said, at the end of *Dracula*, there is a look of sadness on Van Helsing's face... He has suddenly achieved his life's quest, and now what is he going to do? I can tell you that I didn't have that in mind at all when we were shooting the film. I stand there and run my hand through my hair and look down out of exhaustion. But that critic was absolutely right. Something in me was communicating that to the

Frankenstein introduces Doctor Hans Kleve (Francis Matthews) to the hunchback Karl (Oscar Quitak) in *The Revenge of Frankenstein* (1958)

audience, and the audience fills in the rest.'[6]

The film premièred under its American title *Horror of Dracula* in Milwaukee, Wisconsin on 8 May 1958, taking $1,682 on its first day. The film opened in Britain at the Gaumont Haymarket, with a spectacular front-of-house display featuring Christopher Lee, on 22 May 1958 and on Broadway a week later.

The *Daily Telegraph's* review mixed compliments with outrage. 'The new version outdoes its Bela Lugosi predecessor in bizarre horror ... There is much erudite play with vampire repellents and crosses and ... stakes; and by way of a climax, we see the Count, several centuries old, with face and hands crumbling to dust. This British film has an "X" certificate. This is too good for it. There should be a new certificate "S" for sadistic or just "D" for disgusting. But I must add that the film is most efficiently produced and is well acted by Peter Cushing, Christopher Lee...'[7] The *Times* found Cushing 'tight-lipped and resolved' and the film 'by no means an unimpressive piece of story-telling'[8] while *Variety* said Cushing was 'impressive as the painstaking scientist-doctor who solves the mystery.'[9] The *New York Daily News* remarked that the film had 'allocated time, thought and talent to an enterprise which successfully recaptures the aura and patina of yesterday's middle-Europe ... some of the photography is good enough to frame.'[10] The *New York Herald Tribune*, on the same day, said 'the cast play their roles straight and capably, giving the impression that they believe every line.'[11] *Daily Cinema* was similarly impressed. 'Not a second is

wasted in giving Bram Stoker's great novel the treatment it deserves. Performances are in the right key throughout. Peter Cushing is a dominant figure as the doctor, and Christopher Lee never misses as the horrifying Dracula. This is a classic example of how out-and-out screen thrills can be relayed with a happy combination of punch and conviction. *Dracula* will have audiences terrified in their seats from Land's End to New York.'[12]

Even before the cinematic release of *The Curse of Frankenstein*, word from the studio was so positive that Hammer was planning a sequel. In March 1957, the company's three-picture co-production deal with Columbia promised *The Blood of Frankenstein*. Jimmy Sangster wrote the script, which was eventually retitled *The Revenge of Frankenstein*. In the same way that James Whale accentuated the black comedy and eccentricity present in *Frankenstein* to create the sequel *Bride of Frankenstein*, Terence Fisher used a gleeful injection of humour to give his new scares an added relish. 'There are ... wonderful opportunities to put in intentional laughs,'[13] Fisher told the press. Producer Anthony Hinds promised 'all the shake, shudder and wallop'[14] of the first *Frankenstein*, and the public were not disappointed.

The story of *The Revenge of Frankenstein* follows directly on from the finale of *Curse*. The Baron, under sentence of death for the crimes committed by his Creature, was led to the guillotine, but Terence Fisher wisely did not to show the actual execution. As *Revenge* begins, Frankenstein escapes death with the help of a hunchbacked guard, Karl, who is promised a 'perfect' new body. Under the alias 'Doctor Stein', Frankenstein then establishes a respectable medical practice in the town of Carlsbruck, while secretly using the inmates of the poor hospital as donors for his experiments. Assisted by the young Doctor Kleve, Frankenstein transplants Karl's brain into its new body, but when the 'new' Karl is attacked and his brain is damaged, he becomes savage, exposes Frankenstein and dies. The Baron is attacked by the patients at the poor hospital, and beaten nearly to death, but Kleve is able to transplant Frankenstein's brain into a new body before they escape to London to begin work anew.

On 6 January 1958, just three days after the completion of shooting for *Dracula*, Bernard Robinson's lavish *Dracula* sets were re-dressed and used for the filming of *The Revenge of Frankenstein*. The new cast included Francis Matthews as Kleve, Eunice Gayson as Margaret and Michael Gwynn as the new Creature. The idea of a recurring Frankenstein 'monster', so prominent a feature of the Universal cycle, was dropped, since Christopher Lee's Creature had been utterly destroyed at the conclusion of the last film. Continuity in Hammer's *Frankenstein* cycle was to come from the character of the Baron – and Peter Cushing's Baron, at that. As an extra twist, Sangster has Frankenstein becoming his *own* Creature at the conclusion of *Revenge*.

The work was always of paramount importance to Cushing but with a sympathetic director, a supportive atmosphere and a familiar crew, he is clearly enjoying every second of *The Revenge of Frankenstein*. He revels

in some priceless lines, too, though there is never a hint of send-up and Cushing's timing must have been the envy of many comedians. When a pickpocket complains that the loss of his arm will mean losing his job, Frankenstein tells him flatly 'You'll have to find another job ... or use the other hand.' Later, Frankenstein explains to Kleve that after he put the brain of an orang-utan into a chimpanzee, the animal developed cannibal tendencies and ate his wife. 'He ate another *monkey*?' gasps Kleve. With a look of mild outrage, the Baron replies 'What *else* would he be married to?'

Francis Matthews recalls the shooting of the film with great affection. 'The main memory I have of Terry and Peter together is the sheer fun we all had! The seriousness of the material meant that between shots, we all behaved in a ludicrously infantile

Monkey business with Lucy the chimp, watched by her trainer Molly Badham, at Bray Studios for *The Revenge of Frankenstein* (1958)

manner – games, practical jokes and running gags.' In the breaks there were *Times* crosswords and games of battleships (with sound effects) and there was bread-and-butter pudding in the canteen. 'My impression of Peter was of a happy, contented and professionally fulfilled man. He made me feel at home instantly ... It was one of the happiest working relationships I have ever enjoyed.'[15]

Oscar Quitak remembers Cushing fondly too. 'He was wonderful to work with. He was always prepared for every shot, a complete perfectionist.' Quitak, who had to endure painful make-up for the role of the hunchbacked Karl, retreated into Cushing's dressing-room after one shot to find Baron Frankenstein babysitting their simian co-star, Lucy the chimpanzee. On another instance, Cushing was practising his trepanning techniques on a cabbage. 'He was sawing through this cabbage pretending it was a head and it was making such a noise that it was actually worse.'[16]

In several instances, Cushing displays his unerring ability to carry on with a bit of 'business' while sustaining the performance perfectly. After 'staking' his cigarette-case in *Dracula*, in *Revenge*, he uses his buttonhole to symbolise Frankenstein's aspirations to acceptance and respectability. In the first scene, in the 'posh' consulting room, we see Cushing take up a flower, shake off a drop of water, carefully place it in his coat and sniff it. He repeats this action at the end of the film when Frankenstein has established a practice in Harley Street. But when Frankenstein has been discredited by the medical council, and his consulting room is empty, Cushing flings the buttonhole away in contempt. The Baron is a dandy and a socialite, but strangely, after his womanising in *Curse*, he doesn't give a second glance to his new leading lady. Even when forced to plunge headlong into the bosom of Vera Barscynska, he merely gives a resigned sigh and looks at his watch. Although still shot in glorious Eastmancolor, Terence Fisher lightens the colours in his palette a little for this film, just as the Baron's character is lightened enough to let him escape with honour at the end, beginning his work anew in London.

The supporting cast is once again excellent, including many members of Hammer's repertory company. The effete president of the medical council is played by Charles Lloyd Pack, who had played Doctor Seward in *Dracula* and was also in the cast of *Richard of Bordeaux*, as was George Woodbridge, who here plays a brutal janitor. Other notables include Richard Wordsworth as a garrulous patient with Lionel Jeffries and Michael Ripper as a pair of grave-robbers.

For such a funny, pricelessly cast, artfully played piece, the film did not go down at all well with the critics, particularly C A Lejeune, who seemed to take the film as a personal insult. 'This the sequel to an earlier and almost as regrettable Frankenstein travesty made by the same company; and Peter Cushing, who

can be an actor of parts when he so chooses, again demeans himself by playing the hero ... The actors are more to be pitied than criticised. The whole thing is to my taste a vulgar, stupid, nasty and intolerably tedious business. A crude sort of entertainment for a crude sort of audience. Films of this kind are the last refuge of unimaginative producers who have lost the art of communicating individually with human beings and have fallen back on the appeal to mass hysteria.'[17]

Some critics took things less seriously, like Peter Burnup who noted Frankenstein was 'played again by Peter Cushing in forbidding fashion. Miss Eunice Gayson also drops in now and again on the proceedings. Quite why I couldn't quite make out.' (Gayson's reduced role was due to an injury sustained when she was thrown from a horse on set. She subsequently had to wear an uncomfortable brace under her costume.)

There were the inevitable comparisons to the 1931 model too. 'I am afraid it can't hold a grave-snatcher's candle to the earlier Karloff prototype,' said the *Evening Standard*. 'His was a very terrifying Thing (or so it seemed when I was 12). Frankenstein's revenge is purely to vindicate himself in the eyes of science. He intends to show his product off to the whole medical world in a spirit of They Laughed When I Sat Down To Build A Monster. Peter Cushing is now artistically dedicated to this species of blood chiller.'[18]

At the time of the film's release there was a great deal of negative criticism levelled at the horror genre, with Hammer's James Carreras dubbed the 'King of Nausea' and protest groups frothing at the ever-more-gory front-of-house posters, which in many instances were far more gruesome than the films they advertised. There was a refreshing note of common sense, however, in this review of *The Revenge of Frankenstein* from the *Daily Express*. 'Frankly I'm not one of those who see anything to worry about in these horror films. This film is preposterous and never tries to be anything else. Moralists can look to life and find their problems there. Here is fantasy. Those who like this sort of thing will love this one, those who don't won't and needn't go.'[19]

On 23 January 1958, Cushing sent a telegram from Ealing Studios (*Revenge of Frankenstein* was shot at Bray) to Rudolph Cartier about the forthcoming production of Terence Rattigan's *The Winslow Boy*. 'Please consider Gwen Watford Love Peter Cushing' On 28 January 1958 Kenneth Cleveland wrote to Cartier determining that Cushing should get sole star billing above the title of *The Winslow Boy*.

Cushing was so busy and so much in demand at this period that for his appearance on the BBC's popular quiz show *What's My Line* on 9 February, he had to be ferried from the set of *The Revenge of Frankenstein* at Bray.

The Winslow Boy began rehearsal on 20 February 1958, nearly a fortnight before the completion of filming for *The Revenge of Frankenstein*, necessitating some juggling on the BBC and Hammer's part. Cartier, who won the Guild of Television Producers and Directors Award for best drama producer of 1957, had already produced *The Winslow Boy* in Germany in 1956, when it was hailed as 'a shining example of the working of British democracy, showing as it does how even the small man can fight against bureaucracy.'[20] Cushing played the eminent KC Sir Robert Morton, described by Rattigan as 'a man in his early forties, cadaverous and immensely elegant. He wears a long overcoat, and carries his hat and stick. He looks rather a fop, and his supercillious expression bears out this view.' Morton brings the first act to a close with his interrogation of young Ronnie Winslow, who has been accused of stealing a five-shilling postal order, and it is easy to hear Cushing's cadences in Sir Robert Morton's lines. It's a safe bet that the Cushing digit was held aloft more than once.

The initially severe character who turns out to be a formidable ally was a role that Cushing would play over and over again. It would be satisfying to think that there was more than a little of Van Helsing's steel in Sir Robert and vice-versa.

The Winslow Boy was reviewed in The *Times*: 'Mr Cartier's deliberately suave production laid out the play for inspection ... he avoided commentary by camera and entrusted the play to his excellent cast.

'A man who's good for 14 years stays good to everlasting.' Not so with the downtrodden Harry Quincey in the BBC's *Uncle Harry* (1958)

Mr Peter Cushing played Morton without the savagery associated with the part; it was an icy and mercurial performance which preserved the character's paradoxical combination of ruthlessness and gentle reserve.'[21]

The Winslow Boy was the last play of Cushing's BBC contract but he was soon involved in another – Thomas Job's play *Uncle Harry*, again co-starring Mary Morris with Rona Anderson, Beryl Measor and Hugh Morton. The play was set in a small town on the Welsh border and was to be broadcast from the BBC's studios in Cardiff. The *Radio Times* had this to say: '"I've known Harry Quincey" says a character in tonight's play "for 14 years and a man who's good for 14 years stays good to everlasting." As events turn out, this proves to be faulty reasoning, for Harry Quincey – Uncle Harry to everybody because he is such a quiet, gentle sort of chap – lives under a strain, suffocated by the attentions of two quarrelsome sisters, and turned down by the woman he loves. Then one day he conceives a desperate plan to free himself from his bondage.'[22]

The transmission of *Uncle Harry* was unexpectedly put back until 10.00 pm. There was a replay of Manchester United's match against Milan, just days before United's appearance in the FA Cup Final. The BBC were adamant. 'As a rugby fan,' wrote assistant head of drama Norman Rutherford to Cushing on 1 May, 'I cannot expect you to appreciate the significance of this game played with a round ball. But there it is. We must accept it as fact. I asked if we could telerecord *Uncle Harry*, but my request was not granted.' However, Rutherford was convinced that 'Mary will hold them to the screen. I am looking forward to the production more than most I will have viewed during the past year as I have always felt that this is a part which you would bring to life most vividly on the television screen.' There was a PS for rugby fan Cushing. 'I am sure you were delighted with Blackheath winning the Middlesex "Sevens" this year!'

'What a skilful re-creator Peter Cushing is!' enthused the *Daily Telegraph*. 'He is always being given characters in television plays created on the stage by a Gielgud, an Emlyn Williams or an Eric Portman, and always putting them successfully through "the sieve of his own personality" as Granville Barker put it. In Thomas Job's psychological murder play *Uncle Harry* on BBC television last night, he was following Michael Redgrave who took the name part in the London production some 15 years ago. This part of a weak, middle-aged bachelor who plans ingeniously to get rid of his two over-possessive spinster sisters so that he can marry suited him far

In the heat of battle, Captain Pearson of the *Serapis* offers his antagonist a chance to surrender in *John Paul Jones* (1958)

better than some heroic or romantic role, and indeed he gave one of his most satisfying studies. Rona Anderson was also well in character as the girl who attracts him and Mary Morris reminded us what an incisive actress she is as the sister condemned to death for the murder she does not commit – that of her own elder sister.'[23]

With the international success of *The Curse of Frankenstein* and the eagerly anticipated opening of *Dracula*, the Cushings were enjoying unprecedented financial security. They decided to buy a seafront property in the Kent seaside town of Whitstable, where Cushing could paint and where the sea air would help Helen's breathing. On 26 May, Cushing's birthday, this was reported in the *Standard*. 'Actor Peter Cushing, who is 45 today, has bought a white clapboard house on the beach at Whitstable, Kent. He is turning the top floor into a studio. Cushing is an accomplished water colourist and has painted many Whitstable scenes on his visits there in the past 15 years. He says "Now, instead of sitting on a breakwater

to paint, I shall be able to work in comfort. I may attempt the wonderful sunsets over the Isle of Sheppey which inspired Turner. It is worth buying a house in Whitstable just to see them!"'[24]

On his birthday, however, Cushing was in New York for the Broadway opening of *Dracula*. The *News of the World* stated that '*Dracula* has ... most profitably ... set the West End of London back on its heels.' While in the US, Cushing was to take part in 'a series of coast-to-coast networked television appearances' promoting *Dracula*, 'not to speak of "personals" before avid Broadway reporters. There'll be quite an ordeal for our Mr Cushing. But so it goes. To the delight, doubtless, of the Chancellor of the Exchequer, Cushing and the goose-fleshed chiller-killer-dillers in which he figures have become rich dollar earners for Britain. The first of the horrific series – *The Curse of Frankenstein* – has already earned 3,000,000 dollars in America.'[25]

Cushing's next job in July and August 1958 was the role of Captain Pearson in *John Paul Jones*, directed by John Farrow. The film is part sprawling American epic and part US Navy propaganda with Robert Stack as the Scottish-born merchant captain John Paul Jones who is adopted as a Naval captain by the newly independent Americas.

Cushing was 'fined down', as he put it, by a mild bout of dysentery at the location of Denia in Spain, but looks resplendent in powdered wig and period British Naval uniform. The score even gives us a bar or two of 'Hearts of Oak' when he appears. It is 1779, Britain is at war with the Americas, and Pearson, captain of the *Serapis*, engages Jones in a terrific sea battle off Flamborough Head. Jones loses most of his crew and many of his friends. When Pearson hails him to ask for his surrender, Jones gives the film's signatory quote 'I have not yet begun to fight!'

The night-time battle is realistically staged, although Cushing remembers in *Past Forgetting* that the explosive charges on deck were sometimes a little too close for comfort. Captain Jones is victorious, and there is a look of real resignation from Cushing as he admits grimly 'it's useless to shed more blood.' Jones refuses to accept Pearson's sword in surrender and later, the erstwhile enemies join in the reading of the burial ceremony over their dead. Given Cushing's love of swashbuckling action he must have been very happy to make a film like *John Paul Jones*. It was his last prominent role in a big-budget American movie until *Star Wars* in 1976.

Chapter Thirteen

Elementary Exercises

Cushing had been collecting toy soldiers from childhood, and by the late 1950s had an extensive collection. He introduced Alan Ladd to collecting while they were filming *The Black Knight*, and every Cushing co-star who was invited to dinner was given an impromptu review of 'the troops'. Cushing's theories about toys and hobbies were well thought out and somewhat revolutionary for the time, when miniatures were not common, and there is a strong indication of his Peter Pan personality in a piece entitled 'Toys? They're Not Child's Play – says Peter Cushing' which he wrote for the *TV Mirror's* 'On My Soap-Box' column. Cushing changed the column's title to 'On My Hobby-Horse'.

'Hobbies? "Oh," you sigh, "Peter Cushing is going to tell us about his toy soldiers again! ... Just kid's stuff. It's nothing to do with a bold Soap-box subject, surely?" Now I have a theory about hobbies and toys, and I'm quite prepared for you to scoff at me. The theory is quite simple. It is that toys are given to children when they are too young to appreciate them and that because most men "put away childish things" as they reach adulthood, they miss a great deal of happiness at a time in their lives when, because of greater maturity, they are actually in a much better position to enjoy their toys and hobbies.

'The tragedy is that far too many men are hobby-less ... Without the escapism which comes only from dabbling with adult toys, their minds are prey to all the frustrations and fears of the working day. From my hobby-horse, I do not say that men would be *better* if they kept to their toys in adult years; but certainly they could be happier ... So many, it seems to me, lose happiness as they grow up. Their entire absorption in their careers and adult responsibilities bring lines of worry and premature old age. It is not silly or childish to have an interest in hobbies ... some men develop a passionate interest in costly 35mm cameras and in veteran and vintage cars, but what are these things except toys of a rather larger and dearer sort? I am not particularly mechanically-minded, so although I do have a certain interest in mechanical models, I get much greater contentment from miniature figures and costumes. I love collecting old manuscripts and books on period costume too, but of course, that's a branch of art, and not a subject for my hobby-horse.

'H G Wells ... wrote a most interesting book entitled *Little Wars*, which was a serious satire designed to make real war impossible. There is a British Model Soldier Society, including youngsters of nine up to colonels of ninety, and who manoeuvre the soldiers according to the rules which H G outlined in his book, rules which have changed little since the days of Napoleon. Played according to these rules, the wars of these tin soldiers become a vast game of chess. When I come home at night and find the TV news or the newspaper headlines more than usually anxious and alarming, I sometimes get out my soldiers and start solving international problems on my lounge carpet. Fearful problems which ... cause international strife at UNO, are settled in a quiet half-hour with my

Cushing with some of his beloved model soldiers, in a picture taken to publicise *The Black Knight* (1953)

'It's a marvelous opportunity,' said Cushing when offered the part of Sherlock Holmes in *The Hound of the Baskervilles* (1958)

private armies of military men, who are as clever, bold, strategic, and victorious as I can make them, although they are only 2-and-a-half inches high. One day, I may be tempted to send to Whitehall, to Washington and to the Kremlin, so that statesmen can find the key ... But no. I have no wish to challenge anyone's opinion. I have my own inner contentment with this world-in-miniature ... And you could too. It's not a thing to shout or campaign about, but to discover privately, and to enjoy in one's own heart.'[1]

Cushing's next film concerned another subject close to his heart. He was to star as Sherlock Holmes in Hammer's adaptation of *The Hound of the Baskervilles* directed by Terence Fisher. 'Many people said I should play Holmes,' Cushing admitted. 'When I was offered the part I was thrilled. It's a marvellous opportunity when you've got so much detail to base your character on.'[2] If Cushing played Van Helsing 'more or less as myself,' then Holmes is definitely a performance as a wholly different character. 'Impish, waspish and Wildean'[3] was how *Films and Filming* described it. It is theatrical and not a little arrogant, but appropriately catches the aloof genius of the world's greatest detective. With quizzical expressions and flamboyant gestures, Cushing is perfect for the role. André Morell, reunited with his co-star from *Nineteen Eighty-Four* on much more agreeable terms, is a perfect foil as Watson, redefining the character as a

canny lieutenant to Holmes after the well-meaning bumbler of Nigel Bruce.

Kenneth Hyman – son of the American financier Eliot Hyman, James Carreras's partner – acted in a senior role during the production of many Hammer films. *The Hound of the Baskervilles* was one of the few where he took an on-screen credit as producer. Ken Hyman's company Seven Arts had purchased the film rights to *The Hound of the Baskervilles* from Sir Arthur Conan Doyle's estate, and had secured money from distributor United Artists. The film was announced as a forthcoming attraction in March 1958 replacing another proposed literary adaptation – a remake of *Dr Jekyll and Mr Hyde*. Cushing was signed on 1 August, and James Carreras promised 'I shall get him to sex it up a bit.'[4]

While Anthony Hinds said, however, that Holmes would be played 'realistically, not romantically'[5], Cushing told the *Evening Bulletin* about his research for the role. 'I've based all my costumes on the original *Strand* magazine pictures. Everything is right, down to the old mouse-coloured dressing-gown, which I charred with cigarettes to get the burns Holmes made during his experiments. When he's on a case, he is like a dog following a scent. Holmes is not the pleasantest of characters either. He doesn't suffer fools, and he must have been insufferable to live with.' Cushing gleefully included canonical details like Holmes writing memos to himself on his shirt-cuff and lighting his pipe with a coal from the fire. The storyline, however, plays rather footloose with Doyle to introduce several 'horrific' elements like a tarantula spider, sacrificial rites (reported but unseen) and a man with a webbed hand.

Following a prologue, which illustrates the story of wicked Sir Hugo Baskerville in the expected Hammer style, we are placed into Bernard Robinson's enchantingly accurate Baker Street set. Cushing is first seen with his hand over his face, smoking his pipe while he listens to Doctor Mortimer (Francis De Wolff) explaining the legend. Holmes solves a chess problem with a snort, and turns to Mortimer with a look of bored indifference. 'There must be hundreds of similar folk stories,' he enunciates fiercely. 'I fail to see why I should find this one of singular interest.' Mortimer explains that Sir Charles – the latest resident of Baskerville Hall on Dartmoor – has recently been found dead, a victim of the 'hound of Hell' that is supposed to take vengeance on all of Sir Hugo's heirs. While he listens to Mortimer, Holmes seems preoccupied with straightening a crooked picture, running his finger through the dust and checking his correspondence which is transfixed to the mantelpiece with a dagger. He later admits that he was deliberately goading Mortimer to find a significant clue – that Sir Charles died of heart failure. Later, Cushing makes Holmes positively coquettish to charm further information out of Mortimer.

As Holmes agrees to meet the Baskerville heir, Sir Henry, the following day, Cushing suggested that they insert an original line from the Doyle 'canon' to send Mortimer on his way – 'My professional charges are on a fixed scale, I do not vary them, except when I remit them altogether.' Christopher Lee makes an attractive hero out of the thankless role of Sir Henry Baskerville, and clearly enjoys his scenes with Cushing. The Cushing digit is brought to bear on Sir Henry as he issues the warning, 'under no circumstances are you to venture out onto the moor at night!' – a definitive Holmes moment in a splendidly enjoyable Cushing performance.

One of the problems with the story of *The Hound of the Baskervilles* is that Holmes is missing for a large chunk in the middle while Watson accompanies Sir Henry to Baskerville Hall – Holmes is meanwhile hiding on the moor, observing and gathering information. For the reunion between Holmes and a baffled and angry Watson, Cushing appears in a long black cloak – not unlike his Frankenstein rig. 'Forgive me if my dramatic entrance startled you,' says Holmes with a smile. 'It's been rather lonely up here!' Meanwhile, Sir Henry has fallen for a local girl, Cecille (Marla Landi), daughter of

the farmer Stapleton. Following an intuition, Holmes investigates an abandoned tin-mine and realises that the legendary hound is far from supernatural...

Scriptwriter Peter Bryan's revision of Doyle gives Cushing some bonus scenes, including one with Miles Malleson as the fluttery entomologist Bishop Frankland. 'Allow me to shake the hand of the country's greatest detective,' chortles his Grace, who has clearly been following Holmes' exploits avidly. 'That case of the Bermondsey forgery,' he hoots, 'that was a first class piece of work!' Next to the fluffy Bishop with woodworm in his belfry, Holmes seems particularly steely: 'My Lord ...' he insists. 'I am fighting evil, fighting it as surely as you do!' Once again, it can be seen how players of Malleson's calibre ennoble Hammer's early horror output.

Terence Fisher repeats the style of *Dracula* but, apart from his deft storytelling abilities, stays in the background once again. The settings for the film are magnificent though economical, and Jack Asher's photography is gorgeous, filling the nooks and crannies with an array of weird colours – particularly the saturated reds and greens which add an other-worldly eeriness to the studio-bound moorland.

Cushing greets a member of the Sherlock Holmes Society (left) and his old ENSA sparring partner Humphrey Morton (right) on the set of *The Hound of the Baskervilles* (1958)

Throughout, James Bernard's driving score gives a real sense of energy and excitement.

The only stumbling-block was the climactic appearance of the hound. There were in fact two dogs – one, a great dane called Colonel was, it transpired, rather too mild-mannered to be a hound of hell. An attempt to film him in a scaled-down set with child actors standing in for Holmes, Watson and Sir Henry produced footage more laughable than horrible. A second dog was provided by trainer Barbara Woodhouse, but even with the addition of a rabbit fur mask made by Margaret Robinson, wife of designer Bernard, it failed to terrify. Cushing maintained that the Hound had never been realised on screen adequately.

Despite Hammer's hopes that the film may lead to a series of Holmes movies, the response to the film was mixed and plans were dropped. In 1968, how-ever, Cushing was involved in a series of 15 Holmes adventures for television, one of which was a 100-minute adaptation of *The Hound of the Baskervilles*.

Among the reviews for Hammer's version, *Newsweek*'s was particularly encouraging. 'The latest revival of the hair-raising ... classic has among its distinctions actor Peter Cushing, who seems likely to strike oldsters as the best Sherlock Holmes yet ... Tense and taut, with a steely glint on his close-shaven cheekbones, Cushing is the epitome of the classical detective ... A living, breathing Holmes.'[7]

Cushing, in the field, paints a water-colour landscape at his portable easel

The *Observer*, however, found deficiencies in the film. 'It would seem hard to make a dull picture of *The Hound of the Baskervilles*, but Hammer ... have done it. By cunning changes in the relationships of character, by the invention of new scenes of no relevance whatsoever ... they have managed to evolve a script which misses almost all the salient points of the original. Peter Cushing is the new Sherlock Holmes. Curiously, for he has shown authority in other parts, he seems fussy, finicky and indeterminate in this one. André Morell is the Doctor Watson, and he works hard to avoid the buffoonery in the part. *The Hound of the Baskervilles* is a betwixt-and-between picture; unsatisfactory to the Holmes expert, and providing no full feast to the horror-gobblers.'[8]

The *Sunday Times* found Cushing 'too oversprightly' as Holmes in a 'very mild shocker; a few nocturnal howls, hints of nameless sacrificial rites ... the rest is whodunit and poor hungry doggie.'[9]

While Cushing was facing the 'poor hungry doggie', the BBC were busily planning a production of George Du Maurier's *Trilby* for Christmas 1958, with Cushing as the hypnotist Svengali (a role which had been played in the 1954 film by Donald Wolfit). On 9 September Angela Hepburn, now Cushing's television agent, wrote to Michael Barry. 'I have some more information from Hammer as to their plans for Peter's next production for them, which ... is to be *The Man in Half Moon Street*. At present they plan to start shooting this picture on or about the 10 November (six to seven week schedule – generally six.) *Hound of the Baskervilles*, on which he has just commenced work this week – and the start of *Half Moon Street* gives an available period 20 October – 9 November approximately.'

Despite these restrictions, the BBC was still very keen. 'Svengali belongs to a period that requires the breadth and colour which I believe Peter would join me in appreciating.' Barry explained to Hepburn, adding that they would even postpone *Trilby* from transmission on Boxing Day to accommodate Cushing.

But it was not to be. The state of play was spelt out in an exasperated letter from Angela Hepburn to McMaster on 27 November 1958. 'It is with the greatest regret I have to tell you that Peter Cushing will not be available to play Svengali for you on the proposed filming date. As you may or may not know, Peter is under contract to Hammer Films to do five pictures for them within a period of 18 months. This means virtually that he has approximately ten days to a fortnight off between each film and therefore his periods of availability are not only limited but also spaced far apart. In actual fact the film he is about to do (on a 12-week schedule) is not for Hammer but for another company – and therefore it follows that as soon as it is completed he has to return immediately to Hammer to start work on his next film for them. I ... explain this to you so that you can see how very little point there appears to be in postponing your production with the idea of Peter being available at a later date. I have just talked with him on the telephone and he liked the script very much indeed, and he is extremely sorry that he will not be able to play it.'

The trouble with *Trilby* seemed to disincline the BBC from involving Cushing in new productions. There would be various inquiries on his part, and an abortive attempt to relaunch *Cyrano de Bergerac*, but he would not appear in a major BBC production until 1963.

There seems no readily apparent reason, either, why Cushing did not make Hammer's *The Man in Half Moon Street,* which was renamed *The Man Who Could Cheat Death*, and the lead role was taken by Anton Diffring. There is nothing more about the non-Hammer film that Angela Hepburn mentions, and Cushing did not start work on another film at Bray until the New Year. Perhaps he wished to devote his attention to a rather different West End appearance. On 3 December 1958, 'Here and There – An Exhibition of Water-Colours by Peter Cushing' opened at the Fine Art Society, New Bond Street.

The exhibition comprised 54 paintings, many of them views of Whitstable. There was also a painting completed in the garden of artist Edward Seago, studies of the Thames including Lambeth Bridge and a backwater near Richmond, and several scenes around Altea near Alicante, painted while Cushing was filming *Alexander the Great*. Among the visitors to the exhibition was the assistant controller of the BBC, Cecil Madden, who wrote a letter of appreciation. 'I came along to your water colours at Bond Street. You certainly are a versatile chap! I particularly enjoyed the Spanish pictures.' Cushing replied from Whitstable. 'Thank you so much for going to see the exhibition. I was very sorry not to see you there but I was an hour and a half late due to the fog. I look forward to seeing you again ... with any luck Helen and I will be back in London early in the New Year.'

The last job of the year *was* for the BBC, however, but on radio. On 17 December Cushing recorded his selection for one of broadcasting's hardiest perennials, *Desert Island Discs*.

Desert Island Discs was first broadcast in 1942 and even by 1958 was something of an institution. Each week, presenter Roy Plomley interviewed a celebrity 'castaway' who chose eight gramophone records to help him (or her) while away the hours on a desert island.

Cushing's selection was a mixture of light classics and popular music including the overture 'Donna Diana' by Reznicek and a piece from Joseph Strauss' *Die Fledermaus,* of which he said: 'It's just so delicious ... It reminds me rather of a Christmas stocking. Whenever you dip into this wonderful piece of music something new and refreshing comes out. It's an

awfully difficult choice to take one tiny bit out of such a jewel.'

Cushing apologised to Plomley for being a poor Robinson Crusoe, admitting that he would be 'absolutely shocking, dear boy, dreadful' because his wife did everything for him. As the rules of the island were genially dictated to him, Cushing entered into the spirit of the thing, although he was rather concerned for his creature comforts, chiefly a cup of tea. He used his next choice, Sibelius' Symphony Number 1 in E minor, to illustrate the feeling he had in America of wanting to get back to England. 'Sibelius always seems to me to have this incredible longing – a longing for something he wants to get to and can't. I'm sure, I know, it was the feeling I had when I was in America – and the same feeling I'll have on this island of yours, to get back to England.' Then, it was 'from the sublime ... to the sublime' – Jimmy 'Schnozzle' Durante singing 'I'm a Vulture for Horticulture'. 'He's so full of vitality and really the best on the variety and vaudeville stage. You can't help but just go along with Jimmy, he really has something!' Cushing's fifth record was from Richard Strauss' *Der Rosenkavalier*. 'One of my favourite waltzes, from the third act. Amongst all the records that I love, perhaps I love this one a little bit more.'

There was a change of mood again, to 'El Limpiabotas', a mambo sung by Cuates Castilla, the Mexican Singing Twins. This was followed by Yvonne Printemps singing 'I'll Follow My Secret Heart', from Noël Coward's *Conversation Piece*. 'This is enchantment!' Cushing enthused. 'It is from the era of the theatre that was my favourite and which I loved most dearly. I think it'll come back one day, but I think it's what this time is missing and I'd like a little memory of that, please.' The final selection was 'The Royal Hunt and Storm' from Berlioz' *The Trojans*. 'I think it's most majestic and inspiring and I think it'll help me a lot.'

Cushing opted for the Sibelius as his choice if he were only allowed one record, although he complained that the decision was difficult. In choosing his luxury item, he tried to get one over on the canny Plomley by requesting a full-sized Sopwith Camel aeroplane and a manual on how to fly it. Plomley told him no, so Cushing swapped the complete works of Shakespeare (supplied to all castaways) for a painting set. He also requested his toy soldiers as a luxury item, although 'I'm sure,' he said, 'if that lot was on board it's what sank the boat!' Cushing's *Desert Island Discs*, which also included plugs for the exhibition and *The Hound of the Baskervilles,* was broadcast on 23 February 1959. Three weeks later, the castaway was Ernest Thesiger, Cushing's co-star from *The Silver Whistle*. Thesiger's luxury item was also a painting set.

The Cushings stayed in Whitstable over Christmas and through January 1959. They returned for 25 January, when Cushing was back at Bray for his fifth film with Terence Fisher – *The Mummy*.

Chapter Fourteen

That C-r-e-e-p-y Character

'That C-r-e-e-p-y Character' was how David Stone described Cushing in *Everybody's* magazine in February 1959, although he discovered that there was really nothing creepy about him at all.

'It was at his Whitstable home that I talked to the 45-year-old Peter Cushing. Comfortably clad in a thick sweater, old trousers and fur-lined bedroom slippers, he told me about the hard road he has travelled to reach his present perch at the top. We chatted in the studio which Cushing has built at the top of his house. One wall, almost entirely of windows, floods the room with light, and at the other end of the room is a large work-table, laden with all the apparatus an artist needs.

'The critics like to describe him as "suave" "polished" and "silky",' wrote Stone. 'He is all these things, and it seems to come from an inner contentment. It is no effort talking to Cushing. He bubbles with a young man's enthusiasm for the world around him. Offstage his voice is surprisingly soft, and he has a tendency to guffaw when something amuses him. He would much rather talk about his hobbies than about himself ... and values his solitary rambles through the English countryside far more than the West End's tinsel glamour.

'It would be impossible to imagine him bothering with "psychological" acting or explaining his art in

Joseph Whemple (Raymond Huntley), Stephen Banning (Felix Aylmer) and his son John examine a relic from the tomb of Ananka in *The Mummy* (1959)

fancy terms. His approach is essentially that of a man doing a job of work." He is now Peter Cushing Productions Ltd, and in the happy position of having work in the theatre, films and TV as far as the eye can see. But his success does not weigh on his mind in any disturbing way. "I wouldn't mind if I didn't have it, you know. I've got so much more."'[1]

At 45, just five years after his father had made that dread pronouncement of failure, Cushing was a worldwide success. He was greeted with cheers when he visited America with Christopher Lee for the première of *Dracula*, and had signed autographs long into the night. He had little trepidation about following the horror path and becoming typecast; his concern was for Helen, who, after supporting him for so long, deserved something in return. 'Helen's life had been a riches to rags story,' he said. 'I wanted to restore some of the riches again, after all she'd been through.'[2]

Cushing's next project, Hammer's *The Mummy*, began filming on 25 February 1959. It was a lengthy shoot that lasted until 16 April, but he was back with old friends. Christopher Lee was playing Kharis, the Mummy of the title, and Terence Fisher was once again behind the camera.

Cushing had first achieved fame as a romantic actor, and *The Mummy* features one of his gentlest film roles as John Banning, a quiet and scholarly man who is suddenly confronted with the living embodiment of 'the sins of the father'. We first see Banning on an archaeological expedition in Egypt with his father Stephen (Felix Aylmer) and uncle, Joseph Whemple (Raymond Huntley). John has broken his leg but is still full of boyish eagerness and enthusiasm to see the dig. (Because he refuses to have his leg set, he later walks with a limp.) Cushing manages by his wide-eyed performance to portray a young man far better than he did in *Richard of Bordeaux*, though he is clearly abetted by some 'beauty' make-up, courtesy of Roy Ashton, who had taken over from Phil Leakey as Hammer's chief make-up artist. Jimmy Sangster's script has some rather subtle jokes, too. When Cushing delivers Banning's wistful line 'I seem to have spent most of my life among the dead,' perhaps Sangster was quietly commenting on Cushing's newfound reputation as a graveyard-dweller.

To give 'some sort of logic' to the beam of light passing through the mummy in Hammer's poster, Cushing asked that a scene be included where he drove a harpoon through Christopher Lee's Kharis in *The Mummy* (1959)

Stephen Banning has discovered the tomb of Queen Ananka, but a vengeful Egyptian, Mehemet Bey (George Pastell) warns of the ancient curse – 'He who robs the graves of Egypt dies!' Stephen enters the tomb and discovers the Scroll of Life but, unseen to him, a hidden door swings open. When the old man is later found by Whemple, Stephen has been driven out of his mind. The old man is committed to an asylum, but three years later he suddenly regains his wits and warns John about a living mummy in Ananka's tomb. There is a touching scene between Banning and his father with Cushing clearly delighted to be performing with veteran actor Aylmer, his co-star from *Hamlet*. Filled with hope that his father is sane, John is bitterly disappointed. 'You're a fool, John,' says Stephen – Cushing visibly winces. Later, when John is informed that his father will have to put in a padded cell for his own protection, Cushing does a turn-into-shot again, as he did in *Dracula*.

The Mummy has been brought to England by Mehemet Bey, but the crate in which it is contained is accidentally dropped into a marsh. This blood-red

bog, filmed at Shepperton because there was no tank facility at Bray, is the focus for one of the film's definitive scenes – the Mummy rising from the mud, sent off by the Bey to destroy the desecrators of Ananka's tomb. The subsequent attack on Stephen Banning in his cell is frighteningly savage. Dripping slime, the Mummy bends back the bars of the cell, slithers in and strangles the old man. Although Kharis is an automaton of bandage and bone, and moves with an appropriately robotic gait. Christopher Lee once again manages to invest a creature with a personality and motivation using only his eyes. There is no little sadness at his inevitable destruction.

In Banning's study, John is going through his father's papers. Cushing has a long exchange with Raymond Huntley, during which time he moves about, lights a cigarette, empties his ash-tray into the fire – and the whole speech is filmed in one continuous take. It is a startling achievement that goes almost unnoticed. Cushing then relates the legend of Ananka, and we see Christopher Lee as the High Priest Kharis, looking magnificent in his Egyptian regalia.

When the Mummy attacks his home, Banning can only watch in horror as Whemple is strangled. He rushes to the gun cabinet and empties a pistol into the monster, but it has no effect and convinces the dogged Inspector Mulrooney (Eddie Byrne) that he is dealing with 'fantasies out of Edgar Allan Poe!' Later, as Banning awaits the Mummy's return, he realises that his wife is the image of Queen Ananka – Cushing has a tender scene with Yvonne Furneaux as Isobel. 'She was considered the most beautiful woman in the world,' says Banning, smiling as he adds, 'mind you, the world wasn't such a big place then.' He kisses her and sends her to bed so he may face his enemy alone. The tension is difficult to bear as Banning paces up and down awkwardly on his twisted leg, waiting for the Mummy. The thing duly crashes in and goes for Banning – he is only saved by the intervention of Isobel, whose likeness to Ananka confuses the creature.

Cushing was alarmed to see that the publicity material for the film showed the Mummy with a large hole in his midriff, and a beam of light passing through it. 'This was never referred to in the script,' he recalled, 'so I asked how it got there. "Oh," said the publicity man. "That's just to help sell the picture." Oh, I thought – that's just not on.' Cushing asked Terence Fisher if he could take the harpoon from the wall in Banning's study and drive it through the Mummy's body, giving at least the idea that light *could* pass through the creature, 'thus giving some sort of logic to the illuminated gap on the posters.'[3] Cushing was always concerned about logic in scripts, believing that it was unwise to treat the audiences as idiots. 'The people who see horror films are very critical,' he noted, 'and they don't like just any old nonsense.'[4]

Yvonne Furneaux added that it was Cushing, diplomatically adding ideas to Fisher's set-ups, that saved the film. 'He was so tactful,' she says. 'Every time I was there, I could see that Peter had the ideas. He should have directed films.' Furneaux came to the film thinking it *would* be nonsense. When she found herself working with people like Peter Cushing and Christopher Lee, who treated the material with absolute seriousness, she abruptly changed her mind. 'From the start I should have cared just as much as Christopher and Peter.'[5]

The film benefits greatly from the care taken on it in all departments. Felix Barker's review of *The Mummy* in the *Evening News* noted that Cushing 'holds the whole tottering fabric of splendid nonsense together with his sincerity.'[6]

Three days before the completion of filming of *The Mummy*, on 16 April, Cushing recorded an interview at Bray for the BBC World Service. Broadcast as *Calling Australia* number 211, the subject was 'H for Horror'. Cushing was paid five guineas. Later in the year he was featured in the Light Programme show *Dateline London*, interviewed by Angus McDermid about his collection of model soldiers.

On 25 May 1959, Cushing joined director John Gilling for Robert S Baker and Monty Berman's production of *The Flesh and the Fiends*. Gilling, Baker and Berman formed Triad Productions specifically for this film, which marked the first instance of a company poaching Cushing from Hammer to take advantage of his new reputation.

In comparison with Cushing's last film *The Mummy* – which for all its Eastmancolored elegance is limited to several interior sets and a handful of actors – *The Flesh and the Fiends* in black-and-white is something of an epic, in widescreen, with huge interior and exterior sets stuffed with extras.

The Flesh and the Fiends is set in Edinburgh in 1828, where the 'brilliant, aggressive, provocative, verbose' Doctor Robert Knox teaches medicine and employs the resurrectionists Burke and Hare to acquire bodies for his anatomy classes. Cushing was already familiar with Knox, as he had used the surgeon as one of the components for his portrayal of Frankenstein. 'He was fundamentally doing something for the good of mankind,' Cushing said, 'but against all odds, because the villagers always seem to come and knock on his door and shout "You beast! You beast!"'[7] Knox's plight, Cushing said, helped him to give credibility to his performance as Frankenstein, and you can hear the Baron's metallic tones in Knox's lines: 'Emotion is a drug that dulls the intellect. Approach the science of medicine with a more clinical mind.'

Although the film's middle section is devoted to the performances of Donald Pleasence as Hare and George Rose as Burke, the first quarter-hour is given over almost entirely to a lengthy speech from Cushing as Knox. 'Miracles, gentlemen, are an apology for ignorance and a retreat for fools. To primitive man, the human body was a miracle. To us, it is a structure ... a complicated structure, yes, but no longer a miracle.' Knox rarely shies from an insult or an arch observation, and in a searing exchange with the hypocritical Edinburgh elders, spits, 'I can show you the heart, my dear Reverend – can you show me the soul? Beneath the armpit? Between the eyes, deep in the abdomen?'

In support are Melvyn Hayes (who had played the young Baron Frankenstein) as the idiot boy Daft Jamie, Reneé Houston as the ill-tempered Mrs Burke and Billie Whitelaw as the ill-fated barmaid of the 'Merry Duke'. 'I don't think I have worked with a finer cast,'[8] said John Gilling. And inspired by his actors, he creates an appropriately Dickensian atmosphere of delinquency in the dingy Edinburgh backstreets, with some startlingly brutal scenes. In one, Burke suffocates drunken old Aggie (Esma Cannon) and later, Pleasence gets to copy Cushing's 'terror' scene from *Nineteen Eighty-Four* when Hare sees a rat and goes berserk. And as Burke and Hare bring their newest body in, 'as fresh as a new-cut cabbage', Knox, roused from his bed, appears in a dressing-gown, waving his handkerchief against Burke's reeking breath.

When Burke and Hare are eventually arrested, Hare immediately turns King's evidence and denounces his former friend, who is hanged. But the mob is not satisfied – they round on Hare and blind him. Knox meanwhile has to face the medical Council, whose only concern is the honour of the profession. Threatened with gaol, Knox is fluorescent with rage. 'Croak your miserable way to the law-courts, if you dare,' he spits. 'I will meet you on the steps with a torchlight to scorch into your souls, and leave them bare as a warning to your future victims.'

Heading home after walking out of the hearing, Knox meets an urchin begging for ha'pennies. The doctor has no money, and asks the girl to come back with him to his house. 'No thank you,' she says politely, 'you might sell me to Doctor Knox!' Knox rises, tears running down his face. Unlike Frankenstein, Knox can still see his soul, can still connect with other people and so is redeemed. 'I've just heard the voice of conscience,' he admits back at the Academy. 'From a small child I heard the truth. It said "You are an ogre, Doctor Knox. You have killed humanity."' Knox is resigned to facing an empty lecture-room, but it is full of his students who applaud as he enters.

The film was another success, with Cushing's performance singled out for more praise than usual, although it was once again remarked upon that Cushing was 'an expert in this sort of fare.' With so many 'horror' performers already sending the genre up, *Variety* noticed that 'Cushing knows … parody is fatal and plays the part with straightforward sincerity, dignity and authority.'[9] The *Times* noted that Gilling's competent direction and concise script was 'well supported by Mr Peter Cushing as the … sarcastic and autocratic authority figure.' However, the review found fault with Burke and Hare, 'this grotesque and evil pair lose reality in their moments of sardonic humour, and thus step out of character in a way the director should never have allowed.'[10]

Cushing's next role was Charles Norbury in William Fairchild's play *The Sound of Murder*, directed at the Aldwych Theatre by Fred Sadoff, beginning in August 1959. Norbury, a writer of children's stories, is a cruel tyrant whose despotic behaviour drives his wife Anne

'You are an ogre, Doctor Knox. You have killed humanity.' Cushing as the Edinburgh anatomist who turns a blind eye to grave-robbing and murder in *The Flesh and the Fiends* (1959)

(Elizabeth Sellars) to contemplate murdering him. Terence Longdon played Anne's lover Peter Marriott with Patricia Jessell as Norbury's secretary Miss Forbes, who discovers Marriott's murder plot and blackmails him. David Jackson, who later appeared in the successful science fiction series *Blake's 7*, played PC Nash.

'It's Murder – But It's All Respectable' wrote W A Darlington in the *Daily Telegraph*. 'For years I have been misjudging the inhabitants of Surrey. I imagined behind those smug mock-Tudor facades or in those graciously-beamed cottages the living was gracious and the characters soft. But now I know better – or worse. Successful Charles Norbury... refuses his wife a divorce then within about ten minutes, she and her lover plan to murder him. Neither turns a hair. Obviously violent death is all in a day's work for them. None of the people ... is given any humanity but as cogs in the machine they do their work well enough. Peter Cushing does ... very efficiently his appointed job of

The finger of suspicion points to Lucy Byrne (Virginia Maskell), Professor Sewell, Doctor Shole (Kenneth Griffith) and Bob Marriott (Tony Britton) in the Boulting Brothers' *Suspect* (1959)

being more unpleasant in a shorter space of time than would be credible in an ordinary play. Elizabeth Sellars makes the bloodthirsty Mrs Norbury look like an advertisement for gracious living.'[11]

A review in the *Times* criticised the play's use of technology in the plot. 'It can do no harm to say that the initial breakdown of this plan for a "perfect murder" is brought about by a tape-recording machine. Obviously these modern instruments, which are so easily left on when they should be turned off, will sooner or later have to be banned from the stage, and the sooner the better. The tele-phone has served the dramatist well, but there can be no future for the mechanical eavesdropper.' The review approved of several ingenious surprises along the way, however, and while 'the moderately clever will anticipate what the penultimate surprise will be ... they will in all probability miss the final turn of the screw and may even be morally aghast at its nature.' Nevertheless, the reviewer found the play 'skilfully directed and no less skilfully acted. Mr Peter Cushing succeeds in making a distinguished writer in the Beatrix Potter vein so odious in his vindictive sadism that he almost deserves to be shot in cold blood.'[12]

The play was popular, and ran until February 1960. In December, however, Cushing started work on *Suspect* for the Boulting Brothers, and after one particularly hair-raising drive from the studios to the stage door decided that it was not sensible to appear on stage while filming. He took advantage of a get-out clause in his contract and was replaced in the role of Norbury by Michael Goodliffe, who had appeared in *The End of the Affair*.

In the summer, the Cushings had moved house as the lease on their flat in Airlie Gardens expired. They opted to stay in Notting Hill and found a property in Hillsleigh Road, which they had converted to provide a studio with a large window for painting. Reporter Vivien Hislop had a regular feature in the *Evening News*, in which she visited celebrities' homes, commenting on their décor and illustrated her article with a pen-and-ink picture. Hislop visited the Hillsleigh Road house for a piece entitled 'So *this* is Frankenstein's Real Castle'.

'From actor Peter Cushing, that master of spine-chilling suspense on stage, TV and films, came an invitation the other day. To see his new home, an old house high on Campden Hill. I found a yellow front door in a whitewashed gable end, halfway up a charming street so steep and narrow it could have been in the depths of the country. Peter's wife, actress Helen Beck, welcomed me in and told me about their "find". It was once a coach-house, then an artist's studio, and it is only a stone's throw away from the two rooms which she and Peter had shared for the past 15 years. First they had to have the builders in. They simply "imported" five local workmen from Whitstable (where they have a white clapboard house right on the beach) and installed them in the attic for ten weeks. "They had wonderful fry-ups at night" says Helen. All the decorating ideas have been hers, except the tiny hall which was planned round Peter's choice of wallpaper – a deep pink pattern of harlequins. The floor is tiled in big black and white squares and the size of the room doubled by a huge old mirror of carved wood and brass. Through the open hall door there is a view of the living room with the spacious north-lit studio beyond.

'All the rooms have Helen's feminine touch. In the living room it is a soft crushed raspberry coloured carpet, pink and white striped wallpaper and graceful regency and early Victorian furniture. Helen loves collecting. Most of her furniture she has bought for a song from a favourite antique dealer in Whitstable. She has a few heirlooms too. One is her great-grandfather's bell-pull, an elaborately beaded affair which she hung for fun near the fireplace.

'The studio is Peter's domain. For an actor who has made a name scaring people out of their wits, Peter is a surprise. He is a quiet, gentle man who lives in a world of his own, an artist and a dreamer whose passion is not the study of murder but model-making.

A long glass-fronted showcase holds some of the hundreds of model soldiers he has made or collected since he was a boy. He builds model planes too. They hang overhead suspended from lengths of fishing-line, so high that he keeps an aluminium ladder handy to reach them. Nearest to the roof was a big bomber. "I often take pot shots at it with a model gun" Peter confided. Next we inspected his shipping – model docks, cranes, tugs and liners set out on a sheet of blue plastic. A pair of binoculars was thrust into my hand – upside down for an 'aerial' view. The Cushings have Sir William Russell Flint as a friend and neighbour and somehow Peter finds time to paint in water-colour too.'[13]

On Boxing Day, 26 December 1959, Cushing began work on the thriller *Suspect,* directed by Roy and John Boulting. The Boulting brothers were responsible for such popular British films as *Brighton Rock*, *The Magic Box* and *Lucky Jim*, and had recently turned to satire with *I'm All Right Jack* starring Peter Sellers. Later in the 1960s they became directors of British Lion Films.

On completion of their latest movie the brothers found that the studio space was still theirs for three weeks. A £1000 wager was made between them that they couldn't complete a film in three weeks, but they did, and *Suspect* was the result. 'It really was one of the quickest pictures I appeared in,' Cushing remarked, 'but it stands to this day as a lesson that such budgets and tight shooting schedules can sometimes work.'[14] The end result is sound but as limited in its setting as a television play of the time would have been. Apparently the strain of working on *Suspect* as well as the *Sound of Murder* in the West End took its toll. Co-star Ian Bannen remembered Cushing repeatedly forgetting his lines on the first day of filming.

For his role as Professor Sewell, Cushing is playing an older man, with a moustache and a severe grey wig. Sewell is a biologist who has developed a cure for bubonic plague but is not allowed to publish his findings for fear of terrorism. Early in the film there is a lengthy exchange on the subject of nationalism with Raymond Huntley (his co-star from *The Mummy*) as the bluff Sir George Gatling, the Minister of Defence. 'You tell me it'd be treason to publish my work because some lunatic might use it to kill Englishmen,' says Sewell. 'It could save half a million lives outside this country, then I say it'd be treason to those half million if I don't!" Like Huntley and Cushing's scenes in *The Mummy*, these exchanges were filmed in lengthy continuous takes, a money-saving device only expedient with the most reliable of actors.

While the settings and the script remain relentlessly grey, *Suspect* relies on its performances to make up for its shortcomings. Sewell is a somewhat flamboyant character with his bow tie and watch-chain, and in emphasising his odd manner it seems that Cushing is trying his best to give a bit of colour to the part.

Thorley Walters is good value as a flustered police inspector and Ian Bannen plays an embittered amputee who manoeuvres young scientist Tony Britton into unknowing espionage. The treasured Spike Milligan, who was still working on *The Goon Show* on radio, provides the comic relief as an Irish janitor and has several scenes with Cushing. Also in the cast were Donald Pleasence, Geoffrey Bayldon, Sam Kydd and Anthony Booth, all of whom would work with Cushing again.

At the beginning of 1960, Cushing was about to start work on Hammer's *The Brides of Dracula* and was scheduled to join the BBC's new production of *Cyrano De Bergerac* shortly afterwards. Then he learned that there was, finally, to be a BBC production of *Journey's End* and wrote to Michael Barry on 10 January. 'I don't know if the rights are now available, whereas most actors' ambition is to play Hamlet, mine has always been to play "Stanhope"! I do realise of course that he is a much younger man than me, although life on the Western Front has aged him prematurely beyond his years. However, I would be very happy to play Osbourne, if the march of time has left its mark too much on me! The biggest fly in the ointment is the question of when you are to transmit this production. As you know, I will be filming up to the point where I begin rehearsing for *Cyrano*, so if it is possible to find a date for *Journey's End* fairly soon after April 10th, I would hold myself available. If I miss this opportunity, it will not come again for the next decade!' He concluded, 'Helen and I are so looking forward to your coming for a meal at our new house as soon as we have a little more free time.'

Despite Cushing's offer to hold himself available, his timing was a little adrift. *Cyrano De Bergerac* proved beyond the BBC's means once again, and the drama department no longer had the luxury of altering transmission slots to accommodate their stars. Michael Barry wrote sadly to Cushing on 14 January: 'No doubt because of your work at the studios you had not heard about *Cyrano*, although I had made sure the word was sent from here as soon as I was given a decision at the end of last week. For three weeks we had been battling with the cost of mounting *Cyrano*. Not until we had striven to solve the problem from every angle did I have to accept the fact that we could not produce. I know this will be a bitter disappointment to you. These financial matters – much as they can affect us all – should not concern you especially when working. I wish I could, in the next breath, come back with *Journey's End*, but it must be done between Monkhouse's *The Conquering Hero* on 28 February and *The Fanatics* on 13 March. I cannot postpone without losing the chance of linking the trilogy of plays together. Sorry, Peter.'

There wasn't long to worry about *Journey's End*, however, with a new adventure for Van Helsing just around the corner…

Chapter Fifteen

Swashing My Buckle

After the runaway success of *Dracula* in 1958, the sequel was inevitable. For reasons that remain unclear, Anthony Hinds requested a script that did not rely on the participation of Christopher Lee. Early in 1959 Jimmy Sangster presented *Disciple of Dracula*, featuring a vampire called Baron Meinster. The Baron preyed on the female attendees of a girl's school until he was confronted by the hero, Latour, who summoned Dracula to do away with his disciple. *The Hound of the Baskervilles'* screenwriter Peter Bryan then rewrote the script, and changed the title to *The Brides of Dracula*. Bryan ousted Latour and brought in Doctor Van Helsing, who destroyed Meinster with a swarm of killer bats summoned by an appeal to the powers of darkness to 'do justice to their code'.

It was decided that if Peter Cushing reprised his role as Van Helsing it would provide the necessary continuity in the series. However, Cushing was reportedly unimpressed with the rewritten script. Hinds engaged playwright Edward Percy (whose stage work Cushing admired) to add a final polish and shortly before the film went into the studio on 26 January 1960, Hinds himself did further work on the script. The resulting screenplay is one of Hammer's most lyrical and witty, and Terence Fisher excels himself in creating a shadowy netherworld in which an iconic hero takes on a monster – the quintessence of fairy-tale.

The story sees Van Helsing protecting the young schoolteacher Marianne Danielle (Yvonne Monlaur) from the unholy attentions of the vampire Baron Meinster (David Peel). While Van Helsing's bursts of swashbuckling activity were more or less limited to the last reel of *Dracula*, here the whole film is a showcase for Cushing's heroic athleticism. There are a couple of terrific fight sequences – a deft bit of gun-slinging as he slides a cross along a table to block the vampire's escape and he fights off a monstrous bat with his vampire hunter's bag. At the finale, Van Helsing leaps onto the sails of a burning windmill, bringing the mill's shadow into the shape of a cross that destroys the vampire. For that feat, at least, Cushing stood aside for a stunt double.

As Marianne is discovered unconscious in the forest, Cushing appears from a coach in his opera coat and high-crowned hat, immediately handsome, reassuring and determined. He makes much of little details like breaking open a phial of smelling-salts and gets some of the best opening lines Hammer has to offer. 'You've been badly frightened, haven't you? But there's nothing to be afraid of now. I'm a doctor. Doctor Van Helsing...' The audience are in need of an ally by this point. In the prologue, Marianne discovers Baron Meinster chained up in his Chateau, apparently by his jealous and cruel mother, the Baroness. Marianne frees the handsome aristocrat, whereupon he immediately kills his mother and escapes into the night. In the Baron, Terence Fisher created a

Van Helsing ministers to student teacher Marianne Danielle (Yvonne Monlaur) in *The Brides of Dracula* (1960)

powerful foe whose appearance switches suddenly from a blonde-haired, Wildean decadent to a red-eyed monster trumpeting with fury. A huge close-up of the Baron, fangs bared, hissing and spitting like a cat cuts to a shot of his grimly determined opponent. For all Christopher Lee's success in *Dracula*, his presence is not really missed here.

Van Helsing tells the troubled local priest (Fred Johnson) that he is studying a strange sickness '… partly physical, partly spiritual…' – the cult of the undead. Cushing has to explain the vampire lore all over again, but in this film he does so while unpacking a suitcase – prop 'business' is used to great effect. Cushing makes the fantastic details about Vampires and How to Kill Them seem all the more believable because as he is explaining them, he is putting a bundle of shirts into a wardrobe.

In the climactic fight in the Baron's windmill hide-out, the vampire hunter is bitten by the vampire.

His strength failing, Van Helsing hauls himself to a brazier and places a branding-iron into the coals. He sears the bite with the iron and throws holy water on the burn which miraculously heals. Camera operator Len Harris recalled how Cushing put a real poker in the fire then, out of shot, swapped it for a wooden prop which he then brought to his neck. 'The strength of the shot is in Peter Cushing's acting, because when he puts the poker on his neck you really feel it!'

'The cast is too good for the material'[1] snorted the *Times* review. It would take some material to match this cast. Second billing goes to Martita Hunt as the imperious Baroness, whose formidably chiselled exterior hides an almost unbearable loneliness. The Baroness has sheltered and protected her son, procuring victims for him. In return for her indulgence, the (literally) spoiled boy takes everything from his mother, reducing her to a white-faced shadow who shyly hides her vampire fangs from Van Helsing in a gesture of weirdly ambiguous sexuality. (The *New York Herald Tribune* noticed 'dabs of Freud and Tennessee Williams.'[2]) Hunt was best known for her role as Miss Havisham in David Lean's 1946 film of *Great Expectations,* a role which informs the Baroness' wistful recollections of the 'gay times, balls, dinners … life' that used to fill Chateau Meinster.

Cushing shares a powerful scene with Martita Hunt and matches her note for note. On the trail of the vampire, Van Helsing arrives at the chateau and the undead Baroness creeps into view in the background. 'Who is it that is not afraid?' she asks.

'Only God has no fear,' Van Helsing states.

'There's no release from this life which isn't life … or death,' states the Baroness. 'And I know I shall have to do whatever hideous thing he asks me to!' Van Helsing brings peace to the Baroness in the only way he can, with a stake through the heart – and with

With grim purpose, Van Helsing drives a stake into the vampirised Baroness Meinster in *The Brides of Dracula* (1960)

little more than an intake of breath to steel himself, Cushing conveys to the audience the horror of his work. As cock-crow signals daybreak, Van Helsing takes up a stake and a mallet. Then with a single downward stoke, in an attitude like a Pre-Raphaelite knight, he hammers in the stake. As the blood seeps out, Fisher suddenly, momentarily, fills the screen with scarlet – a close-up of a red curtain which Van Helsing pulls down to lay over the dead Baroness.

This is the first of Fisher's horror films to have a number of good roles for women. As well as Yvonne Monlaur as Marianne and Andrée Melly as the doll-faced student teacher Gina, Freda Jackson plays Greta, the Baron's old nurse, whose hysterical, triumphant cackles in the prologue set the appropriate key for the events that follow. Later, in the graveyard, a bedraggled Greta hugs the ground as she coaxes the vampire girl out of her coffin. 'The Master's waiting for you…' she coos, 'come on my precious, my little love…' as a white hand claws its way obscenely out of the ground. Just as precious is Cushing's ever-widening stare of horror as the coffin lid opens. This is another of Fisher's definitive sequences, a scrap of nightmare committed to film.

Other cherishable members of the cast include Miles Malleson as the hypochondriac Doctor Tobler, whom Fisher uses to contrast with the horror of the

Captain Judd supervises the test of veteran pilot Captain Gort (Bernard Lee) in the thrilling *Cone of Silence* (1960)

Baroness's death. (The Doctor briefly becomes a kind of surrogate Watson to Van Helsing's Holmes.) Henry Oscar, Cushing's old ENSA boss, makes something marvellous of the pompous schoolmaster Herr Lang, accompanied by Mona Washbourne in full flutter as his wife. While Lang huffs and puffs, Cushing remains perfectly still – then deftly presents a visiting card from a silver case. Immediately, Lang is all smiles. 'Leiden University?' he coos, 'How could I be expected to recognise a doctor of philosophy, a doctor of theology, a professor of metaphysics by the cut of his trousers?'

Malcolm Williamson provided the score, favouring a reedy organ theme for the suspense sequences at the chateau and the graveyard which adds a faintly ecclesiastical atmosphere to these scenes. To match this, the film is presented in the stained-glass window colours of Jack Asher's luminous photography, never finer than here. The entrance of Chateau Meinster was filmed at Oakley Court, the Victorian Gothic house near to Bray Studios, which appeared briefly in *The Curse of Frankenstein* and *The Mummy*. Over the years the house would appear in almost as many horror films as Peter Cushing.

Once again, however, Terence Fisher was without honour in his own country. The *Observer* called the film 'ludicrous monstrosity following a spoor of Technicolor blood, which lead farther and farther away from the force, pity and near dignity of Bram Stoker's novel.'[3]

This was Cushing's last Hammer horror for some time. He made a conscious effort to make different kinds of films, sensing that the public were not responding to what he knew was work of some quality, not just from him but from all the Hammer personnel. He would continue to make films for Hammer, but when *The Brides of Dracula* completed filming on 18 March 1960, Cushing would not make another film with a fantasy horror subject for three-and-a-half years.

Cushing's next production, the Bryanston/British Lion film *Cone of Silence*, brought him back down to earth even though it concerned a group of aircraft pilots. The film captures a charming late-fifties *milieu* of Morris Minors, tea bars and aerodromes and the cast includes a host of familiar faces including George Sanders, Bernard Lee, Noel Willman, André Morell and Marne Maitland with Cushing's good friend Gordon Jackson as another pilot. The film was shot in March and April, directed by Charles Frend, who was an editor for Hitchcock and directed such films as *The Magnet* and *The Cruel Sea*.

The film's title plays on a double meaning. The 'cone of silence' refers to an area of radar black-out which pilots must find while flying 'blind' and also to the cover-up of a potentially dangerous aeroplane. The film was given the rather more literal, and rather more mundane title *Trouble in the Sky* in America. Bernard Lee plays the veteran flyer Captain Gort, who crashes on one of the initial flights of a new plane – the *Phoenix*, designed by Nigel Pickering (Noel Willman). Pickering knows that his career will be finished if the safety of the *Phoenix* is called into question, so he has deliberately been witholding information about a defect in the take-off equipment. Cushing plays Flight Captain Clive Judd, a smarmy customer who has all the classic traits of a school sneak. Judd charms stewardess Joyce Mitchell (Delphi Lawrence) to get inside information about a romance between Captain Hugh Dallas (Michael Craig) who is investigating the *Phoenix* case and Captain Gort's daughter Charlotte. 'Old Judd's a great organiser but he's not exactly my idea of a gay evening out,' says Dallas.

There is a compelling take-off scene in the *Phoenix*, with Cushing in the full pilot's rig and headphones – the danger that the plane could suddenly go out of control makes the subsequent landing equally heart-stopping. Satisfyingly, Judd gets his come-uppance in the end. Gort was supposed to have caught a piece of hedge in the wheels of his plane at Calcutta, but it transpires that it was Judd's take-off which clipped the hedge.

The film has several thrilling sequences, and the black-and-white photography adds a documentary feel to the whole. Producer Aubrey Baring, of the Baring's banking family served in a similar capacity on *The Abominable Snowman*.

On 23 May 1960 director Terence Fisher began work on *Sword of Sherwood Forest*, Hammer's Megascope adaptation of the television series *The Adventures of Robin Hood*. The show was one of the first great successes of independent television, making a star of actor Richard Greene in the title role. (Greene acted as co-producer for the Hammer film.) Cushing was cast as the villainous Sheriff of Nottingham, the role played by Alan Wheatley in the series. Wheatley and Cushing played many similar roles in their careers – Wheatley had previously played Sherlock Holmes and Mr Darcy for the BBC. Terence Fisher had directed several episodes of the TV series so obviously knew the style, but the film is a disappointment. The locations, at County Wicklow in Ireland, are flat and uninteresting, the storyline is convoluted and the dialogue is pallid. Even in widescreen, several elaborate action sequences fail to create any excitement.

As the Sheriff, Cushing looks immaculate in a silver beard and long black wig, but despite one scene where he offers a man a free pardon and then shoots

him, he never does anything particularly wicked. It seems as if Fisher and Cushing are trying very hard to make the Sheriff a three-dimensional human being, in a film where a black-hearted rogue might have served their purpose better. Cushing's fee, in second billing, was £3,500.

Nevertheless, Cushing's Sheriff is a relaxed and entertaining performance, particularly in the scenes with Maid Marion (Sarah Branch) whom he always calls 'Madam'. All the familiar gestures are present and correct – he bites his thumb in contemplation and holds his finger aloft to emphasise that Robin Hood is 'a *very* dangerous criminal'. And clearly no expense was spared on the Sheriff's costumes, designed by John McCorry. In almost every scene the Sheriff is wearing a different ensemble in velvet and leather. He also appears in a long robe that looks like a flock-wallpaper dressing-gown and wears a black-and-white number with chains for the assizes. The real villain of the piece, in a plot to kill the Archbishop of Canterbury, is the Earl of Newark,

Cushing as the less-than-black-hearted Sheriff of Nottingham in *Sword of Sherwood Forest* (1960)

played at a simmer by Richard Pasco. His henchman is the effete Lord Melton, played by Oliver Reed with an ill-advised 'snide' accent which is unfortunately comic rather than menacing.

When Robin and Little John seek sanctuary in a priory, the prioress turns out to be Newark's cousin – she's suspicious from the outset because she's got *lipstick* on. Newark is ready to kill off the outlaws but the Sheriff cannot bring himself to murder in cold blood. In a sudden, startling turn, Melton stabs the Sheriff in the back and kills him, denying Cushing the traditional last-reel swordfight between Robin and the Sheriff, or indeed (as seems more likely) some sort of reconciliation.

Filming for *Sword of Sherwood Forest* concluded on 8 July and the film was released for the Christmas holidays on 26 December 1960. *Kinematograph Weekly* correctly called it 'jolly, disarmingly naïve adventure comedy melodrama'[4] while in America, *Variety* stated rather baldly that Cushing 'plays the Sheriff the way the Sheriff should be played.'[5]

Later in the summer of 1960, Cushing joined the cast of *The Hellfire Club* for Regal Films, directed by Robert Baker and Monty Berman who had made *The Flesh and the Fiends*. The British cast was headed by Peter Arne and Adrienne Corri, with Australian Keith Michell – who was brought to England by Olivier in 1948 – making an impressive starring début as the brawny hero. There is indispensable support from the likes of Bill Owen, David Lodge and Francis Matthews, with Cushing given rightly-earned 'Guest Star' status in the credits. The script was by Jimmy Sangster and Leon Griffiths from Sangster's storyline.

While all concerned were doubtless keen to find some potential scares in the legendary coven of debauched noblemen that was the Georgian Hellfire Club, there's more sin in the first five minutes of *The Hound of the Baskervilles* than in the whole of this film. Jason Caldwell (Michell) the heir to Netherden Hall, has been ousted from his country seat by his wicked cousin Thomas (Arne) who carries on the rituals of the Hellfire Club. Jason, who has grown up in a travelling circus, uses his old friends to help him

reclaim his title, despite Thomas' associates in the club – 'some of the most influential men in the British government.'

When Lord Netherden dies in 1766, Jason cannot his prove his claim to the estate other than with a locket that belonged to his mother. He visits the family lawyer Mr Merryweather (Cushing) who initially gives him short shrift. Cushing looks handsome in his beard and black wig, making great play of his snuff-taking and Latin quotations. Merryweather is a wily bird but an endearing ally, like a rather more grave version of Cushing's Doctor Who. 'Look at you,' says Merryweather, assessing the future Lord Netherden. 'You're dressed like a country clod-hopper! Documents? Nothing! Just some wild story and a locket. Call that proof? I call it impertinence, sir!' Jason vows to prove his case, and Merryweather, recognising in Jason his

Cushing as the canny lawyer Mr Merryweather in *The Hellfire Club* (1961)

'mother's spirit and his father's temper' agrees to help. The chief piece of evidence in Jason's claim is a letter at Netherden which proves his identity. Merryweather has a plan. 'If one was dishonest, which of course one is not, one could steal the letter ...'

'And what if one was caught?' says Jason.

'Then one would need a very good lawyer, my Lord.'

Later, Cushing enjoys himself in a courtroom sequence with Miles Malleson as a hanging judge. Merryweather seems to lose the case, and Jason is sent to Newgate to await execution, but this is all part of the lawyer's plan to keep the young Earl out of danger. Merryweather's trump card is to bring in his friend William Pitt, the Earl of Chatham, who has consented to raise the matter of Jason's title in parliament.

The film is not badly made or badly acted – it's a standard British swashbuckler of the time – but there's something magical in Cushing's handful of scenes that makes the rest seem dull when he's not about. The *New York Herald Tribune* found the film 'nothing more than a routine derring-do melodrama. What went on in those Hellfire caves would have made Fanny Hill blush. The film simply plays up the club as a background ... but the orgies are strictly for Grandma!'[6] The debauchery in the commonly-seen print is tepid, but there was a spiced-up version of the

Mr Evan Wrack presents the case for the prosecution in Michael Anderson's *The Naked Edge* (1960)

film, with bosoms bared, produced for Europe. The location used for Netherden Hall was Moor Park Golf Club, which would turn up again in Hammer's *The Vampire Lovers*.

Cushing's role in *Im Namen des Teufels* (*The Devil's Agent*), a German/British co-production, is not known, which is a shame because the cast included Peter Van Eyck, Christopher Lee and Billie Whitelaw and the film was directed by John Paddy Carstairs, who had commented so favourably on Cushing's performance in *Beau Brummell* for the BBC. Cushing's scenes (if indeed he shot any) were deleted and he does not feature in the finished print. He listed the film in his filmography, but could recall nothing about it in later years, and Christopher Lee states that did not meet his Hammer co-star when the film was made in Ireland.

In *The Naked Edge*, however, Cushing *can* be seen, again as a lawyer. The film was directed by Michael Anderson at the end of 1960 with Gary Cooper and Deborah Kerr. Anderson was well-known for directing popular successes like *The Dam Busters* and *Around the World in Eighty Days* and significantly, directed the 1955 film of *Nineteen Eighty-Four* in which American

actor Edmond O'Brien took Cushing's role of Winston Smith. Anderson's Hitchcock-influenced direction mixes a gritty sequence shot in a tenement block with negative shots for flashbacks, shots through water and diagonal shots. The film was based on Max Ehrlich's novel *Last Train to Babylon,* adapted by Joseph Stefano, who came to the film riding high on the success of his screenplay for *Psycho.*

Donald Heath (Ray McAnally) is on trial for the murder of a co-worker and the theft of £60,000. George Radcliffe (Gary Cooper) is Heath's employer, on whose testimony Heath is ultimately convicted. Some years later, an old blackmail threat comes to light, implicating Radcliffe in the murder and the theft. Radcliffe's wife (Deborah Kerr) begins to suspect her husband and contacts the blackmailer, but in doing so places her own life in grave danger...

Cushing plays Evan Wrack, prosecuting counsel in Heath's trial, shot for the most part in close-up and looking splendid. Wrack is flamboyant of gesture and pedantic of speech, smugly anticipating victory in an open-and-shut case. Shifting his robe on his shoulders when going in for the kill, Cushing deliberately removes his glasses, then uses them as a prop to enunciate his speech for the prosecution. 'Mr Heath, after observing this inhuman, *immoral* effort you are making to save your own neck, I doubt there remains in this court one person who can continue to believe in your protested innocence!'

The film again is a showcase for some excellent characters, notably Wilfrid Lawson (from Cushing's play *The Road*) Hermione Gingold as a blousy madam and Sandor Eles (who would appear with Cushing in *The Evil of Frankenstein*) as her fey fancy-boy. Cushing enjoyed a brief reunion with Deborah Kerr, his co-star from *The End of the Affair*, who made *The Naked Edge* before starting work on the supernatural chiller *The Innocents* in February 1961.

In April, Cushing was back at Bray for the shooting of Hammer's *Cash on Demand*, directed by Quentin Lawrence. This short black-and-white film, which began shooting on 4 April 1961, was based on an ITV play by Jacques Gillies called *The Gold Inside*, also directed by Lawrence, which had been broadcast on 24 September 1960.

Crisply photographed on a handful of tiny sets in a fortnight, the film is no little achievement and shows just what the Hammer personnel were capable of. It features two fascinating central performances from Cushing and his 'Watson' André Morell (who had

'What is it you want?' asks bank manager Fordyce. 'Just some *money...*' replies wily crook Colonel Gore-Hepburn (André Morell) in Hammer's modest masterpiece *Cash on Demand* (1961)

appeared in the TV version) in a Pinteresque story of deception and emotional manipulation.

Cushing plays Harry Fordyce, manager of the City and Colonial Bank, Haversham Branch, a petty, vindictive, joyless character who holds the threat of dismissal over his staff because it is practically the only power he has. On the day before Christmas Eve, Fordyce is visited by a man who calls himself Colonel Gore-Hepburn, an inspector from the bank's insurance agency. But Gore-Hepburn, played by Morell at his foxiest, is really a confidence trickster of the most cunning kind.

We first see Cushing looking like black beetle in his bowler hat and steel-rimmed spectacles. He fastidiously cleans a smear off the bank's brass name-plate, and berates his staff for keeping a rusty pen on the counter ('This isn't a post office, you know!') Cushing clearly enjoys playing such a small monster and Morell seems to like playing the real brute, mixing avuncular charm with effortless cruelty,

although cameraman Len Harris pointed out that the leads could have swapped roles and the piece would still have worked.

By a faked telephone call, Gore-Hepburn makes Fordyce believe that his wife and son are held hostage. As Morell elaborates with grisly details, there is more than a touch of O'Brien from *Nineteen Eighty-Four*. 'There are two men at your house,' he explains. 'At this moment your wife has an electrode attached to each side of her head. If you fail to co-operate with us in any way whatever they will pass a charge through the circuit. It is extremely painful and I'm afraid the effects of it are permanent. She would never recover her wits.' Lawrence uses several telling close-ups of Fordyce's appalled, panic-stricken face. 'What is it you want?' he bleats. Gore-Hepburn merely smiles. 'Just some *money...*'

It is difficult enough to believe that Fordyce has a home life, never mind a wife and child, but he seems fiercely devoted to them. 'If anything happens to my family, I'll kill you, I swear I will...' he spits.

Gore-Hepburn shows Fordyce how he intends to steal the money – a plot that will involve Fordyce's collaboration in a criminal act.

When, after the suspenseful robbery, Gore-Hepburn has escaped with the loot, the chief clerk, Pearson (Richard Vernon), makes Fordyce admit that he has helped to rob his own bank. In pleading for Pearson's support, Fordyce is reduced to a grizzling wreck – with his hands clenched together in despair. When the police arrive with Gore-Hepburn in handcuffs, the staff rally round Fordyce, who at the end of the experience is changed for the better – 'What is the usual sentence? For completely failing in my duty towards my staff?' In a film that echoes *A Christmas Carol* and *It's A Wonderful Life*, we discover that there is gold inside Fordyce after all.

There is some considerable dexterity on Cushing's part with keys and suitcases, but his performance is still rather theatrical. Possibly because of the tight filming schedule, or perhaps because Fordyce's only characteristic is his meanness, there are occasions when he seems over-mannered and rather comically prim. Cushing is playing a little older than his age, but he looks older here, in black-and-white, than he would in colour in *Frankenstein Created Woman* five years later.

Columbia released *Cash on Demand* in America on 20 December 1961, with screenings in New York as late as April. In Britain, however, the film was not released for another two years, although it was well-received on release as a well-crafted, unpretentious second-feature. *Kinematograph Weekly* said 'the film creates considerable tension and excitement without any violent action and without straying at all from the back itself ... a credit to the script, direction and sound acting by all the cast, especially Peter Cushing as the tortured bank manager and André Morell as the suave robber.'[7] In his 1997 book *An Autobiography of British Cinema*, critic Brian McFarlane described this little-seen movie as 'possibly the best "B" film ever made in Britain.'

Fury At Smugglers' Bay was Cushing's next project, reuniting him with director John Gilling for a rather run-of-the-mill British swashbuckler filmed on location at Fishguard in Wales, doubling for nineteenth-century Cornwall. Cushing gets top billing as Squire Trevenyan in buckled boots, tricorn hat and a scraped-back wig with a pigtail. His character is something of a martinet, and in the early scenes there seems little logic for his severe behaviour towards his son Chris, played by John Fraser. It eventually transpires that Chris is illegitimate – but Trevenyan has kept this secret from his son. A pirate called Black John (Bernard Lee) was a former groom of Trevenyan's, and knows the secret. The pirate blackmails his former employer, who as justice of the peace, 'the chief arbiter of law in the county' is able to turn a blind eye to Black John's smuggling activities.

Cushing gets one good scene with Bernard Lee when the old pirate reveals the Squire's wife's indiscretion. 'You hate it, don't ya?' leers Black John – Lee's performance has more than a touch of Robert Newton's Long John Silver – 'It's twisting you, like a knife in the guts.' Cushing simmers with fury, then snaps and smacks Black John with his horsewhip. There's no humour in Trevenyan and Cushing's expressions throughout are stiff and unengaging, so different from the sprightly and beguiling Mr Merryweather.

Cushing may have enjoyed these films but he really should not have been making them at this time. His Hammer involvement is often blamed for keeping him from 'legitimate' roles, but childish nonsense like this may well have done his career more harm. None of the films in his abdication period from horror have the quality or the staying power of *Dracula* or *The Mummy*.

As Cushing pointed out, it was a British Western. 'The scenario contained all the traditional ingredients: lots of shootin', the inevitable brawl in the saloon, a *High Noon* confrontation between duellists using swords instead of six-shooters and the cavalry charging to the rescue in the nick of time. I had the grumpy-old-dad-who-turns-up-trumps-in-the-end Lee J Cobb part.'[8]

Cushing as Squire Trevenyan in *Fury at Smugglers' Bay* (1961)

There are notable appearances by George Coulouris as an 'honest' smuggler, William Franklyn as a highwayman known only as 'The Captain' and Miles Malleson, who plays the Duke of Avon as another of his memorably funny screen hypochondriacs. On the debit side there are some poorly-choreographed fights and possibly the worst-day-for-night footage ever committed to film. Perhaps the poorest element of the film is the flat script, which allows little in the way of character development for anyone.

At the finale, everybody ends up in Smugglers' Bay for a shoot-out between the smugglers and soldiers. The Captain kills Black John, but not before Trevenyan is shot defending his son. Cushing executes a neat turn as he falls and makes a meal of a rather protracted death-scene in which he manages to give a parting glance to each of the assembled company before rolling his eyes aloft. 'You rode your horse very well, dear fellow,' Cushing recalled Christopher Lee telling him after a television showing of *Fury At Smugglers' Bay*, 'and the expression on your face when you died

'Even your cloth can't sanctify the mark of the hangman's rope.'
Captain Collier (Patrick Allen) feels Dr Blyss's collar in *Captain Clegg* (1961)

He plays two distinct characters – the whimsical Blyss (something like Mr Merryweather), and Clegg, a strong and heroic figure who uses the profits from smuggling to help the poor of the village. The result is a fast-paced and thrilling swashbuckler – exactly the sort of film Cushing would have been happy making for the rest of his life – featuring the familiar Hammer production values and an excellent cast.

We first see the Reverend Doctor Blyss lustily conducting his flock from the pulpit. We also see Oliver Reed as the Squire's son Harry, lusting after the Innkeeper's adopted daughter Imogene, played by Yvonne Romain. The Reverend gently chivvies his congregation, warning that 'war with France is more than just a possibility,' as the King's revenue men arrive, led by Patrick Allen as Captain Collier. Collier spent many years in pursuit of the notorious pirate Captain Clegg, who is buried in Blyss's churchyard. As the soldiers interrupt the service, Cushing immediately turns his mild steel on Collier. 'Would you be kind enough to remove your hat?'

There is a meeting of the smugglers to decide what to do with the contraband already in the village. Clegg enters, with Cushing perfectly timing the slam of the door behind him to punctuate his first line to the smugglers. Clegg orders that their plans are not changed. The smugglers (including Michael Ripper as Blyss's right-hand man Jeremiah Mipps the coffin maker and Martin Benson as the weasely innkeeper Rash) disguise themselves and their horses as the 'Romney Marsh Phantoms' to frighten away the suspicious. The film features some of Hammer's finest day-for-night shooting and the phantom riders are an unexpectedly chilling image.

Cushing effortlessly slips in and out of the benign expression of Doctor Blyss and cheekily makes Collier hold his stick and bible in a priceless bit of prop business. 'They are very devout here,' he explains later of his flock. 'They don't care to meddle with the forces of darkness!' When Clegg sends Collier off on a false trail, Cushing throws his head back in a wild, soundless laugh. Here, as throughout the film, Cushing is every inch the hero. A long black wig with a white streak emphasises the shape of his face and enables him to look both angelic and fierce.

was exactly the same as when you were told what your salary for the film was going to be.'[9]

John Fraser warmly recalls Cushing's enjoyment of the film and his enthusiasm for the swordfights and horseback chases. 'Peter was the perfect gentleman ... He told me his mother brought him up almost as a girl, and it's a miracle he didn't grow up gay – which of course he didn't – but having missed out a bit on a boys' childhood, his passion was for toy soldiers and boys' games. Every Saturday he used to walk from his home in Holland Park to Hamley's in Regent Street to buy more model soldiers. He had a whole battlefield laid out in his attic. He was a darling man!'[10]

On 25 September work began on another blood-and-thunderer for Cushing when he took the lead in Hammer's *Captain Clegg*, directed by Peter Graham Scott. This was an adaptation of Russell Thorndike's novel *Dr Syn*, which had already been filmed in 1937 with George Arliss as the Dymchurch vicar who secretly practices smuggling on Romney Marsh. Walt Disney Pictures had also secured the rights to the *Dr Syn* title for a film with Patrick McGoohan, so Hammer's smuggler was cosmetically slapped with the alias of Doctor Blyss. In all other respects, including the name 'Captain Clegg', Thorndike's story was unchanged.

Cushing adored the chance to tackle the *Dr Syn* story, adding much to the film with his own research.

When Harry is arrested as the smugglers' look-out, Clegg takes his phosphorescent friends out for a last ride. They distract the excise men long enough to rescue the boy, and the wild ride concludes with an iconic shot of Cushing pulling off his skull-like mask.

Back at the church, with the revenue men's net tightening, Blyss conducts an impromptu marriage between Imogene – who is in fact his daughter – and Harry. Again, the details are everything – Cushing raises an eyebrow when he realises Mipps has used a curtain ring for a wedding ring. Cushing was coached in the wedding service by none less than the vicar of Bray himself. As the service ends and the young couple escape, Collier bursts in again, and tears off Blyss' collar to reveal the scars left when Clegg escaped the hangman's rope. Clegg addresses his people. 'No man can stand on the gallows without coming face-to-face with his soul. On that day, truly, the old Clegg died. What the new Clegg has done, you all know. When I first came here, I found you in wretchedness and poverty, deprived by harsh laws and heavy taxes of the simple comforts all men have a right to expect. I took upon myself the task of changing all that at the expense of the Revenue. What I did, I did for the good of you all.'

Cushing finally gets the swing-on-the-chandelier finale that was denied him in *Dracula*. However, he is, in rapid succession, shot by Collier and then harpooned. The Captain dies heroically saving Mipps, who carries his fallen comrade to the grave that awaits him.

Variety made a good

Cushing studies the marriage service with the Reverend Sidney Doran, watched by director Peter Graham Scott, during the filming of *Captain Clegg* (1961)

point about Hammer films in general when praising the film. 'Pure escapism of course, but notable in that the Hammer imprimatur has come to certify solid values in all production departments, and there's no mystery why these films rate audience allegiance. The histrionics are generally convincing, especially Peter Cushing as the pirate-cum-vicar.'[11]

Director Peter Graham Scott remembers Cushing's particular contribution to a crucial scene in *Captain Clegg*. 'Peter Cushing was a very interesting man. I knew his work, but I had not met him before. He must have been getting on for 50 when we worked

with him. He was a proper actor, he was a very good actor, and he knew that those films wouldn't have worked without that. Before we started, [producer] John Temple-Smith and I went and saw Peter, and he showed us his soldiers, laid out in the battle of Waterloo. He explained that Blucher was arriving on the right and it was all tremendously interesting. We met Helen, whom he adored, there was no question about it, it was sheer *worship*. She was a lovely woman – I wouldn't have been, let's say, "down on the knee" about her, but there you are, *c'est la vie*.

'Peter said he liked the script, but there were several things he didn't like about it. He said that there wasn't any real characterisation for the Captain. We got a woman called Barbara Harper, an extremely good writer who'd done things for me on television, in on it, and we worked on that, but there was still a sticking point. We had built up the tension and Doctor Blyss was delivering his sermon in the pulpit. And I said well, fine, he can start the sermon and then we'll get the Navy to burst in, but Peter said "No, he *must* deliver the sermon." And so I said why? We've got the tension going, and the speed going. He said "No, we must stop the film, and wait while he delivers the sermon." I said well, what are the Navy doing? They're just coming through the forest. He said "It'll just have to be a bigger forest."'

'Of course, the day arrived to shoot it and he said "By the way, I've just jotted down a few lines for me to actually utter." So I thought, fine, I'll just let him start off with "My brethren..." and cut away to the excise men. And he delivered this speech, which he'd written, and he delivered it beautifully. I didn't rehearse it, I just said "we'll do it". He told the villagers how when he arrived they had been oppressed by heavy taxes, the Napoleonic wars were going on, they were starving, he had brought them prosperity, they could feed their children, he had done all this for them, on the basis of the smuggling. At this point, the doors burst open, and the revenue men burst in. I thought Peter, you are a crafty old sod. It was the best speech in the film.'[12]

Chapter Sixteen

Abdication, Restoration

On 9 January 1962, Patricia Lewis wrote in the *Daily Express*: 'After a five-year reign as "The King of Horror" actor Peter Cushing plans to abdicate. But not without a courtly bow to the Draculas and Frankensteins who made him an international star. "I was sort of carried along with the cycle," explained this fast-talking greying man of most un-actorish habits, like living in Whitstable, drinking only orange juice and carrying a briefcase. "It was wonderful to work steadily on from one film to the next, but then a few weeks ago I realised that out of the 10 movies I had made for Hammer, six were "X" certificate. Though they made a spectacular impact on the box-office I don't want the public labelling me solely as 'that horror man'." He approaches every role with the same respect but "I have a tremendous eye on the takings" he says. "I don't mind being connected with an artistic success so long as it also takes money. I say to myself 'My ego may want me to play Hamlet, but will people pay to *see* me play Hamlet?' If I were offered two plays at the same time and one was *Macbeth* and the other was *Rookery Nook*, I'd do *Rookery Nook* because I believe it is more attractive for the general public." Cushing studies all his parts with the same attention that he says he would give to *Hamlet*. "But now I'd like to do a film comedy. It's time I got a new identity. Particularly as I have never been the monster in any one of those films."'[1]

The film comedy was, sadly, not forthcoming. Neither was anything else. In a 1965 interview, Cushing wrote of a 'terrible slump in the industry … three years ago'[2] when he was out of work for 18 months. Cushing had achieved worldwide success but, unbelievably, was unable to find work at home.

On 20 February 1962, Angela Hepburn wrote to the BBC to enquire about the possibility of Cushing appearing on the radio programmes *Frankly Speaking*, *Woman's Hour* and *Let's Find Out*. 'For some time he has wanted to appear on the programmes.' Nothing came of the suggestions immediately, and there was no more enthusiasm from Norman Rutherford, Acting Head of Drama, when Cushing wrote on 21 April to suggest a possible role in a play. 'It is getting on for four years since my last!' he wrote, and suggested the plays *Charles the King* by Maurice Colbourne and

J B Priestley's *They Came To A City* (which he had played at the 'Q'). As was common before, Cushing asked for a list of the forthcoming plays for summer and the autumn, to see if there were any parts he knew and would like to play.

'I am not particularly excited, nor were my council, by the suggestions you have made,' replied Rutherford. 'We have gone a considerable way now in the development of writing for television. The majority of work lies with new writing, so a list of plays would be fruitless as they would mean nothing to you.' Rutherford's reply reflects the changing times at the BBC. New plays were the future of television drama, consequently 'stage' plays and 'stage' actors like Cushing were less and less in demand. And there could more than likely have been a touch of prejudice at Cushing's success in what the BBC must have regarded as low-brow entertainment. This exile, if such it was, did not last long. There was still a need for theatre-trained actors, and the following year they were glad to welcome him back to the fold to play Cassius in *Julius Caesar*.

Cushing only made one film in 1962, *The Man Who Finally Died*. In this, he was again working with director Quentin Lawrence although there is less tension in this rambling tale of middle-European intrigue than in the concentrated atmosphere of *Cash on Demand*. The film was based on a 1959 ITV serial by Lewis Greifer, which originally starred Michael Goodliffe. For the film, Goodliffe's role was taken by Stanley Baker, with strong support from Mai Zetterling, Eric Portman and Niall McGinnis.

Joe Newman (Baker) arrives in Konigsbaden, Bavaria, following a message from his father Kurt Deutsch, whom he believed had died in 1943. Newman is told that his father was a prisoner of war in Russia for 18 years, and on his escape back to Germany was taken in by Doctor Peter Von Brecht (Cushing), with whom he stayed until he died of a stroke. Von Brecht initially comes across as a completely decent, urbane, generous man, but it soon becomes clear that he is being *too* nice. Deutsch's young widow Lisa (Zetterling) and Police Inspector Hofmeister (Portman) encourage Newman to leave as soon as possible, but as he begins to investigate he

'Pass the marmalade'. Frankenstein at breakfast with Elizabeth (Hazel Court)
in *The Curse of Frankenstein* (1956)

Victor Frankenstein with Paul Krempe (Robert Urquhart)
in *The Curse of Frankenstein* (1956)

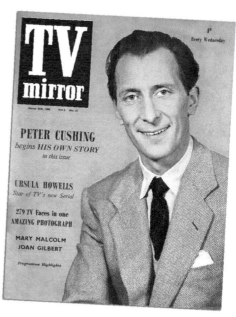

'Peter Cushing begins his own story in this issue'
TV Mirror, 27 March 1954

Captain Pearson with John Paul Jones (Robert Stack) in *John Paul Jones* (1958)

Von Brecht and Joe Newman (Stanley Baker)
feature on the cover of John Burke's novelisation
of *The Man Who Finally Died* (1961)

Major Horace L Holly in *She* (1964)

A publicity shot for *Dr Who and the Daleks* (1965)

FRANKENSTEIN
CRÉA LA FEMME SCHIEP DE VROUW
/ FRANKENSTEIN CREATED WOMAN /

PETER CUSHING / SUSAN DENBERG   THORLEY WALTERS · JOHN ELDER · ANTHONY NELSON KEIS · TERENCE FISHER

A SEVEN ARTS·HAMMER PRODUCTION   RELEASED BY 20th CENTURY-FOX   COULEURS DELUXE KLEUREN

Frankenstein brings Christina (Susan Denberg) back to life
in *Frankenstein Created Woman* (1966)

The Belgian poster for *Frankenstein Created Woman* (1966)

Lancelot
Canning and
Ronald Wyatt
(Jack Palance)
in a segment
called *The Man
Who Collected
Poe* from
Torture Garden
(1967)

Sir John Rowan
with his fiancée
Lynn Nolan
(Sue Lloyd) in
Corruption
(1967)

Sherlock Holmes on Dartmoor in the BBC's adaptation of *The Hound of the Baskervilles* (1968)

Inspector Gregson (George A Cooper), Sherlock Holmes and Dr Watson (Nigel Stock) in *A Study in Scarlet* (1968)

Mr Grimsdyke entertains the local children in *Tales from the Crypt* (1971)

The mysterious Mr Smith dabbles in the occult,
with tragic consequences, in *Asylum* (1972)

Count Gerard De Merret in *Orson Welles Great
Mysteries – La Grande Breteche* (1973)

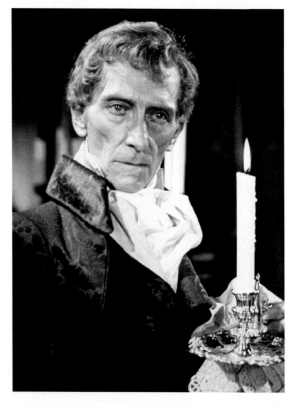

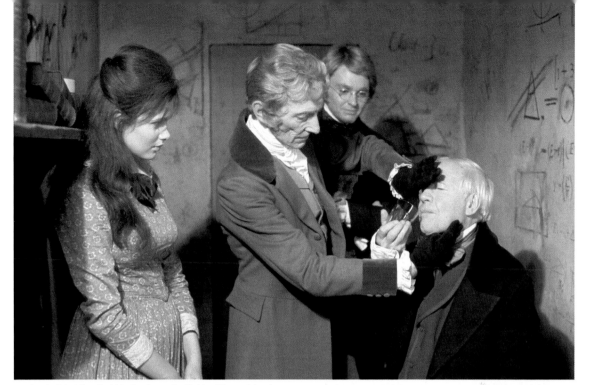

Sarah (Madeline Smith), Frankenstein, Helder (Shane Briant)
and Durendel (Charles Lloyd Pack) in *Frankenstein and the
Monster from Hell* (1972)

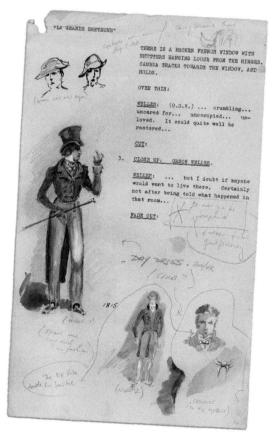

Professor Abner Perry in *At the Earth's Core* (1976)

Cushing's own annotations and watercolour sketches for his
costume, on his script for *La Grande Breteche* (1973)

Chuck Spillers (Brian Cox) with Martin Blueck in *Hammer House of Horror – The Silent Scream* (1980)

Air Commodore William Raymond in *Biggles* (1985)

A portrait of Cushing from the late 1980s

finds that no-one is telling the truth. Is it possible that his father is still alive?

The convoluted story betrays its origins as a television serial with every new twist presumably relating to cliffhanging episode endings. As the film wears on, the dialogue becomes more and more forcedly mysterious with a thump on the harpsichord signifying each new revelation.

It is not a taxing role for Cushing, who looks elegant in a dinner suit in the early scenes and who works well with his beautiful Swedish leading lady Mai Zetterling. 'I was never involved in a crime,' says Lisa, as she is forced to lie for Von Brecht. 'You're lucky,' he says wearily, recalling his work in the concentration camps. 'I was involved in six million...'

Cushing gets to stand up to Stanley Baker in one grim scene in a displaced persons' camp and they are subsequently present at a disastrous disinterment for which Von Brecht is blamed. 'I played quite a good chap really,' said Cushing of Von Brecht. 'Although I still went around with a gun in my hand. I have no doubt that people will remember me in this picture as the villain.'[3] It doesn't help that the real villain is kept under wraps until the last reel, while Cushing plays a very obvious, very villainous red herring.

Footage from *The Man Who Finally Died* was turned into Cushing's 1987 Holsten Pils television commercial mixed with newly-shot footage of Griff Rhys Jones. The sequence used in the advert comes from near the beginning of the film when Von Brecht is talking about a fine liqueur ('It's pre-war,' he says, 'I've only got one more bottle left in the cellar...') although Cushing's lines in the commercial are transposed from their original order.

Cushing's next role was his first for independent television – which had now been running for more than seven years. *Peace With Terror* was a Sunday night play in the *Drama 62* strand, a story about a religious fanatic who plots to blow up the War Office.

An interview in the *TV Times* featured Cushing at home 'inspecting the guard', his collection of model soldiers that 'crowd a glass-fronted cupboard the length of his studio. The British Army is represented through the ages on one shelf. On another are models

Cushing as Peter Von Brecht with Lisa Deutsch (Mai Zetterling) in *The Man Who Finally Died* (1962)

forming a Coronation procession. Their appeal for Peter Cushing is not in detail but in their atmosphere of pageantry and contemporary history. Does Peter Cushing enjoy visiting toy shops? "The only sort I ever do visit," he admitted. "My wife has to buy all my clothes!" In spite of the model firearms and gun carriages Cushing is a peaceable man. "Not even soldiers enjoy war," he said. "Only a fanatic ... would think that a bomb in the War Office would do any good – even as a gesture of protest."[4]

Peace With Terror was another play by Jacques Gillies, and the director was once again Quentin Lawrence. (*Cash on Demand* had not yet been released in the UK.) Frederick Parsons (Cushing) heads a sect called The Union for Peace. As accomplice in his bomb plot, Parsons hires Henry Warblow (Brian Wilde), recently released from prison for assaulting a policeman at a disarmament meeting. But Warblow turns out to be an awkwardly large, rather weak character, caught up only accidentally in the disarmament fracas. The chapter-and-verse quoting Parsons is not deterred, however, and goes ahead with his plan.

To research the role, Cushing went on a Sunday morning visit to Speakers' Corner in London's Hyde Park to hear the soap box orators to get some real-life atmosphere into his part. 'There they were,' he said. 'Half a dozen religious fanatics like Parsons.'[5] The cast for the play also included Sheila Manahan as Parsons' indignant wife and George Woodbridge, who was last with Cushing in *The Mummy*, as Sergeant Greenfield. Brian Wilde had also worked with Quentin Lawrence on *The Man Who Finally Died*, but he had no scenes with Cushing.

The play did not go ahead smoothly. An item in the *Daily Telegraph* on 4 June 1962 read: 'Unsuitable ITV Play Postponed'. 'The play *Peace With Terror*, by Jack Gillies [sic], was withdrawn by Associated Television last night, because it dealt with a religious fanatic. A spokesman said: "We decided this theme was not entirely suitable for a Sunday evening." It will be broadcast later in the month on a weekday. Peter Cushing was to have taken the part of the fanatic. He had a leading role a few years ago in George Orwell's

'Et tu, Brute?' Brutus (Paul Eddington) and Cassius lead the assassination of Caesar (Barry Jones) in the BBC's *The Spread of the Eagle* (1963)

Nineteen Eighty-Four which caused a public outcry when it was televised by the BBC.' ATV kept a copy of the play, which is preserved in their archive and was subsequently acquired by Polygram.

On 10 October 1962, radio producer Charles LeFaux wrote to Cushing suggesting a role in a radio production of M R James' classic ghost story *Oh Whistle And I'll Come To You*, which was later adapted for television by Jonathan Miller for *Omnibus*, starring Michael Hordern. 'We are planning a series of half-hour plays and want to have a very good name above the title. I'm sure we could do it in one day in the studio.' Cushing read the play but declined the role.

In January 1963, Cushing embarked on his most involved project for some time. It was a three-part BBC adaptation of Shakespeare's *Julius Caesar*, part of the nine-part cycle called *The Spread of the Eagle*, which included *Corialanus* and *Antony and Cleopatra*. The producer and director was Peter Dews, who in 1960 had overseen a massive and prestigious production called *An Age of Kings* comprising Shakespeare's *Richard II, Henry IV, V* and *VI*, and *Richard III*, starring Sean Connery and Robert Hardy.

In *The Spread of the Eagle* Cushing was to play Caius Cassius, one of the conspirators in the murder of Julius Caesar. Cassius is described by Caesar as having

'a lean and hungry look' – an appropriate description for Cushing. Fellow conspirator Brutus was Paul Eddington, with Barry Jones as Caesar and Keith Michell as Mark Antony.

The setting is Rome 44 BC, where 'the Colossus' – Julius Caesar – is urged to accept supreme power. However, the republicans, including the plain-thinking Brutus and the coldly intellectual senator Cassius, think they see another tyrant in the making. So a conspiracy is forged to assassinate Caesar, while strange supernatural events warn the citizens that tragedy is impending. Caesar's death brings about civil war, and the Republican army led by Brutus and Cassius must confront the forces of Mark Antony, loyal to Caesar's memory. Brutus, troubled by conscience and ghostly visitations, has little heart for the fight; neither has Cassius. The battle goes well for them at first, but their enemies prevail and both conspirators die by their own hands.

With its 1960s graphics and elaborate camera set-ups, *The Spread of the Eagle* boasts a deliberately modern approach, showing how much more sophisticated television production had become since Cushing's last performances. The acting is naturalistic, and Cushing brings force and passion to his delivery of Shakespeare's text, investing the complex speeches with emotion and meaning. In his black wig he looks severe, and the television cameras are noticably less kind to his face than film cameras.

Before rehearsals started on 25 February, Cushing was in contact with Peter Dews to check the pronunciation of certain lines. The series was recorded in Studio 4, Television Centre on 8 March, 25 March and 5 April 1963, with Cushing's fee at 563 guineas per episode. The production was recorded 'as live', which meant that recording breaks were kept to a minimum (to avoid costly editing) and small mistakes had to be worked through if possible. Paul Eddington remembered the problems created by having real horses in the studio – they tended to slip on the rubberised flooring that was used for the battlefield. While Cushing and Eddington struggled to continue with their performances, Keith Michell was fighting a losing battle to keep his horse out of shot. Michell called Cushing's Cassius 'one of the finest Shakespearean performances I have ever seen,' remembering that during rehearsals, Cushing wore doormats and fire-irons in place of his sword and armour, leading the bluff Northerner Peter Dews to remark that he looked like a hearth-tidy.

The newspapers picked up on the return to television of Peter Cushing. This chirpy piece was from James Green in the *Daily Mirror*: 'A few words today from Cassius. Not Cassius Clay of boxing fame. He never said just a few words about anything. This Cassius is the one with the lean and hungry look. Mr

The Spread of the Eagle (1963) – Cassius lends an ear to Mark Antony (Keith Michell)

Peter Cushing will play him tonight on BBC TV in the Shakespearean play cycle *The Spread of the Eagle*. It is five years since Cushing last acted for the BBC. But having decided that they can be no worse than the horror films he is back with a bang. Mr Cushing as Senator Caius Cassius, will be on view for three Fridays in succession. Take a close look at the togas being worn on TV. If you buy a ticket to see Elizabeth Taylor in *Cleopatra* you will spot the same garments. "The TV people decided to use the film company togas and we had to wait for them to arrive from Rome" says Cassius Cushing. "I suppose if togas have got to come from anywhere they might as well come from Rome. They arrive in two sizes," he explained. "Large and small. All that needs altering is the hem length. They have an advantage over suits that fittings are not required. The more I wear togas the more I like them. The real thing takes a long time to wind round but

these film jobs were in simplified form. A toga is loose and comfortable, does away with collars and ties, and it's easy to learn to swing the train over the left arm." Peter Cushing lives at Whitstable and for much of the year enjoys – if that is the word – a daily swim. He is a kind of Pied Piper to the local children and often joins in their beach games. In fact, the mob can sometimes be seen pushing him into the water. Cassius of the wet and watery look.'

When he had finished *The Spread of the Eagle*, Cushing made an appearance on the BBC's *Living Today* programme on 16 April 1963. He talked about his paintings with interviewer John Anthony.

On 10 September 1963, Cushing recorded a contribution to the *New Comment* radio programme – *The Macabre* was broadcast on the Third Programme on 21 September. On 22 September he began location filming for a *Comedy Playhouse* episode called *The Plan*, written by Richard Harris and Dennis Spooner, former scriptwriters from Tony Hancock's ITV series. *Comedy Playhouse* was used as a kind of testing-ground for new comedy situations and characters, some of which (including *Steptoe and Son*) were turned into continuing series. Perhaps there wasn't much mileage in Cushing's character of Albert Fawkes, a disgruntled descendant of the gunpowder plotter, whose appearance in *The Plan* was to be his first and last.

The *Radio Times* introduced *The Plan* thus: 'Just suppose there was an Albert Fawkes who became fed up with having his leg pulled and decided to get his own back. Suppose he enlisted the aid of an ex-member of the IRA, by name Seamus McMichael, in a second attempt to dissolve Parliament the speedy way. Albert's 1963 gunpowder plot is the plot of tonight's *Comedy Playhouse*, written by a team new to BBC-tv – Richard Harris and Dennis Spooner. That well-known Irish actor P G Stephens plays the part of Seamus... "I came over with me young heart bursting to strike a blow for freedom and the only time I've struck in 20 years was for a longer tea break."'

Francis Matthews, who had enjoyed his association with Cushing so much in *The Revenge of Frankenstein* and had a small role in *The Hellfire Club*, appeared as Captain in *The Plan*.

'The only thing I recall about *The Plan*,' he says, 'was the isolated comedy scene which Graham Stark and I played "outside Number 10 Downing Street".

We only saw Peter briefly at the read-through. Stark and I were a couple of "whizzo" idiot officers attempting to defuse a bomb.'

Cushing's fee was £420. *The Plan* was rehearsed in the first week of October, recorded on the 7th in Studio 3, Television Centre, and transmitted close to Guy Fawkes' Night on 2 November. The play is effectively a comic cousin of *Peace With Terror*, and it says much of the times that, in 1963, an ex-member of the IRA would have been considered an acceptable supporting character in a half-hour comedy.

On 14 October work began on *The Evil of Frankenstein*, Cushing's return to Hammer after nearly two years. Helen's worsening illness and its treatment was Cushing's highest priority and this made regular money a necessity – whatever the work.

The Evil of Frankenstein was Cushing's only *Frankenstein* movie not directed by Terence Fisher, who was meanwhile contracted to make two films for Hammer's former co-production partner Robert Lippert. Fisher was replaced by Freddie Francis, who had spent many years as a lighting cameraman (including work on Cushing's films *Moulin Rouge* and *Time Without Pity*) and had already directed the psychological thrillers *Paranoiac* and *Nightmare* for Hammer.

Anthony Hinds provided the script for this film, which ignored the Baron's carefully constructed backstory established in *Curse* and *Revenge*. Under the terms of a distribution deal with Universal, Hammer were now allowed to use a variation of Jack Pierce's famous Frankenstein monster make-up, which they did, despite the fact that the first two films had done perfectly well without it. Thus Cushing's Frankenstein

is suddenly lumbered with a huge, bolt-necked Creature, which neither the character nor the canon needed. The story was a pastiche of the Universal Horrors, but unfortunately taking a cue from the point when Universal were starting to parody themselves. Even Don Banks' bombastic score recalls the musical fanfares of Franz Waxman.

At the beginning of the film, Frankenstein's latest experiments in a jerry-rigged watermill laboratory are destroyed by a zealous priest, the Baron determines to return to his former home in Karlstaad with his assistant Hans (Sandor Elès). There he discovers his property ransacked but his old laboratory intact, and preserved in ice nearby is his first half-formed Creature. The monster is restored to life, but is mindless. A hypnotist, 'Professor' Zoltan (Peter Woodthorpe) is engaged to activate the Creature's brain, but instead he sends it out to steal and murder. Eventually the creature kills Zoltan, gets drunk on brandy, accidentally drinks chloroform and finally, in agony, sets fire to the laboratory, apparently destroying the Baron in an inferno.

As Frankenstein, Cushing looks older, often tired and unshaven, some way from the dandy of *Revenge*. In this film the Baron faces nothing but betrayal, failure and disappointment – he successfully animates his monster but it is abused by everybody else. Hinds determined to 'put more compassion into our horror films'[9] but Frankenstein is only given an out-of-character streak of sentimental self-pity. He is made to seem foolish by deliberately antagonising the citizens of Kalstaad, and then complains when they bother him. All the characters are underwritten, however, and Peter Woodthorpe can do little even with the role of the roguish Zoltan.

Cushing worked on the script, to ensure that Frankenstein was 'basically the same chap'[10], and there is nothing at all wrong with his performance, except a couple of moments of straight-to-camera eye-boggling. There are occasional saucy lines: 'He has a good brain and excellent eyes,' Frankenstein tells the mesmerist about his monster. 'I won't tell you where I got them, but I can assure you they're perfect.' Cushing's expression on discovering the monster frozen in ice is full of wonder and a later stand-off with the monster has at least a little of the old Olivier-trained flair.

Director Freddie Francis supervises Sandor Elès and Cushing on location for *The Evil of Frankenstein* (1963)

Terence Fisher directs Cushing on the set of *The Gorgon* (1963)

Francis admits that he had little connection with the material. It was, he says, a case of 'here is the monster, here is the mad lab and away we go, so to speak.'[11] The 'mad lab' itself is genuinely magnificent, a great cathedral of blue glass, valves and lightning, with Cushing dashing around in the middle trying to keep up with it all. The monster is less effective, a blundering automaton with big boots, a *papier mâché* head and a rigid expression. Nevertheless. Francis marshals some clever sequences, particularly the lead-in to the flashback of the first experiment, which tracks over Cushing's shoulder, down the deserted corridors of the chateau to the laboratory. Unforgivable are the shoddy last-act process shots of Cushing driving a gig, and worse, the long-shot of an obvious stand-in driving the gig on location. It is sadly obvious, as the credits roll that Cushing, rather than being an integral part of the cast, has carried the entire film.

'*The Evil of Frankenstein* ... has its moments,' considered the *Times*. 'Particularly the full-blooded opening. One or two of the actors get quite out of control, but Mr Peter Cushing is, as ever, authoritative as the idealistic misunderstood Baron and the script ... is engagingly aware of its own absurdity.'[12]

The Evil of Frankenstein finished shooting on 16 November. At the beginning of December, Cushing was reunited with Christopher Lee and Terence Fisher for *The Gorgon*.

Cushing plays Doctor Namaroff, chief medical officer at the Vandorf Medical Institution. He is an ambiguous figure, devoted to his work but crippled by his love for the doomed Carla Hoffmann, who is possessed by the spirit of the Gorgon Magaera.

'Namaroff was not a neurotic raving villain,' Cushing remarked, 'but a reserved, thinking man, shy, retiring, rather sad and without much to say. Yet he had the power to collect and sustain around him an aura of undiluted menace. Namaroff sends a cold shudder down your back.'[13] Though Namaroff does indeed have an 'aura of menace', what he knows or doesn't know about Carla's condition is very ambiguous. Namaroff never smiles – he has none of Van Helsing's beguiling charm – it is as if in loving Carla he has been turned to stone already.

Fisher adores the trappings of the ruined Castle Borski where the Gorgon has her lair – there is a thrilling scene in a rainstorm where Paul Heitz (Richard Pasco) sees Mageara in reflection, scored with thunderclaps and bursts of James Bernard's

Barbara Shelley and Cushing entertain Columbia's Bill Scott, a visitor to Bray Studios, during shooting of *The Gorgon* (1963)

hypnotic novachord-and-percussion score. The idea of a Gorgon who turns bodies to stone is more than usually nonsensical, it is only the conviction of Cushing, and Barbara Shelley as the beautiful, tormented Carla that makes the conceit believable. Terence Fisher encouraged his cast to play it for absolute truth. Christopher Lee, in a heavy grey wig, turns up as Professor Meinster to badger the locals and eventually see right prevail. He is effectively playing the Van Helsing part, although the plot is not properly set up to accommodate one. There are no real heroes or villains in Vandorf.

Filming on *The Gorgon* was completed on 16 January 1964 at Bray Studios. Despite the relentlessly downbeat atmosphere of the film it seems to have been a happy shoot – Barbara Shelley remembers Cushing singing Gilbert and Sullivan – Giuseppi's song from *The Gondoliers* and the Nightmare song from *Iolanthe* – and taking him on in ferocious contests to see who could sing the fastest without dropping a word. 'It was Chris in the morning with operas and Peter in the afternoon with Gilbert and Sullivan,' Shelley recalls. 'And impersonations of Sylvester the Cat!' Cushing was up to his old cabbage-cutting tricks again, too. 'He did his surgery on this cabbage *perfectly* – and I was expected to keep a straight face. He did, but I couldn't.' Shelley invited Cushing to participate in a drawing game that she had found. 'You were given two vertical straight lines and you had to incorporate them into a drawing. Most people made the trunk of a tree or something, and you could tell

things about their character by what they drew. Peter made the linked letters P and H, for Peter and Helen. No great psychology needed there. I said "You love your wife very much."'[14]

Richard Pasco had first met Cushing at the 'Q' Theatre in 1943, and worked with him and Fisher on *Sword of Sherwood Forest*. He recalled that much of the climactic swordfight between Paul and Namaroff was choreographed by Cushing. *Films and Filming* noted that while Christopher Lee was miscast, Fisher had given the film a 'romantic glow'[15] and that the acting was unusually sensitive.

Cushing went back to the BBC in March, but there is some mystery surrounding his contribution to the children's programme *Star Story*, a short-lived precursor to *Jackanory*. Star readers in the series included Prunella Scales, Andrew Cruikshank and Stratford Johns, Cushing read a ghost story called *The Yellow Cat* by Michael Joseph. Six stories were broadcast but the seventh, – Cushing's – did not go out. Possibly the story, or Cushing's telling of it, was considered too frightening for the children's television slot. In November 1980 the story was read by Robert Powell in an unashamedly creepy children's series called *Spine Chillers*.

Cushing did appear on television in June, however, as Elijah Baley, one of science fiction's most beloved heroes, in one of Isaac Asimov's famous 'robot' stories. The BBC 2 adaptation of *The Caves of Steel* in the *Story Parade* series marked Cushing's first association with young Hungarian director Peter Sasdy, with whom he would make the film *Nothing But The Night* in 1972. Asimov's story was adapted by young writer Terry Nation, who had made a name for himself the previous Christmas by devising the Daleks for the new children's science fiction series *Doctor Who*. In May 1965, Cushing would take the role of the Doctor in the film adaptation of Nation's first *Doctor Who* story.

The setting for *The Caves of Steel* is New York City in the distant future. Fourteen million humans live beneath a protective dome, with a workforce of positronic robots. The city-dwellers fear the outside world and the threat from the 'Spacers', the former colonists who live in the Outer World, and who wish to free humanity from the domes – their 'caves of steel'. Detective Elijah Baley (Cushing) is called in to investigate the murder of an eminent Outer World scientist, Doctor Sarton. To see a fair investigation, Baley is assigned an unconventional partner – a lifelike robot called R Daneel Olivaw, who will act as an observer for the Spacers. Baley later discovers that Olivaw was a prototype for a sophisticated new Outer World robot created by Sarton in his own image. After identifying and arresting a rabble-rouser called Clousarr, who belongs to an anti-technology 'medievalist' group, Baley is framed for an attack on another robot. Baley learns that his superior, Commisioner Enderby, is involved with the medievalists and seeking to discredit the Outer Worlders by destroying their crowning achievement – R Daneel. In the nick of time, Baley uncovers the truth – Enderby killed Sarton, believing he was his own robot.

The Caves of Steel was rehearsed from 15 April to 4 May, with filming (for a chase sequence) on 17 April. The play was recorded in Studio 1, Television Centre on 7 May with John Carson as R Daneel and Kenneth J Warren as Enderby. Cushing's fee for the 75-minute play was £787.

The *Daily Telegraph* noted that *The Caves of Steel* 'proved again that science fiction can be exciting, carry a message and be intellectually stimulating.'[16] Although the play no longer exists in the BBC archives, several scenes extracted for use in *Horizon* and *Tomorrow's World*, have been preserved.

In the mid-1950s, American producer Milton Subotsky suggested to Hammer that they remake *Frankenstein*, submitting his own script for their approval. They rejected Subotsky's draft but went ahead with the remake anyway – the rest we know. Although Subotsky remained philosophical about it, Hammer's subsequent worldwide success no doubt stuck in his craw. As soon as he was able, he set to work making horror films himself with his own company, Amicus, run with fellow American Max J Rosenberg. Their intention was to produce movies on Hammer lines, even if this meant borrowing Hammer stars Cushing and Lee.

At the end of May, Cushing appeared in his first film for Amicus – *Dr Terror's House of Horrors*. This 'portmanteau' film, produced in the style of Ealing Studios' *Dead of Night*, saw the actor reunited with director Freddie Francis and Christopher Lee at

Shepperton Studios. Also in the cast were Roy Castle, Donald Sutherland and *Pick of the Pops* DJ Alan Freeman.

It is fair at least to say that *Dr Terror's House of Horrors* is not *Dead of Night*. It is a garish, lightly comic concoction, for which Cushing provides the linking banter, peering out from under a formidable pair of bushy eyebrows as Doctor Schreck – literally 'Doctor Terror'. This polite stranger joins five men in a railway carriage and produces a tarot deck ('I call it my house of horrors') to show each of them a glimpse of their futures. Each of the five 'futures' forms a story – the subjects, voodoo, a werewolf, a creeping vine, vampires and a crawling hand. By far the best excerpt stars Christopher Lee as Franklin Marsh, an arrogant and venomous art critic who is publicly humiliated by one of his 'victims', the artist Eric Landor (Michael Gough). Landor continues a campaign of embarrassment until eventually, Marsh runs him over, destroying his right hand and his livelihood. Then a

Franklyn Marsh (Christopher Lee) nervously selects a card from *Dr Terror's House of Horrors* (1964)

disembodied hand begins persecuting Marsh, giving Lee plenty of opportunity for nervous agitation and horrified reaction. Marsh eventually throws the hand on the fire but its sudden reappearance on the windscreen causes him to crash his car. Marsh, who initially told us 'I live by my vision', is blinded in the crash.

Cushing's small role must surely have been a disappointment for fans, drawn in by his prominent position on Amicus's lurid poster. He makes the most of every line, though, with a lilting German accent and an owlish expression. Eventually, the train pulls up – but the men in the carriage do not recognise the station. 'Why have you done this? What do you want? *Who are you?*' demands Marsh. Cushing turns to the camera and in extreme close-up, smiles 'Have you not guessed?' Schreck's face is replaced with a grinning skull – their futures have already happened and he is the Grim Reaper. The *Daily Cinema* found 'a lot of fun and irony' in the film, and Cushing 'the ideal choice for the shabbily sinister Doctor Schreck.' *Monthly Film Bulletin* praised Cushing's 'unshaven, mittened Death who ties the stories together, and the denouement has an appropriately apocalyptic flavour.'[17]

Chapter Seventeen

Men of Steel

After a short break following *Dr Terror's House of Horrors*, Cushing was back with Hammer to play Major Horace L Holly in their adaptation of Henry Rider Haggard's *She*. Location filming took place in Israel from 24 August 1964, returning to the ABPC Studios at Elstree and finishing on 17 October. The film was directed by Robert Day and starred Ursula Andress as the immortal Ayesha with John Richardson, Bernard Cribbins, Christopher Lee and André Morell.

The film begins in Palestine, 1918. Following an encounter with a mysterious and beautiful woman, newly-demobbed Leo Vincey (Richardson) embarks on a quest for the lost city of Kuma with his friend Major Holly and Holly's batman Job (Cribbins). After crossing the desert they are captured by the savage Amahaggers but rescued by Bilali, High Priest of Kuma (Lee). Balali takes them to the 2000-year-old Ayesha, Queen of Kuma, known as 'She Who Must Be Obeyed'. She believes Leo to be the reincarnation of her lost love Killikrates, who must now fulfil his destiny and join her in the flame of eternal life.

After a lacklustre Frankenstein and the emotionally petrified Namaroff, *She* gives Cushing the chance for some traditional derring-do in the sort of entertainment he adored. In this unashamed 'family' film, he proves once more that he could enliven any genre, and that he was particularly suited to action and adventure. The Peter Pan quality that so many have remarked upon in Cushing is at its clearest here, and Major Holly on the back of a camel in the Negev desert is not so very far from little Peter 'Brighteyes' on his bike in Kenley.

In the opening scenes, the three soldiers relax in a hostelry full of dancing girls. ('Well, we've survived the war,' says Holly heartily, 'let's hope we survive this place!') Cushing's expressions calculatedly mix ambiguous feelings of loss and yearning, possibly even premonition, before the reflective mood is dispelled by the girls around him – 'I say, chaps, look at that!' Holly has clearly been a bit of a rascal in his time, and, advising Job to take his hat off, he joins in with the dancing. The Cushing shimmy is worth the admission price alone.

Working in the desert was gruelling. The actors had to start filming at 8.00 am because the afternoon heat was unbearable, perspiration evaporated almost immediately and they all had to eat salt to prevent dehydration. Cushing had trouble with a truculent camel called Daisy. In the staging of the spectacular Bedouin attack, a mistimed explosive charge peppered Bernard Cribbins' backside with shrapnel and blew one technician's finger off.

The political situation in Eilat at this time was potentially explosive too. 'The Arabs just sat there with their machine guns in their laps,' said Cushing. 'In the meantime we were popping off our prop guns and hoping we would not be attacked. We were lucky that they seemed to enjoy watching us. It was quite an exciting period.'[1]

'I say, chaps, look at that!' Major Holly, Job (Bernard Cribbins) and Leo Vincey (John Richardson) are entertained by a belly dancer (Lisa Peake) in *She* (1964)

John Doran of ABPC Elstree reported on the location filming for *Film Review* magazine, March 1965. 'Standing behind the camera, Bob Day acted each of the parts being played before him; grunting and groaning when things didn't go according to plan, enthusing when it went as planned. Peter Cushing sat in the shade and talked. It is a measure of his ability ... that so gentle a man can chill the blood with performances in the horror films with which his name is synonymous. A highly intelligent man, Peter talked ... about the autobiography he has thoughts of writing, a work for which Bernard Cribbins has suggested the title *I'm All Right, Drac*.'[2]

Elstree's interior sets struggled to match the grandeur of the desert exteriors, but Cushing's expression of wonder on entering the halls of Kuma distracts from the deficiencies of the sets. It is alarming, however, to see the familiar face of André Morell (as the Amahagger leader) speaking with the equally familiar overdubbed voice of George Pastell.

At Ayesha's side, Christopher Lee positively glows with power as the noble Bilali, who is ultimately corrupted by his desire for immortality. Cushing and Lee share a short but memorable scene when Holly finds Bilali praying amongst the mummies of the previous high priests. Cushing's offhandedness is matched by Lee's restrained strength and the effect is electric. The actors had only shared dialogue in three films thus far, despite co-starring in seven.

Holly has several lengthy speeches on immortality and director Robert Day remembered that Cushing was line-perfect. Leo seeks Holly's advice when Ayesha offers him eternal life, and Cushing's gentle delivery infuses the words with wisdom. 'It's age of the mind that's important, not the body,' Holly says. 'The joy of living is not to be denied, but to know that it will be there for all time, without change – life at a standstill. It's not quite the same thing.' Holly also discourses on the subject of love and Cushing contributed his own lines here. 'Have you ever been in love, Holly?' asks Leo. 'Oh, many times, and *truly* once,' he smiles. 'A deep sincere love will last most people a lifetime, but even that changes from the frantic yearnings at its beginnings to a quiet unspoken understanding at its end. The physical side of human love wasn't designed to last forever.' Holly is not always so poetic, however. He maintains a constant simmering glare of defiance at Ayesha's cruelty and rages at her when she

Holly and Job (Bernard Cribbins) look on as Ayesha crumbles to dust at the conclusion of *She* (1964)

sacrifices the handmaiden Ustane. Cribbins provides another excellent foil for Cushing and their double-act in *She* is tremendously entertaining. No mean actor, Cribbins equals Cushing's expression of horror as Leo and Ayesha bathe in the blue flame, and She Who Must Be Obeyed withers into hideous old age.

The downbeat ending and several overlong dance sequences hamper the film, but the performances and a heart-warming 'bank holiday' feeling to the whole count for much. There is also one of James Bernard's most inspiring and lyrical scores, with its two main themes. The 'Desert Quest', which effortlessly captures Holly's boundless spirit of adventure, is matched by Ayesha's fanfare, which trumpets her name – 'She Who Must Be Obeyed!' Bernard stated that he particularly enjoyed this film because it allowed him to use a more romantic palette. Among many effective moments is the point when Leo bids goodbye to Holly, a plaintive echo of the desert theme underscores their farewell.

She was Hammer's most expensive production to date, and went on UK release on 18 April 1965. Although it was one of the top films of the year, it received a critical pounding. 'Ridiculously old-fashioned' spouted the *New York Times*.[3]

On 3 September, while still filming *She*, Cushing was a guest on the Light Programme's *Let's Find Out*. Produced by David Carter, the show was broadcast on 20 October 1964.

Laughs all round – Patrick Wymark, Cushing, director Freddie Francis, Nigel Green and Patrick Magee between shots on *The Skull* (1965)

In August, radio producer Charles LeFaux wrote to Cushing offering a part in *Loyal Servant*, a BBC tribute for Sir Winston Churchill's 90th birthday in the form of a specially commissioned play about Churchill's ancestor the Duke of Marlborough. 'Ever hopeful, I am pursuing you once more,' wrote LeFaux, 'believing that the terrible waste of such a splendid actor cannot go on indefinitely.' Cushing replied: 'I received your letter just before I left home (sadly!) for location work in Israel. I am delighted at the prospect of working with you again and am so glad that you should think of me for this most exciting project. Unless the company's "first call" on my services intervenes, I should be free.'

Loyal Servant, by Ian Rodger, was recorded on 8 November and broadcast on the Home Service on 30 November. Cushing's fee was 60 guineas. Afterwards, LeFaux sent a letter of congratulation. 'It was a splendid performance on Sunday!' Cushing replied 'I'm surprised *Loyal Servant* hasn't been done already on sound or television...' concluding, 'now, on with the gardening!'

On 14 December 1964, Cushing recorded an interview at the TV Theatre, Shepherd's Bush for the BBC 1 series *First Impressions*. It was transmitted on

5 January 1965. Cushing's fee for this show was 25 guineas, plus a return fare London-Whitstable.

On 18 January, Cushing began work at Shepperton Studios on his second Amicus production, *The Skull*, based on a short story by Robert Bloch. Freddie Francis was once again the director and the supporting cast included Patrick Wymark, Christopher Lee, Jill Bennett and Peter Woodthorpe.

Writer Christopher Maitland (Cushing), a wealthy collector of arcane literature and relics, acquires the skull of Donatien Alphonse François, the infamous Marquis de Sade – 'the man whose name has become the symbol of cruelty and savagery in all of us.' His friend Sir Matthew Philips (Lee) warns him that De Sade was possessed by an evil spirit which still inhabits the skull. During the nights of the new moon, the skull is animated by beings from another realm, driving whoever possesses it to murder...

Milton Subotsky stated that he had always wanted to make a movie without dialogue, and *The Skull* is very nearly it. In this respect, the film has much more in common with the continental horror film-making of Mario Bava than the script-and-character-driven Hammer films. As a cost-cutting measure, Subotsky usually wrote the scripts for his pictures, and the submitted script for *The Skull* was about half-an-hour short. Also there were few stage directions. This was not a problem for Freddie Francis, who maintained that scriptwriters put in too many stage directions and he generally ignored them anyway. He followed the maxims of John Huston (with whom he had worked) that every shot had to tell its own story, and had to be filled with as much information as possible. So, much time is given over to Cushing's appalled grimace and lingering shots of grotesque artefacts, including the skull itself. Occasionally though, Freddie Francis pulls off a genuine cinematic *tour de force*.

In one harrowing scene, made all the more distressing by Cushing's face of horrified confusion, Maitland is taken to a weird courtroom by two police officers. There, he is compelled to bring a revolver to his head. Francis closes in on Cushing's vivid blue eyes – he fires, but the chamber is empty. The bewigged judge laughs insanely, gas pours through a grille and, as the walls close in, the skull floats towards him with horrible purpose. It is the realisation of a nightmare, prefiguring by several years the bold colours and disorientating dream-imagery of *The Prisoner*. Later, as Maitland is dispatched to steal a statue from Philips, the skull bobs cheerfully out of its cabinet and settles itself down with De Sade's awful grimoire. Seen through the skull itself, Cushing's expression of utter dread dissolves into bland, hypnotised compliance. Francis had a specially-made cowl over the camera to present a 'skull's-eye view' – it is an obvious, almost childish, cinematic device, but its ghoulish simplicity makes it work.

Cushing plays Maitland as a rationalist, whose refusal to believe in every successive horror perpetrated by the spirit makes his fate at once harder to bear and all the more inevitable. There is a very genuine feeling that he is losing his mind. His final stand, as the skull closes in for the kill has distinct echoes of the conclusion of *Nineteen Eighty-Four* just over ten years before.

In France the film was improbably called *The Dreadful Crimes of the Marquis de Sade*. In May 1966, the *Times* reported that a Paris court had ordered the title changed again after complaints from Count Xavier de Sade, a descendant of the Marquis, a

landowner in the Aisne district. *Variety* (4 August 1965) hailed a 'classy shudder film ... script is sound except for dragging in some scenes for effect only. The right ascetic approach is given by Peter Cushing as the determined collector.'[4]

During the filming of *The Skull*, Cushing made a guest appearance on Bernard Cribbins' television show. Cribbins had been impressed with Cushing's renditions of music hall songs and invited him on the programme. Cribbins was well-known for his comic songs 'Hole in the Ground' and 'Right Said Fred', both of which went top ten in 1962. The show, simply titled *Cribbins*, was recorded on 5 and 6 February in Studio 4, Television Centre.

In the early 1960s, Hammer had scored a considerable hit by issuing pirate movies (*The Pirates of Blood River*, *The Devil-Ship Pirates*) specifically timed to meet the demands of children on the school summer holidays. Milton Subotsky, who had successfully taken on Hammer at the horror game, saw the potential to rival these holiday films too. He acquired the rights to the first Dalek story from the BBC's *Doctor Who* series and gained co-financing from another American, Joe Vegoda, whose chief specification was that the films go out under the Aaru name rather than Amicus. Realising that they still needed an international name to front the picture, Subotsky cast Cushing as Doctor Who without an audition.

'I cannot guarantee your safety, but I can promise you unimagined thrills!' Doctor Who and his granddaughter Susie (Roberta Tovey) are held captive on the planet Skaro in *Dr Who and the Daleks* (1965)

Cushing considerably softened William Hartnell's portrayal of Doctor Who, making the mysterious time-traveller into a kindly, forgetful, distinctly *terrestrial* boffin – in his white wig, corduroy frock-coat and with perpetually bowed legs, he looks something like an elderly Wild West sheriff. Subotsky revised and simplified Terry Nation's TV script, making it unequivocally family entertainment. While missing the intensity of the black-and-white television serial, it remains a charming and endearing children's film, bursting with colour and spectacle and catching, at several moments, a real sense of the magic of outer space.

In his home-made time machine TARDIS (Time And Relative Dimension In Space) the eccentric Doctor Who transports his grand-daughters Barbara and Susan, plus Barbara's accident-prone boyfriend Ian, to

Roy Castle, Jennie Linden, Roberta Tovey and Cushing at Shepperton Studios during the filming of *Dr Who and the Daleks* (1965)

the distant planet Skaro. Here they encounter the mutated Daleks, who inhabit robotic shells, and the blond, humanoid Thals. Thousands of years of war have reduced the planet to ashes, and the Thals have become pacifists. But now the Daleks plan to explode a neutron bomb to wipe out the Thals once and for all.

The film was shot between 12 March and 23 April 1965 at Shepperton Studios. The director was Gordon Flemyng, with Roy Castle as Ian, Jennie Linden as Barbara and Roberta Tovey as Susan.

There is some irritating comic business at the beginning with Castle (Cushing's co-star in *Dr Terror's House of Horrors*) but once in his stride, Cushing is in total command. He gives an expression of undiluted wonder on seeing the surface of Skaro for the first time, and a terrific wink to Susan as he suggests they explore the futuristic city that they have seen in the distance. The petrified jungle set filled the whole of Stage H at Shepperton, at that time the biggest sound stage in England. It was partly lit from below with concealed lighting, and the anamorphic lenses were removed from the cameras for the jungle scenes to give a weird distortion to the picture. Director of photography John Wilcox came straight to the picture after finishing *The Skull*. Roberta Tovey remembered that there was a magical atmosphere on the set. 'Peter Cushing was a great flower man,' she recalls. 'For the scene when Susan finds a flower in the forest, he phoned up the Royal Horticultural Society and found the name, which I then had to remember.'[5] Before finishing the film Cushing agreed to do a sequel, on the condition that Tovey repeat her role as Susan.

The stars of the film are undoubtedly the Daleks themselves, possibly the most malevolent and certainly the most melodramatic robot-creatures in science fiction. ('The Daleks are beyond reason,' states the Doctor, 'they wish only to conquer!') £4500 of the budget was assigned for building the Daleks from the BBC's plans and they look magnificent. Most importantly, the Daleks' easily-imitated electronic voices were preserved intact from the television version, and in the echoing city they are genuinely unnerving.

Bryan Hands was one of the Dalek operators and had to control the Black Dalek during the climactic battle. 'I suppose being the Dalek leader was a kind of honour,' he said, 'except that I was still inside it when it exploded!' He remembers that Cushing was enthusiastic on set, and was concerned that the 'Dalek boys' were looked after. 'He would occasionally join us in the canteen but would generally take to his dressing-room when not required.'[6]

There are some breathtaking mattes for the crags of Skaro, Malcolm Lockyer's music is equally monumental and at times strangely moving. There is also a grim moment when the Doctor realises that the travellers are dying of radiation sickness from the planet's poisonous atmosphere. While this revelation is not quite as harrowing as it was on television, it is still a chilling touch for such an upbeat film.

Cushing provided a bewitching narration for the trailer – 'Come with us into that strange new world. I cannot guarantee your safety ... but I can promise you unimagined thrills!' – and, riding on the success of the Daleks on television, the film was one of the top ten British films of the year. Like *Dracula,* there were queues round the block at cinemas. 'Kids will love it,' said the *People.* 'Their parents will find this gigantic schoolboy lark Dalektable!'[7] 'The dotty Doctor is played by Peter Cushing rather in the manner of a mad hatter looking for a lost tea party,'[8] wrote Leonard Mosely in the *Daily Express* on 23 June.

Although Terry Nation had reservations about the big-screen version of the Doctor, he was on a percentage of the profits and recalled with some amusement that the film's blockbusting success meant that Subotsky was forced to pay up with the royalties after the first year.

There was a windfall for Cushing from the Hammer film *Dracula Prince of Darkness.* This was the film that saw the return of Christopher Lee to the role of Dracula and it featured, as a prologue, the conclusion of the original Hammer *Dracula* with Cushing and the candlesticks. Cushing was formally contracted for the re-use of this footage on 1 July 1965 – in *Past Forgetting* he recalled that he needed work done on the roof at Hillsleigh Road and James Carreras generously covered the cost of the work as a 'repeat fee'.

Then, after his battle with the Daleks, there were more science fiction capers for Cushing in his next film, *Island of Terror,* which was directed by Terence Fisher and co-produced by Richard Gordon, who had produced *Corridors of Blood* and *Grip of the Strangler* with Boris Karloff.

In *Island of Terror*, Cushing plays the eminent pathologist Doctor Brian Stanley, who is informed of a boneless corpse found on the remote Petrie's Island off the Irish coast. Stanley travels to the island with bone specialist Doctor David West (Edward Judd) and West's girlfriend Toni (Carole Gray). There they discover that scientists working in secret to develop a cancer treatment have accidentally created a tentacled organism that eats bone. Worse, the silicone-based creatures, called silicates, are impervious to firepower and can multiply indefinitely.

Cushing was heartened, no doubt, by the presence of his friend Fisher and some old acting comrades including Eddie Byrne and Niall McGinnis. He gives a very relaxed performance as the modern-thinking doctor, who goes through the picture with an easy manner and a wry quip for every occasion.

The film is encumbered with often tortuous dialogue and a wildly improbable plot, but Fisher somehow manages to ride these problems out. Cushing, of course, delivers the scientific terminology as if it were Shakespeare and his wide-eyed disbelief as the silicates multiply in front of him makes up for the fact that they are distinctly uninspiring lumps of rubber festooned with spaghetti. But Dr Stanley, who is shyly fond of Toni himself, is not so very brave. At the scientist's laboratory, he is all for sticking together. 'I wouldn't want to stay out here alone – it's too damn creepy!'

Fisher does not shirk from the chills, either. As Stanley and West gather the radiation samples that they believe will destroy the creatures, a prowling silicate's tentacle grabs Stanley's wrist. The organisms are as strong as steel, so West has no choice but to chop off Stanley's hand before his bones are liquefied. Even this doesn't dampen Stanley's spirits, however, and after his arm has been bandaged, he complains 'One more transfusion and I'll be a full-blooded Irishman.'

Doctor Brian Stanley is attacked by a silicate in *Island of Terror* (1965)

Malcolm Lockyer's thunderous music is very like his score for *Dr Who and the Daleks*, but fits the action and adventure well. Barry Gray, the composer of the *Thunderbirds* theme who had also worked on sound effects for the Dalek movie, adds more electronic whoops and warbles here, plus some genuinely unpleasant sucking noises that add a horrible touch to the silicate attacks.

While not on a par with Fisher's Gothics, it is an appealing and exciting film. When it was released in the US (as late as March 1967) *Variety* was generous with its praise for the star. 'Cushing, whose performances in this type of role are always above average, is properly brusque and with a wryly objective point of view. He also varies between heroism and cowardice, creating a character with natural, not exaggerated fears and hesitations.'[9]

Despite Cushing's problems with appearing on stage in *The Sound of Murder* while filming *Suspect,* he was shooting *Island of Terror* while appearing on stage.in the Ben Travers farce *Thark*. This production began a short run at the Yvonne Arnaud Theatre, Guildford and was directed by Ray Cooney. The cast included Alec McCowen (who had appeared in *Time Without Pity* as Michael Redgrave's son) Ambrosine Philpotts, Jennie Linden, who followed Cushing from *Dr Who*, and the veteran comedy actress Kathleen Harrison.

When the play transferred to London's Garrick Theatre at the beginning of August, Harold Hobson reviewed it in the *Sunday Times*. His review shows further evidence of Cushing's worldwide popularity in connection with the horror genre, and his particular attraction for the French. 'Tuesday's performance of *Thark* at the Garrick was a Travers triumph. My enjoyment owed nothing to nostalgia. It was fresh, vital, a thing entirely of today. It was a considerable pleasure to see Peter Cushing, who plays the part of a middle-aged gentleman with roving eyes. In these grievous times we should reverence all actors who build up Britain's reputation abroad. Though they remain in Britain, they are cultural exports. Mr Cushing is the idol of the *Midi-Minuit Fantastique* mob, and the mere mention of his name, coupled if possible with that of Christopher Lee, is enough to raise spirits in the Rue du Cherche-Midi. His rufous countenance, his formidable but flustered commands certainly raised mine. I wondered now and again why he was appearing in Mr Travers' girl-friend burlesque of the twenties instead of some tale of freezing horror. Mr Cushing falling off the whirlwind and misdirecting the storm with exasperated confidence is an inspiring sight. If only Mr Lee had emerged from the grandfather clock on that ominous staircase, my pleasure would have been perfect. What am I saying? It *was* perfect.'[10]

Cushing remembered that the play called for his character, Sir Hector Benbow, to share a four-poster bed with nephew Ronnie (McCowen) in the 'haunted house' of Thark. The rake on the stage at Guildford was exceptionally steep and the bed, on castors, would edge closer and closer to the edge. 'We were,' wrote Cushing, 'in danger of going "over the top".'[11] Cooney's suggestion was that they push the bed back up the stage, to the encouragement of the audience.

Cushing had been engaged in an ongoing correspondence with the BBC since the *Cribbins* show because Moss Bros kept charging him for the hire of a suit used in that production. The situation was eventually resolved, with effusive apologies all round, by the time Cushing began rehearsals for a play in BBC 2's *30 Minute Theatre* series. It was called *Monica*, by Pauline Macaulay, and was rehearsed between 27 October and 3 November 1965. It was broadcast live on 4 November from Studio G, Lime Grove. The director was Naomi Capon and Cushing's fee was £378. The play was thus described in the *Radio Times*: 'Simon (Gary Bond) is furious with his girlfriend Monica and fakes suicide, knowing that she will arrive in the nick of time to save him. A man arrives instead and what was intended as a joke takes a sinister turn.'[12]

The BBC had planned to repeat Cushing's groundbreaking performance in *Nineteen Eighty-Four* in 1962, but it was considered that the quality of the telerecording was not acceptable for rebroadcast. The only viable alternative was to remount the production, retaining the Kneale script, with a new cast. The production eventually went ahead on 28 November 1965, directed by Christopher Morahan, with David Buck as Winston Smith, Joseph O'Conor as O'Brien and Jane Merrow as Julia. 'It was excellent,' Cushing remarked of the new production, 'with a good cast, but nobody turned a hair. Time had moved on. It just wasn't frightening any more.'[13] Cushing appeared on *Late Night Line-Up* on BBC 2 on 27 November 1965 in a programme devoted to the old and new productions of *Nineteen Eighty-Four*. André Morell, Yvonne Mitchell, Nigel Kneale and Rudolph Cartier were all interviewed, along with Buck, Merrow, O'Conor and Morahan. Cushing delightedly pointed out that filming for his version of the play took place on the buildingsite that eventually became Television Centre.

After Christmas, Cushing was back at Shepperton Studios from 31 January to 22 March 1966, facing the Daleks again in his second film as Doctor Who – *Daleks' Invasion Earth 2150 A.D.*

Once again, the film was based on a story from the television series (1964's *The Dalek Invasion of Earth*) and again, Gordon Flemyng was the director. To match increased audience expectations, the film required exterior filming and a huge model of a Dalek flying saucer so the budget was duly increased. Joe Vegoda came on board once again and the Sugar Puffs company added finance in return for prominently placed posters in the film advertising their cereal. The film was shot on Studio B at Shepperton. In Studio A they were shooting *Casino Royale* with a host of stars including Cushing's former leading ladies Ursula Andress and Deborah Kerr.

The film sees policeman Tom Campbell (Bernard Cribbins) stumbling into TARDIS after being attacked in a smash-and-grab raid. Doctor Who, with Susan and his niece Louise (Jill Curzon), takes Tom to London in the 22nd Century, where they discover that the Daleks have invaded and subjugated the people of Earth. The film (shot under the title *Daleks Invade Earth 2150 A.D.*), is rather more gritty in tone than its predecessor, with a strong supporting cast including Andrew Keir, Ray Brooks and Godfrey Quigley as the anti-Dalek freedom fighters. Bernard Cribbins once again makes a good partner for Cushing, and the Doctor is somewhat less eccentric with him. For the latter part of the film, however, Cushing is teamed up with Ray Brooks and they work less well together. Key scenes like a London street full of Daleks are interesting, but there is noticeably less dialogue in this film than

Doctor Who and Tom Campbell (Bernard Cribbins) are apprehended by Robomen on the banks of the Thames. Worse lies in store in *Daleks' Invasion Earth 2150 A.D.*

the first, and the conclusion, diverting the Daleks' planet-splitting bomb, seems rushed and muddled.

'I'm really a very gentle character, fond of long walks and reading. But no one believes it,' said Cushing, interviewed by William Hall for the *Evening News* (25 March 1966) behind-the-scenes on *Daleks' Invasion Earth 2150 A.D.* 'Outside his dressing room in darkest Shepperton, they were waiting for him to tangle with those grotesque pepperpots who never seem to take Not Wanted for an answer. Mr Cushing smiled thinly and said "A lot of people have accused me of lowering my standards but I've never felt I'm wasting myself. You have to have a great ego to want to play Hamlet all the time, and I just haven't got that ego. Challenge me on this, and I'll say: "Well, I've kept working." And surely that's the important thing. It was no surprise to me to learn that the first *Doctor Who* film came into the top twenty box-office hits last year, despite the panning the critics gave it. That's why they've done the sequel, *Daleks Invade Earth 2150*. And that's why they're spending almost twice as much on this one."

'At 50, Mr Cushing is reconciled to the oddities of show business. "I played Winston Smith in *Nineteen Eighty-Four* on TV and it was probably the high spot of my television career. I'd like to have done the film

version, but they gave it to Edmond O'Brien. I still don't know why. Now I'm playing Doctor Who while Bill Hartnell is doing it on TV. But that's the way it goes. Down one minute up the next. After a time you get used to it." Today Mr Cushing has reason to be content. Having saved the world (a novel touch, using the earth's magnetic centre to pin the metal Daleks to the core) he is now considering several parts that will keep him occupied throughout the summer. "Among them – a Roman general, a French Legionnaire and dear old Frankenstein again."

'He hooked his thumbs into his luridly fancy waistcoat, sat back comfortably and said "It's nice to have people fighting over you. Rare too. Three years ago during that terrible slump in the industry I was out of work for 18 months. I'll never forget it. But ours is an unpredictable world. That's why I keep working."

Apart from lone hikes in which he memorises the next day's lines (his wife Helen, 23 years married, waved him away this week on a 13-mile 'Fieldfare' walk) Mr Cushing's hobbies are collecting model soldiers and operating the miniature theatre he has built at his beachside cottage in Whitstable Kent. "We have no children and no animals. But all the kids and all the dogs in Whitstable are my mates" he said. They're used to having a monster in their midst.'[14]

Cushing fell ill during the making of the film, requiring Subotsky to re-arrange scenes so that they could be shot around him. Subotsky was able to claim £30,000 on the film's insurance policy for a two-day hold-up until Cushing had recovered. *Daleks' Invasion Earth 2150 A.D.* went on general release on 5 August 1966, with a strident trailer that set the mood: 'Planet Earth has been bombarded by meteorites, subjected to cosmic rays, savagely invaded by men of steel, who have no flesh to pierce, no blood to spill! 2150 A.D. – a year that will thrill you and terrify you!' However, the craze for the Daleks was waning, and this movie was considerably less successful than the first Dalek film. The *Times* mentioned the 'long-suffering, ill-used Peter Cushing,'[15] but Alexander Walker in the *Evening Standard* said that 'the sets are quite an eyeful, so are the special effects, and director Gordon Flemyng can teach Disney a lot about packing in the action.'[16]

Chapter Eighteen

Back to Baker Street

Of the list of roles Cushing anticipated in the *Evening News* on 25 March 1966, it must have been aggravating to Cushing that the only one to come to fruition was 'dear old Frankenstein again'. Cushing was at Bray at the beginning of July to begin his fourth Frankenstein film, *Frankenstein Created Woman*, a project that was mooted as early as 1958, when James Carreras coined the title as Hammer's answer to Roger Vadim's *And God Created Woman*. Cushing's contractual fee for the film was £5000.

Terence Fisher was back at the helm as director and the film is a definite return to form for the series. As if to prove the point, Fisher begins the film with a shot of a guillotine, as he did in *Revenge*. Anthony Hinds' script rids Frankenstein of the mawkish sentiment displayed in *Evil* and the Baron is back in total command, having now turned his attention to the soul. He even appears to *have* a soul – he certainly doesn't kill anyone, and his work here seems almost philanthropic. But he is still some distance from understanding human nature, and the forces of love and revenge are ultimately his undoing.

In this film, Frankenstein thinks nothing of experimenting on his own body, subjecting himself to freezing to prove that the soul can survive death. As the Baron is revived by his associate Doctor Hertz

Frankenstein rises from the slab while Doctor Hertz (Thorley Walters) and Hans (Robert Morris) look on in *Frankenstein Created Woman* (1966)

(Thorley Walters) with a massive electrical charge and some smelling salts, Cushing rises from his coffin rubbing his neck in a now-familiar bit of business to signify weariness or discomfort. Frankenstein's assistant Hans (Robert Morris) is sent to fetch champagne from the local café, setting the plot in motion as he encounters three wealthy, idle young 'bloods' who are taunting the scarred Christina (Susan Denberg), daughter of the café owner Kleve. Later, the bloods break into the café and kill Kleve, but Hans is accused of the murder and executed at the guillotine. Hertz acquires the body and Frankenstein captures the young man's soul. Christina, who was in love with Hans, commits suicide shortly after witnessing his execution. Frankenstein retrieves Christina's body and cures her disfigurement, but places Hans' soul inside her body.

At Hans' trial, Frankenstein appears before Peter Maddern's ferrety police chief. As ever with Cushing, the details are everything. He idly flicks through the bible when Frankenstein should be swearing on it, and when asked 'What is your occupation?' he replies 'I am a busy man.' In place of the buttonhole from *Revenge*, Cushing now uses the Baron's black opera cloak as his chief prop, swirling it flamboyantly or pulling it straight for effect on several occasions. There is continuity with *Evil* in that the Baron's hands have been burned and are useless for surgery.

The science is never elaborated upon, and the talk of 'frames of force' to give life after death is woolly indeed. Thorley Walters' wide-eyed, child-like Doctor Hertz is agog at every new scientific marvel, and comes very close to stealing the film. The soul-catching apparatus itself consists of two parabolic dishes and a tuning fork, but with Cushing manning it we are compelled to believe, bringing a glimpse of the metaphysical to the Hammer *Frankenstein* canon. And who can complain as Cushing, in black gloves with his sleeves rolled up, ministers to the dead, with the two artfully-teased streaks of grey at his temples giving a subliminal impression of a devil's horns.

Reviewers noted that Walters was playing Watson to Cushing's Holmes, but when the Baron is tending to the newly-beautified Christina – using her as an experimental subject – it becomes clear that this is nothing less than Hammer's *Pygmalion*, with Cushing

Producer Anthony Nelson Keys, Cushing and Susan Denberg on location for *Frankenstein Created Woman* (1966)

as Higgins and Walters as Colonel Pickering. As Hans wreaks his terrible revenge through Christina, murdering each of the bloods in turn, the film takes a grisly and inevitably tragic turn. In one of the most disturbing scenes in any British horror film, Christina is seen kneeling in supplication before the head of her late lover. Then, tormented by her divided personality, she commits suicide by throwing herself off a cliff. As Christine brings his experiment to a premature end, Frankenstein looks on with a flicker of fury, frustration and possibly even sadness in his eyes. Then, with a glance to the Almighty, he sets off alone again.

The film, photographed by Arthur Grant, is beautifully coloured with rich reds and mouldy greens, with the Baron decked out in black-and-white to catch the eye. It is apparent, however, that the number of days Cushing was required on this film were kept to a minimum, as the juveniles (Morris, Denberg and the bloods) are given several long scenes to eke out the length. In the earlier *Frankensteins*, Cushing was barely off the screen for a minute. *Variety* remarked that 'Cushing could walk through the Frankenstein part blindfold by now, but he still treats it seriously as though he were playing Hamlet.'[1]

If there was a point when Cushing should have stepped off the horror treadmill, it should have been here. It is easy with hindsight to see that he was heading for a dispiriting run of low-brow and low-budget movies but it must be remembered that there were few genuine alternatives. In film terms Cushing's name was now synonymous with horror. An alternative would have been films in Europe or America, but he would not – could not – move away from London and Whitstable because of Helen's health.

To his credit, Cushing never denigrated the genre that had made him. 'I believe implicitly in everything I do in terror pictures,' he said later, 'because I believe there is a public demand for this type of escapist entertainment. They are, after all, harmless outlets for what might otherwise be awkward tensions in many people. I believe in the characters I play and the weird and uncanny games they get up to. I have to believe. It is the only way I prevent myself and my pictures being laughed out of the cinemas. By believing in what I'm acting in – an actor should do, whatever his part dictates – I am able to give greater credulity to the character

Holmes and Dr Watson (Nigel Stock) in a 1968 BBC publicity still for *Sir Arthur Conan Doyle's Sherlock Holmes*

charge of greeting the guests, and after a word or two about Cushing's model soldiers, asked 'Have you got anything up your sleeve for us?' Cushing replied 'If I'm allowed to say... I'm going to play Sherlock Holmes. A series for the television. Will you come and be Watson?' 'I wouldn't mind that!' More replied. More's participation in the series was not to be, but the show was destined to be one of the big successes of the BBC's autumn season.

The *Sherlock Holmes* series was one of the first drama serials for BBC 1 to be made in colour. However, as BBC 1 did not start broadcasting in colour until more than a year later, the full effect was not seen until the series was repeated in 1970. For contractual reasons involving the Doyle estate (the Holmes stories were not yet in the public domain) the BBC had to make it clear that these stories formed the second season of *Sir Arthur Conan Doyle's Sherlock Holmes*. The first season had aired in 1965 and starred Douglas Wilmer as Holmes with Nigel Stock as Doctor Watson.

Wilmer declined to appear in the second series, commenting on, as he put it, 'a large amount of

unwisdom at the helm'[6] during the first. So the BBC approached John Neville, who had played Holmes in the 1965 Compton-Tekli film *A Study in Terror*. Neville also declined, but Cushing accepted readily. Cushing was placed under exclusive contract to the BBC for seven months and shooting began in May.

'I think he wanted to raise his profile a bit,' says Donald Tosh, who became script editor and co-producer of the series. 'He had done some films which he thought were not tremendously wise choices. This was a prestige project, back at the BBC, back on his old ground. But it had changed beyond recognition. And I don't think he knew how much he was second choice to Douglas Wilmer, which would have upset him if he had known. Wilmer, good actor that he was, was nowhere near Peter in star terms, he'd just rather coined Holmes for the 1960s.'[7]

Nigel Stock, who had received much critical acclaim for his portrayal of Watson, continued in the role, providing a note of continuity. The 'hook' for the new series was to be its portrayal of 'the savagery of Victorian crime' taking a cue from Patrick Hamilton's

Gaslight. Producer William Sterling fancied a Hitchcockian touch, and advised his directors to watch the Easter Bank Holiday screening of *Psycho* 'As I have been saying to everybody, it is a starting point to my production approach for Holmes.' Cushing agreed to the project on 16 February, and was placed under exclusive contract on 20 May at 735 guineas per programme. The decision to make the series in colour was not finalised until 13 May.

The first scenes filmed were for *The Hound of the Baskervilles*, and took place for the first time on genuine Dartmoor locations, near Newton Abbott in Devon, using a vintage steam train on the Dart Valley Railway. In the programme, the exteriors appear rich and are excitingly shot. While the interior sets are spacious, they are somewhat overlit. In comparing the BBC's production of *The Hound of the Baskervilles* with Hammer's, Cushing is noticeably gentler, which some felt was a mistake, although he still gives an unforgettable spin to lines like 'It's murder, Watson. Refined, cold-blooded, deliberate murder!'

It soon became clear that the project's reach was exceeding the BBC's grasp. The filmed Grimpen Mire sequence was unusable and had to be remounted at Ealing. In the electronic studio, a general unfamiliarity with the colour television equipment led to further expensive delays. For Cushing, who 15 years earlier had been in some chaotic live TV broadcasts from Alexandra Palace, it must all have seemed horribly familiar.

Donald Tosh had worked on the early days of *Coronation Street* and as a story editor on *Doctor Who* and was brought onto *Sherlock Holmes* to replace John Barber, who was leaving to become drama critic of the *Daily Telegraph*. He had something of a baptism of fire, as he recalls. 'The Head of Serials, Andrew Osborn, said, "We've just filmed the two episodes of *The Hound of the Baskervilles* and the series has now overspent by £13,000," which in those days was a *vast* sum of money. I was basically told to re-write the scripts so that the exterior sequences could be done in the studio.'[8]

Plans to feature stars like Leslie Caron, Orson Welles, Sean Connery and Peter Ustinov in supporting roles were quickly dropped. The supporting cast still featured many familiar faces, however, including, Brenda Bruce, Daniel Massey, Juliet Mills, Cecil Parker, Dennis Price, Corin Redgrave, Peter Woodthorpe and Edward Woodward.'

Despite lengthy pre-production for the 100-minute *Hound of the Baskervilles*, the period of time between recording and transmission of subsequent episodes got shorter. Cushing was calmed considerably by the presence of Helen in the studios on 23 August for the recording of *The Second Stain* but ill health prevented her from attending all the recordings.

William Sterling had to supervise the editing of *The Dancing Men* and a studio session for *The Boscombe Valley Mystery* on 23 September. As a consequence, an unfinished edit of *The Dancing Men* was accidentally transmitted on 24 September. when this mistake was reported in the *Daily Mail* the next day, it was used as a stick to beat the BBC with. 'The unprecedented disasters in the showing of this week's *Sherlock Holmes* – they broadcast an unedited recording which included shots at rehearsal – were probably due to divine retribution. No series deserves it more! Admittedly it has some good things, notably the reconstructions of the original *Strand* illustrations and the playing of Nigel Stock and Peter Cushing, although in my judgement Holmes should be colder and more arrogant. Elsewhere it was the crudest attempt the BBC has made to crash the international market ... I was disgusted by the generally low aim of *The Dancing Men*, which stretched itself to fill its time by blowing up the character of the housekeeper into a figure of mysteriously unexplained menace by the crude device of dressing her in black and photographing her outside doors looking fierce. But it made no attempt to visualise Holmes' ingenious solution of the cipher, which was the point of the whole story. The series is even made with transparently obvious breaks for commercials. ITV can justify this sort of thing by reminding us that it is a commercial operation. The BBC operates a public service system and in the past has always refused to cater for the international market at the expense of the British audience. Now it is debasing a famous British literary possession to satisfy a market it doesn't need to sell in. The note of contempt for the mass audience in *Holmes* is nothing new. It indicates a disastrous change of policy towards its fictions which requires an explanation.'

David E Rose, Assistant Head of Series, Drama, wrote a personal letter to Cushing on the matter of *The Dancing Men*: 'I felt I must say how very regrettable it was that there should have been two interruptions to *The Dancing Men* transmission last Monday night; and coming so near to the start of this very important series. I would like you to understand that it was in no way due to carelessness with regard to the programme ... and further measures are being considered against a repetition, not only concerning drama but the service as a whole. May I add on a personal note that, having been close to the series for a couple of weeks, I am elated by your presence as "Holmes" on the screen both individually and together with "Watson"; I am deriving much warmth and pleasure.'

Andrew Osborn found that he had to be rather more hands-on with the project than had been expected. Will Sterling had directed several small films but was very inexperienced as a producer. He was effectively replaced by Osborn and Tosh, although his name was left in the credits. Cushing remained committed to the project but, as always, he liked to have the whole script memorised before the rehearsal period, and was dismayed by the number of last-minute rewrites. 'If I had to change a line,' Tosh

Holmes and Watson (Nigel Stock) consult *Peoples of All Nations* in the BBC adaptation of *The Sign of Four* (1968)

remembers, 'Peter would say "Oh no, I can't take any more. It's too late. I can't make any more changes..." So we said, "OK, Peter, you say it your way, we'll get round it and shave something else." Nigel Stock would take on anything, he just got on and did it. Cushing was the star, he had to carry the whole series, that was why he was there – as a *major* star.'

There was drama off-screen at the conclusion of *The Solitary Cyclist*, however, on 25 November. Tosh recalls, 'Stanley Miller, a big fellow, long since dead, adapted *The Solitary Cyclist*, which has one of the worst endings of all time. The whole deduction hinged on this single line – Holmes suddenly says "I should have realised it was a false beard" or whatever. It really is pathetic, but it's Doyle. Stanley didn't really want to use it and Peter hated it. He said "I'm not going to say it." I said "You've got to say the line, it's the only explanation there is." Peter usually pulled us up because we weren't using the original Doyle lines. And now here was a line that *was* Doyle and he didn't like it. Stanley was jumping up and down in the gallery saying "That man will say that line! It's Doyle!" I think in the end they had to hold him down.

'Peter kept fluffing just before the line, so we couldn't use it. We'd got to about take 19 and somebody said "Do you realise we've got about three minutes and then they pull the plugs, or we're all on overtime?" The director, Viktors Ritelis, decided that he could edit around it and nobody would notice. I said "Don't tell Peter! Don't, for God's sake, say a word." I went storming out of the gallery, down onto the floor and accused Peter of unprofessionalism in front of the entire cast and crew. He was shocked to

the core. He'd probably never been spoken to like that, or certainly not recently. I said "I know you don't want to record this line, but we will record it once, if we have to pay overtime to everybody for the next week." Peter sailed through the rest of the scene, said it very quickly and it was all over and gone and wrapped up and we all breathed a sigh of relief.'[10] Today, director Viktors Ritelis has nothing but happy memories of these troubled times. "I remember the *Holmes* series well," he says. "In fact some of my fondest work-related memories are of Peter Cushing, and his tiny wife who sat behind me in the gallery during recording. When she died he sent me a note thanking me for the way I treated her and it is one of my treasured possessions. Both were lovely people."

The Sign of Four and *The Blue Carbuncle* were the last two episodes of the series to be shot, and considering that emotions behind-the-scenes were becoming more and more strained, it is barely perceivable on screen. *The Sign of Four* was adapted from Doyle's 1890 novella by Holmes aficionados Michael and Mollie Hardwick, and features Ann Bell as Mary Morstan, who – in the book – became Mrs Watson. That particular romantic entanglement is not included in the script, although Stock's Watson is clearly taken with the lady. A lengthy filmed sequence, as Holmes, Watson and Toby the dog track the villainous Jonathan Small, was shot in York Street and Church Road in Twickenham, in Isleworth and on a boat on the Thames at Brentford.

As Christmas 1968 approached, a proposed version of *The Red Circle* by the Hardwicks had been shelved, so Donald Tosh dug out Stanley Miller's adaptation of the Holmes Christmas story *The Blue Carbuncle*. The script was too short and lacked incident, so Tosh rewrote it entirely to return it more or less to Doyle's original story of Mr Henry Baker, whose Christmas goose 'lays a beautiful blue egg' – the Countess of Morcar's priceless jewel, the Blue Carbuncle. The story features one of Holmes's most bewitching pieces of deduction, delineating Baker's entire character and situation by examining his discarded hat, and Cushing presents this with characteristic aplomb.

The Devonshire Club in St James Street was used as a location for the Cosmopolitan Hotel where the jewel theft takes place, while Great Goodwin Farm, near Guildford, became Mrs Oakshott's goose farm. Harry Wilde was engaged to tutor Cushing in miming with the violin and the Salvation Army were paid five guineas for recording carols. The filming was completed on 29 November but the studio scenes were recorded just a week before the programme's transmission.

Despite the problems, the series was a popular success and Cushing was hailed as a definitive Holmes for a new generation. The series received awards in Italy and Hong Kong, with ten of the episodes repeated in colour in the summer of 1970.

Chapter Nineteen

Scientist, Surgeon, Madman, Murderer

Towards the end of the *Sherlock Holmes* recordings, Cushing selected his favourite television moments when he appeared on *Star Choice* for BBC 1, recorded on 10 December for a fee of 50 guineas.

With just a fortnight off, Cushing was back at Hammer for *Frankenstein Must Be Destroyed*, which began filming on 13 January 1969. This was Cushing's fifth appearance as Frankenstein and he was again directed by Terence Fisher, with an exceptional supporting cast including Veronica Carlson, Simon Ward, Freddie Jones, and Maxine Audley.

Although unremittingly grim, the film is a magnificent piece of work and regarded by many as Hammer's finest film. This is also Cushing's most detailed performance – the *Frankenstein* cycle gave Cushing and Fisher the opportunity to refine a characterisation of considerable depth and frightening conviction.

This was Cushing's first film for Hammer since they departed Bray Studios, and as a result, the exteriors (at ABPC Elstree) look bigger, more realistic and genuinely foreign, away from the storybook settings of *Frankenstein Created Woman*. The photography is gritty and grainy, and Fisher experiments with new techniques including many more close-ups. The film's grammar is fluent and more assured, and the script, by assistant director Bert Batt, makes the familiar set-ups fresh and fascinating.

The film opens as a mysterious cloaked figure makes his way through a European square, and James Bernard's hurdy-gurdy music cheekily refers to the 'Harry Lime' theme. As the unsuspecting Doctor Heidecke approaches his consulting-room, the figure raises a sickle – and blood splashes onto the brass name-plate.

As the killer, Cushing's distinctive gait gives him away, as does the delicacy with which he places Doctor Heidecke's head into a hat-box. The close-ups and cuts and hand-held camerawork in this early sequence are not typical of Fisher. We are soon, however, presented with Harold Goodwin as a reassuringly comic burglar. Cushing (his face still unseen) enters the house as the burglar descends into a secret laboratory. With effortless grace, Fisher tricks out the suspense as the Baron stops on the stair.

Goodwin discovers a body suspended in a tank – the first big shock.

Cushing stops in the laboratory, his hand brushing the retorts. With a flourish, we see the Baron's ghastly bald mask. It is a startling, repellent image and the previous shock is effectively topped. The Baron and the burglar fight – knocking over the body in the tank, of course – the whole urgently scored by Bernard. If the masked Frankenstein is occasionally a stuntman – there is no reason why it shouldn't be – there is one shot at least in which Cushing's very obvious body language comes across clearly. The burglar escapes and the Baron tears off his mask in fury. Cushing's wide eyes and panting, sweating face carry a genuine thrill of excitement. The music sounds a fanfare – '*Frank-en-stein Must-Be-Dest-royed!*' – and the Baron sets to work disposing of the body from the tank.

Later, the burglar, almost delirious with terror, is interviewed by Inspector Frisch (Thorley Walters), who rightly suspects that they are looking for a 'mad and highly dangerous medical adventurer.' Meanwhile Frankenstein, impeccably mannered and eminently charming, arrives at a guest house run by Anna Spengler (Veronica Carlson). Under the alias of Mr Fenner, the Baron makes himself at home.

Anna's fiancé, Karl Holst, works at the local asylum with the formidable Professor Richter (Freddie Jones). One of their patients is the deranged Doctor Frederick Brandt, who reputedly practised brain transplants.

Holst is stealing drugs from the asylum to pay for treatment for Anna's invalid mother. Frankenstein immediately seizes this weakness and blackmails Holst into assisting him. Cushing's performance is more measured than the flamboyance of *Created Woman*, informed, no doubt, by the performances before the television cameras in *Sherlock Holmes*. Physically, he looks exactly like Holmes, his costume is almost identical, although his expressions are harder and he speaks in short, clipped sentences. Cushing's own hair is dyed to match the toupée, which he wore as Holmes – as a result, Frankenstein looks very slightly artificial, almost robotic.

It is a tight script, full of highly concentrated action in a short space of time and, significantly, there is no subplot. Frankenstein is on screen nearly all the time.

'Mr Fenner' introduces himself to Anna Spengler (Veronica Carlson) in *Frankenstein Must Be Destroyed* (1969)

On a raid to the asylum to steal equipment for a new laboratory, Frankenstein and Holst are apprehended by a nightwatchman. Panicked, Holst kills him and they flee back to the guest house. 'Who *are* you?' Holst demands. 'I am Baron Frankenstein,' says the Baron, with a glance aloft to an irate Jehovah. He explains that Brandt – with whom he had been in correspondence – had discovered a successful method of transplanting brains. He must now cure Brandt's madness to learn the secret.

The subsequent kidnap of Brandt from the asylum is botched and Brandt suffers a heart attack.

Back at the laboratory, watched by the terrified Anna, Frankenstein massages Brandt's chest. With a single, deft movement Cushing takes out his pocket-watch to time the heartbeats. Before Brandt dies, his brain must be transplanted into another body – more specifically, into the body of another *doctor*, Frankenstein thus exacting his revenge on the medical profession that has disowned him. 'Professor Richter would be ideal...'

A little later, Anna discovers Frankenstein and Karl with Professor Richter's unconscious body. She is sent back to her room, where Frankenstein later rapes her. This scene was included shortly before shooting wrapped at the instruction of James Carreras, who claimed the distributor feared there was not enough

sex in the picture. Ironically, the scene was ultimately cut from American prints.

The rape scene proved exceptionally difficult for Veronica Carlson and Peter Cushing to film. 'I thought the world of Jimmy Carreras, but it was an error,' Carlson remembers. 'Peter didn't want to do it. He took me to dinner one evening to discuss it but it didn't make the scene any easier. I couldn't refuse to do it. Terence Fisher was very understanding but it was totally humiliating. Every alternative was more vulgar than the last ... Terry just said "Cut. That's it," and turned away. Peter and I just stayed there and held on to each other.'

Although the scene sits awkwardly in the continuity of the film, it is undeniably powerful, played with a frenzied conviction by Cushing. Frankenstein repeatedly kisses Anna but there is no passion – the Baron is impotent of emotional feeling, and this is simply a monstrous act of violation. Properly, Anna should afterwards have been revolted by Frankenstein's very presence, but the rape was filmed *after* many of the subsequent scenes.

Frankenstein returns to work and begins surgery to put Brandt's brain in Richter's body, using little more than carpenter's tools – none of the electrical jiggery-pokery of the previous films. Here is some of the grimmest brain-work in any of the Hammer

Frankensteins. As technology had moved on in the 1960s, so Frankenstein's methods seem to have regressed. Cushing handles it all grim-faced – he's even unshaven at this point.

Windsor Davis appears as a policeman, intent on searching the premises with his men. Bernard's strings create a diabolical tension while Davis simply walks up and down. Even after his three murders and a rape, the audience is placed in the unlikely position of *not wanting* Frankenstein to be caught. Even the Baron allows himself a small smile as the police are deflected and the surgery can continue. The experiment is a success. Pleased with himself, Frankenstein goes out for a constitutional. Unfortunately, as he buys himself a buttonhole, he is spotted by Brandt's wife, Ella. Frankenstein's vanity is his undoing once again.

The sudden burst of a water-main at the Spengler house temporarily exhumes the late Doctor Brandt. There is something obscene about Brandt's dead arm flapping in the plume of water that erupts from the flowerbed, and poor traumatised Anna – not far from insanity herself – has to drag Brandt's body out of the sodden earth and hide it elsewhere. Later, when Frankenstein returns, the water repair men have dug up the garden. Momentarily startled, he exchanges glances with Anna. 'There's nothing more to be seen here...' he tells the onlookers, before airily remarking to the workmen 'Ruined my plants!'

In the meantime, Ella Brandt has found a caricature portraying her husband and Frankenstein as vultures and she decides to pay a visit on the Baron. Greeted kindly by Frankenstein, Frau Brandt is taken to her husband – or at least to the bandaged *thing* he says is her husband. Cushing's scenes with Maxine Audley have a special finesse. She was an old friend from the *Caesar and Cleopatra* days and the rapport of these two theatre-trained actors is apparent. Cushing makes it seem that there is concern at the heart of Frankenstein's actions but we are aware that he is manipulating Frau Brandt with meticulous cruelty. The ruse works – he has bought the time they need. After kissing Audley on the hand, Cushing turns back to camera, and his face fills the frame. 'Pack!' he spits. 'We're leaving!'

The next day, Ella returns and realises she has been deceived. Brandt's body is subsequently discovered in the outhouse. Meanwhile, Frankenstein, Karl and Anna have returned with Brandt/Richter to his earlier

Frankenstein rapes Anna (Veronica Carlson) in a scene that disturbed both actors in *Frankenstein Must Be Destroyed* (1969)

laboratory, seen at the beginning of the film. Freddie Jones wakes, pulls off the bandages and looks in disbelief at his 'wrong' hands. In a silver tray, Brandt sees his reflection – but not *his* reflection. Frankenstein discovers Karl in the stables, where the boy is planning his escape, and they fight. Anna encounters the desperate Brandt/Richter and stabs him in panic before he runs off. Frankenstein, discovering what Anna has done, kills her without compunction.

Brandt/Richter goes back to Ella. He hides behind a screen and speaks like a frightened child. Jones carries the role with complete sincerity. 'I have become the victim of everything Frankenstein and I ever advocated.'

The next morning, bidding Ella leave, Brandt/Richter sets a trap. Frankenstein enters. 'I fancy that I am the spider and you are the fly, Frankenstein,' croons Jones. 'Better you had killed me...' A cat and mouse-chase ensues, with Brandt/Richter shying oil lamps onto the petrol-soaked floor. Frankenstein desperately tries to locate Brandt's notes. He finds them, and tries to escape, but Brandt/Richter catches him and carries the screaming Frankenstein back into the burning house.

Work on *Frankenstein Must Be Destroyed* wrapped on 26 February 1969 and the film opened in May. For the *Sunday Telegraph,* brevity was the soul of wit. 'At the Warner, *Frankenstein Must Be Destroyed* – yet again! New monster, old tricks, with Peter Cushing reassuringly in charge.'[1] The *Sunday Times* went into a little more depth. 'If you must have horror films, *Frankenstein Must Be Destroyed* is probably about as good as you can expect ... The good Doctor Frankenstein (Peter Cushing, of course) saws off the top of a victim's head and bores a hole in it with a handy brace-and-bit – the old elements of nausea, in fact, with redeeming ridiculousness. The comic effects in this series, always intentional, here are smarter than usual. After his exercise with the saw Frankenstein orders two lightly boiled eggs for breakfast.'[2]

When the film opened in America, *Variety* wrote enthusiastically: 'there's nothing tongue-in-cheek about the playing of Peter Cushing who gets his effect by an authority which carries along the audience and which he could hardly strengthen even if playing Lear for an Oscar.'[3]

This film shows the depths of Frankenstein's misogyny. He emotionally manipulates Ella Brandt

General Spielsdorf prepares to behead Carmilla Karnstein (Ingrid Pitt)
in *The Vampire Lovers* (1970)

in a rather small ballroom. There seems to be a general lack of attention in some quarters, resulting in shots like the uninterrupted view of the modern tennis courts at Moor Park Golf Club where the exterior locations were filmed, however the acting does much to shore things up and the plot rattles on with conviction. Soon after Mircalla (Pitt) comes to stay at the home of General Spielsdorf, his daughter Laura (Steele) begins to suffer nightmares in which she is molested by a monstrous cat. Soon she is becoming weak, and eventually, despite tender care from Marcilla, she dies.

There is still a relaxed quality to Cushing's performance. He has a good scene with Jon Finch as Laura's beau, Carl Ebbhardt, and later, in a deck-chair striped waistcoat, he discusses Laura's illness with Ferdy Mayne's oblivious doctor, while Ingrid works her wickedness above. Cushing's bedside manner is touching, and spectacularly deft is his ultimate realisation that Marcilla is a fiend. When he rushes to Laura's bedside, unshaven, dressed in a splendid black nightgown, his howl of despair is truly touching. 'It is daylight now,' he breathes, 'and she is dead!' Finding

the bite-marks on Laura's breast, he realises, aghast, what has been going on.

The General goes to consult his friend Baron Hartog (Douglas Wilmer) who seems to be a founder member of the middle-European vampire-hunting chapter of which Van Helsing is later a part. Carmilla moves on to the home of Sir Roger Morton (George Cole) where she begins turning her unhealthy affections to Morton's daughter Emma (Madeline Smith), playing with her, praying with her and eventually preying *on* her. There is excellent support again from Kate O'Mara as Emma's governess Madame Peridot, who bemoans 'the trouble with this part of the world is that they have too many fairy-tales...' before herself being drawn into Carmilla's web of seduction. As Carl becomes informed of Carmilla's evil, he rides to save Emma from the same fate as Laura – and Jon Finch holds his sword hilt like a crucifix, as Olivier did in *Hamlet*.

At Karnstein Castle, the truth is revealed – Carmilla is the last of the vampiric Karnstein family. She is hunted down and there is a wonderful expression of revulsion from Cushing as he plunges the stake into Carmilla – it is his first bit of vampire-dispatching in nearly ten years.

'Often though I have thought to befriend the ill-used monsters of the screen,' wrote the *Sunday Times,* 'I had never thought of keeping a vampire as a pet – or so I felt until *The Vampire Lovers.* This is about a female vampire who battens by preference on the bosom of some sweet girl (vampirism, recognising the need to march or rather nuzzle with the times, has gone nudist). However she is ready to bite anyone of the male sex, too, beginning with a nibble at the ear and proceeding to a sanguinary gnaw at the throat. Pretty Madeline Smith, round-eyed and no wonder, provides some of the bosoms; the versatile vampire is played by Ingrid Pitt; and Peter Cushing is among the hosts who accept without demur her appearance, stunningly draped in scarlet, as a house-guest in the best Styrian families.

Later though, Mr Cushing mucks in, and I use the term advisedly, with the exterminating team. And now the film looks back on an earlier occasion when an executioner collapses, too tired to decapitate another thing. And suddenly you feel that Carmilla, temporary survivor of the massacre, deserves to join the martyred monsters of the screen. Somebody ought to set up a rehabilitation centre for delinquent vampires. Think, after all, of the scene when at breakfast after a night literally bloodthirsty, the sated girl is offered a dish of kedgeree or devilled kidneys. "I'm not hungry," she says pushing it away. You would have to go far to find a cheaper pet to feed.'[4]

Ingrid Pitt recalls her first meeting with Cushing was as he chopped off her head, during the filming of Carmilla's climactic death scene when a dummy was set up for the decapitation. 'I mumbled something silly like "don't get cut up about it", but Peter was terribly sweet and offered to take me to tea to make up for it' The friendship between Cushing and Pitt deepened on meeting Mrs Cushing. 'Helen could speak Russian, and I could manage a smattering, so we began sending cards to each other in Russian, with Peter acting as the postman. He did his job very well. Helen loved roses, and so I was sent cards with roses on them. I hadn't really been in London long, and I was a bit lonely, so it was kind of them to take me under their wing, if only for a short time. Then Peter found out that one of the last days of filming, 3 March, was the 100th anniversary of my father's birth. At the end of the day's filming he brought out champagne and a cake, then took me and Helen off to a little restaurant. It was magical.'[5]

On 22 February, during the making of *The Vampire Lovers*, Cushing recorded *Line-Up* at Television Centre, for the usual fee of 25 guineas.

There was another TV appearance, on *London This Week*, recorded on 5 June, before Cushing started another Amicus portmanteau film, *The House That Dripped Blood*. The film was shot from 29 June at Shepperton Studios. The director was Peter Duffell. Because of Helen's worsening condition, Cushing had attempted to obtain a release from his contract, and while he was freed from Hammer's *Lust for a Vampire* (to which he was contracted and scheduled to begin on 6 July) he was held to the Amicus film.

Cushing appeared in a segment of *The House That Dripped Blood* called *Waxworks*, as retired stockbroker Philip Grayson, who becomes obsessed with the wax figure of Salome in a local wax museum. 'The story was nothing more than a contrivance to get Peter Cushing's head on a plate,' said Duffell. 'I decided to try to give the story a little resonance on the strictly human level by building up the loneliness of the character, taking refuge from the loneliness of life in his books, music and memories ... of the dead girl.'[6] (The music included Schubert's 'Death and the Maiden', which gave Duffell his preferred – and rejected – title for the film.) For the scene when Grayson is seen flicking through some theatre programmes, Duffell provided the programmes including one for Olivier's production of *The School for Scandal*, in which Cushing had played Sir Joseph Surface.

Joss Ackland and director Peter Duffell with Cushing on location for *The House that Dripped Blood* (1970)

The *Waxworks* segment, with able support from Joss Ackland and Wolfe Morris, is a grim enough little tale (based, like the other three segments, on stories by Robert Bloch), but let down by unappealing wax effigies and a thumpingly obvious twist. Of the other stories, Christopher Lee's tale of witchcraft is the best, while Jon Pertwee and Ingrid Pitt team up for a comic horror story about a vampire's cloak. Pitt remembers that, although they had no scenes together, she met Cushing for tea at the studios while filming, and they were together in the dubbing studio when the film was finished. The most affecting part of *The House That Dripped Blood* are the shots of Cushing, standing on a riverbank, lost in grief for his lost love. It is difficult not to think that he was in some way anticipating the unendurable – Helen's death.

The critics were kind. 'Agreeable surprise,' said Dilys Powell in the *Sunday Times*. 'In *The House That Dripped Blood*, four stories go to make up a lively and intelligent essay, far better than its title suggests, in horror and joke-horror. Peter Duffell, directing his first feature film, has dealt admirably with a cast including Denholm Elliott, Peter Cushing, Christopher Lee and Nyree Dawn Porter.'[7]

Chapter Twenty

Losing Helen

W hen the volume of his fan mail had increased to huge proportions, Cushing decided to take on a secretary. But finding one who could stay the course was not easy. 'They came and went in bewildering succession,' he wrote, 'all to have babies (not guilty, m'lud). In September 1959, Mrs Joyce Buten arrived and promptly announced that she also wanted to start a family. In desperation, I told her that it didn't matter how many children she had, so long as she didn't leave us.'[1] In 1974 Joyce remarried, to Bernard Broughton, and would remain as Cushing's secretary for the rest of his life.

Cushing exchanges jokes with the hot-chestnut man between shots on *I, Monster* (1970)

In the late 1960s Helen began a correspondence course of breathing exercises which were improving her condition somewhat, until she was told by a locum doctor that what she was doing was waste of time. 'It was pitiful to see her spirit crumble,' Cushing said of that time. 'Although it wouldn't have made any difference to the inevitable outcome, that slap in the face took the heart out of her, and speeded her decline. Her weight went down to six stone – I had lost three myself – and we were both physically and mentally spent.'[2]

As Cushing no longer had a London home, when he was filming in Shepperton or Pinewood he would stay at Brown's Hotel in Mayfair – 'my favourite hotel in London'[3] he called it – and this accommodation would generally be included in his fee. For his next engagement, the Amicus film *I, Monster*, he did not want to be away from Helen in the evenings so travelled on the milk train from Whitstable at 6.00 am and returned home at 10.00pm at night. Joyce, who was living in Welling at this time, travelled to Whitstable to keep Helen company during the mornings and afternoons.

I, Monster, based on Robert Louis Stevenson's *Dr Jekyll and Mr Hyde*, was filmed from 10 October 1970, directed by 22-year-old director Stephen Weeks, with Christopher Lee in the dual role. In a transparent attempt by Milton Subotsky to duck copyright restrictions (MGM owned the rights to the title), the central characters were re-named – Jekyll became Marlowe and Hyde became Blake – although most of Stevenson's other characters were retained.

Subotsky also determined to make the film in 3-D, using a process that required constant lateral movement within the frame, making conventional film grammar almost impossible. After a while, the process was abandoned so in the finished film several interminable tracking shots are clumsily cut together with static close-ups.

Contact sheet pictures recording Cushing's sole day of filming (alongside Valerie Leon) on the ill-fated *Blood from the Mummy's Tomb* (1971)

Despite the technical problems Christopher Lee gives an excellent central performance. The script, however, wastes no time on the subsidiary characters so Cushing, as Marlowe's solicitor Utterson, spends an inordinate amount of time on the edge of the frame, nodding in agreement with colleagues Richard Hurndall and Mike Raven. Cushing loved the period furnishings, and wore some of his own Edwardian-styled clothes for the film – which were specially tailored for him by theatrical costumiers Montague Burton's – as a result, he seems completely at home in this era. He is even able to reprise the eye-up-to-the-magnifying-glass trick as he compares the identical signatures of Marlowe and Blake.

Although by turns tedious and confusing, the film has several startling scenes. A nightmare sequence features a distorted, faceless Marlowe; there is a spectacular chase through the massive turbines of a water-works and the monstrously ugly Blake's pathetic encounter with a small child in a park. The film has an authentically cluttered look and Carl Davis' lyrical score does much to unify the disparate elements.

Cushing's last job in 1970 was *The Morecambe and Wise Christmas Show*, recorded on 16 December 1970 at Television Centre for transmission on Christmas Day. Eric and Ernie's guests included William Franklyn, Edward Woodward and Eric Porter, with Cushing emerging from a grandfather clock at one point to complain once again that he hadn't been paid.

On 11 January 1971, Cushing began work as Professor Julian Fuchs in Hammer's *Blood from the Mummy's Tomb*, an adaptation of Bram Stoker's *The Jewel of Seven Stars*. The director was Seth Holt. Cushing completed only one day's work on the picture, which is recorded in a handful of stills with leading lady Valerie Leon.

'At the end of the first day,' wrote Cushing, 'Joyce rang to say Helen had been taken into Canterbury Hospital for a check-up, where she would be kept for a few days. She looked tired when I got there in the evening, but comfortable enough.' But that night, Helen had a relapse. 'I begged the doctor to let her come home, and he agreed, pointing out that she would need constant nursing.'[4]

Cushing asked John Redway to cancel his participation in *Blood from the Mummy's Tomb*. He brought Helen back to Whitstable and arranged day-and-night nursing care. 'For a little while, she improved, amid familiar surroundings and loving care, but it was only temporary, like an electric light bulb, that sometimes seems to glow brighter for a few seconds just before the filament burns itself out, and is extinguished forever.' At two minutes past nine on the morning of 14 January 1971, with her husband by her bedside, Helen Cushing died.

'I went out onto the deserted beach,' Cushing recalled. 'It was blowing almost gale force ... I began humming "Happy Birthday To You". I think I'd gone a little mad. I found myself indoors again, wandering aimlessly about the house, then suddenly started rushing up and down stairs as fast as I could, in the vain hope of inducing a heart attack.'[5]

He would consider suicide more than once in the weeks that followed. But, he wrote, 'Deep down I knew I would never take such a step ... It wouldn't be fair, I thought. Someone would have to clear up the grisly mess; it is not allowed by God; it wouldn't get me

Gustav Weil rides out with the Brotherhood in *Twins of Evil* (1971)

The character had something that it wouldn't have had if it had been written for me.'[7] The production of *Blood from the Mummy's Tomb* was dogged by tragedy, as assistant director Derek Whitehurst remembers. 'First Peter left, then we lost the director, Seth Holt [who died of a heart attack on 14 February aged 47. Michael Carreras stepped in as director]. Then one of the art department boys was killed on his motorbike.'[8] The crew of *Blood from the Mummy's Tomb* organised a wreath of flowers to be sent to Helen's funeral.

More than two months would elapse after Helen's death before Cushing was able to return to work in late March 1971. He was reunited with some familiar faces to play Gustav Weil in Hammer's *Twins of Evil* at Pinewood Studios. The gaunt-looking Cushing was clearly very upset, although acute, stupefying grief would not engulf him until some four years later.

Cushing's burden of sadness does not get in the way of his performance; if anything, it lends it an added dimension. Weil is as powerful and detailed a characterisation as Frankenstein, and a return to form after Cushing's unsurprisingly distracted turn as Utterson.

Twins of Evil was the third film in Hammer's Karnstein trilogy. The second was *Lust for a Vampire*, originally intended to be directed by Terence Fisher and to star Cushing – scriptwriter Tudor Gates had written the part of Giles Barton, a student of the occult, especially for the actor. When Fisher suffered a fall and was unable to participate, Jimmy Sangster took over as director, then Cushing declined the role so he could care for Helen.

Twins of Evil, like *Vampire Lovers* and *Lust for a Vampire*, was produced by Harry Fine and Michael Style, written by Tudor Gates, and featured the female vampire Carmilla Karnstein. The film retained the same Styrian locale from the first two Carmilla pictures but under director John Hough the tone was darker than Roy Ward Baker's fairy-tale *milieu*. A Western in all but the trappings it was clearly influenced by Michael Reeves' 1967 film *Witchfinder General* and Weil is not very far in manner and dress from Vincent Price's Matthew Hopkins.

'Peter Cushing takes a protective attitude to the questionable characters he has played over the years,' stated Hammer's publicity material for *Twins of Evil*. 'And his latest is no exception. "This chap is by no

what I wanted, anyway – to be reunited immediately with Helen and in any case I hadn't the necessary courage. Over-riding all these considerations, there was that message that Helen left me in her last letter. 'Let the sun shine in your heart. Do not pine for me, my beloved Peter, because that will cause unrest. Do not be hasty to leave this world, because you will not go until you have lived the life you have been given. And remember, we will meet again when the time is right ... this is my promise.'[6]

Blood from the Mummy's Tomb continued with Andrew Keir in the role of Fuchs. 'The producer, Howard Brandy, rang me to see if I'd help Hammer out,' Keir recalled. 'He said "We've tried to carry on, but it isn't going to work. Peter's very upset." The part was written for Peter, he had his own personality and style and that's what the writer saw. Obviously, if you're writing it for Peter, you must know his work.

means a baddie," he said. "He's a fanatical puritan and believes that what he's doing is absolutely right. His religion dictates that the way to rid the evil or sin from people is to burn them – a dreadful thing to do but he is not just doing it out of vengeance.'[9]

Weil does have human feelings, but they are buried very deep and even at his gentlest, he speaks in a kind of controlled roar. Before the credits, the Brotherhood burst in on a helpless village girl who is dragged out and summarily burned at the stake. Cushing gives her an expression of revulsion, pity, resignation – even self-disgust – all in a sneer. Weil can stop the Brotherhood from rioting with a word and then, with a flick of his head, set them off again. Later, he makes the simple act of washing his hands into an affecting gesture. Kathleen Byron is excellent as his gentle wife, who has to put up with a husband who rarely enters a room without first throwing open the door and then standing framed in the doorway, barking abuse. As the story begins, Weil takes in his orphaned nieces, the twins Maria and Freda (Mary and Madelaine Collinson). Maria is virtuous but Freda is wicked, and is promptly seduced and corrupted by the sybaritic Count Karnstein (Damien Thomas), who himself has been turned into a vampire by the spirit of his ancestor Carmilla.

Weil's austerity serves to make Karnstein's debauchery more exotic. 'What kind of plumage is this?' he rumbles, seeing the girls in their travelling clothes 'For birds of paradise?' Damien Thomas counters as a handsome and cultured villain, spitting taunts at his dour adversary. 'Pray for me, Weil. That's what you're supposed to do for sinners, isn't it? *Pray for me!*'

The plotting is rather uneven, Cushing's lines become repetitive and there are three almost identical burnings before the film is halfway through. As in *The Vampire Lovers*, the vampires aren't bothered by daylight, and after a while it begins to seem ridiculous that the entire Brotherhood spend their nights thundering about the countryside riding down every young girl they can find. ('Some men like a musical evening,' Karnstein glitters. 'Weil and his friends find their pleasure from burning innocent girls.') With Karnstein seeing off his share and the Brotherhood burning the rest, it's a wonder there are any girls left in the village at all. The showdown at the finale sees Weil with an axe in his back and Karnstein impaled on a spear – a fittingly grim conclusion to a bleak morality play.

While reviews generally assessed *Twins of Evil* as more of the same, the burgeoning fan press, which now included genre magazines like *Cinefantastique*, gave the film due credit for shifting the goalposts – Cushing was particularly praised for bringing sympathy to the 'twisted witch-hunting uncle [who] travels the lonely road of evil-doing in the Lord's name.'[10]

On 11 July, a short item appeared in the *Sunday Express*. 'On most days around lunchtime, actor Peter Cushing cycles away from his home in Whitstable. He returns after four or five hours and goes straight to bed. "My wife Helen died in January and I cycle to stop thinking about her. I set off in one of three directions, towards Faversham, Margate or Canterbury. It's about 14 miles there and back to Canterbury. I stop off for cups of tea in tea shops I used to go to with Helen. Everywhere I cycle holds memories of her. We went everywhere together. She's with me all of the time ... I've given up many of the things we used to do. The memory is too harrowing. That's why I cycle every day."'[11]

Thus the general public was informed of the desperate straits of one of its most beloved stars. There was immediately an enormous outpouring of affection. 'I have been deeply moved by the many letters I have received following the article last week,' wrote Cushing to the *Sunday Express* on 18 July 1971. 'I shall answer them all in time. No doubt through my own fault, I was misquoted. I never could – and would never try – to forget my beloved wife Helen. My cycling is for a number of reasons but not that. I suffer a great deal of remorse for certain things done, and certain things not done – and it is these destructive elements which I am trying to exorcise. If self-pity crept into what I said then it must be true. But I had no wish to give that impression. If it were not the certain Truth and Knowledge that I shall be reunited with my loved one when my pilgrim journey

Cushing in his award-winning role as the persecuted junk man Grimsdyke in *Tales from the Crypt* (1971)

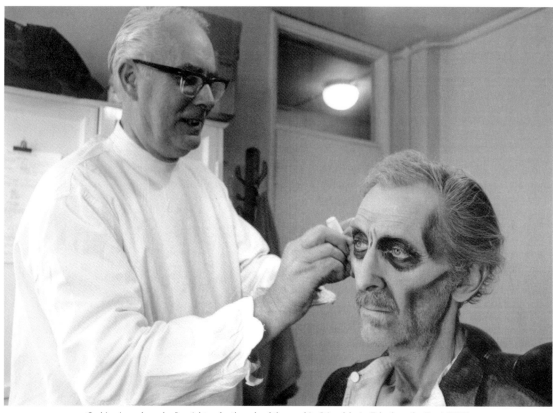

Cushing is made up by Roy Ashton for the role of the zombie Grimsdyke in *Tales from the Crypt* (1971)

on this strange land is finished – then I could not face up to anything. Without that promise, the whole of this life would be a mockery and a waste. The best is yet to come for all of us. In the mean time, this life must go on. And I shall endeavour to give of my best in work and diverse activities. Thank you again for your kind thoughts of me. May God's blessing be with you always.'[12]

On 27 July 1971, Cushing travelled to Harpenden to film the BBC 2 *Nature Spectacular* for producer Richard Brock. The fee was £100 (plus the rail fare from Whitstable to London, £2.10).

'Work – a problem to solve is all I ask. Give me work.' So said Cushing as Sherlock Holmes at the conclusion of *The Sign of Four*, and Cushing, perhaps also remembering Holmes' advice to Watson that 'work is the best antidote to sorrow', launched himself into a gruelling schedule of five films in the next four months. An unmade project from this period was Peter Bryan's script *Dead...?* which would have seen Cushing as Mainard, the leader of a psychic society who becomes involved with the horrible consequences of a séance at a carnival.

At the beginning of September he was back with Amicus and director Freddie Francis for *Tales from the Crypt*, a $500,000 adaptation of five stories from the American EC horror comics. (Cushing's name had been linked with these maligned publications as far back as the *Nineteen Eighty-Four* outcry.)

Cushing was sent the script but disliked the part he was offered – the role of Ralph Jason in the *Monkey's Paw*-styled episode *Wish You Were Here*, which was eventually taken by Richard Greene. He spotted the role of Arthur Grimsdyke in the *Poetic Justice* story and asked John Redway to suggest this. 'The role in the script,' Cushing said, 'was originally nothing. The story as written was about the young man. Subotsky said, "Of course, let him have it!"'[13] With the assistance of Freddie Francis, Cushing virtually ad-libbed the part. 'I based the character of Grimsdyke on an old man I once knew. He was rich but wore shabby clothes all the time, and was good to the kids in the neighbourhood.'[14]

Grimsdyke is a poignant creation, meticulously drawn and played with care and subtlety. The plucky old man is first seen entertaining the local children while his spoiled and affluent neighbour James Elliot (played by Robin Phillips) looks on and decides to destroy him for no reasons other than jealousy and spite.

Dressed in a blue bobble-hat and threadbare cardigan, with stubbly grey whiskers, Grimsdyke is everyone's favourite grandad – the accent is basically Doctor Who-with-the-corners-taken-off. 'As written, all his lines were spoken to himself,' said Cushing of Grimsdyke. 'A lonely sad figure, with only his faithful dog for company, but somehow the situation didn't ring true to me. I drew inspiration from personal experience, as I was in similar circumstances, apart from the dog. I found I could address some of the dialogue to this pet, as one so often does in real life, but for the major portion, I needed something else. At home, a photograph of Helen hangs on the wall above my writing-desk, and during those dark days I often found myself looking at it and speaking to her. I thought this would be the answer to my problem with Grimsdyke, and Freddie Francis agreed. We didn't use Helen's picture, as it would have been wrong "casting", but a suitable face was found and put in a cheap wooden frame, upon which the old boy whom I was to play could gaze longingly.'[15]

It is difficult to watch the scenes where Grimsdyke's hands tremble over a ouija board to contact his late wife (who, of course, is called Helen) but the scene is undeniably powerful. Her message warns of danger and Cushing's eyes widen in terror. 'Danger? Who to? Is it one of the children?' Like Job, Grimsdyke bears his persecutions stoically – by Elliot's machinations, the old man loses his job, his pension, his beloved dogs. Even the children are told to stay away from him. 'Just one more turn of the screw' promises Elliot.

Then, on Valentine's Day, Grimsdyke receives a bundle of cards. 'But you're my only sweetheart,' he tells his wife. The cards are full of hateful verses. Cushing reads and re-reads them in bewilderment. 'Some people live in the country, some people live in the town. Why don't you do us a service? Jump in the river and – ' The final, disbelieving, heart-broken quiver of his mouth is profoundly moving.

Grimsdyke hangs himself and Elliot discovers the body. Cushing helped to choreograph the details – one shoe off, revealing a woolly sock, a withered pot-plant and the shattered frame of the wife's photograph. Grimsdyke, who studied books on spiritualism, has the last laugh, however, and a year later he rises from the grave set on revenge. The old man's resurrection is double-exposed, capturing the half-glimpsed quality of a nightmare. Then the zombified Grimsdyke

Van Helsing and his arch enemy Dracula (Christopher Lee), reunited in 1970s Chelsea for *Dracula A.D. 1972* (1971)

approaches Elliot in his study, stepping stiffly from the blackness of the shadows and placing his rotting hand delicately on the desk. It was, as Mark Gatiss wrote in *Shivers* magazine, "able to reduce a noisy audience at an NFT screening to stunned silence."

'Peter Cushing – What would a horror film be without him?' asked the Amicus press notes. 'Certainly my public image overshadows reality,' admitted Cushing, 'but that's what the movie business is all about, isn't it? It means I'm doing something right.'[17]

In *Cinefantastique*, Dan Scapperotti stated '*Poetic Justice* was the best of the five tales. Freddie Francis elicits the finest performance from Cushing as the aged Grimsdyke. The veteran actor presents a character both pathetic and noble. As the persecuted junk man, Cushing maintains his dignity as his world crumbles around him.'[18]

The *New York Times* thought that *Tales from the Crypt* was not 'strictly speaking, a horror film at all, although it has its share of silly supernatural effects. Its people are small and spiteful and their bad ends exhibit the kind of heavy morality I associate less with fine horror fiction than with cautionary literature designed to persuade children to brush their teeth.'[19]

Cushing went from Amicus straight back to Hammer to reprise the role of Van Helsing for the first time since 1960 in *Dracula A.D. 1972*. Filming started on 27 September at MGM-EMI Elstree (formerly ABPC), directed by Alan Gibson, with Christopher Lee as Dracula, Michael Coles, Christopher Neame and Stephanie Beacham. The producer was Josephine Douglas who, as a BBC producer, had worked with Cushing in the 1950s.

Dracula A.D.1972 begins well as Dracula and Lawrence Van Helsing fight it out on top of a coach in 1872 – the coach crashes and Dracula is impaled on a broken carriage-wheel. Cushing is wide-eyed as Dracula decomposes in front of him once again, before a classic double-take-and-fade-away as Van Helsing drops dead of his exertions. It is a thrilling sequence, lent a bluish phosphorescence by the day-for-night filters. If the film had maintained this pitch it would have been much the better. As it is, the first modern scene is completely inappropriate and almost unwatchable.

We first see Lorrimer Van Helsing, grandson of the above, approaching in long shot – a rather

Lee and Cushing on Hadley Common with producer Josephine Douglas,
during filming of the prologue for *Dracula A.D. 1972* (1971)

Helsing pelts up and down the King's Road before falling exhausted against a shop window in a state of genuine despair. There's even a touch of the old Van Helsing's fierce athleticism in the fight between Cushing and Christopher Neame. 'I think it's valid ... that Van Helsing should be viewed by Scotland Yard as an elderly eccentric,' Cushing said. 'Any man who leaves home in the morning with a doctor's bag filled with crucifixes and sharpened stakes just in case he should run into a few vampires ... He's got a few problems of his own.'[20]

In his handful of scenes, Christopher Lee looks magnificent as Dracula, but has practically nothing to do. In the final confrontation with Van Helsing, however, the vampire is as animalistically savage as in 1958, and even gets a genuine Stoker line – 'You would play your brains against mine? Against me, who has commanded nations?' Cushing conceded that the role of Van Helsing offered much more potential than the role of Dracula.' Christopher doesn't want to keep playing the sort of Dracula films he has been playing – *Dracula in the Dark, Dracula Meets Frankenstein, Search the House for Dracula*. All he has to do as Dracula is stand in a corner, show his fangs and hiss.'[21]

Marjorie Bilbow, in *Cinema TV Today*, found the film 'a not particularly convincing attempt to bring old Drac up to date that even undemanding addicts are unlikely to find very exciting.' Her review encapsulates the contemporary opinion of the film, although there is high praise for Cushing. 'The idea of Count Dracula coming to life in the present day is good and it is perfectly feasible to assume that the vogue interest in the black arts should provide him with his chance to return. The film would be much more successful if it did not make such desperate efforts to be up-to-the-minute with slang expressions that manifestly do not come naturally to the cast or the characters they are portraying, or waste so much plot time on party and disco scenes that are old-hat telly. What with music that is more bang-bang thriller than spooky, and direction that emphasises the crime and detection element rather than the supernatural, Dracula and his activities get pushed into the background. Only Peter Cushing, moving serenely

old-fashioned-looking figure in the London of 1972. He berates his grand-daughter Jessica (Beacham) for putting her feet on his writing-desk and reading his books – 'This is my place of work, not W H Smith and Son' – but becomes genuinely concerned when he discovers that she is dabbling with the occult.

Cushing's almost imperceptible expression of confusion as Jessica tells her grandfather 'I've never dropped acid, I'm not shooting up...' shows a man struggling to keep up with a changing world.

Cushing has several fine scenes, particularly an exchange with Michael Coles' Inspector Murray that gives the lie to the theory that Cushing was out of his depth in a modern setting. When it becomes clear that Dracula has been resurrected, Van Helsing visits a church to fill a bottle of holy water from the stoup and Cushing's slightly guilty look around as he adds to his vampire-hunting accoutrements is priceless. When Jessica is kidnapped by Dracula's minions, Van

and sincerely through the thicket of trite dialogue and over-anxious performances, achieves moments of chilling conviction.'[22]

On 30 September, Cushing appeared on Radio 2's *Late Night Extra* programme to talk about the new Hammer *Dracula*. A week later he was interviewed at Brown's Hotel by John Doran for *Be My Guest,* broadcast on Radio 2 on 19 November. On returning to Whitstable, he was interviewed at home for a documentary on comics in BBC 2's *Man Alive* series, recalling the days of the *Gem* and the *Magnet* with examples from his own collection.

Another assignment for Hammer followed quickly, with a film called *Fear in the Night*. Jimmy Sangster was producer, director and co-writer, with a small cast comprising Judy Geeson, Ralph Bates and Joan Collins – although all of Cushing's scenes were with Geeson. The film was shot between 15 November and 17 December 1971 on location and at MGM-EMI Elstree. The total budget for the film was a mere £141,000, and Cushing's fee for four days' filming was £1000.

The story involves the fragile Peggy Heller (Geeson) who, while recovering from a nervous breakdown, is attacked in her home by an unseen assailant – all she can remember later is tearing off the attacker's false arm. However, because of her emotional state, her claims of the assault are disbelieved. She goes to stay at the school where her husband Robert (Bates) works, but there she discovers that the school has no pupils, and the headmaster has an artificial arm...

Cushing's place in the story, as the improbably named headmaster Michael Carmichael, is simply to play the bogeyman, but this he does very effectively indeed. His initial appearance, as he looms out of nowhere, is splendidly creepy. In a rigid, fake-looking wig, Cushing maintains a suitably robotic bearing, and adds off-putting little touches like sniffing Geeson's hair. Carmichael is one of the rare instances of Cushing playing a genuinely damaged character. We learn that the headmaster was injured in a terrible fire at the school and that the whole building is kept operational, with tape-recordings standing in for the pupils, for him to play-act his former role.

Unfortunately, *Fear in the Night* is a case of very little meat and an awful lot of gravy. "We had such fun on the set," says Jimmy Sangster. "Judy Geeson was rather a dear and Peter was just super. The problem was when we'd nearly finished shooting and I realised it was likely to be very short. So I had to hold a lot of walks and entrances and exits far longer than one normally would."[23]

On 20 November 1971, Cushing travelled to Bristol to take part in a series called *Sounds Natural* for Radio 4. He was interviewed on his interest in wildlife and the countryside, and the talk was illustrated with sound recordings from the BBC Sound Archive.

In November of the previous year, director Robert Fuest had wanted Cushing to play Doctor Vesalius in Vincent Price's art-deco horror extravaganza *The Abominable Dr Phibes*. Cushing had declined the role to spend his time nursing Helen, and Vesalius was played by Joseph Cotten. In December 1971, however, Cushing filmed a cameo at Elstree for the second Phibes film, *Dr Phibes Rises Again*, again directed by Fuest.

Disfigured genius Anton Phibes (Price) is racing against time – and the mysterious archaeologist Biederbeck – to reach the sacred 'river of life' in Egypt, where Phibes intends to revive his late wife Victoria. On board a passenger steamer, the Elsinore Castle, Phibes sees off a meddlesome scholar of antiquities called Ambrose, dumping him overboard in a giant gin bottle. Cushing appears as the ship's captain in a short scene with Robert Quarry as Biederbeck, insisting that they continue looking for Ambrose. Biederbeck says, on the contrary, that they must continue on their way with all speed. Cushing looks smart and sober in his captain's uniform, with a moustache (his own) neatly trimmed. He gets one joke in his minute-and-a-half-long conversation. "I suppose," he asks Biederbeck of the late Ambrose, "he never ... touched the bottle?" Renowned tippler Hugh Griffith, Cushing's co-star on television in *The Moment of Truth*, played Ambrose.

'You must think me a very dry old stick.' Michael Carmichael meets Peggy Heller (Judy Geeson) in Jimmy Sangster's *Fear in the Night* (1971)

direct connection back to the climax of *Nineteen Eighty-Four*.

On 6 and 7 April 1972, Cushing was at Shepperton for his role in another Amicus portmanteau film, *Asylum*. This was directed by Roy Ward Baker from a script by Robert Bloch, again from his own short stories. Cushing played Mr Smith in a segment called *The Weird Tailor* with his old friend Barry Morse.

Morse plays the tailor Bruno who is instructed, by a strange and insistent client called Mr Smith, to make a suit from a bizarre shimmering material. Bruno must follow the instructions in an ancient book, and can only work during the hours of darkness. It transpires, however, that Smith is a diabolist, and the suit is intended to raise his son from the dead. As Mr Smith, Cushing keeps his expressions bland and benign and wears his own black-rimmed glasses. His voice is gentle but his diction is of course, impeccable. Initially, Smith seems like Bruno's saviour, but we are given clues to Smith's bizarre intentions – he enters Bruno's shop in silhouette, and later leads the tailor to his bare study in a low-shot full of foreboding. Smith cannot pay Bruno. His research into the forbidden arts, he explains, his voice breaking with emotion, cost him his fortune. He draws a gun and insists that Bruno give him the suit. Roy Ward Baker creates a touching and iconic set-up with Cushing clutching a revolver and with tears in his eyes, standing over the white cadaver of his dead son.

'I believe that reactions must be instinctive rather than planned,' Cushing revealed, 'because I do not find planned reactions believable. The unschooled actor or director would have the character ... with tears running down his face, moaning "I can't go on." When my wife passed away I was very quiet, almost stunned. Mr Smith in *Asylum* loses his son and does not go to pieces, he quietly seeks a way to regain his son by means of this occult book and magic suit. I don't approve of the occult business but the reaction of Smith is entirely my own, based on my own experience ... more believable than if I played it for histrionics.'[4]

Cushing listed his costume on the script as 'Blue 3-piece suit (red stripe, white piping), shirt (cream),

'I play rather an impetuous gentleman with the wonderful name of Mr Smith,' said Cushing of his role in *Asylum* (1972)

tie (blue), blue socks, black shoes, overcoat, black trilby hat (hair piece when not wearing hat), dark suede gloves'. As an indication of Smith's penurious state – 'no watch and chain'.

Cushing's next film was for a new company in the horror field, but the faces behind it could not have been more familiar. 'I hear that Christopher Lee is to become the temporary "boss" of his friend Peter Cushing,' the *Evening Standard* reported in March 1972, 'Mr Lee has formed a production company with producer Anthony Nelson Keys to make a film called *Nothing But The Night*. They have asked Mr Cushing to appear in it. "It's a psychological thriller," says Cushing, "I play a pathologist, which I have never done before, and Chris is an ex-Army officer with Special Branch connections. I am happy to say that Hammer films are not at all disturbed, in fact they are bending over to help us. It will be the third consecutive film I've made with Christopher in three months. We've become a sort of Laurel and Hardy act."'[5] Lee and Nelson Keys' company was christened Charlemagne Film Productions, and shooting began on 18 April on location and later at Pinewood, under the direction of Peter Sasdy. The diverse cast included Diana Dors, Duncan Lamont, Georgia Brown and Fulton MacKay. Cushing plays Sir Mark Ashley, who investigates a series of deaths linked to the wealthy patrons of the Van Traylen orphanage. Eventually it becomes clear that the orphans themselves are part of a plan by the patrons to achieve immortality by transferring their minds to the bodies of the children.

The film, based on a novel by John Blackburn, is effectively a whodunnit, but so relentlessly does the script mislead and misdirect on the way (throwing all the suspicion onto Diana Dors' character, Anna Harb) that when the twist is revealed the viewer is inclined to feel roundly conned. Cushing plays the pathologist character well, even shouting Christopher Lee down at one point, but the character is flatly written and does nothing in second half of the film. Diana Dors and Georgia Brown work very hard and to the credit of director Peter Sasdy, there are some lingering

Cushing hitches a lift in a wheelchair in *Nothing But The Night* (1972); co-star Diana Dors and director Peter Sasdy can be seen behind him

images. At the conclusion of the film, the children, dressed in the uniforms of the adults who have possessed them, realise the folly of the experiment and one by one, jump over a cliff to the deaths. *Nothing But The Night* is clearly a film ahead of its time but is hampered by an impenetrable and humourless script. It suffered from poor distribution and was not widely seen. Sadly, it was Charlemagne's only film.

During the filming of *Nothing But The Night* at Pinewood, Cushing gave his first significant interview on the subject of Helen's death to Ray Connolly of the *Evening Standard*. 'They say that time heals, well, in this case it hasn't,' he said. 'Not after a year and three months ... Mediums? I neither believe in them nor disbelieve. But I would never go to one. And sometimes one might think what is one doing here? and why one doesn't do what dear George Sanders did the other day, or what poor Tony Hancock did. But I know I've been left for a reason. There is no waste. No waste.'[6] In July the *Standard* reported that Cushing had persuaded his close friend Paddy Smith – his stand-in and driver – to take his wife and small son on holiday in Cushing's Jaguar. 'I can't bear waste' said Cushing. 'It seems such a shame to have

the car lying idle in my barn. I used it quite a lot to take Helen for treatment and for quiet holidays. But it's only done 25,000 miles since I bought it ten years ago which is ridiculous.'[7]

After an appearance as the 'mystery voice' on Radio 4's *Twenty Questions*, recorded on 2 June 1972, and an appearance on BBC TV's amiable antiques quiz *Going for a Song*, recorded on 9 June in Bristol, Cushing started work on another film for Amicus. Based on the novel *Fengriffen* by David Case, it was known for a while as *Bride of Fengriffen* before eventually coming to the screen as *~~And Now The Screaming Starts!* Roy Ward Baker was the director and the cast included Patrick Magee, Herbert Lom, Rosalie Crutchley, Stephanie Beacham and Ian Ogilvy. Filming began on 17 July 1972 at Shepperton, with Oakley Court standing in as the Fengriffen family pile.

In 1785 Charles Fengriffen (Ogilvy) brings his new bride Catherine (Beacham) to live at the family estate. Soon she is having hallucinations – an eyeless spectre appears outside her window and a severed hand attacks her. She later learns that she is pregnant and fears that she has somehow been impregnated by the ghost. The family Doctor, Whittle (Magee) sends for a doctor from London 'well versed in a new science' – psychiatry. Doctor Pope (Cushing) arrives and discovers that the debauched behaviour of Charles' grandfather has led to a curse on the bride of Fengriffen.

This simple story of 'the sins of the fathers visited upon the sons' is told in convoluted style, enlivened by Cushing's gentle performance – in Regency duds and a rather effeminately tousled blond hair piece. 'Can you cure unhappiness, Doctor?' asks Stephanie Beacham's troubled Catherine. He cannot, sadly, despite spending three-quarters of an hour trying. Cushing's scenes with Beacham are touching but the film is repetitive and wearing.

Derek Whitehurst was assistant director on the picture – the first of three in a row with Cushing. 'After Helen's death,' he says, 'I can't say Peter became difficult to work with, but you had to be careful. There was never a question of his grief interfering with a film or a part. He would always learn the script, which was a very rare thing, but he became very concerned about eyelines. When he was acting, if he caught someone's eye behind the camera, even me, who'd worked with him before, it would put him off. In the end everybody had to duck out of sight so that he wouldn't see them. He would call me to one side very gently, and I'd have to move the sparks out of the way, and they would complain that their tea was getting cold. It became a bit of a routine. Perhaps it stopped him working with people who didn't know him. But there wouldn't be any drama. He was still easy-going, gracious to other actors, there was no camera hogging, no exasperation with lines being forgotten or people that weren't very good. And he was still always charming to the young ladies – we had many in

Dr Pope amidst the graves of the Fengriffen family (on the Shepperton backlot) in *~~And Now The Screaming Starts!* (1972)

Hammer films, and some of them were pretty grim."[8]

A new *Frankenstein* was on the cards at Hammer for Terence Fisher, in an early 19th Century setting. On 31 August 1972, Cushing wrote from Whitstable to producer Roy Skeggs about reusing the honey-coloured hair piece from *~~And Now The Screaming Starts!* which was hired from a London company called Wig Creations. 'They are keeping it for me, and I would be grateful for your confirmation.' The next day there was another note to Skeggs, listing props for Baron Frankenstein and surgical instruments required for the operation scenes. By 6 September, Cushing was installed at Brown's Hotel. In the few days before filming began on 18 September Cushing worked on Anthony Hinds' script with Skeggs and Fisher.

Frankenstein and the Monster from Hell would be Hammer's final *Frankenstein* and Terence Fisher's last film. In finishing, it returned to the very beginning of the canon – *Frankenstein and the Monster* was the title of the Milton Subotsky script that led to *The Curse of Frankenstein* in 1956. The title was rejected in 1956, but with the words 'from Hell' added it obviously passed muster in 1972. Cushing, ever one to expose the wiles of the front office, observed 'But people will be expecting a Monster from Hell, and we haven't got one.'[9] Terence Fisher rationalised that the monster came 'from Hell, from evil, from Frankenstein's mistaken belief that he is the creator of man, which of course he isn't, and will never succeed in being.'[10]

Cushing here gives a last, rather distant performance as the Baron. When Simon Helder (Shane Briant) a follower of Frankenstein's theories, is committed to an asylum for the criminally insane, he discovers that the Baron is resident in the asylum also.

To introduce Frankenstein, Fisher uses a powerful three-step cut, from long-shot, to mid-shot, to close-up, drawing us into Cushing's porcelain face. James Bernard's strings weave their spell too, giving an immediate, though subtle, familiarity. The Baron has the run of the asylum and is cynically manipulating the inmates to engineer his newest creation. Helder joins him enthusiastically. However, after years of being a rational, driven scientist – always coldly sane – Frankenstein has finally tipped over the brink into irredeemable madness.

Fisher's revelation of his new Creature echoes the unveiling in *Curse*. But David Prowse as the monster, eyeless and slumped in his cage, looks unfortunately like some hairy old soak wearing a rubber mask from a joke shop. Prowse's performance is better when the Creature is sighted and standing up, and he is at best an improvement on Kiwi Kingston's monster in *The Evil of Frankenstein*. Frankenstein and Helder are aided by a mute girl called Sarah, known to the inmates as the Angel. She is played by Madeline Smith, who had prevously appeared in *The Vampire Lovers*. Smith has a thankless task, running around after everyone, and

Van Helsing confronts Christopher Lee's Dracula for the last time in *The Satanic Rites of Dracula* (1972)

yet she still manages to invest Sarah with a kind of luminous innocence.

'I look at that film now and wonder who the girl is,' says Madeline Smith. 'With her very dark hair, a bit podgy in the fizzog, nothing like me at all! I remember that Peter was lovely to work with, but I was still rather nervous because he was such a big star. He got on well with Shane, who was as ferocious in his way about what he did as Peter was. It was terrible to see what grief had done to Peter. He was so painfully thin, and it was as if the light had gone out of his eyes. With Helen gone, he was half a person. I remember also that he used to cover his script with the most beautiful, tiny writing, like a little old mathematician or the Brontës! He paid no heed to the hoot-and-hollerers, and just got quietly on with the business of making our little film.'[11]

Frankenstein fits his monster with a new brain and Cushing is almost licking his lips as Helder's saw slices through the skull – he later kicks over the old brain in a gesture of supreme indifference. Then as the monster awakens, to a plaintive fiddle motif from James Bernard, there is a glitter in Cushing's eye as Frankenstein faces his creation. Suddenly, the Creature turns on Helder with a broken bell-jar and Cushing displays his old, familiar athleticism as he smashes a bottle of chloroform into his coat and leaps onto the monster's back.

With the Creature subdued, Frankenstein explains his latest and most insane scheme – to mate Sarah with the creature and finally produce a perfect human being. The Baron smiles as he reveals his plan to Helder, but

there's something dead and dreadful in those water-blue eyes. Cushing was concerned about the logic of Frankenstein wanting to mate his creature with a mute girl, and rewrote two pages of the script to explain that Sarah's inability to speak was due to a shock, not a physical condition. Outside in the asylum the inmates are on the rampage, having suspected foul play from the Baron for some time. They eventually round on the Creature and tear it to pieces, echoing the similar scene in *Revenge*. As the monster lies in a heap, Frankenstein repeats his first line 'Go back to you rooms, now. There's nothing more for you to see. It's all over.'

The film is preoccupied with failure and death, following the downbeat trend of *Frankenstein Must Be Destroyed*. It is Fisher's last grim fairy-tale, with genuine moments of power and poetry, providing a fitting conclusion to the story of the Baron that does not disgrace the director or the star. Derek Whitehurst could see that it was the end of an era. 'Terry said he didn't think he'd be directing any more,' he recalls. 'The strain was just too great for him. In a few years, the film business had changed completely, and we'd lost a lot of the old Hammer personnel. It was rather a sad atmosphere when we finished that one.'[12] For Cushing and Whitehurst however, it was straight on with 'the next one'.

On 13 November, Cushing began work as Lorrimer Van Helsing again, in *The Satanic Rites of Dracula* (in production the film was known as *Dracula is Dead and Well and Living in London*). Cushing's fee was now £6000, plus accommodation at Brown's Hotel and £25 per week for his driver. The director was *A.D. 1972*'s

Alan Gibson, with Christopher Lee and Michael Coles also returning from that film. Stephanie Beacham was not available to play Jessica Van Helsing so the role was taken by Joanna Lumley. Old comrades Freddie Jones, Patrick Barr and William Franklyn also joined in.

'My family have an affectionate joke with me about Peter,' Franklyn remembers. 'If I eulogise about someone, praising their character, humour, etc, they say in unison "it's one of Dad's 'Peter Cushing' saints." Because in my professional lifetime I've seldom met a person of such generosity of spirit, humour, natural courage and non-judgemental reactions. He was an icon of the non-egotistical, totally professional and immensely companionable actor team-spirit. On a film set, Peter always wore an immaculate white glove, as if being expected to serve crumpets and pour tea. As if by magic, it disappeared the moment the preparation for a take was sounded, and on the word "print" from the director it would miraculously appear again, with the inevitable cigarette lodged between the first and second fingers. A nicotine-stained professor of whatever branch of horror was, to Peter, unthinkable.

Unless forbidden by the director on safety grounds, Peter would always do his own stunts. We have ridden and jumped and sworded with the same fun that we swapped anecdotes on military manoeuvres and board games. He was a leading consultant on the subject. Knowing him and remembering him brings warmth and smiles.'[13]

In *The Satanic Rites of Dracula,* Van Helsing is called in once again by Inspector Murray when several well-known establishment figures are involved in a black mass at a country estate called Pelham House. One of the sect is an old friend of Van Helsing's, the Nobel Prize-winning bio-chemist Professor Julian Keeley (Freddie Jones). Van Helsing visits Keeley who is in a state of terrified agitation having developed an accelerated strain of *bacillus pestis* – bubonic plague. Murray and Jessica discover vampirised girls in the cellar at Pelham house, and it is revealed that Keeley's research was sponsored by a reclusive tycoon called D D Denham. Van Helsing confronts Denham and exposes him as Dracula, but is captured and taken to Pelham House. Here, on the 23rd day of the 11th month, the Sabat of the Undead, Dracula will release the plague and fulfil the biblical prophecy of Armageddon.

Cushing's scenes here are limited again, but there is a marvellous exchange with Freddie Jones as the dribbling, cow-faced Julian Keeley, who is totally in thrall to Dracula. 'Evil and violence are the only two measures that hold any power...' he drools. 'And nothing is too vile, nothing is too dreadful. You need to feel the thrill of disgust, the beauty of obscenity.' Cushing seems a little bored with relating the anti-vampire precautions yet again, and the list of items that can repel Dracula has now taken on ludicrous proportions. But there is real steel in Van Helsing's confrontation with 'D D Denham' as he draws the pistol to fire the silver bullet. Lee looks powerful and attractive, and his delivery reveals nothing of his almost complete disillusionment with the role and Hammer's treatment of the character. This was the last film in which Lee and Cushing would face each other as Van Helsing and Dracula.

Cushing gets perhaps the best line in the film when facing William Franklyn's disbelieving Colonel Torrence, who asks if they are dealing with 'hob-goblins and witches and things that go bump in the night'. 'Hobgoblins are fantasy creatures of the nursery,' states Van Helsing. 'As for witches they certainly exist, although 90 per cent of them are charlatans. Things do go bump in the night. Quite often.'

Again Cushing was responsible for rewriting Van Helsing's lines. He was notably concerned about the line which says that the vampire lives in mortal dread of silver. 'This bothers me,' he wrote on

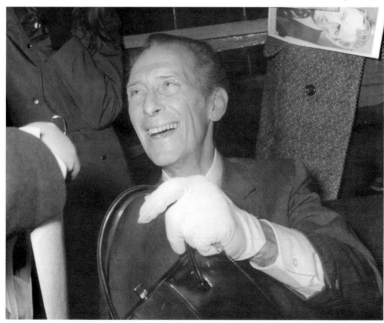

Gentleman Cushing obliges with a lady's handbag during an autograph session at the NFT.
Note his white smoking glove, worn to prevent nicotine stains on his fingers

Vincent Price with Cushing on location at Pyrford Manor for *Madhouse* (1973)

the script 'because of the silver ring Dracula wears,' but the reference remained unchanged. Cushing clipped a biblical quotation from a newspaper and pasted it into his script. It read 'Be not overcome of evil, but overcome evil with good. Romans XII, 21.'

Cushing began 1973 with two BBC television shows in one day. On the afternoon of 4 January, he was a guest on *Ask Aspel*, in which children requested clips from favourite TV shows be shown again. In the evening, Cushing appeared on the magazine programme *Nationwide*, to talk about his recent films.

In mid January, Cushing took to the stage of the National Film Theatre in London to take part in one of the John Player Lectures sponsored by the famous tobacco company. He spoke at length about his early life, his trip to Hollywood and his stage career, although there was little about Hammer or his horror roles. A transcript of the interview with David Castell would form the basis for his autobiography, which he began after Helen's death 'as a form of therapy.'[14]

A fortnight later, on 5 February 1973, Cushing was back at the BBC recording another *Morecambe and Wise Show* – broadcast in March. In this programme, Cushing tells Eric and Ernie, 'I'm not letting you out of my sight until I get paid. Until I get my money, wherever you go, I shall go.' ('That'll be a bit awkward at about 11 o'clock

tonight,' says Morecambe.) As a result, Cushing has to join in the song-and-dance routine 'We're a Couple of Swells'. He is a little unsteady, but he seems to be enjoying himself greatly. Suffice to say, even by the end of the show, he has still not been paid.

In April, Cushing attended The Second International Horror Film Festival in Paris, organised by Alain Schlockoff, and on 17 April received a standing ovation as he collected the Licorne D'Or award for best actor in a horror film (for *Tales from the Crypt*) and a special award for his horror film work over the last decade. While in France he visited the Riviera to film the location work for an episode of ITC's adventure series *The Zoo Gang* entitled *The Counterfeit Trap*. Here Cushing played another Frenchman, Judge Gautier, who has fallen on hard times. He is painfully insecure about his much younger wife (played by Jacqueline Pearce) and becomes involved with a smuggling ring to keep her in luxury. The episode was directed by John Hough (from *Twins of Evil*) and the regular cast of *The Zoo Gang* included John Mills and Barry Morse.

On 14 May, Cushing began work at Twickenham Studios on *Madhouse*, an Amicus production based on Angus Hall's novel *Devilday* and directed by Jim Clark. Filmed under the rather more evocative title *The Revenge of Dr Death* it featured Cushing as Herbert Flay, an embittered screenwriter and former actor. Flay plots a diabolical revenge on horror star Paul Toombes (played by Vincent Price) whom he believes has robbed him of the chance of stardom in the role of 'Dr Death'. When a figure dressed up as the Dr Death character begins committing murders, Toombes is a suspect but Flay is the killer all along. The film is peppered with clips from Roger Corman's Poe movies (starring Price), features several grisly deaths and a climactic fight between Flay and Toombes which Cushing described as 'a titanic ding-dong'[15] and which finishes with Flay tumbling into a tank of spiders. 'It was me,' Cushing told his American fan club, 'and I like spiders.'[16]

Perhaps *Madhouse* is an appropriate title after all for a film which involves everybody in an inordinate amount of running around. Because Cushing is the real villain of the piece, he plays it very quietly while the many red herring characters (including Robert Quarry, who became friends with Cushing during the filming) go hell-for-leather. Location filming was carried out at Pyrford House in Surrey (for Flay's mansion) and at the London Weekend Television Studios on London's South Bank. The BBC's cinema programme *Film 73* featured a behind-the-scenes item on the filming of *Madhouse*, with director Jim Clark, Cushing and Price. Clark acknowledged his debt to the 'gods' of the horror genre, Tod Browning and James Whale, and said of his stars 'One couldn't work with easier people. They respond marvellously to direction and know instinctively what to do. They're both extraordinarily pleasant people anyway, and one is terribly lucky to have them.' Price revealed that at the time he was 'very anxious to do a ...thriller for children, where there is no blood, but with all the marvellous old things like creaking doors... Kids are

the biggest audience in the world.' 'Look how they love *Doctor Who*!' Cushing chips in. 'Do you know it? We did two films and it's been such a success on television.'

While shooting *Madhouse*, Cushing took part in an episode of Price's BBC radio anthology *The Price of Fear*. Entitled *The Man Who Hated Scenes* and recorded on 16 June 1973, the story presented Cushing as a cuckolded husband again, a timid man who will go to any lengths to avoid a 'scene' but who nevertheless takes an appalling revenge on his adulterous wife. The radio work reveals a rapport between Cushing and Price which is perhaps not apparent in their film work.

On 14 May, Cushing wrote from Twickenham Studios, in reply to an invitation from Kay Evans, producer of *Woman's Hour*, to be guest of the week on 20 June. 'My belovèd wife derived so much enjoyment from *Woman's Hour* over the years and so did I. I am currently engaged on two films with overlapping schedules – either one could require my services on 20 June. Hope I will be free!' Kay Evans was prepared, if need be, to record the interview 'between shots at the studio'. Cushing wrote again from the Royal Station Hotel in Hull on 3 June to inform her that he would be at Shepperton Studios on 20 June (filming *From Beyond The Grave*).

The interview was recorded at Broadcasting House on 18 June with presenter Sue MacGregor and was clearly an emotional experience. 'Dear Miss MacGregor,' wrote Cushing the following day, 'thank you for your compassionate interest in the interview. I do hope the end result is what you desired.'

In Amicus's film *From Beyond the Grave*, a weird curio shop called Temptations Antiques provides the linking device for the four stories, and in his role as the proprietor of this emporium, Cushing has excellent co-stars like Ian Carmichael, Ian Bannen and David Warner to play against. This is one of the strongest Amicus portmanteau films, directed by Kevin Connor and based on stories by R Chetwynd Hayes.

Cushing as the exceedingly odd proprietor of Temptations Antiques with unwary customer William Seaton (Ian Ogilvy) in *From Beyond the Grave* (1973)

As David Warner enters the shop to buy an old mirror, Cushing appears from out of the knick-knacks in bushy eyebrows, wielding a crocodile and a peculiar Northern accent. '250 pound...' he drawls, sucking on his pipe, 'a *gen-you-wine* antique...' Warner knocks him down, swindling the old man, and

Professor Lundgren prepares to hunt the Beast, watched by Davina Gilmore (Ciaran Madden), in *The Beast Must Die* (1973)

as a result, meets a grisly end. The extravagantly made-up Cushing appears even more goblin-like when seen through a wreath of smoke or the dimpled glass of the shop-window. 'You have *cer-tiffy-cate*?' he enquires of Ian Bannen, who is attempting to buy himself a Victoria Cross. 'Otherwise every Tom Dick and Harry would be after one, and that wouldn't be *fur*, would it?' Bannen nips back and steals the medal anyway. Cushing is unimpressed. '*Naughty...*' he tuts to himself. 'Shouldn't have done that...' And Bannen duly receives his comeuppance. For Ian Carmichael, who swindles him out of a silver snuff-box, Cushing has the glorious parting shot 'I hope you enjoy snuffing it!'

On 12 July 1973, John Redway wrote to BBC producer Anthony Cornish about a radio script by Brian Hayles called *Lord Dracula*. 'Peter Cushing thought it very good and even talks about it as the basis for "a splendid, definitive Dracula epic film". He would be interested to take it further as a radio series.' Later, it was proposed that the script be reworked as a one-off *Saturday Night Theatre* production, but by this time Cushing was no longer involved. Hayles had provided the script for *Nothing But The Night*, and later wrote *Arabian Adventure*. Hammer reworked the story as a screenplay called *Vlad the Impaler* which

spent over 20 years in the development wilderness, never to be produced.

On 16 July 1973, Cushing began work on Amicus's werewolf film *The Beast Must Die*. This was directed by Paul Annett and starred Calvin Lockhart as millionaire big game hunter Tom Newcliffe, who invites a disparate group to his country estate knowing that one of them is a werewolf. Cushing plays Doctor Christopher Lundgren, a Norwegian expert on werewolf lore, and is required to deliver a lengthy, dull treatise – most of it nonsensical – about the lymphatic system and the science of werewolfism. Calvin Lockhart is powerful and enigmatic, but even he has little to do. The film features some agonisingly poor day-for-night shooting, a considerable amount of running around and an embarrassingly fake-looking werewolf played by a large dog. The film features a 'werewolf break' – a gimmick like those used by the horror film huckster William Castle – which serves only to protract the agony. Cushing, with no character to fall back on, seems unsettled and out of place, although as usual, his script was covered with annotations. 'Be – don't act, eyes up – don't look aslant or down. Smile when I can.' The following month he would be back on fine form, in 1815 costume, in a segment of the *Orson Welles Great Mysteries* TV series called *La Grande Breteche*.

Chapter Twenty-Two

Treading Time

Orson Welles Great Mysteries was a collection of 25 half-hour stories produced in the UK by Anglia Television, with guest stars including Claire Bloom, Donald Pleasence, Dean Stockwell and Christopher Lee. Orson Welles' role in the series was merely to loom into view in the pre-filmed introductory sequences which were shot in Paris by Peter Bogdanovich. *La Grande Breteche* is the story of Count Gerard de Merret (Cushing) and his faithless wife Josephine (Susannah York) who is having an affair with a Spanish prisoner from the Napoleonic war. Knowing that Josephine's lover is hiding in her closet, the Count makes her swear on a crucifix that the cupboard is empty, then proceeds to have it bricked up. The story, which recalls Poe's favourite theme of burial alive, was adapted from Balzac by Martin Worth and the director was Peter Sasdy, who the previous year had worked with Cushing on *Nothing But The Night*.

Again Cushing's physical appearance is startling. His Regency coat hangs on his frail shoulders, his skin is almost transparent and his cheeks are quite hollow. But even in a half-hour playlet, he was mindful of his character's motivation. 'Get across love for Josephine' he wrote on his *Grande Breteche* script, 'and the reason for his great jealousy.' He annotated the script with a wealth of detail, including three watercolour drawings of costumes from 1815 and sketches on how to tie a cravat and how to wear and carry a bicorne hat. His list of personal props includes gloves and cane and a fob-watch and winding-key, many of which he provided himself.

By 1973, Hammer were finding money difficult to come by from their English and American backers. With hopes of making inroads into the successful kung-fu genre, chairman Michael Carreras struck a co-production deal with the Shaw Brothers of Hong Kong for two films, to be made in the colony. In his position as Hammer's remaining trump card, Cushing was contracted to appear in both, playing Van Helsing in *The Legend of the 7 Golden Vampires* and British agent Rattwood in the kung-fu thriller *Shatter*.

Before he left for Hong Kong, Cushing was involved in Carreras' plans to create a Hammer museum. Cushing's famous model-building skills were to be showcased prominently, and he was asked to produce a series of 1:24 scale tableaux representing Dracula's castle, two prehistoric scenes and the vampires' temple from *7 Golden Vampires*. The deadlines were very tight and Cushing worked for five weeks on the first model, which was the temple. Cardboard, paper and balsa wood were the principal materials, with a variety of nails, nuts and washers used for fixtures and fittings. Cushing was determined not to let Carreras down, and became so completely preoccupied with the project that he worked all day and frequently all of the night. When the model was completed he had to burn his clothes. Sadly, the plans for the museum came to nothing and the other models were never made. A full-sized wax model of Cushing as Baron Frankenstein was later featured in an exhibition co-organised by Carreras and mounted in the cellars of the London Palladium. Cushing admitted that he would not go to see his effigy, because 'I'd be too embarrassed!'[1]

The Legend of the 7 Golden Vampires began filming on 22 October 1973 on location in Hong Kong and at the Shaw Brothers' studios. The director was Roy Ward Baker, working on his final Hammer assignment.

China, 1904. While giving a lecture in Chung King University, Professor Laurence Van Helsing meets Hsi Ching (David Chiang), a young man whose ancestral village of Ping Kuei is at the mercy of the legendary seven golden vampires. Van Helsing joins an expedition to Ping Kuei, financed by the wealthy Vanessa Buren (Julie Ege) but discovers an old foe – Count Dracula (John Forbes-Robertson) – controlling the vampires and zombies that plague the region.

The Legend of the 7 Golden Vampires has many powerful and strange moments, and Cushing brings his usual quiet dignity to the bizarre conclusion of the Hammer Dracula cycle. But the film was made under the most extreme circumstances, as Roy Ward Baker told *Shivers* magazine: 'It could have been much better. Michael Carreras was in charge and was trying to freshen it up – very bold and praiseworthy – but the whole set-up was slip-shod and nobody knew what anyone was doing. The Shaw Brothers' studios weren't soundproofed. They were huge but they were made of corrugated iron ... and nobody had thought it through whether to shoot direct sound or dub it all afterwards ... The film was a failure, an absolute failure.' Baker

Van Helsing journeys to the village of Ping Kuei with kung-fu fighting vampire slayer Mai Kwei (Shih Szu) in *The Legend of the 7 Golden Vampires*

had some praise for Cushing, however. 'I made several films with Peter and he was an absolute charmer. Before his appearance in every scene, he would check how he was dressed, what he had in his pockets. Meticulous detail. He was very straightforward, but strait-laced, I'd say. A nice person who made a career by specialising, and what he did he was very good at.'[2]

This Edwardian incarnation of Van Helsing contradicts Hammer's continuity (he was supposed to have died in 1872), but the Professor has lost none of his old vampire-hunting zeal. In his grey wig and russetty velvet coat, however, Cushing is charmingly like a rather more sober Doctor Who. He doesn't drop a stitch here, though, and while slighter in frame, is no different from the Van Helsing of *The Brides of Dracula*. Cushing is at his best in the quiet scenes, musing by the campfire over whether he has been sent by divine intervention, or feeling a prickly sensation in his neck when evil is approaching.

The scenes of corpses pulling themselves out of the grave are very good indeed, owing much to the Chinese tradition of 'hopping' vampires, and there is something unsettling about the mixture of styles. However, the muddle of religion and vampirology gives rise to some amusing conjecture. 'They abhor anything which has a holy significance,' Van Helsing explains. 'In Europe, the vampire walks in dread of the crucifix, here it would be the image of the Lord Buddha.' Thankfully he was not called upon to knock two candlesticks together and make one of those.

As the battle gets underway, Van Helsing grabs a flaming brand and has a go at the vampires himself. Cushing falls into a bonfire at one point, which looks exceptionally dangerous. The stunt is cut short on screen, and looks alarmingly impromptu. Otherwise, Cushing seems to be enjoying himself in the lengthy fight sequences, punctuating the martial arts mayhem with shouts of advice – 'strike at their hearts!'

The chief let-down in the film is the representation of Dracula. The Shaw Brothers insisted that the Count was included simply for the box-office, but the character is shoddily represented and given nothing

A warm greeting for an old friend as Cushing appears on Christopher Lee's *This Is Your Life* (1974)

Morse. Guest stars for the series included Joan Collins, Christopher Lee, Roy Dotrice and Leo McKern. Cushing played Raan, an ancient alien, with Joanna Dunham as his daughter Vana.

Cushing admitted that he did not read science fiction, but he seemed to enjoy playing it, and he was doubtless attracted to the role of Raan, a 508-year-old scientist who lives in a city made of light. Raan is described in Edward Di Lorenzo's script as 'an interesting character... on the surface he is all charm and rather amusing. However, there is an underlying menace about him – it is not intentional, but nevertheless it weaves through his words somewhat like a surgeon describing the operation to a patient before actually performing it.' Raan intends to study Koenig as an example of the missing link between primitive man and his civilisation, but Vana will not let her father experiment on a living specimen. 'The perfect balance between thought and feeling must be found,' Raan admits. 'Both our worlds have yet to discover it.' Cushing's costume for Raan consisted of a diaphanous gown and a long white wig, and the make-up used a heavy gold face-paint which proved very difficult to remove.

Cushing was back in more familiar costume, and on fine form in his second Tyburn film, *The Legend of the Werewolf*, as Paul Cataflanque, police pathologist and amateur detective. The film was directed by Freddie Francis from 19 August 1974 at Pinewood Studios co-starring Ron Moody, Roy Castle and Hugh Griffith.

Cushing seems to be enjoying himself enormously – almost all of his scenes, until the last, have a ghoulish humour about them. It is never forced, it is just a witty, clever, concentrated performance. Cataflanque is eating his tea as the newest cadaver is brought in. 'Ooh dear,' Cushing clucks, with his mouth full, peering under the sheet, 'that's very nasty...' He gets rid of his pompous superiors by mischievously presenting them with a gullet and when he does a bit of undercover research in the local brothel he is left bashfully holding a frilly garter. Perhaps his best one-liner is his resigned 'C'est la vie' as he destroys his silver walking-stick handle to make a silver bullet. David Rintoul plays the wolf-boy Etoile, whose torment at becoming a werewolf is carefully presented.

Unfortunately, though beautifully shot in parts, *The Legend of the Werewolf* is a clumsy, haphazardly-plotted film, over reliant on repetitive red-filtered werewolf's-point-of-view shots. The film has much in common with its stablemate *The Ghoul*, but Cushing seems much happier than he was in that film, and his performance as Cataflanque is one of his most enjoyable in the 1970s, a classic example of the actor being a great deal better than the lines he is given to say.

After the collapse of the Hammer museum project, Michael Carreras was busy looking for other outlets for the Hammer name. He followed the lead of another

asked Freddie Francis, the director, if we could use some photographs of Helen, and he thought it a marvellous idea. They blew them up and sepia'd them, and had these marvellous close-ups of Helen ... So at last we made a film together.'[6]

Quite whether this blurring of art and life was a sensible idea or not is debatable. Veronica Carlson recalls that when Cushing had to deliver the lines about Mrs Lawrence's death, he was so overcome that he broke down in tears and had to leave the set. 'I wanted to go up to him and just give him a hug,' says Carlson. 'But you couldn't. He wanted to be on his own.'[7] Watching Cushing as he breathes the line ' My wife is dead...', there is the uneasy feeling that his very private grief was being rather cynically exploited, but he went on record in *Past Forgetting* to say how enormously grateful he was to Kevin Francis for his continued support, and actor and producer enjoyed a warm friendship until Cushing's death.

Also during *The Ghoul*, Cushing appeared with Carlson on a *This Is Your Life* programme to pay tribute to Christopher Lee. Other guests included Vincent Price, Oliver Reed and Trevor Howard and the programme was broadcast on 3 April 1974. At Easter, Cushing followed the lead of Spike Milligan and Cliff Richard to appear on a late-night religious programme called *What Was He Like?*, explaining his own interpretation of the life of Christ. There were also appearances on the BBC's *Film 74* and *Horizon* programmes.

In May 1974, at Pinewood Studios, Cushing starred in an episode of Gerry and Sylvia Anderson's big-budget science-fiction series *Space: 1999* entitled *Missing Link*. The series starred Martin Landau as Commander Koenig with Barbara Bain and Barry

great British institution, the *Carry On* films, and began plans for a theatre show. When the popularity of the *Carry Ons* in cinemas began to wane, producer Peter Rogers staged *Carry On London*, which enjoyed a successful run at the Victoria Palace Theatre in London in 1973. A Hammer stage show might have been a going concern if Cushing had participated, but he wrote an apologetic letter to Carreras on 25 April 1975. 'My dear Michael, John Redway has told me of your kind thought regarding your new venture, and I want you to know how much I appreciated it. But I'm afraid the 'legitimate' theatre is now a thing of the past as far as I'm concerned. Many years ago, it was part cause of a nervous breakdown I had, which – perforce – kept me out of work for nearly twelve months. I have of course, been on the stage many times since then and each occasion was anathema to me. I wish you good luck and great success in all you assay.' The letter was signed 'Helen and Peter'. At this time, Cushing was also offered the role of Sherlock Holmes in a Broadway production of *The Crucifer of Blood*, based on *The Sign of Four*, which he also declined.

From the beginning of June 1975, New York independent filmmaker Ken Wiederhorn made a $300,000 film provisionally called *Death Corps* – later retitled *Shock Waves* – shot on 16mm and blown up to 35mm. Wiederhorn, who with partner/producer Reuben Trane had won an Oscar in 1973 for the Best Dramatic Student Film, sought advice on making a low-budget horror film from producer Richard Gordon, who had made *Island of Terror*. Gordon recommended Cushing, who readily agreed – 'I felt if my name could help them at all, it would be a good thing to do.'[8] Cushing's four days of shooting took him to Florida's Biscayne Bay, where he kept a low-key presence on set, making coffee for the cast and crew and helping the ladies in the cast through the swamp.

The film stars Brooke Adams as Rose, who joins a group of friends to charter a seedy yacht for a cruise (The boat's curmudgeonly captain is played by John Carradine). One night the boat is rammed by the hulk of a freighter which has run aground near a small island. Exploring the island, the friends discover an abandoned hotel, whose single inhabitant keeps the secret of a bizarre Nazi experiment from the Second World War.

As the classical music from a gramophone bleeds through the colonnades of the deserted villa and slurs to a halt, Cushing's voice rings out 'Why have you

In *Trial by Combat* (1975) Ben Willoughby (Neil McCarthy) and Sir Edward Gifford educate the young John Gifford (Marc Harrison) in the ways of chivalry

come to this place?' It is an entrance to match Christopher Lee's in *Dracula*. In a gently lilting German accent, he continues, 'I am waiting. You will please answer my question.' Cushing here plays a strange and sinewy figure, but an undeniably powerful one, even in his ragged clothes and filthy neckerchief. He is surprisingly athletic too – as can be seen when he sprints across the beach later in the film. He is made-up with a livid scar across his forehead and right eye. This weird recluse is a former SS commandant, who was in charge of a division of troops which were surgically altered to exist underwater, to crew submarines which would never have to surface. 'They were the most vicious and bloodthirsty of all the SS divisions,' the commandant explains. 'We created the perfect soldier from cheap hoodlums and thugs and a good number of pathological murderers and sadists as well. We called them the *Toten Corps* – the Death Corps – creatures more horrible than any you can imagine. Not dead, not alive, but somewhere in between.'

The collision with the cruiser has awakened the Death Corps, who stride across the seabed toward the island. The underwater scenes of the zombies (photographed by Irving Pare) have a balletic grace and a fairy tale otherworldliness. These sequences, accompanied by discordant synthesized score (by Richard Einhorn) are as compelling as any Hammer scene and the albino zombies, with their pallid, goggled faces, were described by *Fangoria* as 'one of the best monster gangs to come down the pike in a long time'.[9] Some of the acting, however, is unintentionally hilarious and the zombie who pursues and finally drowns the commandant looks suspiciously like David Hockney. But *Shock Waves* is not a bad film, and prefigures many of the late 1970s horrors. The commandant provides Cushing with a chance to play a menacing character, but one who is haunted by a terror from the past. His tiny, guilty glance to the swastika banners that decorate his retreat is exceptional. It is one of his last really satisfying horror roles.

On his return to Britain, Cushing was to have starred in a film version of Dennis Wheatley's *The Satanist* for Tyburn, with a planned cast including Shirley Bassey and Orson Welles. This film fell through at the last minute, so Cushing was able to film two cameo scenes as Sir Edward Gifford in Kevin Connor's film *Trial by Combat*. The film stars Donald Pleasence as the leader of the Knights of the Order of

Ebullient director Costas Carayiannis with Cushing, Donald Pleasence, Luan Peters and Costa Skouras during the filming of *The Devil's Men* (1975)

Avalon, who recreate medieval jousts in full armour. But these displays have nothing to do with pageantry – the knights of the order are being used as a kind of vigilante group, bringing 'justice' to criminals who have escaped the law. Director Connor was obviously keen to work with Cushing again after *From Beyond the Grave*, it is a shame, however, that he could not be given more to do. Sir Edward is effectively the embodiment of the knights' true code and as such is seen off even before the credits have run. Cushing appears later in a flashback, as Sir Edward's son remembers how his father taught him fencing and the importance of chivalry. The film features John Mills as the unconventional ex-Scotland Yard man Bertie Cook, and with knights on horseback seeing off underworld criminals, has the feel of an extended episode of *The Avengers*.

Cushing made several appearances on television in 1975. He appeared on *The Amazing World of Cinema* in a show entitled *The Mad Scientists* for VPS/Polymedia. He was also a guest on *Looks Familiar*, the nostalgic quiz game hosted by Denis Norden in which a panel of celebrities recall personalities, films and events from the early part of the century. Cushing also provided the on-screen narration for Paul Annett's documentary on the supposedly-haunted *Herstmonceaux Castle*.

Despite telling Michael Carreras that his career in the 'legitimate' theatre was over, in October Cushing took one last turn on the boards to pay tribute to a favourite actress. He had watched and enjoyed the television series *Edward the Seventh*, starring Timothy West, and he was particularly taken with the actress Helen Ryan's portrayal of Princess Alexandra. 'Miss Ryan,' he wrote 'played the royal personage as if she had lived and breathed and had her being during that

period of ... history. I was deeply impressed by this remarkable recreation and wrote her a fan letter.'[10]

Ryan was married to Guy Slater, who was about to start a season as director of the Horseshoe Theatre in Basingstoke. Cushing suggested that they open their season with *The Heiress*, a play by Ruth and Augustus Goetz, based on *Washington Square* by Henry James. Set in 1850, the play tells the story of the dominating Doctor Austin Sloper (Cushing) and his awkward daughter Catherine (Ryan), and her one chance for escape and fulfilment with former playboy Morris Townsend. Is he the reformed character and honourable suitor he claims to be, or is he merely after her money?

The Heiress played to full houses between 21 October and 1 November 1975 and Cushing stated that the few weeks he spent on the production were the happiest he had spent since 1971. Helen Ryan remembers 'Peter was wonderful, super in the play, but he was so terribly nervous. The play opened at 7.30 and Peter would be at the theatre three hours beforehand to check his props and his costume.'[11]

Later in November, Cushing was the star guest at 'Monstercon', a New York event run by horror fan and *Famous Monsters of Filmland* editor Forrest J Ackerman. This gave many American fans their first chance to meet Cushing in person. Ingrid Pitt and Michael Carreras were also guests, and Pitt remembers Carreras taking herself and Cushing to a jazz club where Carreras displayed his exceptional talent for playing the trumpet. At the convention, Carreras unveiled plans for a new Hammer film based on the comic strip *Vampirella*, to star Cushing, directed by John Hough. This, like so many Hammer plans at the time, never came to fruition. While in America, Cushing made a guest appearance with Ackerman on

Tom Snyder's *Tomorrow* TV programme in New York. They were joined by Professor Leonard Wolfe, author of *The Annotated Dracula*, who dominated the conversation. Although Snyder had little knowledge of the genre, Cushing played along cheerfully, and rightly scoffed at Wolfe's theories of the sexual connotations of vampire-staking.

Shortly afterwards, Cushing went to Greece to film *The Devil's Men*. This muddled story of ancient rites and blood sacrifice was directed by Costas Carayiannis with Donald Pleasence, Luan Peters and Nikos Vewrlekis, with Cushing as the occultist Baron Corofax, a nobleman from Dracula's homeland of Carpathia. Corofax is sinister and severe, but Cushing seems far too noble to be a villain. He is given little to do, but maintains a great stillness when delivering his lines, giving them a subtle, implied menace. 'I have little in common with the local people...' he coos to the heroine, Laurie Gordon (Luan Peters). 'I am an exile – you being an American will find that hard to understand.' Pleasence plays Corofax's opponent, the Van Helsing figure Father Roche – a sympathetic, heroic priest with a core of steel.

The sound in the film is hollow and indistinct, the photography clumsy and the script feeble. The camera prowls around picture-postcard ruins, underscored by Brian Eno's unsettling synthesised score and far too much is made of the pagan idol, a pint-sized statue of a minotaur with two gas-burners up its nose. There are several big close-ups of Cushing's green-tinted face, shot through distorted lens, and he looks formidable striding through the caves in his crimson robes. 'The old customs remain,' he intones endlessly, 'and the ancient gods live on.'

Corofax's invulnerable disciples cannot be killed even by the force of an oncoming car, but in a nice reversal of fortune, Cushing is stopped in his tracks when Pleasence brandishes a crucifix. In a final insane twist, Corofax and his people are sprinkled with holy water and literally explode. The film could have done with more touches like this earlier on. Only three years later, John Carpenter made *Halloween* with a teen heroine, an unstoppable robot-like killer and a synthesized score. He wanted Peter Cushing too, for the lead role of psychiatrist Doctor Loomis but Cushing turned the role down, as did Christopher Lee – although Lee later admitted this was a mistake. The part of Loomis went to Donald Pleasence, but it would have been interesting if Cushing had completely made the transition from old horror to the new. He had gone some way with *Shock Waves* and *The Devil's Men*, although it was clear that this new style wasn't really *his* style.

Back in England after Christmas, Cushing was filming from 20 January 1976 in an AIP/Amicus co-production based on Edgar Rice Burroughs' *At the Earth's Core*. The director was Kevin Connor again. Cushing plays the eccentric Doctor Abner Perry, who has invented a fantastic burrowing machine, nicknamed the 'Iron Mole', with which he intends to drill through a Welsh hillside. We first see Perry in his dust-coat supervising the building of the machine, when Cushing somehow manages to sum up the inventor's whole character with a little wave of encouragement.

The mole is launched and immediately goes out of control, depositing Perry and his American backer David (Doug McClure) in a palaeolithic jungle with a pink sky. ('The land of pink jelly' the *Evening Standard* called it.) It might as well have been another world and Doctor Who's TARDIS that took them there. Cushing all but repeats his Doctor Who performance, and he is the right age to be convincingly doddery now. 'This cannot be the Rhondda valley', Perry mutters gravely, before declaring 'David, we are not *on* Earth ... from my observations, dear friend, I can positively state that we are *under* it – at the Earth's core!' As they dismount the Mole and explore the new terrain, Perry and David are interrupted by the appearance of an enormous dinosaur, of the man-in-a-rubber-suit variety, which lumbers about on a back-projection screen while Cushing and McClure charge about in the foreground. Escaping the beast, David and Perry are captured and imprisoned by a group of vicious, pig-faced creatures called Sagoths.

Producer John Dark with Cushing on the set of *At the Earth's Core* (1976)

'They're so excitable...' says Perry, 'like all foreigners.' (As the Sagoth guard approaches later, Cushing, clearly ad-libbing, clucks 'Oh no, here comes cheerful Annie again!') The travellers meet fellow captives Ghak (Godfrey James) and Dia (Caroline Munro) who tell them that the land is called Pellucidar, and it is ruled by the Mahars, a savage race of telepathic reptile-birds. Soon Perry and David are leading the rebellion against the Mahars and the scenes of Cushing drilling the Pellucidans in archery are delightfully funny. So too is his line, delivered into the impassive milky eye of the chief Mahar, 'You cannot mesmerise me, I'm British!' The *Standard* concluded that the film-makers should have 'success with the wide-eyed child that is in all of us.'[12] while the *Telegraph* praised the 'often very funny Peter Cushing.'[13]

'You'll have to kill me first...' Doctor Mebach Von Claus contemplates the immortality of evil in *The New Avengers: The Eagle's Nest* (1976)

Milton Subotsky's name is down as screenwriter, but Cushing recalled that (as ever with Amicus) there wasn't much of a script. He had to make up his own lines – chiefly 'By jove!' or shouts for help from the thick of various predicaments. Mike Vickers creates a score of electronic bleeps and burbles and a stirring orchestral theme, ideal for this sort of scientific romance. Quite what veteran cinematographer Alan Hume – who had photographed many Cushing films – thought of filming this tomfoolery is not recorded.

However, there is still something wonderfully nostalgic in this very British genre of brass-bound Victorian derring-do, which was all but obliterated by the coming of *Star Wars*. There was even the potential for a sequel in Perry's innocent enquiry to David 'Have you ever thought of going to the moon?' When the film was released at end of July in time for the school summer holidays, Thames TV's cinema programme for children *Clapperboard* dedicated a whole show to behind-the-scenes footage from *At the Earth's Core*.

In 1975, producers Brian Clemens and Albert Fennell had made a deal with French television backer to bring *The Avengers* back to the screen after a break of nearly seven years. *The Satanic Rites of Dracula*'s Joanna Lumley was the new *Avengers* girl, with Gareth Hunt on hand for the fisticuffs, as Patrick Macnee, now 53, was considered to be too old for that kind of thing. The series went under the title of *The New Avengers*, but in most respects, the old order was unchanged. Clemens wasted no time in inviting Cushing back as a guest star for the first episode of his new series, *The Eagle's Nest* which was filmed in April on location on the Isle of Skye and at Pinewood studios. 'It was sad to see how fragile Peter was,' Clemens remembers. 'He told me he was just treading time until he could join his wife.'[14]

Cushing plays Doctor Mebach Von Claus, an eminent German scientist whose field of expertise is suspended animation. It's a gently humorous performance, and there is a good deal of fun with a deep-frozen frog called Albert in a scene that recalls a similar revivification in *The Curse of Frankenstein*. Von Claus is kidnapped and taken to the Scottish island of St Dorca, where Father Trasker (Derek Farr) leads a group of Nazis disguised as monks. Von Claus is asked to attend to a sick member of the order who has been placed in cryogenic suspension, little suspecting he is part of a plot to resurrect the greatest evil of the Twentieth Century – Adolf Hitler.

To leaven the wilder excesses of the plot, there is some artfully-played comedy that shows the series is back on top form. Joanna Lumley shares a beautiful scene with Sydney Bromley (as the bewildered old local who saw Hitler's plane come down) while Macnee interrupts a squadron of jackbooted, saluting Nazis with a hopeful 'Rule Britannia?' *The Eagle's Nest* is a more complex piece of work than *Return of the Cybernauts*, the action more realistic and less cartoonish. Von Claus is beaten up savagely – and gives a reaction of genuine horror when he discovers that the monks have nothing less than Hitler's body in suspended animation and need Von Claus to revive him. 'It is hideous! Obscene!' Cushing spits, on seeing the Fuhrer's face for the fist time. 'You'll have to kill me first...'

It was rarely easy for Cushing to discern, on the studio floor, the fate of the film he was making. Occasionally, he had been upset when he felt that the context of his performances had been changed (*Corruption*, for example) and he even maintained that *The Curse of Frankenstein* could have been 'another picture that came and went and nobody took any notice.'[15] What importance did he place, then, on one week's filming at the beginning of May 1976 on a children's science fantasy adventure? The sets were small and the young American leads were homesick and disgruntled at their lack of direction. But from its troubled beginnings, the film became one of the biggest cinema sensations of all time. That film was *Star Wars*.

Chapter Twenty-Three

Still Dancin'

Cushing did have an inkling of what to expect from *Star Wars*, perhaps. 'I thought the kids would adore it'[1] he said. He was not wrong. A lot of kids adored it very much indeed. And a lot of adults too.

With *Star Wars*, George Lucas – who wrote, produced and directed – changed the face of filmmaking. The movie became one of the highest-grossing pictures of all time, and audiences came to expect action and spectacle. The developments in special effects required for the film set new standards for the industry, and John Williams' sweeping orchestral score raised the film soundtrack to the status of classical music.

The adventures of young farmboy Luke Skywalker (Mark Hamill), 'a long time ago, in a galaxy far, far away....' have become a modern myth. Luke dreams of leaving the desert planet Tatooine and joining the rebellion against the oppressive forces of the evil Galactic Empire. He acquires two robots which have escaped from a rebel ship – one of them, R2-D2, is carrying the plans to the Empire's secret weapon, a massive battle station of terrifying power called the Death Star. Luke's journey sees him join forces with the exiled Jedi knight Obi-Wan Kenobi (Alec Guinness) and the space pirate Han Solo (Harrison Ford) to face the evil Darth Vader.

In his script, originally entitled *The Star Wars*, Lucas mixed elements of classic fairy-tale and Arthurian legend with knowing cinematic references. He assembled elements from all his favourite childhood films – the dog-fights from *Tora! Tora! Tora!*, the cliffhangers from *Flash Gordon*, the bar-room brawl from any number of Westerns. And the golden age of horror was represented by Peter Cushing.

Lucas originally considered Cushing for the role of Obi-Wan Kenobi before deciding that his lean features would be better employed as the villain, Grand Moff Tarkin. ('I've often wondered what a "Grand Moff" was,' said Cushing later. 'It sounds like something that flew out of a cupboard.'[2]) Tarkin is a charming and calculating villain, at his best in a confrontation with Carrie Fisher as Princess Leia. 'Governor Tarkin,' she spits. 'I recognised your foul stench when I was brought on board.' 'Charming to the last,' replies Tarkin. 'You don't know how hard I found it signing the order to terminate your life.'

Tarkin's second-in-command is the Sith Lord Darth Vader, a character who would achieve greater significance as the *Star Wars* trilogy continued. Here, though, Tarkin exerts some control over Vader – with a word, he stops him from telepathically throttling an underling and Leia observes that Tarkin is 'holding Vader's leash'. By an occasional haunted glance, however, Cushing is able to imply that Vader holds the real power, and Tarkin is uneasy in his presence. Thus both characters are made more frightening.

'Peter Cushing is a very good actor...' George Lucas said in an interview for *Rolling Stone* magazine. 'Adored and idolised by young people and by people who go to see a certain kind of movie. I feel he will be fondly remembered for the next 350 years at least.'[3] Cushing was fondly remembered by everyone who worked with him on *Star Wars*, including *Monster From Hell* David Prowse (Darth Vader), Don Henderson (General Tagge) and Leslie Schofield (Imperial Commander). Carrie Fisher remembers that Cushing was very kind to her, giving her the benefit of his years of experience in film acting.

There is a final shot of Tarkin, a split second before Luke and his friends destroy the Death Star, as he stands alone, having refused to abandon the station 'in our moment of triumph'. With his hand at his mouth, he is almost chewing his nails. In his moment of quiet terror, we see the humanity of the monster – classic Cushing.

Cushing's filming at the EMI-Elstree Studios (formerly MGM-EMI) was sandwiched between *The New Avengers* and flying to America for a cameo in the TV miniseries *The Great Houdinis*. Like all the 'guest stars' apart from Guinness, Cushing was on a specially arranged flat fee for *Star Wars* of £1000 for the week, and he received no further payment.

'One spares a grain of compassion for Grand Moff Tarkin, Governor of the Imperial Outlands, despite his unconscionable villainy,' said *Films and Filming*, 'simply because he is so excellently played by the immaculately-spoken Peter Cushing, who regardless of their cross purposes in the plot, seems in effect to share with Guinness a Movement Towards The Perpetuation Of Clear Speech.'[4]

General Tagge (Don Henderson), Darth Vader (David Prowse) and a contemplative Governor Tarkin aboard the Death Star in *Star Wars* (1976)

Cushing's chief memory of *Star Wars* was the trouble with his boots. Close to the opening of *Star Wars*, the *Evening News* revealed: 'The reason Peter Cushing's size twelves led to a knees-up', accompanied by a helpful picture of the Cushing feet. 'Sharp-eyed cinema-goers may note, when the fabulously successful film *Star Wars* opens here at Christmas, that Peter Cushing only ever appears on screen filmed from the knees up. The reason is that wafer-thin Mr Cushing – he is six feet tall but weighs only nine stone – has such enormous feet that the film's wardrobe department was unable to cater for him. As the Grand Moff Tarkin ... the man who made horror respectable was supposed to wear proper dictator-style riding-boots and the wardrobe duly supplied a pair of size nines. "But alas, I have taken a size twelve since my youth," Cushing said. "When I crammed on the size nine boots I could hardly walk. So I persuaded the director George Lucas to shoot me from the knees up – which meant I could wear comfy plimsolls." Surprisingly, Mr Cushing's partner in horror, Mr Christopher Lee, who can give him a good four inches in height, takes only a size eleven – and a *narrow* at that.'[5] For the record, Cushing is seen wearing the boots in one brief long-shot.

Between 12 – 15 May Cushing was in Hollywood, invited by 20th Century-Fox to appear in *The Great Houdinis*, a TV movie on the life of the celebrated illusionist Harry Houdini. *Starsky and Hutch*'s Paul Michael Glaser played Houdini, with Ruth Gordon, Wilfred Hyde-White, Bill Bixby, Vivian Vance, Sally Struthers and Clive Revell. Cushing played Sir Arthur Conan Doyle – the *Sherlock Holmes* author who investigated spiritualism and the occult with Houdini – while Maureen O'Sullivan played Doyle's wife.

Cushing arrived in America on Tuesday 11 May and was called the following day at 7.00 am. 12 May was Wilfred Hyde-White's birthday, which was celebrated with a party on set at which Cushing cut the cake. On 13 May scenes were filmed in a prison cell set on Stage 20 at the Fox studios. By this time, the film was over budget and behind schedule due to problems with a séance sequence, and work went on until midnight on all of Cushing's filming days. Behind the scenes, Cushing once again chatted to his American fans, recalling his days on stage with Tod Slaughter in *The Gay Invalid* and his recent experience in *Tendre Dracula* while revealing his fondness for buckwheat pancakes.

At this time, the American Peter Cushing Club Journal featured a revealing section in which Cushing answered readers' questions. In a simple question and answer fashion, Cushing gave brief responses on a host of subjects. He seemed to find the questionnaires taxing, would rarely be drawn on a particular topic but by his occasionally terse replies would often say much by saying nothing. As witnessed here –

Is humour an important ingredient in a horror film? 'It is an important ingredient in all walks of life.'

What is the first step to make a good horror film? 'Sincerity.'

Have you ever considered ending your career in horror films like Mr Lee? 'No. Nor has Mr Lee, I think you'll find.'

Do you think young adults aged 13 or 14 should be able to see your 'R' ('X') rated films? Why or why not? 'I have a feeling they *do* – on television if not in the cinema.'

You have stated that you avoid seeing certain types of movies. Would you mind giving examples of these types? '*The Exorcist, Last Tango in Paris, Shampoo, The Graduate*, etc.'

What did you think of the film *Jaws*? 'First-class entertainment.'

How did you like being guest of honor at the Famous Monsters Con? If asked would you make a return visit? 'It was a most wonderful and moving occasion. I was completely overwhelmed by the warmth of the welcome I received and the genuine affection extended by all those in attendance. Indeed I would come again if asked and circumstances allowed.'[6]

Cushing later revealed to the fan club that he did not watch fantasy movies, but nevertheless that he would consider appearing in another *Frankenstein* if the script was good. He explained that he no longer had his collection of toy soldiers, which were sold after Helen's death. He expressed his preference for ragtime music and thought the BBC's production of *War and Peace* 'Quite excellent – beautifully produced.' He also revealed that he had read Nicholas Meyer's speculative Sherlock Holmes novel *The Seven Per Cent Solution*. 'It was very ingenious and had a style of its own, and as such I thought it was splendid. But to my mind no one has ever been able to catch the atmosphere of the original Conan Doyle stories.'[7]

On 28 August 1976, Cushing appeared on the *Jim'll Fix It Bank Holiday Special* for the BBC. In the show, flamboyant disc jockey Jimmy Savile helped to grant the wishes of viewers. Two boys wrote in wanting to know about horror make-up. They were duly made-up to look monstrous, but they had a further request – to scare Peter Cushing! Cushing's generous participation in the show would have a happy coda in a subsequent edition nearly ten years later.

In the autumn of 1976, there was a reunion for Cushing with Vincent Price for a radio serial called *Aliens in the Mind*. Developed from an idea by former *Doctor Who* script editor Robert Holmes, the serial is a *Quatermass*-like story of a genetic mutation on the remote Scottish Island of Lewigh which breeds a race of powerful telepaths. Cushing plays Doctor John Cornelius, an eminent British brain surgeon and Price plays Professor Curtis Lark, a bohemian American explorer, scientist and Nobel Prize winner whose research has been in the field of telepathy and telekinesis. Together they form a rather waspish Holmes and Watson partnership, with Cornelius gently educating Lark in the finer points of British life while facing a mysterious and relentless foe. Richard Hurndall from *I, Monster* also starred, with Cushing's good friend Irene Sutcliffe.

As the British film industry continued to decline, Cushing increasingly found that he had to travel abroad more and more to find work – only one of his next seven films was made in England. In October 1976 he travelled to Spain to play another German, Major Von Hackenberg, in Ottokar Runz' film *Die Standarte* (*Battleflag*). Cushing joined several former Hammer co-stars, included Simon Ward (*Frankenstein Must Be Destroyed*) and Jon Finch (*The Vampire Lovers*) for this lavish production, which was filmed in German and Spanish. We see Cushing striding across the battlefield, in a splendid grey uniform, kepi and boots – the proper size, it is hoped. 'Will the gentlemen permit me to join them?' he inquires politely as he languidly lights a cigarette. He begins interrogating the senior cadet officer Count Max Emmanuel Heister, claiming some abilities in fortune-telling, looking at the soldier's hand and stating 'one should always be prepared for death, fella. Some people seem to know when it will intervene.' By a series of questions, Von Hackenburg exposes Count Heister as a fraud – his father was a gypsy. 'I have no doubt that there are normal men among the gypsies,' says the major, 'but they don't try to pass themselves off as aristocrats.' Von Hackenburg orders that Heister surrender the standard to Menis (Simon Ward), who must now guard the battleflag with his life. Menis' adventures take up the rest of the film.

In November Cushing flew to Canada for *The Uncanny*. This was yet another portmanteau picture – produced by Milton Subotsky as an Anglo-Canadian co-production, and directed by Denis Heroux. It was originally entitled *Brrr!* and was based on Michel Parry's short story anthology *Beware of the Cat*. Cushing's scenes were filmed on location in Senneville and at the Panavision Studios, Montreal, from 16 November 1976, although the 'Malkin' segment was filmed at Pinewood Studios.

The Uncanny saw Cushing back in top-billed position, and once again providing the linking device for a series of eerie tales. In this instance he is Wilbur Gray, a down-at-heel eccentric who believes that cats are agents of the Devil. With Canadian locations, the film looks very different from the usual home-grown

Heinrich Haussner sizes up a recruit in *Hitler's Son* (1977)

product and Cushing's performance of barely-controlled hysteria is eminently watchable – in other hands it could have been merely aggravating. He makes the idea of a man hunted by cats convincing and rather disturbing.

Gray takes the evidence to his wearily sceptical publisher Frank Richards (Ray Milland). 'It's all here!' he tells him. 'Years of research! Evidence from all over the world proving beyond a shadow of doubt that cats have been exploiting the human race for centuries!' Richards, himself a cat-fancier, says that the public may not yet be ready for such tales. 'You said that about my book on flying saucers!' wails Gray, and proceeds to present the evidence from his manuscript. The first, and best, story is set in London in 1912, starring Joan Greenwood as Miss Malkin, a wealthy, bedridden old lady who is ultimately nibbled to death by her charges. The following black magic episode with Chloe Franks is dull and the third segment, a film studio farce with Donald Pleasence and Samantha Eggar set at 'Haemorrhage Film Productions', becomes a histrionic runaround. The whole is saved by Cushing's detailed performance of preoccupied seediness – he is wearing two cardigans, wipes his nose on his gloves – but because his theories are proven true, Gray ultimately achieves a kind of nobility. In several scenes, Cushing directs his lines to a low camera and seems to be carrying on a suspicious 'conversation' with his feline tormentors. Gray meets a grisly end when his is set upon by a pack of moggies and falls down a flight of steps.

In 1977 Cushing returned to Australia to make a ten-part documentary series called *A Land Looking West* with John Izzard of Swan Television. Cushing

enjoyed making the series, and recalled how they had to use a small plane to cross the vast areas of outback between their Perth base and the various locations. 'On our way to Dampier Land up in the North Western region I sat next to the pilot, who after about half an hour in the air, leant back, closed his eyes and dozed off for a spell. When he awoke he turned to me and said "I orlways hev a kip over thet stretch – gets a bit boring doin' it every day and the plane knows the way" There's faith for you, I thought.'[8] (When they travelled by road, later, the experience was repeated!) Cushing fell in love with the bright stars in the inky night sky 'down under' and had a hilarious run-in with a nicotine-loving ostrich, which snatched the cigarettes from his lips as soon as he lit up!

For his next role, in *Hitler's Son*, Cushing travelled to Munich's Arri Studios in September 1977. The premise of the film is that Hitler's naive son Willi (played by Bud Cort) is taken in by a group of neo-Nazis and used as a figurehead for their new Reich. Filmmakers were eager to follow the success of black comedies like Mel Brooks' *The Producers*, but *Hitler's Son*, filmed under the rather less incendiary title of *Return to Munich*, is a surprisingly charming film.

Cushing looks fit and seems genuinely happy to be doing something different, although the 'exiled Nazi' role would become a typecasting headache as much as the 'stitcher of limbs'. Cushing enjoys the comedy in the part, and has a sublimely funny running gag involving several perfectly-timed comic falls.

Cushing played Heinrich Haussner, the leader of the Fascist League, but even in the wake of *Star Wars*, little was made of his contribution. *Hitler's Son* was featured on the cover of the May 1978 edition of *Films and Filming*, but Cushing was nowhere to be seen, even in the two-page photo spread. Shooting on *Hitler's Son* over-ran by six weeks, causing Cushing to miss an appearance in John Dark and Kevin Connor's Edwardian science-fiction adventure *Warlords of Atlantis*. Cushing was to have played Atraxon, Imperator of the Supreme Council of Atlantis, a ruthless Martian scientist who intends to pervert the course of human development. (Part of his scheme involves the rise of Nazi Germany.) The part would have been a good cameo in a popular and well-publicised film, which was a great summer holiday hit in the post-*Star Wars* summer of 1978. Atraxon was eventually played by Daniel Massey, the cast also included Cyd Charisse, Peter Gilmore and Doug McClure.

At the end of 1977, Cushing wrote to his British and American fan clubs requesting that they be disbanded. He felt that he was too old, and that his work – now mostly cameo appearances – did not warrant such attention. The British club concurred with his wishes, but the Americans embarked on a campaign to prove that their star was still loved and wanted. After heartfelt letters from club organiser Deborah Del Vecchio (née Bennett) and the members, appealing to Cushing to let the club continue, he, of course, agreed. Del Vecchio and Tom Johnson went on to write the first detailed, invaluable Cushing filmography in 1992.

On 27 July 1978, Cushing flew to Zambia to take part in a film called *A Touch of the Sun*. This low-budget comedy was directed by Peter Curran, who had been a film editor on Hammer's *When Dinosaurs Ruled the Earth*, later becoming a producer with films including *Male Bait* (1971) and *Penelope* (1975). *A Touch of the Sun* was something of family affair as Curran wrote, directed and edited the picture, which was produced by his wife Elisabeth. Unfortunately, the film, also known as *No Secrets*, is a shambolic piece of work, with added-on softcore porn sequences that look as if they were filmed in a suburban living room.

With his solar-powered ray, Emperor General Samumba of the African state of Akasuba (Edwin Manda) downs a US space capsule and holds it to ransom for $25 million. US Captain Nelson (Oliver Reed) and CIA Agent Coburn (Bruce Boa) are sent to retrieve the capsule, allying themselves with the wily District Commissioner Potts (Cushing), who was left behind in his jungle outpost when World War II ended and has no idea that Akasuba is independent. The role of Commissioner Potts was originally intended for comedy actor Terry-Thomas, who had to drop out because of other commitments.

Most of Reed's slapstick, with a bawling Keenan Wynn as General Spellman, is unbearable. However, it is difficult to dislike a film which features Cushing's broadest comedy performance. In shorts and pith-helmet, Cushing does some Oscar-class double-taking and ad-libs wildly, whether singing along to Samumba's propaganda broadcasts or complaining that the war is stopping his deliveries of champagne. 'I've been writing to Winston for 20 years,' he says, 'but he never replies.' Captain Nelson politely points out that the War ended in 1945 and Churchill has died.

However, Potts is still a sly old bird, attempting to turn every situation to his financial advantage. He ropes in a group of local Chief Zawe's tribesmen as bearers and charges the Americans $1000. ('What's that in Sterling?' he inquires, twirling his beard furiously.) When they later run into Samumba's solar-powered force field, Potts knocks on it with his swagger stick and remarks that Captain Nelson has been 'reading too much H G Wells'.

Amidst all the mayhem, though, there is a touching scene as the commissioner expresses his bewilderment with the modern world. 'I think I'm goin' mad...' he says. 'Stark starin' mad. First the war's over. Then Winston's dead, then invisible sun-walls...' When he discovers all the off-duty Zawe tribesmen wearing smoking jackets and drinking cocktails, it's the final straw. 'Now all my bearers think they're Noël Coward!'

'The quiet Zambian temperament appeals to Cushing,' explained the publicity brochure for *A Touch of the Sun*. 'He finds the local people gentle, sympathetic and more inclined to be content without the luxuries of life than their European counterparts. Cushing describes himself as an old-age pensioner from the seaside village of Whitstable in Kent. The colours of Africa are glorious, and as a painter Cushing delights in the purple bourgainvillaes, scarlet poinsettias ... flame trees, and the endless vistas of green forests under pale blue skies. The prospect of handling some of the country's wild creatures, such as a cheetah and a python, in his role as the animal-loving Potts, bothers Cushing not at all; nor does the heat, which is nothing compared with the scorching air of Israel where he has been on location before.'[9]

The film was obviously well intentioned, and has some touches of inspired craziness – like General Samumba's troops dressed as Highland pipers travelling in a double-decker London bus marked '11A – Piccadilly to Akasuba via Oxford Circus.' Melvyn Hayes appears as a camp Tarzan, with his accident-prone mate Jan (Mike Cross) but Commissioner Potts remains delightfully unfazed. 'Last week he thought he was Ginger Rogers,' he tuts. 'Wonderful "Black Bottom".'

Cushing's only other role in 1978 was in *Arabian Adventure*, filmed in September at Pinewood Studios, directed by Kevin Connor. A reworking of the *Arabian*

Christopher Lee and Oliver Tobias join Cushing (in costume as the Wazir, with added smoking glove) behind the scenes on *Arabian Adventure* (1978)

Nights stories, it is set in the fictional region of Jadur where the evil wizard Alquazar (Christopher Lee) sends a young prince, Hasan (Oliver Tobias) on a quest for the magical blue rose of Elil. Cushing appears in a cameo as the deposed ruler of Jadur, the imprisoned Wazir Al Wuzara. He pops up in a dungeon cell near the beginning of the story, where Prince Hasan has been confined by Alquazar. When Hasan says 'Allah helps those who help themselves' the Wazir retorts 'Well, he doesn't seem to have done you much good, has he?'

The film is exciting enough, but in the post-*Star Wars* days there was little time for any film that did not deliver androids, spaceships and laser battles. In referring back to Alexander Korda's 1940 film *The Thief of Bagdad*, *Arabian Adventure* allowed Christopher Lee to pay tribute to one of his boyhood heroes by taking the role originally portrayed by Conrad Veidt. Lee is magnificent, and Cushing (with the white whiskers he grew for Commissioner Potts) is delightful when he is on screen – which is not long enough.

On television meanwhile, Morecambe and Wise had made a highly publicised departure from the BBC, joining Thames Television for a new series. Cushing continued as a regular guest, with his old routine, still demanding money for his original appearance. Cushing appeared in the show broadcast on 18 October 1978, with guest stars including Donald Sinden and Judi Dench, and Cushing's co-star from *Nineteen Eighty-Four*, Leonard Sachs.

Apart from providing the narration for a short film called *The Detour*, directed by Rodney Holland, which concerned the adventures of a young boy and his dog (whom the boy believes to be a reincarnation of the Egyptian god Anubis) Cushing did no more work until mid-1980.

In 1979, with Hammer Film Productions in receivership, former board-members Roy Skeggs and Brian Lawrence formed an alliance between their own company Cinema Arts and ITC. The result was a series of 13 50-minute horror films for television called *Hammer House of Horror*, produced 'in association with Hammer Film Productions'. With its memorable ponderous theme, high production values and many old Hammer personnel, the series was a fitting last hurrah for the old firm. The series was filmed from 28 June 1980 on location in Buckinghamshire.

The Silent Scream is the best-remembered of the *Hammer House of Horror* episodes, doubtless because of the participation of Cushing. The actor is reunited with

Alan Gibson, director of the modern-dress Draculas and the familiarity is obviously reassuring. Cushing gives a masterfully underplayed performance, once again with a German accent as benign pet shop owner Martin Blueck, who says he was a former inmate of a concentration camp. Blueck is a genuinely horrific figure, all the more so for the hint of pathos that remains even after his true colours are revealed. Francis Essex's script gives Cushing and a young Brian Cox some excellent interplay, and the claustrophobic pet-shop setting (which recalls the *What Big Eyes* episode of Nigel Kneale's *Beasts*) is disturbing from the outset. The story has several unexpected twists and the gruelling ending provides the series with one of its most potent and lingering images. Producer Roy Skeggs recalls that Cushing was initially reluctant to take on the role, another Nazi, but participated out of loyalty to Hammer.

Following *The Silent Scream*, Cushing worked on the Hallmark Hall of Fame TV production of Charles Dickens' *A Tale of Two Cities*. This was directed by Jim Goddard, written by John Gay and filmed from 30 July 1980 for six weeks at Shepperton Studios and on location in England and France.

In Paris, shortly before the French Revolution, Doctor Alexander Manette (Cushing) is released from wrongful imprisonment in the Bastille and is reunited with his beloved daughter Lucy (Alice Krige). Lucy

Martin Blueck falls into his own trap in *Hammer House of Horror: The Silent Scream* (1980)

marries a French nobleman, Charles Darnay (Chris Sarandon), who has left his title in France to live in England. But when Darnay returns to France to rescue a faithful servant from the hands of the revolutionaries, the aristocrat is himself captured. Doctor Manette cannot save him, but a dissolute English lawyer, Sidney Carton – who resembles Darnay – switches places with him in the prison of La Force, knowing that this means certain death at the guillotine.

This film features a cast of Britain's finest actors. Billie Whitelaw is a powerfully malicious Madame Defarge, Kenneth More bumbles endearingly as Jarvis Lorry, while none less than Flora Robson, Robert Urquhart and Barry Morse fill the minor roles. In the last great role of his career, Cushing gives an understated and unsentimental performance as the long-suffering Doctor Manette. First seen in straggling beard and long matted hair, he plays the reunion between Manette and his daughter with consummate skill, turning his face out of shadow as a flicker of recognition crosses

Doctor Manette appeals to the revolutionaries of France in *A Tale of Two Cities* (1980)

his vivid blue eyes. There is an obvious affection between Cushing and Krige. 'She is everything to me,' Manette says of his daughter, 'more than life itself.' When Manette suffers a relapse, he is compelled back to his old prison trade as a cobbler. Director Goddard again lingers on a haunting close-up of Cushing's eyes as the horror of his imprisonment clouds his reason.

In his best scene, Cushing enthusiastically rouses the revolutionaries and pleads for Darnay's life. 'For sixteen years I was a prisoner in the Bastille. I know the pain, I know the suffering you endure!' He is taken up on the shoulders of the mob. 'I beg you ... as a citizen ... as a patriot, not to take his life!'

Chris Sarandon later played a powerful vampire in the horror comedy *Fright Night*, in which he was opposed by Roddy McDowell as movie vampire-hunter 'Peter Vincent', a gentle Cushing/Price parody.

It was possibly a conflict of schedules with *A Tale of Two Cities* that stopped Cushing from taking the role of Robert Miles in Lucio Fulci's Italian horror film *Il gatto nero* (*The Black Cat*) which was due to film from 11 August. The script, by Harry Alan Towers and Biagio Proietti, was sent to Cushing in May, and as usual he meticulously annotated it with costume requirements and instructions to himself on his performance ('Play Miles oddly. Slightly mad to start with'). As ever, Cushing's notes show his concern for his co-stars ('No cruelty to cats – vet standing by') and in red letters across the top of the script it reads 'Helen' 'Us'. It is unlikely anyway that Cushing would have been comfortable with the explicit gore of the

Italian horror school, but whatever his reasons for declining, the film went ahead without him and his role was taken by Patrick Magee.

After *A Tale of Two Cities*, Cushing travelled to Spain for *Misterio en la isla de los monstruos* (*Mystery on Monster Island*, sometimes simply *Monster Island*), directed by Juan Piquer Simon.

Cushing plays William Kolderup, a shipping magnate and 'the richest man in America' – and as if to prove it, almost as soon as he appears, he is seen buying an island for five million dollars. The island is reputedly infested with monsters, but Kolderup's rival Taskinar knows that hidden on the island is a fortune in gold. Kolderup's heir is his nephew Jeff, who is eager to see the world before his impending marriage and despite his uncle's reluctance, Jeff is sent off for a trip on a ship called the *Dream*. After some days, the boat is attacked by monstrous fish-like humanoids and is seen to explode, leaving Jeff and his dance tutor Artelett ship-wrecked on Kolderup's 'Monster Island'. The pair meet a female castaway, rescue a man from cannibals, build a stockade to defend themselves from predatory dinosaurs and battle masked marauders. In the nick of time, Kolderup arrives to declare that the whole set-up has been a sham, a test of manhood for young Jeff, but he has reckoned without the greedy and devious Taskinar.

For the few scenes in which he appears, Cushing plays the richest man in America with panache, but *without* an American accent. He wears several suits best described as 'natty', and it is a shame he didn't get some more scenes. His dialogue with Ian Serra's endearingly vulnerable hero is strong and affecting. Terence Stamp is as underused as Cushing, but smoulders with style as the villain, and gets to squareoff against Cushing in the finale.

The film is a close cousin of *At the Earth's Core*, although the dinosaurs here are clumsier and even more rubbery. And though Cushing doesn't face the monsters in this outing, Doctor Abner Perry could easily have replaced the twittering dance master who is embroiled in the action. The creatures that attack the *Dream* are ludicrous sub-*Doctor Who* costumes with grumpy-looking faces – we are later informed that they were made by a San Francisco toymaker. On the plus side, there are some very interesting monsters composed of seaweed, which rise up in great slippery heaps from the beach and pursue Jeff and his friends.

In *Starburst #27* Tony Crawley made a spectacularly vitriolic outburst about the forthcoming *Monster Island*. 'Now the bad news ... Jean Piquer is making a new movie. Piquer, as you may not need reminding, is a Spaniard who thinks, for some incomprehensible reason, that he knows how to direct films. He'd have difficulty directing traffic as evidenced in ruining Jules Verne in his tawdry version of *Journey to the Centre of the Earth* with Kenneth More...'[10] Crawley did however report that James Stewart was to star in *Monster Island* – Cushing replaced Stewart in the role of Kolderup.

Juan Piquer was interviewed by Manuel Valencia for *Cinefantástico y de terror espanol 1900-1983*. 'What surprised me ... was the tremendously professional approach of Peter Cushing during shooting of *Mystery on Monster Island*. I was really amazed. As a person he was a true gentleman, so charming and kind. Being who he was, a genuine living legend, and as advanced in years as he was, his enthusiasm during the shoot was unbelievable. I remember ... he told us that he believed in reincarnation and that he wanted to die so that he could join his wife who had died some time before. I recalled this story years later and used it as the beginning of *Cthulhu Mansion* (1991)'[11]

Mystery on Monster Island featured a cameo by another genre star, Paul Naschy, who is still as big a horror hero to the Spanish as Cushing was to the British. He warmly recalls the first meeting of two 'terror titans'. 'Peter Cushing was the first person to congratulate me when I won the Méliès award at the Paris Festival in 1972 (Best Actor for his portrayal of Gotho in *El jorobado de la morgue*/*The Hunchback of the Morgue*). Oliver Reed, Christopher Lee and Terence Fisher were all present, but Peter was the first to come over with all his usual elegance and style and shake me by the hand. On one occasion I dined with Peter and Terence Fisher and I have very fond memories of them. Some years later we both appeared in *Mystery on Monster Island* although we didn't actually have any scenes together. In fact I was a sort of 'special guest star' and Peter didn't have much screen time

either but Piquer is a cunning devil and he knew full well the 'marquee value' of the names Terence Stamp, Paul Naschy and Peter Cushing...'[12]

Back home, Cushing was a guest on the *Morecambe and Wise Christmas Show*, which went out on Christmas Day 1980. An exceptional guest cast included Peter Barkworth, Jill Gascoine, Peter Vaughn, Gemma Craven and Alec Guinness.

At the end of 1980, Cushing went to Spain for the Cinespana production *Asalto al casino* (*Black Jack*) directed by Max H Boulois. The film concerns an attempt on a casino by a gang disguised as a rock group, and the attempts by a dogged policeman to foil them. Cushing's character of Sir Thomas Bedford is behind the robbery, and sits at the gaming table while the heist is underway. Cushing appears at the beginning of the film, and at the end, with a couple of lines in the middle. 'There are only two pleasures in life,' he says. 'A good whisky and a good horse.' The heist fails, but Sir Thomas at least escapes with his freedom.

Francisco R Gordillo, assistant director on *Black Jack* and later director of Paul Naschy's *Licántropo*, recalls: 'Peter Cushing worked on that film for three days. I remember between scenes Peter and I were talking, with the aid of an interpreter, because my English isn't good and Peter only knew a few words of Spanish, but we had quite a lengthy conversation about the *cinefantástico* genre that he'd done such a lot of great work in. It's a funny thing that in the space of that one conversation we became so friendly. Peter told me that he would like to work with me again in a new film I was then trying to get off the ground, *El cepo* (*The Trap*, 1982, in which Jack Taylor played the proposed Cushing role). I felt really flattered by that because Peter didn't know me at all ... but I thought that was a most generous gesture on his part. Unfortunately *Black Jack* didn't have much luck. As far as I know it was never shown theatrically – I don't really know what happened to it.'[13]

The only other British actor in the cast was Brian Murphy, at the time a national hero as the henpecked husband George in the TV comedy *George and Mildred*. Murphy had no scenes with Cushing, and they did not meet during the filming, but the actor's 'star treatment' gives a clue as to how Cushing was looked after. Murphy remembers 'I was rushed over to Spain to be included in the film because *George and Mildred* was a huge success in Spain and it was thought at the time to get hold of Murphy was a great coup! As to what the story was about, I had very little idea, but the money was excellent – and they wined and dined me. I suspect I was cheaper than Alec Guinness.'[14]

Cushing's career would only take in four more films. Among those, however, there was the chance for a last reunion with the three other great names of horror cinema – John Carradine, Vincent Price and Christopher Lee.

Chapter Twenty-Four

A Saint in Retirement

In May 1982, Cushing was rushed by ambulance to the Kent and Canterbury Hospital. His left eye had become swollen to about three times its normal size. It was, he remembered, 'not a pretty sight and extremely painful' but with his usual deference, he decided that 'as this eruption occurred on a public holiday... I didn't want to pester the overworked doctors.'[1] Thinking the swelling to be merely an oversized stye, Cushing bathed his eye and laid down on the couch. He was found unconscious the next day by his housekeeper, Maisie, who rang for a doctor. Finally, having been examined by no less than three doctors, he was taken to hospital. He was diagnosed with prostate cancer, which was affecting his eye, and given – at best – 18 months to live. He was looked after by Mr Darvill and Doctor Rake of the Cancer Care Unit and put on a permanent course of drugs. To the amazement of the doctors, and without surgery, Cushing made an almost complete recovery. He nearly lost his eye but it was saved, although he was left with slight double vision. His secretary Joyce Broughton and her husband Bernard, who were now taking a more active role in the day-to-day running of things, requested that the specialists did not tell Cushing of the seriousness of his condition. They managed to keep the details of his illness from him for nearly four years, by which time he had completely outstripped the doctors' expectations anyway.

Joyce Broughton remembers that the upheaval of the illness was responsible for rousing Cushing from ten years of grief. 'He came out of his "blue study" as he called it, when he was really ill,' she says. 'He hated hospital and desperately wanted to come home, but the specialist said he could not go home alone, so he came to live with us in Hartley. Suddenly he was thrown into a household with two teenage girls, cats, dogs and many friends around, I don't know how the poor man coped after living a quiet and orderly life then coming almost to a madhouse with telephones ringing, different music in different rooms, boyfriends and girlfriends always around. But he was marvellous, and he began to slowly enjoy life a little more, although he continued to miss his beloved wife until the day he died. After this period he would come and stay for a few days most weekends. But eventually we

moved to Whitstable to be near him and he only came to us when he wasn't well. He loved his home so much with his books and things around him. Thankfully ... with the tremendous care of Doctor John Ribchester, he lived for another 13 years.'[2]

'I must record how deeply touched I've been,' Cushing wrote, 'and always will be, by the love and devotion showered on me by Joyce and Bernard Broughton. I am so grateful to them, and so blest.'[3]

By August 1982, Cushing was well enough to take part in *House of the Long Shadows*, with John Carradine, Vincent Price and Christopher Lee, which was filmed on location at Rotherfield Park, East Tisted, Hants. The film was directed by Pete Walker for the Cannon Group, with a script by Michael Anderson adapted from Earl Derr Biggers' novel *Seven Keys to Baldpate*. Walker had been successful in the 1970s with a series of grisly low-budget shockers including *House of Whipcord*, *Frightmare* and *House of Mortal Sin* and Sheila Keith, who appeared in these three films, took a part in *House of the Long Shadows* that was originally intended for Elsa Lanchester.

Author Kenneth Magee (Desi Arnaz Jr) bets his publisher Sam Allyson the sum of $20,000 that he can write a novel in 24 hours. Allyson suggests that Magee stay at the isolated Baldpate Manor in Wales, but when Magee arrives at Baldpate, he suddenly finds it 'busier than Times Square'. Gradually, the Grisbane family, the original owners of the Manor, assemble – father Elijah (Carradine) daughter Victoria (Keith), sons Sebastian (Cushing) and Lionel (Price). They are met on this night because 40 years ago they imprisoned the third son, Roderick, in his room after he murdered a pregnant girl. But Roderick's room is empty – and who is the mysterious Mr Corrigan (Lee), who claims that he now owns the property?

Cushing plays the timid and tipsy Sebastian Grisbane with an endearingly affected lisp. When Price appears, resplendent in cloak and fedora, to announce 'I am Lionel Grisbane', Sebastian gives an exasperated 'Oh, Lord!'. After years of playing commanding characters, Cushing revels in a poor soul who is frightened of his own shadow. 'I've never been a particularly cou*wage*ous man,' he stammers. 'And the events of this evening have been most disconcerting.'

Wicked Roderick (Christopher Lee), timid Sebastian (Peter Cushing) and flamboyant Lionel (Vincent Price) – three Grisbanes who are not what they seem. *House of the Long Shadows* (1982)

He creates a real sense of pathos as he says 'It's a tewwible thing you know, living one's entire life in a state of fear. It is all I have ever known, fear...'

All the principals work hard – they are playing to their reputations, but what reputations! Price is glamorous and Lee has authority, both are magnificently lit by Norman Langley, and despite some wearing performances from the juveniles and a bland script, the film staggers on. There is an unnecessarily grisly death scene involving a washstand full of vitriol, but Walker manages a fine crescendo of horror as Corrigan reveals that he is the wicked brother Roderick, then runs amok with an axe. As Lee takes a climactic tumble down the stairs, however, and finishes up with an axe in his chest, the whole thing is revealed as a hoax. The Grisbanes are all actors, and the events of the night are a mere charade to inspire Magee to write a better novel. So why do several murders take place when Magee is not

even present? The film and its stars are thrown away for the sake of the cheesiest 'happy ending' in film history and a few limp comic scenes. Reviewers quite rightly felt cheated. Derek Malcolm in the *Guardian* said the film 'brings together Price, Cushing, Carradine and Lee for the first time. It then proceeds to waste them utterly. The worst thing about the film is its total lack of ambition.' The *Sunday Telegraph* thought the 'daft-beyond words plot' could not give the quartet 'anything remotely worth getting their teeth into.'[4] It should have been so much better.

Cushing followed this with a role in *Sword of the Valiant,* another Cannon production and another wasted opportunity. The film was made in Ireland, Wales and France, in September and October 1982, with Miles O'Keeffe as Sir Gawain who, after an encounter with the mysterious Green Knight (Sean Connery) embarks on a quest to the ends of the Earth. The film was directed by Stephen Weeks, the 'poor dear boy' who had struggled to make something out of *I, Monster*, and who had already made a film of *Gawain and the Green Knight* in 1972, starring Murray Head as Gawain and Nigel Green as the Knight. Cushing is wasted in a handful of blink-and-you-miss-'em scenes – it is possible he took part simply as a favour to Weeks. He plays Gaspar, Seneschal to the Lord Fortinbras (John Rhys Davies). Ronald Lacey plays Fortinbras' son, reuniting the two stars of *Raiders of the Lost Ark* (1980), although Rhys Davies was ten years younger than his 'son' Lacey. Apart from one mordant scene opposite Lacey, Cushing is reduced to twittering around Fortinbras as he stomps about a huge model castle and knocks over armies of toy soldiers. The film is ultimately sunk by O'Keeffe's leaden central performance and even Connery, spectacular in gold-green make-up and a twiggy beard, cannot save the day.

Cushing's icon status was played upon in his next film *Top Secret!*, a frantic, gag-a-minute comedy from Jim Abrahams, Jerry Zucker and David Zucker, the directors of *Airplane!* Val Kilmer is rock star Nick Rivers, who foils a plan by the lunatic General Streck (Jeremy Kemp) to take over the world. Lucy Gutteridge also stars, with cameos by Michael Gough and Omar Sharif. Cushing appears in a brief scene as a bookshop proprietor who is in league with the resistance. The whole bookshop segment is a gag however – the scene was recorded backwards, with the actors, Cushing, Kilmer and Gutteridge, going through a series of pre-rehearsed movements to finish 'at the beginning'. The scene begins by spoofing Cushing's magnifying glass trick. The proprietor has a magnifying glass at one eye, then when he removes the glass, the prosthetic eye is still huge. 'We had to do the whole scene in *one take*,' Cushing recalled. 'We had to do everything backwards. We had to walk backwards. If a book was thrown up it was really thrown *down*. I knew that this magnifying glass was going to be there at the end of every take we did. And it terrified me!'[5]

Cushing's next assignment was a rather more gentle experience, in *Tales of the Unexpected*. This was Anglia's follow-up to the *Orson Welles* mystery series and was originally produced by John Rosenberg. The first two series were fronted by Roald Dahl, who introduced half-hour dramatisations of his famous stories with chilly geniality. By the time Cushing appeared in the series, it had moved away from Dahl's grisly fables and was using stories by other authors. *The Vorpal Blade*, shown on 28 May 1983, was adapted by Robin Chapman from a story by Edward D Hoch and was directed by John Jacobs, the producer for *La Grande Breteche*. In a castle garden, an elderly German, Von Baden (Cushing), recounts his university days at Heidelberg as a member of the White Corps, led by the brilliant and tyrannical fencing champion Rudolf Cassan (Anthony Higgins). Cushing looks fragile, but

brings a poignancy to his sedate role as narrator, sharing his scenes with another television veteran, John Bailey. Anthony Higgins would show his fencing prowess again as Moriarty in the film *Young Sherlock Holmes* (1985), and would play the Great Detective in a series of 'updated' Holmes TV movies.

Cushing was a studio guest on the BBC's *Breakfast Time* on 14 June 1983. The interview included clips from *House of the Long Shadows* which was on release at this time.

Then Cushing went to Hollywood for the cameo role of Professor Copeland in the television biopic *Helen Keller: The Miracle Continues,* directed by Alan Gibson.

The film was shot in 1983 with Mare Winningham as Helen Keller, the blind and deaf girl who overcame the odds to become a celebrated scholar and lecturer, with Blythe Danner as Annie Sullivan, Keller's beloved 'Teacher', who interpreted the outside world to the girl via touch-signing. Keller enrolls in Radcliffe College in 1904, where the potential of her work is spotted by Professor Copeland. He is responsible for

Cushing as Von Baden in *The Vorpal Blade* episode of Anglia TV's *Tales of the Unexpected* (1983)

getting Keller her first professional commission – a series of magazine articles which are then collected as a book. Cushing looks elegant in his academic gown, and gives Copeland a wry sense of humour. He screws in a monocle to examine the dull essays submitted by the other Radcliffe girls. '*Spring finds Cape Cod?*' he hoots. 'I wasn't aware that it was lost!'

Back in 1980, plans had been announced for Cushing to appear again as Sherlock Holmes, in a project that would have seen Holmes being encouraged out of retirement by Watson for one last case. This idea ultimately emerged in 1984 as Tyburn's *The Masks of Death*, a film for Channel 4 directed by Roy Ward Baker, who described the project as a film made by Holmes enthusiasts for Holmes enthusiasts. Cushing played an elderly but still spry Holmes, with John Mills as Dr Watson and Anne Baxter as Irene Adler. Production started on 21 July 1984.

In 1913, Holmes and Watson uncover a plan by the German nobleman Graf Udo Von Felseck to leak poison gas into London's homes through the domestic gas supply. Cushing gives a surprisingly active final performance as Holmes, adopting various disguises including a bespectacled parson and a swarthy boatman with an eyepatch. (Make-up by Roy Ashton, who created Grimsdyke.) There are several strong horror moments, such as the ravings of Russell Hunter's inebriated tramp Mr Coombes, who has seen demons on the streets of London – 'Devils! With bodies of men but faces of pigs ... holes for eyes and snouts for noses. Evil ones in search of evil!' Holmes eventually deduces that 'the masks of death' are gas-masks, used by the workers in the Graf's diabolical plan.

The script was by N J Crisp from a story by Anthony Hinds, but the dialogue is mostly unmemorable and the few good lines are shamelessly hi-jacked from Doyle. Cushing's scenes with Mills have a dewy-eyed sentimentality, as if all concerned knew that this was a farewell performance of sorts.

Even though Jeremy Brett was making a very good job of playing Holmes in the award-winning Granada series at the same time, the *Times* on Christmas Eve 1984 was full of praise for *The Masks of Death*. 'Peter Cushing and John Mills were combined with what are known on television as "special guest stars", to suggest that only the great can be on familiar terms with Conan Doyle – or for that matter, with his most famous creation. After all the attempts at parody and the no less frequent inflictions of sexual innuendo or psychoanalysis, Holmes has emerged unscathed – the reason that he has so vigorous and emblematic a character that he can be neither diluted nor obscured. He has even survived the transition to television, which is more than can be said for most real people. And as Peter Cushing proved last night, age cannot wither him; he was Prospero in this production rather than Hamlet, but none the worse for that. Once

again, the Holmes adventure becomes an opportunity for the exploration of characters and settings on a Grand Guignol scale, And once again it can become the vehicle for that peculiarly English combination of genuine horror and spirited comedy.'[6]

Cushing was filming again from 21 January 1985 on *Biggles*, directed by John Hough. For a fee of £35,000, Cushing played Air Commodore William Raymond, with a young cast including Neil Dickson, Alex Hyde-White (son of Wilfrid), Fiona Hutchison and Marcus Gilbert. Rather than produce a straight adaptation of Captain W E Johns' stories about the World War I flying ace James 'Biggles' Bigglesworth, the film-makers unwisely decided to update the character. The result looks just as badly dated for being set in 1986 as if it had been set in 1917.

However, Cushing is on fine form as Raymond, who appears during the credits in a thunderstorm, walking deliberately with a stick. Raymond arrives at the New York apartment of Jim Fergusson (Hyde-White) and politely introduces himself, saying 'It should have happened by now.' Fergusson is a busy man, however, and sends the old man away, then moments later is time-warped back to the Western Front in 1917 where he rescues Biggles from a crashed plane. When Fergusson is subsequently warped back to New York, he wastes no time in locating the Commodore in his London home – inside Tower Bridge. ('When they raise the bridge it gets a bit noisy' Raymond admits.) Cushing then has to explain that Biggles and Fergusson are 'time twins'. The time-travel business needs someone like Cushing to make it believable, and as ever, he does it brilliantly. 'I do not know *why* it happens,' he says, a flicker of firelight catching his cheek, 'only that it *does*.' Raymond served with Biggles many years ago and maintains 'he is a fine officer. You'll be in good hands,' before sending Fergusson on his way with a thump on the shoulder. When Biggles is later reunited with Raymond, there are tears in the Commodore's eyes – and doubtless the audience's – as he says, with complete sincerity 'How I've missed you, old friend.'

The *Times* review said pertinently 'Just when British films seem to be doing so well, *Biggles* comes along to show the other side of things ... The flying ace might well have been made over into a sort of period James Bond, instead there is a misguided and inept attempt to give the film an appeal for imagined mid-Atlantic teenage audiences ... The script is witless, the direction is showy and the performances of the twin heroes are weakly amiable.'[7]

The film is slightly better than its reputation. The dogfights are exhilarating, especially the scrap between a modern helicopter and a German biplane. The sonic weapon, which the Germans are developing in secret in No-Man's Land, is a genuinely frightening conceit. On the downside, the synthesised score is weak and aggravating, and the scenes set in New York but filmed in London are truly excruciating. Cushing rises above it all as Commodore Raymond, who keeps a raven and takes tea beneath a huge portrait of Queen Victoria. It is nothing less than an amalgam of Cushing's on and off-screen personas – initially sinister but ultimately strong and reassuring, as British as the flag and yet slightly out of place in the modern world. It is an appropriate salute. *Biggles* was Peter Cushing's final film.

Nevertheless, the actor was still going strong. In late 1985, he achieved a personal ambition when he came back to *Jim'll Fix It* as a 'Fixee'. One of his remaining ambitions was to have a rose named after Helen, and he had written to Jimmy Savile hoping that the programme could 'grant the wishes of people who were over 70 as well as those who are 7'. Cushing had helped Saville out on a previous occasion, and Savile returned the favour gladly. Rose-grower Christopher Wheatcroft took Cushing around the rose beds at his nursery to choose an appropriate bloom to bear the name 'Helen Cushing', and a solitary whitish rose with pink edges was eventually settled upon. It was, said Cushing 'a beautiful way to keep in perpetuity and loving memory the name of a most wonderful lady.' He thanked the team by producing handmade 'medals' for Savile, Wheatcroft and producer Roger Ordish.

In 1985, Stephen Weeks wanted Cushing to appear as Professor Hodgson in his film *The Avalon Awakening*, which Cushing described in his notes on the script as a cross between *Nineteen Eighty-Four*, *Star Wars* and the legend of King Arthur. A young woman called Lynda is troubled by disturbing dreams and consults Hodgson. It transpires that Lynda is possessed by the spirit of Guinevere and calls on Merlin to arise. Cushing made extensive notes, but the film was never produced.

Another near miss was *A Drop in the Ocean*, Don Houghton's proposed satirical TV pilot about the tiny island of Valtaray, off the coast of Scotland, which existed in isolation for many years until oil was discovered in the harbour. Cushing would have played Neil MacNaughton, 18th Thane of Valtaray, and Houghton provided him with a set of documents outlining the invented culture and history of the island. Cushing had also been suggested for the role of President Borusa in the *Doctor Who* story *Arc of Infinity*, a role eventually taken by Leonard Sachs, and, in 1985, Cushing was considered for a role in the TV series *Knights of God* that was ultimately taken by another Doctor Who, Patrick Troughton.

March 1986 saw the publication of Cushing's first volume of autobiography by Weidenfeld and Nicholson. He had begun writing his life story in the 1960s, and had taken up the task as a form of therapy after Helen's death. The finished volume is very similar in structure to *The Peter Cushing Story*,

published in instalments in the *TV Mirror* in 1955, as well as the transcript of the John Player Lecture from 1971. In some cases, the same story is remembered with different details in each. By 1986, many fans had grown up who knew little about Cushing's early life, and came new to *Peter Cushing – An Autobiography*.

It is a warm and often funny book, detailing his early life and influences, his adventures in America, his meeting with Helen and his rise to fame in the theatre and on television. With uncompromising honesty, he described his early hardships, his nervous breakdown and the anguish of Helen's death. On first reading, many admitted they were moved to tears. Some fans were disappointed, however, that the book said little about Cushing's work at Hammer, and that Cushing chose to end the story in 1971, when he said 'my life, as I knew and loved it, ended.' To promote the book, Cushing embarked on a nationwide round of book-signings and was interviewed on television and radio and in the national press. The book was a massive success.

'The book could have been rather mawkish,' wrote Quentin Falk in the *Guardian*, 'if it was not for the disarming sincerity which Cushing still brings to everything he does. Not only his book but his work – even if the framework has often been frankly mediocre – and his demeanour which is unreservedly and endlessly lauded by that most cynical body of men, film technicians.' Falk also accurately pointed out that 'if it wasn't for the brilliantly-crafted screen persona that was forever transplanting him into exotic mittel-European settings, Cushing might forever have been locked into Semi-Detached Suburban Mr Brit.'[8]

'I never dreamed I'd end up sitting here,' Cushing told *Time Out*, 'with everyone interested in such a very old man's memoirs.' The interview described the actor as 'dressed in muted early Dr Who style, with a discreetly floppy bow tie, checky sort of trousers and watch-chain.' In the interview, Cushing expressed his dismay at the horror inherent in modern life 'watching a *Dracula* picture made 25 years ago must be rather like watching *Noddy in Toyland*' but admitted guarded admiration for Jeremy Brett's Holmes. 'He obviously went into tremendous detail, everything is dead right, but *you don't like the man*. You should like Holmes. Whether he was nice or not doesn't matter.'[9]

Cushing was delayed on his way to the BBC's Birmingham studios for *Pebble Mill at One* on 24 March 1986, but this only meant that his interview with Paul Coia received an even more rapturous reception. In this interview, Cushing was more outrageous than usual, playing to the audience and even impersonating Kenneth Williams at one point. He stated however that 'the only thing I was ever good at was playing rugby. Union, I hasten to add.'

Also on 24 March, an interview appeared in the *Daily Express* in which Cushing made several heartfelt revelations. 'Was Helen as much mother as lover?' asked Victor Davis. 'Oh, very much so,' Cushing admitted. 'I'm so glad that comes across in the book because it is the truth. It wasn't the coddling of a mother's boy but her whole instinct was motherly. She realised that in me, here was someone who needed taking in hand.'

Davis continues; 'In the memoir ... there's a cryptic line that suggests something other than devotion to Helen. It reads "There were times when I was human and erred." Does this mean what I think it means? He doesn't look like a man who had erred. "Bless you but I'm afraid I did. I didn't want to dwell on it, but I felt compelled to tell the truth." Was this a one-off temptation? Sigh. "About two or three one-off temptations. They were actresses and I was about 35-years-old. It is not something I'm proud of. I never intended it to happen. The first time I rang Helen from the nearest phone box and said 'I've done something terrible. I'll be home in a while, put the kettle on.' I told her the same evening. You see it was too much on my conscience. Helen's reaction was truly amazing." Hadn't she biffed him with a saucepan and called her lawyer? "Oh no. She said, 'There is too much sorrow in the world to worry about a little thing like that. You must get things in proportion. If you left me and had babies all over the place, that would distress me terribly because I like and respect you. But what has happened is no more important than cleaning your teeth. It is a natural bodily function. Forget it'." Once might have been an accident, twice a misfortune but *three* times going home to confess? Says Peter, "I don't say I did not hurt her. She would not have been human. But she never let it be apparent. And she meant it when she said I was just being a bit of an old fuss-pot. Mind you, I'll never forgive myself. I was human and she was divine."'[10]

On Tuesday 25 March, Cushing was on the main stage of the National Film Theatre at Waterloo for a *Guardian* Lecture, interviewed by Wayne Drew. This interview covered similar ground to the John Player Lecture and was preceded by a brief signing session for the autobiography. At the end of the lecture, Cushing received a standing ovation from the capacity audience, and was visibly moved to tears.

At the charity première of *Biggles* on 22 May 1986 Cushing was presented to the Princess of Wales at the Empire cinema, Leicester Square, when he broke with protocol to bend and kiss her hand. The Princess was delighted. Prince Charles remarked how much he had enjoyed Cushing's portrayal of Sherlock Holmes.

Cushing was once again interviewed about the autobiography on the BBC's regional programme *Look North* on 5 June 1986. He later appeared on the BBC's *Everyman* documentary *The True Story of Frankenstein*, which looked at the character of Mary Shelley herself (shown on 19 October 1986) and took part in an

excellent documentary in the *Omnibus* strand, *Hammer – The Studio That Dripped Blood*. This included comments from Christopher Lee, Anthony Hinds, Jimmy Sangster, Aida Young, Ingrid Pitt and James Bernard. Cushing was interviewed at his home in Whitstable. On the Bank Holiday edition of *Wogan*, 22 May 1987, Terry Wogan hosted the first part of a two-show celebration of the *Golden Days of British Cinema*, with a star cast including Cushing, Christopher Lee, Bryan Forbes, Bernard Cribbins and Irene Handl.

On 1 June 1987, *Today* quietly reported the announcement of Cushing's retirement. 'After making some of the world's best-known horror films during his 50-year career, Peter Cushing has decided that he will never make another movie. He's just finished filming two television advertisements and he says the experience is enough to make him realise enough is enough. "I did them because I'd been offered two film parts and I didn't know if I was going to be up to the work," he admits. "I didn't want to let anyone down so I thought I'd cut my teeth on these commercials. But having spent four days shooting, I've decided not to do any more films. These adverts will be my swan song. It's just too much for me." In the adverts, for Borthwick's roasts and steaks, Cushing plays a professor who discovers a Neanderthal man. "It sounds bizarre, doesn't it," he laughs. "I have never done a TV commercial before – even though film clips of me were used in the Griff Rhys Jones adverts for Holsten Pils. I thought it would be rather fun. And I was amazed at the amount of money they spend on just one commercial. Hammer could have made a whole film on the budget we had!"[11] Another film that went by the wayside as Cushing retired was Tyburn's proposed Holmes adventure *The Abbot's Cry*, which Cushing described as the story of a village menaced by the wandering ghost of a monk.

May 1988 saw the publication of Cushing's second volume of autobiography, *Past Forgetting: Memoirs of the Hammer Years*. This book did little to make up for the lack of attention paid to Hammer in the first autobiography, but it did contain another range of funny stories and theatrical anecdotes. The *Scotsman* carried a perceptive review which said 'Peter Cushing is one of those actors we take for granted ... he has never attained the glamour of a Connery or the critical respectability of a Guinness. However the subtitle of his second volume ... is a misnomer. Hammer's initial *Dracula* is not mentioned. A more reasoned examination of the subject would have been particularly interesting as the criticisms of the Hammer films were much the same as those levelled at the original books when they appeared. This book ... is never more than a collection of random memories, unstructured in a way that suggests a perverse game of word association, so illogical at times is the link between one anecdote and the next. What does emerge is the confirmation of the screen persona of a gentleman, sometimes lofty, sometimes child-like. This is the combination which made his performances as Dr Who so effective. He quotes an interview with his late wife in which she says that he loathes gossip, and there is not a malicious word in the book. His peers are "magnificent" "excellent" and "outstanding". Through this short, rambling volume shines the warm personality of one of the nice men of the movie business.'[12]

In the *Daily Telegraph*, Jeffrey Richards stated 'Peter Cushing is a star cherished by millions as if he were an old family friend, for the very odd reason that he has been frightening the life out of them for the past 30 years ... Cushing's considerable gifts as an actor have been insufficiently appreciated because of his long association with the unfashionable genre of horror films. But his acting has a precision and classical purity. There are glimpses of real distinction in the recordings that survive of his haunted Winston Smith and Cassius in *Julius Caesar* ... It is high time that his achievement in British cinema was publicly recognised. A knighthood would not be an inappropriate reward for a man who has become one of the best-loved and most widely respected of British film actors.'[13]

There was no knighthood, but on 30 December 1988 Cushing was informed that he was to be awarded the Order of the British Empire in the Queen's New Year's Honours List. A mishap on the very same day, however, put him back in hospital and ended his daily routine of a bicycle ride through Whitstable – he fell off his bike as he swerved to avoid a runaway dog. Cushing revealed that the accident happened as he was cycling to the bottle bank with an empty bottle of brandy. 'I'm virtually teetotal,' he said, 'but my doctor said it would do me good, so I have a watered down brandy with sugar on Sunday as a little treat. After the crash Bernard brought me in half a bottle to the hospital and the doctor rang my GP to find out how much I drink. To this day, in his mind, I'm a drunk.'[14]

On 22 March 1989, Cushing was duly presented with the OBE by Her Majesty the Queen at Buckingham Palace. In appreciation of all the messages of good wishes he had received, Cushing wrote a letter to the *Whitstable Times*. 'I wish I could thank everyone personally,' he said. 'But that is not

Cushing out and about in his beloved Whitstable

possible ... I suppose I am an incurable romantic, because I would like to have slain a dragon or saved the Queen's life, or done some other brave deed which would make me feel I really deserve this honour. But I love this country of ours and its people so very much, and am deeply proud of this recognition, because it must mean that I have done something during my life for it and for them.'[15]

Cushing's last association with Tyburn was the filmed interview *Peter Cushing: A One-Way Ticket to Hollywood*, shown on Channel 4 on 4 June 1989. This comprised 90 minutes of Cushing in conversation with writer Dick Vosburgh, illustrated with photographs and excerpts from Cushing's performances including *Vigil in the Night*, *Hamlet*, *Nineteen Eighty-Four*, *Dracula* and the Tyburn films. As a record of his engaging, sincere, rambling style of conversation, the interview is priceless.

'I hadn't expected to be trotting around until the summer,' Cushing told Katie Ekberg for her article 'The Rather Friendly Baron Frankenstein' in the *TV Times* which dealt chiefly with his recent accident. 'The doctor said to me "Don't forget an anaesthetic puts you as near to death as possible and then brings you back again" and at my age that's no fun. I'm a bit short of breath now but there's no pain, just an ache. I'll always have a limp so I'll just have to play the wounded soldier in my next role. No more cycling though. The doctor said anyone over 70 shouldn't really cycle and to be honest I've lost my confidence.' On 4 June 1989, the same day that saw *A One-Way Ticket to Hollywood* screened, Cushing took part in 'The Great Hip Walk' for the British Orthopedic Association. 'Everyone walks a mile' he explained. 'That's three times round the Kent County Cricket Ground, though I think I'll be lucky to make it once.'[16]

There is one sadness in Cushing's later life that he mentions only in passing in his autobiography, but one on which some light was shed by Christopher Lee. 'He didn't really talk about family matters to me,' Lee recalls. 'He was closer in that respect to Peter Gray. But he said to me once, "I'm sorry I don't see my brother any more." I said "What do you mean, you don't see your brother?" He told me that his brother's wife didn't approve of actors, and wouldn't have anything to do with him, so he hadn't been in contact with his brother for many years. It seemed very sad indeed.'[17] Perhaps if Cushing had been able to re-establish contact with David it might have alleviated the sadness of Helen's passing a little. David Cushing died in 1987.

This Is Your Life featured Cushing on 21 February 1990. The guests included a statuesque Ursula Andress, who reminded him that her character was called 'She Who Must Be Obeyed'. 'Yes, darling, and you still are,' said 'Saint' Peter with a saucy grin, 'what would you like me to do?' Also appearing were Caroline Munro, David Rintoul, David Prowse, Joanna Lumley, Freddie Jones, Kevin Francis, Gwen Watford, a hale-and-hearty Peter Gray and Peter Ustinov. John Mills and Christopher Lee sent pre-recorded announcements – Lee telling Cushing that he was 'a delight and a despair ... the only actor who can read the *Times*, drink his whisky and soda, light his pipe and deliver his lines all at the same time'. Lee finished with the Holmesian advice – 'Step out!'. Roy Ward Baker, Anthony Hinds and Sir James Carreras were also among those present. Joyce revealed that Cushing was actually aware beforehand that he was going to be featured on the programme, and was worried that he would not appear sufficiently alarmed when Michael Aspel presented him with the famous red book. His actor's talents were undimmed, and when 'surprised' he delivered the priceless – if unlikely – line, 'It's just as well I wore my toupée, isn't it?'

Also in 1990, TVS's series *The Human Factor* featured Cushing in a special programme called *For the Love of Helen*. Cushing talked about his life and his faith, and displayed some of his paintings. As part of his recuperation after the cancer treatment and the accident, he had taken up painting again.

As late as 1990, Cushing was still defending causes close to his heart. On 12 July 1990, *Newsroom South East*, BBC 1's regional news programme for London and the South East reported on the threat of demolition hanging over Bray Studios, and Cushing was interviewed along with another longstanding Bray 'resident', cameraman Len Harris. Later, on 9 August 1990 on the same programme, Cushing officially joined the fight to save Bray Studios from closure.

On 29 December 1990, Cushing's last acting assignment was transmitted. To commemorate the 50th anniversary of the Battle of Britain, BBC Radio Kent broadcast *Human Conflict*, a dramatisation of the life of Air Chief Marshal Hugh Dowding, commander-in-chief of Fighter Command (played by Laurence Olivier in the film *Battle of Britain*). Alan Dobie played Dowding and Cushing played a fictional character, a former RAF pilot obsessed with restoring the Air Marshall's reputation. Michael Bath, the producer, told the *Times*: 'Both are working virtually for nothing. They are doing it out of respect for

Dowding. The play portrays him as one of the great men of the 20th Century, the man who won the Battle of Britain.' Cushing added, 'I looked forward to taking part in such a moving tribute to a much maligned man to whom so much is owed.'[18] Because of Cushing's increasing fragility, the play was recorded in his Whitstable home.

Cushing never considered himself as a singer, and thought rapping was 'something you got round a parcel'.[19] Nonetheless, at the age of 78 he provided the rap for rock single 'No White Peaks'. The single began life as a poem about a homesick Gulf War soldier by Peter Kayne. Cushing was asked to record the poem, which was used under a rock track by Assegai Records and released on 11 November 1991. Cushing made an appearance on Granada's magazine show *This Morning* around the same time, promoting the single and turning his still considerable charm on co-presenter Judy Finnegan.

In early 1992, Cushing's long association with Whitstable was commemorated when a newly built sea-viewing platform at Keam's Yard was officially named 'Cushing's View'. 'Incurable romantic' Cushing donated a special bench, designed for two canoodlers. The seat bears a plaque saying 'Presented by Helen and Peter Cushing, who love Whitstable and its people so much.' Cushing's 80th birthday on 26 May 1993 was celebrated by a magnificent party organised by the Broughtons, attended by friends including Peter Gray, Michael and Ann Redington, Don Henderson, Paul Eddington, Ernie Wise and many more.

The next year, his 81st birthday saw the publication of *The Bois Saga*, his phonetic history of Britain, which had begun life with 'silly old Bloggs' locked in the lavatory in 1950. Five hundred copies of 'The Saga of the Famully Bois and Their Rival Fakshun The Poleish Born Blogs' were printed, and comparisons were made between Cushing's book and the work of James Joyce.

Cushing's last professional engagement was, appropriately, in celebration of Hammer films, and reunited him with Christopher Lee. On 17 May 1994, the 'old firm' of Cushing and Lee provided the narration for *Flesh and Blood: The Hammer Heritage of Horror*, an American documentary co-produced with Hammer and directed by Ted Newsom. Those who saw Cushing at the recording session in Canterbury were alarmed at how painfully gaunt the actor appeared and his voice, on the finished commentary, is almost unrecognizable. No one, other than Christopher Lee and Joyce Broughton, knew how terribly ill he was. The cancer, valiantly kept in abeyance for so long, had returned. Nevertheless, Cushing insisted on attending the scheduled recording, and kept bright throughout the session, ad-libbing and joking with Lee. The exertions of the day kept Cushing in bed for two days afterwards and Joyce admitted that she couldn't fathom how he had done it. The broadcast of the documentary was well-publicised in Britain, with a photo-feature in the *Radio Times*. The programme went out in two instalments, on consecutive Saturday nights in August.

Shortly before the first part of *Flesh and Blood* went out, Cushing was taken into the Pilgrim's Hospice at Canterbury. 'We always promised to keep him at home for as long as was possible' Joyce recalls, 'and he would decide when things became too much for him. This we did by me staying with him all day and Bernard all night. We kept our promise until he told us that he was ready to go into the hospice ... The hospice staff were wonderful, not only to him but to everyone in their care, and to Bernard and to me.'[20] After a fortnight in the hospice, and between the two instalments of *Flesh and Blood*, the long fight with cancer came to an end. Peter Cushing died on 11 August.

Obituaries in the national newspapers were uniformly enthusiastic in their praise – 'He was a considerable actor,' said the *Telegraph*, 'whose precise, unapologetic theatrical technique was a boon to Hammer's potentially risible subject matter ... He could imbue superstitious rituals with sincerity and spiritual force, and in all his Gothic efforts kept his tongue very firmly out of his cheek.'[21] The BBC assembled a sensitive and very moving tribute from various carefully chosen clips, from *Nineteen Eighty-Four, Hamlet, Dracula, The Ghoul, Dr Who and the Daleks* and more, scored with John Williams' poignant violin theme from *Schindler's List*. The montage was broadcast after the second part of *Flesh and Blood*.

Some unsavoury newspaper speculation followed when it was discovered that Helen's headstone had been removed from its place in the churchyard at Seasalter. Joyce Broughton later revealed that it was one of Cushing's last wishes that Helen's headstone not become a place for fans to gather. 'He asked us to take certain measures concerning both his own and Helen's ashes and to put them in a secret last resting-place. We have never revealed the details of those instructions, but I can say that we carried them out to the best of our ability.'[22]

Despite Cushing's determination that he did not want a 'big splashy affair', his funeral on 19 August brought Whitstable to a standstill. The funeral

'I'm very old, you know,' Cushing admitted, but the mischevious twinkle was undimmed

procession, led by the frock-coated Mr Terry Davis carrying one of the actor's walking-sticks, first visited Cushing's View which was decked with flowers, then stopped outside Cushing's favourite restaurant, the Tudor Tea Rooms in Harbour Street, which was closed for the day as a mark of respect. Whitstable residents, many of whom followed the cortège on foot, paid warm tribute. In the *Daily Telegraph*, Roger Dilley said 'We were so used to seeing him about the place. I don't think Whitstable will be quite the same without him.' David Ruddock added, 'His were old world values, those of an age of courtesy that has gone.'[23]

On Thursday 12 January 1995, there was a memorial service at St Paul's Covent Garden, 'the Actors' Church', attended by Joanna Lumley, Paul Eddington, Ingrid Pitt and many other friends and colleagues. Christopher Lee and Ron Moody read the lessons, actor James Bree recalled Cushing's early career and Kevin Francis his film work. Rosie Ashe, a young singer whose work Cushing greatly admired and who had sung at his 80th birthday party, sang Noël Coward's 'If Love Were All' accompanied by Jonathan Cohen.

The following summer there was an exhibition of Cushing's paintings and memorabilia, including his painted scarves and playing cards, at the Brook Arts Centre in Chatham, Kent.

'Peter Cushing was one of the handful of actors who defined the horror movie,' said the obituary in the *Independent*. Whether playing Baron Frankenstein, witnessing the awful results of his brilliance or Professor Van Helsing in hot pursuit of Dracula, he brought an air of refinement and nobility to the genre ... His name on the cast list was a constant and reassuring guarantee of quality.'[24]

Peter Cushing was one of Britain's finest actors. He believed in the impossible and compelled us to believe too. On screen, he championed the forces of good or presented a human villain you knew wasn't all bad. His classic films are as popular as ever and his reputation will continue to grow wherever and whenever they are shown. He bore his own private terrors of nerves and grief for so long, but if he is now reunited with his beloved Helen then the Peter Cushing story has a very happy ending after all.

Afterword

Can it really be ten years since Peter Cushing died? It is five years since the first appearance of this book and it is a privilege to be able to revisit it, now elegantly transformed into a hardback and exquisitely refurbished by Peri Godbold.

In finishing this edition, I must express my gratitude to everyone I have spoken to on the subject of Peter Cushing since the first edition, a roll call that now includes Hazel Court, John Hough, Damien Thomas, Tudor Gates, Val Guest and Eunice Gayson. I send my particular thanks to Ann Bell, who wrote fondly of her short time with Cushing on *Sherlock Holmes*, but also told of the fan letter she received from him, congratulating her on her performance in *The Lost Boys*, the BBC's 1978 dramatisation of the life of J M Barrie. Cushing was impressed by the harrowing authenticity of her performance as Sylvia Llewellyn Davies, facing her husband's painful death from stomach cancer. Her letter provides one more example of Cushing's generosity towards his fellow actors and the regard in which he held the members of his profession.

There were many such testaments on display at the Whitstable Museum, which held a new exhibition in the summer of 2004 to commemorate the tenth anniversary of Cushing's death. There were letters from the great and good, and in many cases they were responding to fan letters from him. There was quite an emotional charge in seeing the things on display – the miniature sets, the scarves he painted for Helen, his easel, his watercolours and a strange little figure – a Bois or a Bloggs? – with a head made out of a spoon. Each item illustrated a particular facet of Cushing's character, at once simple and complex.

In the Cushing story there are still a few abiding mysteries – he guarded his privacy so carefully it's surprising there weren't more. Why did he turn down the role of *The Man Who Could Cheat Death*? Exactly which scenes of *Daleks' Invasion Earth – 2150 A.D.* were affected by Cushing's illness – for that matter, what was the illness? Was he ever involved with *The Devil's Agent*? And will we ever see a copy of *Some May Live*? These and other questions I leave as challenges to future biographers.

In the last couple of years, the arrival of DVD has added a new dimension to the appreciation of Cushing's work. There are dozens of his films now available, often remastered, many with marvellous commentaries; *~~And Now The Screaming Starts!* is particularly good. It was a joy to see the BBC release the surviving 1968 *Sherlock Holmes* episodes, all of which stand up remarkably well 36 years on. An enterprising DVD company could do a lot worse than release some 'missing' Cushing films, especially those from the middle Hammer period – *The Brides of Dracula, Captain Clegg, Cash on Demand* – or if they are feeling adventurous, they could delve into the TV archives for *The Spread of the Eagle, Peace with Terror* or *Richard of Bordeaux*.

Thankfully, even now, there is new Cushing material coming to light. From the Pathé newsreel archive come three Cushing items, all in colour. One shows him at a meeting of the 'Waistcoat Club' at the Criterion Restaurant in 1954, alongside the club's founder member Jon Pertwee. Another shows him at home in his 'den' in 1956, making and playing with his model soldiers, a third shows him behind-the-scenes on *Frankenstein Created Woman,* on set with Terence Fisher and reading his script beside the river at Bray.

Filmmaking has changed much since the days of Hammer. How Cushing would have delighted in his colleague Christopher Lee's outstanding success – amounting almost to a whole new career – in the *Lord of the Rings* and *Star Wars* films! In the *Star Wars* saga, which Cushing helped to launch, the story is coming full circle and the newest episode shows the creation of Darth Vader. There is even to be an appearance by Cushing's character, Grand Moff Tarkin, although in this case, an actor wears prosthetic make-up to approximate Cushing's distinctive cheekbones. (We can only hope they got the boots right.) What Cushing would have made of computer-generated sets and characters we can only guess at, but one thing is certain – in today's special effects-driven movies, actors of his calibre are needed more than ever.

After ten years, appreciation for Cushing's work shows no sign of diminishing – George Lucas said that Cushing 'would be fondly remembered for 350 years at least'. So we've a little longer yet to enjoy Frankenstein, Van Helsing, Sherlock Holmes, Doctor Who and all the other characters brought to such vivid life with care, finesse and sincerity by the irreplaceable Peter Cushing.

Inspector Quennell investigates Dr Mallinger's laboratory in *The Blood Beast Terror* (1967)

Chronolgy

New Connaught Theatre, Worthing,
from June 1936
Cornelius by J B Priestley
(*PC as Creditor*)
It Pays to Advertise
(*PC as Johnson*)
Week commencing 15 June 1936
Producer W Simson Fraser
Bees on the Boatdeck
by J B Priestley
(*PC as Mr Tooke*)
Week commencing 29 June 1936
Producer W Simson Fraser
The Man at Six
(*PC as Police Surgeon*)
Week commencing 20 July 1936
Producer W Simson Fraser
Potash and Perlmutter
(*PC as Expressman*)
Week commencing 3 August 1936
Producer Peter Coleman
Aloma
(*PC as Boano*)
Week commencing 17 August 1936
Producer Peter Coleman
The Midshipmaid
(*PC as Kingsford*)
Week commencing 24 August 1936
The Middle Watch
(*PC as Captain Randall*)
Anthony and Anna by St John Ervine

Grand Theatre, Southampton 1937,
including
Lean Harvest
(*PC as John Fairweather*)
Winter Sunshine
(*PC as Elderly Traveller*)
Lady Precious Stream by S I Hsiung
(*PC as Chinese Servant*)
Dick Whittington
(*PC as King Rat*)

with Harry Hanson's Court Players,
including Rochdale 1938
Marigold
(*PC as Army Officer*)

Penge Empire
21-27 March, 1938
Blondie White
*With Betty Bowden, John Ayres, Ursula Gilhepie,
Reginald Marsh.*
28 March – 3 April 1938
The Greeks Had a Word for It
by Zoë Akins
(*PC as Stanton*)
4 April 1938 –
Fresh Fields by Ivor Novello

Nottingham Theatre Royal
30 May – 5 June 1938
This Money Business
by Cyril Campion
(*PC as Mr Lilywhite*)
6 June 1938 –
Love From A Stranger
by Frank Vosper

The Man in the Iron Mask (United Artists)
(*PC as Captain of the Guard*)
Filmed February – March 1939, United Artists
Studios, Hollywood, California
Directed by James Whale
with Louis Hayward, Joan Bennett

A Chump at Oxford (Hal Roach)
(*PC as Jones*)
Filmed April 1939 Hollywood, California
Directed by Alfred Goulding
with Stan Laurel, Oliver Hardy

Vigil in the Night (RKO Pictures)
(*PC as Joe Shand*)
Filmed July – September 1939
RKO Radio Studios
Directed by George Stevens
with Brian Aherne, Carole Lombard

Palm Springs, July 1939, including tour of
West Coast, USA
Love From A Stranger
by Frank Vosper
(*PC as Bruce Lovell*) with Ida Lupino (During
break in *Vigil in the Night*)

Laddie (RKO Pictures)
(*PC as Robert Pryor*)
Filmed at RKO Radio Studios
Directed by Jack Hively
with Tim Holt, Virginia Gilmore

The Howards of Virginia
(Columbia Pictures)
(*PC as Leslie Stevens*)
Filmed at Columbia Studios
Directed by Frank Lloyd
with Cary Grant, Martha Scott, Cedric Hardwicke

The Passing Parade:
Your Hidden Master (MGM) (short)
(*PC as Clive of India*)
Filmed 1940 at MGM
Directed by Sammy Lee
with Emmett Vogan, John Nesbitt

Woman in the House (MGM) (short)
Directed by Sammy Lee
with Ann Richards, John Nesbitt

Dreams (MGM) (short)
Directed by Felix E Feist
with John Nesbitt

Women in War (Republic Pictures)
(*PC as Captain Evans*)
Filmed 1940
Directed by John H Auer
with Elsie Janis, Patric Knowles

They Dare Not Love (Columbia Pictures)
(*PC as Sub-Lieutenant Blacker*)
Filmed at Columbia Studios December 1940 –
January 1941
Directed by James Whale and Charles 'King'
Vidor
with George Brent, Martha Scott
Outward Bound NBC Radio (US)
(*PC as Tom Prior*)

The Grandpa Family (Serial)
NBC Radio (US)
(*PC as Alf, the son*)

Scenes from Bitter Sweet NBC Radio (US)
by Noël Coward
(*PC as The Music Master*)

Summer Season at Warrensburg, New York
State, USA, May – September 1941
Night Must Fall
by Emlyn Williams
(*PC as the Inspector*)

Macbeth by William Shakespeare,
presented in modern dress
(*PC as Banquo and Doctor*)

Pound on Demand
(*PC as the Irish Policeman*)
presented with **Fumed Oak**
by Noël Coward
(*PC as Henry Gow*)

The Ghost Train
by Arnold Ridley
(*PC as Teddy Deakin*)

The Petrified Forest
by Robert E Sherwood
(*PC as Alan Squire*)

Biography
by S N Behrman
(*PC as Leander Nolan*)

Mansfield Theater, Broadway, New York
21 – 29 November 1941
The Seventh Trumpet
by Charles Rann Kennedy
(*PC as Police Constable Percival*)

Canadian Ministry Films
We All Help
(*PC as Captain Roberts, Royal Canadian
Mounted Police*)
Filmed Montreal, February 1942

ENSA Tour, including Wolverhampton,
Canterbury, Dover, Oxford, Taunton,
Oswestry, from April 1942
Private Lives by Noël Coward
(*PC as Elyot Chase*)
*with Sonia Dresdel, Humphrey Morton,
Yvonne Hills, Helen Beck*

Manchester Opera House, July 1943
War and Peace
(*PC as Captain Ramballe and Alexander I,
Emperor of Russia*)
Directed by Julius Gellner
*with Barry Morse, Peter Illing, Paulette Preney,
Frederick Valk*

Phoenix Theatre
War and Peace
6 – 21 August 1943 (20 perfs)

Mendelssohn (BBC Home Service)
(*PC as Paul*)

Broadcast 8 September 1943 from
The Corn Exchange, Bedford
Producer Stephen Potter
*with Basil Langton, Peggy Ashcroft,
Austin Trevor, Deryck Guyler, Carleton Hobbs*

Destination Unknown (BBC Home Service)
Recorded 11 November 1943
at Studio C, Bedford College
Producer V C Clinton Baddely

'Q' Theatre, Richmond
The Morning Star
by Emlyn Williams
(16 – 21 November 1943, 9 perfs)
(PC as Cliff Parrilow)
Produced by Charles Hickman
with Margaret Johnston, Irene Handl

The Lay of Horatius
(BBC Home Service)
Broadcast 16 December 1943
from Studio C, Bedford College
Producer John Burrell

'Q' Theatre, Richmond
The Dark Potential
(transferred as **This Was A Woman**) by
Joan Morgan
(25 – 30 January 1944, 9 perfs)
(PC as Valentine Christie)
Produced by Henry Kendall
with Sonia Dresdel, Shelagh Fraser, Peter Copley

The Fifth Column
by Ernest Hemingway
(27 March – 2 April 1944, 9 perfs)
(PC as Robert Preston)

The Crime of Margaret Foley
by Percy Robinson and
Terence De Marney
(2 – 7 May 1944, 9 perfs)
(PC as Kevin Ormond)
Produced by Richard Bird
*with George Merritt, Percy Robinson, Judy Kelly,
Ian Fleming*

Watch on the Rhine
(13 – 18 June 1944, 9 perfs)
(PC as Kurt Muller)
*with Netta Westcott, Charles Farrell,
Alice Darch*

Private Lives
by Noël Coward
(PC as Elyot Chase)

Cambridge Theatre
Happy Few by Paul Anthony
(from 10 October 1944 –)
(PC as Private Charles, a Free Frenchman)
Directed by William Mollison
*with Wally Patch, Tony Quinn, Derek Blomfield,
John Slater*

Globe Theatre
While the Sun Shines
by Terence Rattigan
(Cushing from December 1944, play opened
8 November 1943)
(PC as Lieutenant Colbert)
Directed by Anthony Asquith
for H M Tennent Productions
*with Michael Wilding, Douglas Jefferies,
Brenda Bruce*

Subsequent tour of **While the Sun Shines**
including Bolton

Criterion Theatre
The Rivals
by Richard Brinsley Sheridan
25 September 1945 – 16 February 1946
(166 perfs)
(PC as Mr Faulkland)
Directed by William Armstrong and
Edith Evans
*with Edith Evans, Michael Gough,
Anthony Quayle, Reginald Beckwith*

The Rivals (BBC Home Service)
(PC as Faulkland)

'Q' Theatre, Richmond
They Came To A City by J B Priestley (one
week, 1946)
(PC as Joe Dinmore)
with Roberta Huby

The Seagull by Anton Chekhov
(one week, 1946)
(PC as Doctor Dorn)

While the Sun Shines by Terence Rattigan
(one week, 1946)
(PC as Lieutenant Colbert)

Tonight at 8.30
by Noël Coward, including:
The Astonished Heart
(PC as Chris Faber)
We Were Dancing
(PC as Karl Sandys)
Fumed Oak
(PC as Henry Gow) with Joan Greenwood

Orley Farm by Anthony Trollope
(BBC Home Service)
(PC as Mr Round, Junior in episodes 3, 5, 6, 11)
Broadcast 24 November, 8 and 15 December
1946, 20 January 1947 from Broadcasting
House
Producer Howard Rose

'Q' Theatre, Richmond
The Curious Dr Robson
by J Lee Thompson
26 November – 1 December 1946 (9 perfs)
(PC as Dr Robson)
Produced by Eileen Pollock

**Wednesday Matinee: A Fourth for
Bridge** (BBC Home Service)
(PC as Henry Forum)
Broadcast 11 December 1946

Theatre Royal, Windsor
The Rivals by Richard Brinsley Sheridan
(PC as Mr Faulkland)
with Peter Gray
The Face of Theresa
(BBC Home Service)
(PC as Blane)
Broadcast 25 January 1947 from the
Langham Hotel, London
Producer Hugh Stewart

Radio Theatre: It Speaks for Itself
(BBC Home Service)
Broadcast 1 May 1947 from Broadcasting
House
Producer Peter Watts

Hamlet (Two Cities)
(PC as Osric)
Filmed May – November 1947 at Denham
Studios
Directed by Laurence Olivier
*with Laurence Olivier, Terence Morgan,
Jean Simmons, Felix Aylmer*

UK Ministry of Information Films
The New Teacher
(PC as Steve)
It Might Be You (aka **Safety First**)
(PC as Doctor)

The High Toby by J B Priestley
(A puppet show)
Single performance at Heals, Tottenham
Court Road
*with Ralph Richardson, Meriel Forbes,
Phyllis Calvert*
Produced by George Speaight

Old Vic tour of Australia and New Zealand
(Depart 14 February – return 16 October
1948)
The School for Scandal
by Richard Brinsley Sheridan
(PC as Joseph Surface)
Directed by Laurence Olivier
*with Laurence Olivier, Terence Morgan,
Vivien Leigh, George Relph*

Richard III by William Shakespeare
*(PC as George, Duke of Clarence and Cardinal
Bouchier)*
Directed by Laurence Olivier and John Burrell
*with Laurence Olivier, Vivien Leigh,
George Relph, Terence Morgan*

The Skin of Our Teeth
by Thornton Wilder
(PC as The Professor/Convener)
Directed by Laurence Olivier
*with Laurence Olivier, Vivien Leigh, George
Relph, Terence Morgan*

Beau Brummell (ABC Radio Australia)
(PC as George Bryan Brummell)

Twenty Questions (ABC Radio Australia)
(PC as guest)

New Theatre, London
The School for Scandal
by Richard Brinsley Sheridan
(in repertory, 20 January 1949 – 4 June 1949,
74 perfs)
(PC as Joseph Surface)
Directed by Laurence Olivier
*with Laurence Olivier, Terence Morgan,
Vivien Leigh*
Richard III by William Shakespeare (in
repertory, 26 January 1949 – 2 June 1949)
*(PC as George, Duke of Clarence and Cardinal
Bouchier)*
Directed by John Burrell
*with Laurence Olivier, Vivien Leigh,
George Relph, Terence Morgan*

The Proposal 'A Jest in One Act'
by Anton Chekhov
(in repertory, 10 February – 1 June 1949,
39 perfs)
(PC as Ivan Vassilyevitch Lomov)
Directed by Laurence Olivier
with Derek Penley, Peggy Simpson

Saturday Night Theatre:
The Alien Corn
(PC as Undergraduate)
Broadcast: 8 October 1949
Producer Hugh Stewart

Opera House, Manchester
from 6 November 1950
Malvern Festival Theatre
1 – 7 January 1951
Garrick Theatre from 24 January –
24 March 1951 (68 perfs)
The Gay Invalid by Sir Barry Jackson and
Robert Brenon
adapted from Molière's *La Malade imaginaire*
(PC as Valentine, an Officer in the King's Guard)
with Elisabeth Bergner, A E Matthews,
Tod Slaughter, Daphne Slater

St James' Theatre: Laurence Olivier's
Festival Season
Caesar and Cleopatra
by George Bernard Shaw
(in repertory, 10 May to 23 October 1951,
76 perfs)
(PC as Bel Affris, later Brittanus)

Antony and Cleopatra
by William Shakespeare
(in repertory, 11 May to 22 October 1951,
76 perfs)
(PC as Alexas Diomedes)

From the London Theatre
excerpt from Antony and Cleopatra
(BBC Home Service)
Broadcast 13 August 1951
(PC as Alexas Diomedes)

PC 49 #10 The Case of the Tenth Green
by Alan Stranks (BBC Home Service)
(PC as Edgar Abigail)
Broadcast 27 November 1951
Recorded 9 November 1951
Producer Vernon Harris
with Brian Reece, Joy Shelton, Leslie Perrins

Eden End by J B Priestley (BBC TV)
(PC as Charles Appleby)
Tx: 2 and 6 December 1951, from Alexandra
Palace
Rehearse 12 November – 5 December 1951,
Inns of Court, Drury Lane
Producer Harold Clayton
with Helen Shingler, Julien Mitchell, Rachel Gurney

When We Are Married
by J B Priestley (BBC TV)
(PC as Gerald Forbes)
Tx: 25 December 1951
Rehearse 10 – 21 December at 60,
Paddington St
Producer Fred O'Donovan
with Frank Pettingell, Raymond Huntley,
Gabrielle Daye

Pride and Prejudice 6-episode serial
(BBC TV)
(PC as Mr Darcy)
Tx: 2, 9, 16, 23 February, 1, 8 March 1952,
from Alexandra Palace
Rehearse 14 January – 1 February 1952 at
Mansergh Woodall Boys' Club
Producer Campbell Logan
with Gillian Lind, Daphne Slater, Prunella
Scales, David Markham

Bird in Hand (BBC TV)
by John Drinkwater
(PC as Cyril Beverley)
Tx: 13 and 17 April 1952 from Studio D,
Lime Grove
Rehearse 31 March – 12 April
Producers Michael Barry and Dennis Vance
with Basil Appleby, Leslie Dwyer

Manchester Opera House, August 1952
The Wedding Ring
by Kieran Tunney and Simon Wardell
(PC as Cyril Soames)
Directed by Robert Helpmann
with Gladys Henson, Irene Browne, Irene Handl,
Shelagh Fraser

Moulin Rouge (Romulus)
(PC as Marcel de la Voisier)
Filming July – September 1952 at Shepperton
Studios and on location
Directed by John Huston
with José Ferrer, Zsa Zsa Gabor, Suzanne Flon,
Christopher Lee

If This Be Error by Rachel Grieve (BBC TV)
(PC as Nick Grant)
Tx: 11 November 1952 from Lime Grove
Rehearse 27 October – 10 November
Producer Stephen Harrison
with Gillian Lind, Shelagh Fraser, Frank Allenby,
Dandy Nicholls

Asmodée by Francois Mauriac,
translated by Basil Bartlett (BBC TV)
(PC as Blaise Lebel)
Tx: 9 December 1952 from Lime Grove
Producer Harold Clayton
with Eileen Peel, Elizabeth Henson,
Michael Meacham

For the Children: The Silver Swan
by C E Webber (BBC TV)
(PC as Lord Henriques)
Episode 1: **Francis**
Tx: 30 December 1952, from Lime Grove
Rehearse 17 – 19 December
Producer Rex Tucker
with David Kossoff

Number Three by Charles Irving,
adapted by George F Kerr and Nigel Kneale
(BBC TV)
(PC as Simpson)
Tx: 1 and 5 February 1953,
from Lime Grove
Rehearse 16 January – 1 February at the
Jewish Lads' Club, 5 Hanway Place,
Lime Grove
Producer Stephen Harrison
with Ursula Howells, Jack Watling,
Raymond Huntley, Terence Alexander

Asmodée by Francois Mauriac (BBC TV)
(PC as Blaise Lebel)
Tx: 17 February 1953
Rehearse 28 December – 16 February
(Released from rehearsal 28 – 31 January)
Producer Harold Clayton
With Eileen Peel, Elizabeth Henson,
Michael Meacham

Epitaph for a Spy
by Eric Ambler (BBC TV)
Episodes 1 – 6
(PC as Josef Vadassy)

1: Arrest Tx 14 March 1953
2: Go Spy the Land 21 March
3: Violence 28 March
4: Ultimatum 4 April
5: All Men are Liars 11 April
6: Epitaph 18 April
Broadcast from Alexandra Palace
Producer Stephen Harrison
with Ferdy Mayne

Wednesday Theatre Presents:
A Social Success by Max Beerbohm (BBC TV)
(PC as Henry Robbins)
Tx: 29 April 1953, from Lime Grove
Rehearse 20 April 1953 – 28 April
Producer John Irving
with Dan Cunningham, Marjorie Stewart,
Audrey Fildes

Rookery Nook by Ben Travers (BBC TV)
(PC as Clive Popkiss)
Tx: 23 May 1953, from Scala Theatre Kingsway
Rehearse 5 – 21 May at North Paddington
Boys' Club
Producer Lionel Harris
with Lally Bowers, David Stoll, Beryl Bainbridge,
David Kossoff

The Road from the play Nationale Six by
Jean-Jacques Bernard, adapted by Alfred
Shaughnessy (BBC TV)
(PC as Antoine Vanier)
Tx: 21 and 25 June 1953
Rehearse 5 – 20 June at Mary Magdalen Hall,
Holloway
Producer Peter Cotes
with Wilfrid Lawson, Josephine Griffin,
Ellen Pollock, Bryan Forbes

Anastasia by Marcelle-Mauret,
adapted by Guy Bolton (BBC TV)
(PC as Piotr Petrovsky)
Tx: 12 and 16 July 1953
Rehearse 29 June – 10 July at 60 Paddington
St, London
Producers Michael Barry, John Counsell,
Rosemary Hill
with Helen Haye, Mary Kerridge, Anthony Ireland

The Noble Spaniard (BBC TV)
by W Somerset Maugham from the French
by Grenet-Dancourt
(PC as the Duke of Hermanos)
Tx: 4 August 1953 from Lime Grove
Rehearse 17 July – 3 August 1953
Producer Stuart Latham
with Frances Rowe, Terence Alexander,
James Gilbert, Elisabeth Gray

Portrait by Peko by P N Walker-Taylor,
adapted by Guy Bolton (BBC TV)
(PC as Seppi Fredericks)
Tx: 23 and 27 August 1953, from Lime Grove
Tx: 31 August from Dusseldorf
Rehearse 5 – 21 August 1953
Producer Lionel Harris
with Patrick Barr, Ursula Howells, Irene Handl,
Basil Appleby

The Black Knight (Warwick)
(PC as Sir Palamides)
Filmed September – October 1953 on
location in England, Wales and Spain
Pinewood Studios from 2 November for
three weeks
Directed by Tay Garnett

with Alan Ladd, Patricia Medina, André Morell, Anthony Bushell, Patrick Troughton, Basil Appleby

Tovarich by Jacques Deval, adapted by Robert Sherwood (BBC TV)
(PC as Prince Mikhail Alexandrovitch Ouratieff)
Tx: 24 and 28 January 1954, from Studio E, Lime Grove
Rehearse 4 – 22 January 1954
Producer Eric Fawcett
with Ann Todd, Clive Morton, Frances Rowe, Andrew Laurence

Beau Brummell by Anatole de Grunwald (BBC TV)
(PC as George Bryan Brummell)
Tx: 14 and 18 March 1954, from Lime Grove
Rehearse 22 February – 13 March
Producer Campbell Logan
with Daphne Slater, Ferdy Mayne, Walter Fitzgerald, David Peel, Prunella Scales

A Book at Bedtime: Natural Causes by Henry Cecil (BBC Light Programme)
Broadcast Monday – Friday 8 – 26 February 1954

Morning Story: The Bride in the Bath (BBC Light Programme)
(PC as narrator)
Broadcast 2 March 1954

The Gay Lord Quex by Arthur Wing Pinero (BBC Home Service)
(PC as the Marquess of Quex)
Tx: 5 April 1954, from Broadcasting House
Recorded 31 March
Rehearse 28 – 31 March 1954
Producer Archie Campbell

May Day (BBC TV)
(PC as narrator)
Tx: 1 May 1954, from Studio E, Lime Grove
Producer Paul Johnston

Men of Mystery (BBC TV)
(PC as Celebrity Guest)
Tx: 14 May 1954, from Lime Grove
Producer Bill Ward
with David Nixon, David Berglas, Chandu

Wimbledon Theatre
31 May 1954
Devonshire Park Theatre, Eastbourne
24 June 1954
The Soldier and the Lady
by Ian Stuart Black
(PC as The Soldier)
Directed by Sam Wanamaker
with Sheila Sim

Woman's Hour: Woman, Lovely Woman 1930 – 1940 (BBC Home Service)
Tx: 24 June 1954
Producer Isa Benzie

The End of the Affair (Coronado)
(PC as Henry Miles)
Filmed 29 June – 10 September 1954
at Shepperton Studios
Directed by Edward Dmytryk
with Deborah Kerr, Van Johnson, John Mills, Stephen Murray, Michael Goodliffe

Down You Go! (BBC TV)
(PC as Celebrity Guest)
Tx: 29 July 1954, from the Television Theatre, Shepherds Bush
Producer Ernest Maxim

The Face of Love (BBC TV)
(PC as Mardian)
Tx: 5 October 1954, from Lime Grove
Rehearse 17 September – 4 October
Producer Alvin Rakoff
with Mary Morris

Magic Fire (William Dieterle/Republic)
(PC as Otto Wesendonk)
Filmed October 1954 on location in Bavaria
Directed by William Dieterle
with Alan Badel, Yvonne De Carlo, Carlos Thompson, Rita Gam

Nineteen Eighty-Four
by George Orwell, adapted by Nigel Kneale (BBC TV)
(PC as Winston Smith)
Tx: 12 and 16 December 1954, from Studio D, Lime Grove
Location filming at Alexandra Palace from 10 November 1954
Rehearse from 22 November 1954
Producer Rudolph Cartier
with Yvonne Mitchell, André Morell, Donald Pleasence, Wilfrid Brambell

The Creature by Nigel Kneale (BBC TV)
(PC as John Rollason)
Tx: 30 January and 3 February 1955, from Studio D, Lime Grove
Filmed Switzerland 3 – 7 January 1955
Filmed Lime Grove 10 January
Rehearse from 17 January, at 60 Paddington St, London
Producer Rudolph Cartier
with Stanley Baker, Eric Pohlmann, Wolfe Morris, Arnold Marle

Find the Link (BBC TV)
(PC as celebrity guest)
Tx: 1 March 1955
Producer Ernest Maxim
with Leslie Mitchell, Josephine Douglas, Moira Lister, Kenneth Horne

The Moment of Truth
by Peter Ustinov (BBC TV)
(PC as the Prime Minister)
Tx: 6 and 10 March 1955
Rehearse from 14 February – 5 March 1955
Producer Rudolph Cartier
with Peter Ustinov, Jeanette Sterke, Donald Pleasence, Hugh Griffith, Noel Hood

Alexander the Great (United Artists)
(PC as General Memnon)
Filmed March – June 1955 in Spain
Directed by Robert Rossen
with Richard Burton, Fredric March, Harry Andrews, Stanley Baker, Claire Bloom

The Browning Version
by Terence Rattigan (BBC TV)
(PC as Andrew Crocker-Harris)
Tx: 12 July 1955
Rehearse from 25 June – 11 July 1955
Producer Campbell Logan
with Joyce Heron, Michael Gwynn, Andrew Ray

Wife for Sale by David Tutaev
adapted from Anton Chekhov's *Live Merchandise*
(BBC Home Service)
(PC as Grigori Vassilich Groholsky)
Recorded 9 September
Broadcast 12 September 1955
Producer Charles LeFaux
with Marjorie Westbury, Deryck Guyler

Richard of Bordeaux by Gordon Daviot (BBC TV)
(PC as Richard II)
Tx: 29 December 1955, from Lime Grove
Rehearse: 5 – 28 December 1955
Producer Victor Menzies
with Jeanette Sterke, Joseph O'Conor, Robin Bailey

Duchess Theatre
The Silver Whistle by Robert McEnroe
(1 – 12 May 1956, 15 perfs)
(PC as Oliver Erwenter)
Directed by Martin Landau
with Ernest Thesiger, Robin Bailey, Alfie Bass, Peter Vaughn, Olga Lindo, Mary Merrall

Time Without Pity (Harlequin)
(PC as Jeremy Clayton)
Directed by Joseph Losey
Filmed from June – August 1956 at British National Studios, Elstree
(PC from 25 June – 28 July 1956)
with Michael Redgrave, Leo McKern, Ann Todd, Alec McCowen

Home at Seven
by R C Sherriff (BBC TV)
(PC as David Preston)
Tx: 12 August 1956, from Lime Grove
Rehearse from 25 July – 11 August
Producer Stephen Harrison
with Helen Shingler, Raymond Francis

House Magazine (BBC TV)
(PC to talk about Film Producers' Award)
Tx: 28 October 1956

The Curse of Frankenstein
(Hammer)
(PC as Baron Victor Frankenstein)
Filmed 19 November 1956 – 3 January 1957, at Bray Studios
Directed by Terence Fisher
with Hazel Court, Robert Urquhart, Christopher Lee

Gaslight by Patrick Hamilton (BBC TV)
(PC as Manningham)
Tx: 13 January 1957, from Lime Grove
Rehearse 27 December 12 January
Producer Stephen Harrison
with Mervyn Johns, Mary Morris, Billie Whitelaw

The Abominable Snowman (Hammer)
(PC as Dr John Rollason)
Filming 28 January – 5 March 1957, at Bray Studios
Directed by Val Guest
with Forrest Tucker, Maureen Connell, Richard Wattis, Arnold Marle, Wolfe Morris

Hobbies: Model Soldiers
(BBC Light Programme)
Tx: 26 April 1957
Interview recorded at home

Picture Parade (BBC TV)
(PC interviewed about **The Abominable Snowman***)*
Tx: 19 August 1957

Violent Playground (Rank)
(PC as Father Laidlaw)
Filmed July – September 1957, at Pinewood Studios
Directed by Basil Dearden
with David McCallum, Stanley Baker, Anne Heywood, John Slater, Melvyn Hayes

Dracula (Hammer)
(PC as Van Helsing)
Filmed 11 November 1957 – 3 January 1958, at Bray Studios
Directed by Terence Fisher
with Christopher Lee, Melissa Stribling, Michael Gough, Valerie Gaunt

The Revenge of Frankenstein (Hammer)
(PC as Baron Victor Frankenstein)
Filmed 6 January – 4 March 1958, at Bray Studios
Directed by Terence Fisher
with Francis Matthews, Eunice Gayson, Michael Gwynn, Oscar Quitak, Richard Wordsworth

What's My Line? (BBC TV)
Tx: 9 February 1958
Presented by Harry Carlisle
with Isobel Barnett, Barbara Kelly, Gilbert Harding, David Nixon, Eamonn Andrews

Follow The Stars (BBC Light Programme)
(PC featured in specially recorded excerpt from Violent Playground*)*
Tx: 9 March 1958
Recorded 5 March 1958
Producer John Simmonds
with Stanley Baker, David McCallum, Terry Scott, Bernard Cribbins

The Winslow Boy by Terence Rattigan (BBC TV)
(PC as Sir Robert Morton)
Tx: 13 March 1958, from Studio D, Lime Grove
Rehearse from 20 February 1958
Producer Rudolph Cartier
with John Robinson, Gwen Watford

Uncle Harry by Thomas Job (BBC TV)
(PC as Uncle Harry)
Tx: 8 May 1958,
from BBC Cardiff Studios
Rehearse 21 April – 8 May 1958
Producer David J Thomas
with Mary Morris

John Paul Jones (Samuel Bronston)
(PC as Captain Pearson)
Filmed May – August 1958, on location in Spain
Directed by John Farrow
with Robert Stack, Marisa Pavan, Charles Coburn, David Farrar

The Hound of the Baskervilles (Hammer)
(PC as Sherlock Holmes)
Filmed 13 September 1958 – 31 October 1958, Bray Studios
Directed by Terence Fisher
with André Morell, Christopher Lee, Francis De Wolff, Marla Landi

Today (BBC Home Service)
(interview about filming of **The Hound of the Baskervilles***)*
Broadcast 10 September 1958

Desert Island Discs
(BBC Home Service)
(PC as castaway)
Broadcast 23 February 1959
Recorded 17 December 1958

The Mummy (Hammer)
(PC as John Banning)
Filming 25 February – 16 April 1959, at Bray Studios
Directed by Terence Fisher
with Christopher Lee, Yvonne Furneaux, George Pastell, Felix Aylmer

Calling Australia: H for Horror
(BBC World Service)
Tx: 13 April 1959
Recorded at Bray Studios

The Flesh and the Fiends (Triad)
(PC as Dr Knox)
Filmed from 25 May 1959
Directed by John Gilling
with Donald Pleasence, Billie Whitelaw, June Laverick, George Rose, Renee Houston

Dateline London
(BBC Light Programme)
(PC as interviewee)
Tx: 17 July 1959

Aldwych Theatre
The Sound of Murder
by William Fairchild
(5 August 1959 to 20 February 1960, 227 perfs)
(PC as Charles Norbury)
Directed by Fred Sadoff *with Patricia Jessel, Elisabeth Sellars, Terence Longden*
(Michael Goodliffe played Norbury after PC left during filming of **Suspect**)

Interview (BBC Light Programme)
(PC interviewed about his collection of model soldiers)
Recorded 28 November 1959

Suspect (Boulting Brothers)
(PC as Professor Sewell)
Filmed December 1959 – January 1960
Directed by John and Roy Boulting
with Tony Britton, Ian Bannen, Raymond Huntley, Thorley Walters, Donald Pleasence, Spike Milligan

The Brides of Dracula (Hammer)
(PC as Dr Van Helsing)
Filmed 26 January – 18 March 1960, Bray Studios
Directed by Terence Fisher
with Yvonne Monlaur, David Peel, Andrée Melly, Martita Hunt, Freda Jackson, Henry Oscar

Cone of Silence
(Bryanston/British Lion)
(PC as Captain Judd)
Filmed March – April 1960
Directed by Charles Frend
with Michael Craig, Bernard Lee, George Sanders, André Morell, Marne Maitland, Noel Willman

Sword of Sherwood Forest (Hammer)
(PC as the Sheriff of Nottingham)
Filmed 23 May – 8 July 1960
Directed by Terence Fisher
with Richard Greene, Niall MacGinnis, Oliver Reed

The Hellfire Club (New World)
(PC as Mr Merryweather)
Filmed July – August 1960
Directed by Robert S Baker
with Keith Michell, Adrienne Corri, Peter Arne, David Lodge, Francis Matthews

The Naked Edge (Pennebaka/Baroda)
(PC as Mr Evan Wrack)
Filmed December 1960, at Elstree Studios
Directed by Michael Anderson
with Gary Cooper, Deborah Kerr, Eric Portman, Michael Wilding

Fury at Smugglers' Bay (Mijo)
(PC as Squire Trevenyan)
Filmed 1961, at Twickenham Studios
Directed by John Gilling
with John Fraser, Bernard Lee, William Franklyn, Liz Fraser, George Coulouris

Cash on Demand (Hammer)
(PC as Harry Fordyce)
Filmed at Bray Studios, 4 April – 26 April 1961
with André Morell, Richard Vernon, Norman Bird

Captain Clegg (Hammer/Major)
(PC as Captain Nathaniel Clegg/Dr Blyss)
Filmed 25 September – 8 November 1961, at Bray Studios
Directed by Peter Graham Scott
with Patrick Allen, Oliver Reed, Michael Ripper

Im Namen des Teufels (The Devil's Agent) (Criterion/Constantin)
PC does not feature in release print
Directed by John Paddy Carstairs
with Peter Van Eyck, Christopher Lee, Billie Whitelaw, Jeremy Bulloch, Helen Cherry, Peter Vaughn

The Man Who Finally Died
(Magna/British Lion)
(PC as Peter Von Brecht)
Filmed 1962, at Shepperton Studios
Directed by Quentin Lawrence
with Stanley Baker, Mai Zetterling, Eric Portman, Niall MacGinnis

Peace with Terror (ABC TV)
(PC as Parsons)
Tx: 3 June 1962 was postponed.
Final Tx: n/k
Directed by Quentin Lawrence
with Brian Wilde

Living Today (BBC)
(interview, 'to talk about your hobby, painting')
Tx: 16 April 1963
Recorded 9 April 1963

The Spread of the Eagle
Episodes 4-6 (BBC TV)
Julius Caesar by William Shakespeare
(PC as Caius Cassius)
Part 4: **The Colossus**
Tx: 24 May 1963
Recorded 7 – 8 March 1963, Studio 4

Television Centre
Part 5: **The Fifteenth**
Tx: 1 June 1963
Recorded 24 – 25 March, TC4
Part 6: **The Revenge**
Tx: 8 June 1963
Recorded 4 – 5 April, TC4
Rehearse 25 February – 3 April
Produced and directed by Peter Dews
with Keith Michell, Barry Jones,
Paul Eddington

New Comment: 'The Macabre'
(BBC Third Programme)
(PC as interviewee)
Tx: 26 September 1963
Recorded 10 September 1963
Producer Joseph Home

Comedy Playhouse: The Plan
by Richard Harris and Dennis Spooner (BBC 1)
(PC as Albert Fawkes)
Tx: 2 November 1963
Recorded 7 Oct 1963 TC3
Rehearse 1 – 6 October 1963
Filming 22 – 23 September 1963
Producer Sydney Lotterby
with Graham Stark, Francis Matthews,
P G Stephens

The Evil of Frankenstein (Hammer)
(PC as Baron Frankenstein)
Filmed 14 October – 16 November 1963, at
Bray Studios
Directed by Freddie Francis
with Peter Woodthorpe, Sandor Elès, Duncan
Lamont, Katy Wild

The Gorgon (Hammer)
(PC as Dr Namaroff)
Filmed 9 December 1963 – 16 January 1964,
at Bray Studios
Directed by Terence Fisher
with Christopher Lee, Richard Pasco, Barbara
Shelley, Patrick Troughton

Star Story
Story Seven: The Yellow Cat
by Michael Joseph (BBC TV)
Recorded 22 March 1964, TC5
Not broadcast
Director David Bellamy

Story Parade: The Caves of Steel by Isaac
Asimov, adapted by Terry Nation (BBC 2)
(PC as Elijah Baley)
Recorded 5 – 7 May 1964, TC1
Rehearse 15 April – 4 May,
Filming 17 April
Directed by Peter Sasdy
with John Carson, Kenneth J Warren

Dr Terror's House of Horrors (Amicus)
(PC as Dr Sandor Schreck)
Filmed 25 May – 12 June 1964 at Shepperton
Studios
Directed by Freddie Francis
with Christopher Lee, Roy Castle,
Donald Sutherland, Alan Freeman

In Town Today (BBC Home Service)
(PC as interviewee)
Tx: 20 June 1964
Recorded 11 June 1964, at Shepperton
Studios
Producer Richard Dingley

She (Hammer)
(PC as Major Horace L Holly)
Filmed 24 August – 17 October 1964, at
Elstree Studios
Directed by Robert Day
with Ursula Andress, John Richardson, Bernard
Cribbins, Christopher Lee, André Morell

Let's Find Out
(BBC Light Programme)
(PC as guest)
Tx: 20 October 1964
Recorded 3 September 1964
Producer David Carter

Loyal Servant by Ian Rodger
(BBC Home Service)
(PC as Lord Churchill)
Broadcast 30 November 1964
Rehearse 6, 7, 8 November 1964
Recorded 8 November 1964
Producer Charles LeFaux

First Impressions (BBC 1)
(PC as interviewee)
Tx: 5 January 1965
Recorded 14 Dec 1964, TV Theatre
Shepherd's Bush

The Skull (Amicus)
(PC as Christopher Maitland)
Directed by Freddie Francis
Filmed 18 January – March 1965, at
Shepperton Studios
with Patrick Wymark, Christopher Lee,
Jill Bennett, Peter Woodthorpe

Cribbins (BBC 1)
(PC as guest)
Tx: 27 February 1965
Rec 5 – 6 February TC4
Rehearse 1 – 4 February
Producer Dennis Main Wilson
with Bernard Cribbins

Dr Who and the Daleks (Aaru)
(PC as Dr Who)
Filming 12 March – 23 April 1965,
at Shepperton Studios
Directed by Gordon Flemyng
with Roy Castle, Jennie Linden, Roberta Tovey,
Barrie Ingham

Yvonne Arnaud Theatre, Guildford
Thark by Ben Travers
(PC as Sir Hector Benbow, Bart, MFH)
Directed by Ray Cooney
with Kathleen Harrison, Jennie Linden,
Alec McCowen
Garrick Theatre
from 3 August – December 1965

Island of Terror (Planet)
(PC as Dr Stanley)
Filmed August – September 1965,
at Pinewood Studios,
Directed by Terence Fisher
with Edward Judd, Carole Gray, Niall
MacGinnis, Eddie Byrne

30 Minute Theatre: Monica (BBC 2)
(PC as Leonard)
Tx: 4 November 1965,
from Studio G, Lime Grove
Rehearse 27 October – 3 November 1965
Producer Naomi Capon

Line-Up (BBC 2)
Tx: 27 November 1965
Interview re **Nineteen Eighty-Four,**
recorded 18 November

Daleks' Invasion Earth 2150 A.D. (Aaru)
(PC as Dr Who)
Filmed 31 January – 22 March 1966, at
Shepperton Studios
Directed by Gordon Flemyng
with Bernard Cribbins, Ray Brooks, Andrew Keir,
Roberta Tovey, Jill Curzon

Frankenstein Created Woman (Hammer)
(PC as Baron Frankenstein)
Filmed 4 July – 12 August 1966, at Bray Studios
Directed by Terence Fisher
with Thorley Walters, Susan Denberg, Robert
Morris

Torture Garden (Amicus)
(PC as Lancelot Canning)
Filmed from 14 November 1966,
at Shepperton Studios
Directed by Freddie Francis
with Jack Palance, Hedger Wallace

The Strong are Lonely
(World Service Drama)
Recorded 27 November 1966, at Bush House
Producer James Vourden
Rehearse 26 November

Some May Live (Krasne)
(PC as John Meredith)
Directed by Vernon Sewell
Filmed 1 January 1967, at Twickenham
Studios
with Joseph Cotten, Martha Hyer

Night of the Big Heat (Planet)
(PC as Dr Vernon Stone)
Filmed from 20 February 1967, at Pinewood
Studios
Directed by Terence Fisher
with Christopher Lee, Patrick Allen, Sarah
Lawson, William Lucas, Kenneth Cope

The Burnt Flowerbed (BBC Radio)
by Ugo Betti
Rehearse 25 February 1967
Record 26 February 1967
Producer Sunday Wilshin

The Avengers: Return of the Cybernauts
by Philip Levene (Telemen/ABC)
(PC as Paul Beresford)
Tx: 30 September 1967
Production completed 15 June 1967
Directed by Robert Day
with Patrick Macnee, Diana Rigg,
Fulton Mackay, Frederick Jaeger

Corruption (Titan)
(PC as Sir John Rowan)
Filmed 15 July 1967 – August 1967, at
Isleworth Studios
Directed by Robert Hartford-Davis
with Sue Lloyd, Kate O'Mara, Noel Trevarthan

The Blood Beast Terror (Tigon British)
(PC as Inspector Quennell)
Filmed 7 August – 12 September 1967, at
Goldhawk Studios, Shepherd's Bush
Directed by Vernon Sewell
with Robert Flemyng, Wanda Ventham

Line-Up (BBC 2)
(PC as interviewee 'about yourself and Sherlock Holmes')
Tx: 29 April 1968

Sir Arthur Conan Doyle's Sherlock Holmes (BBC 1)
Producer William Sterling
(PC as Sherlock Holmes)
with Nigel Stock

1: The Second Stain
Tx: 9 September 1968
Directed by Henri Safran
Dramatised by Jennifer Stuart
with Daniel Massey, Cecil Parker, Penelope Horner, William Lucas
Recorded 23 August 1968 (5th in recording order)

2: A Study in Scarlet
Tx: 16 September
Directed by Henri Safran
Dramatised by Hugh Leonard
with Grace Arnold, Joe Melia, William Lucas, George A Cooper, Edina Ronay
Recorded 2 August 1968 (3rd)

3: The Dancing Men
Tx: 23 September
Directed by William Sterling
Dramatised by Michael and Mollie Hardwick
with Judee Morton, Maxwell Reed, Brenda Bruce
Recorded 2 September 1968 (6th)

4: The Hound of the Baskervilles #1
Tx: 30 September
Directed by Graham Evans
Dramatised by Hugh Leonard
with Gary Raymond, Gabriella Licudi, Philip Bond, Gerald Flood
Recorded 8 July 1968 (1st)

5: The Hound of the Baskervilles #2
Tx: 7 October
Directed by Paul Ciappessoni
Dramatised by Hugh Leonard
with Gary Raymond, Gabriella Licudi, Philip Bond
Recorded 22 July 1968 (2nd)

6: The Boscombe Valley Mystery
Tx: 14 October
Directed by Viktors Ritelis
Dramatised by Bruce Stewart
with John Tate, Nick Tate, Peter Madden
Recorded 23 September 1968 (8th)

7: The Greek Interpreter
Tx: 21 October
Directed by David Saire
Dramatised by John Gould
with Peter Woodthorpe, Nigel Terry, Ronald Adam
Recorded 4 October 1968 (9th)

8: The Naval Treaty
Tx: 28 October
Directed by Anthony Kearey
Dramatised by John Gould
with Dennis Price, Corin Redgrave, Peter Bowles, Jane Lapotaire
Recorded 13 September 1968 (7th)

9: Thor Bridge
Tx: 4 November
Directed by Anthony Kearey
Dramatised by Harry Moore

with Juliet Mills, Isa Miranda, Grant Taylor, Willoughby Gray
Recorded 14 October 1968 (10th)

10: The Musgrave Ritual
Tx: 11 November
Directed by Viktors Ritelis
Dramatised by Alexander Baron
with Georgia Brown, Brian Jackson
Recorded 25 October 1968 (11th)

11: Black Peter
Tx: 18 November
Directed by Anthony Kearey
Dramatised by Richard Harris
with James Kenney, Ilona Rodgers
Recorded 12 August 1968 (4th)

12: Wisteria Lodge
Tx: 25 November
Directed by Roger Jenkins
Dramatised by Alexander Baron
with Richard Pearson, Derek Francis
Recorded 4 November 1968 (12th)

13: Shoscombe Old Place
Tx: 2 December
Directed by Bill Bain
Dramatised by Donald Tosh
with Nigel Green, Edward Woodward, Kevin Lindsay, Peter Miles
Recorded 15 November 1968 (13th)

14: The Solitary Cyclist
Tx: 9 December
Directed by Viktors Ritelis
Dramatised by Stanley Miller
with Carol Potter, Charles Tingwell
Recorded 25 November 1968 (14th)

15: The Sign of Four
Tx: 16 December
Directed by William Sterling
Dramatised by Michael and Mollie Hardwick
with Ann Bell, Paul Daneman, John Stratton
Recorded 6 December 1968 (15th)

16: The Blue Carbuncle
Tx: 23 December
Directed by Bill Bain
Dramatised by Donald Tosh and Stanley Miller
with Madge Ryan, James Beck, Frank Middlemass
Recorded 16 December 1968 (16th)

Star Choice (BBC 1)
(PC as guest)
Recorded 10 December 1968

Frankenstein Must Be Destroyed
(Hammer)
(PC as Baron Frankenstein)
Filmed 13 January – 26 February 1969, at Elstree Studios
Directed by Terence Fisher
with Veronica Carlson, Maxine Audley, Freddie Jones, Simon Ward

Made in Britain
Dracula and Frankenstein Make Money For Britain
(PC as interviewee)
Filmed at Elstree 7 February 1969
Tx 10 February 1969
Interviewer Michael Sullivan
with James Carreras, Veronica Carlson

Incense for the Damned
(PC as Dr Walter Goodrich)
Filmed April – May 1969
Directed by Robert Hartford-Davis
with Patrick Macnee, Patrick Mower, Edward Woodward

Scream and Scream Again (Amicus)
(PC as Benedek)
Filmed from 5 May 1969
Directed by Gordon Hessler
with Vincent Price, Christopher Lee, Michael Gothard

One More Time
(PC, uncredited, as Baron Frankenstein)
Directed by Jerry Lewis
PC's appearance filmed at Shepperton Studios 23 July 1969
with Sammy Davis Jnr, Peter Lawford, Christopher Lee, Percy Herbert

The Morecambe and Wise Show (BBC TV)
Tx: 27 July 1969
Recorded 30 – 31 May 1969
Rehearse 23 – 29 May Forrester's Hall, 269 Kilburn High Rd, London
Producer John Ammonds
with Eric Morecambe, Ernie Wise, Bobbie Gentry, Vince Hill, Kenny Ball, Janet Webb

The Morecambe and Wise Show (BBC TV)
Recorded 16 – 17 August 1969
Rehearse 11 – 15 August
Producer John Ammonds
with Eric Morecambe, Ernie Wise

The Vampire Lovers (Hammer/AIP)
(PC as General Spielsdorf)
Filmed from 19 January 1970 – 4 March 1970, at Elstree Studios
Directed by Roy Ward Baker
with Ingrid Pitt, Pippa Steel, Madeline Smith, George Cole, Dawn Addams

Line-Up
(PC as guest)
Recorded 22 February 1970

While We're On The Subject: Television
(PC as interviewee)
Tx: 26 February 1970

London This Week
(PC as guest)
Tx: 8 June 1970
Recorded 5 June 1970

The House That Dripped Blood (Amicus)
(PC as Philip Grayson)
Filmed from 29 June 1970, at Shepperton Studios
Directed by Peter Duffell
with Joss Ackland, Wolfe Morris

I, Monster (Amicus)
(PC as Frederick Utterson)
Filmed from 10 October 1970, at Shepperton Studios
Directed by Stephen Weeks
with Christopher Lee, Mike Raven, Richard Hurndall, Susan Jameson

The Morecambe and Wise Christmas Show (BBC 1)
Tx: 25 December 1970

Recorded 16 December 1970
Rehearse 11 – 15 December
Producer John Ammonds
with Eric Morecambe, Ernie Wise, William Franklyn, Eric Porter, Edward Woodward

Blood from the Mummy's Tomb
(Hammer)
Filming 11 January 1971
Directed by Seth Holt
(Cushing completed only one day's filming and does not appear)
with Valerie Leon

Twins of Evil (Hammer)
(PC as Gustav Weil)
Filmed 22 March 1971 – 30 April 1971, at Pinewood Studios
Directed by John Hough
with Mary and Madelaine Collinson, Dennis Price, Damien Thomas

Nature Spectacular (BBC 2)
(PC as guest)
Recorded 27 – 29 July 1971
Locations Harpenden, Kent
Producer Richard Brock

Tales from the Crypt (Amicus)
(PC as Arthur Edward Grimsdyke)
Filmed from 13 September 1971, at Shepperton Studios
Directed by Freddie Francis
with Robin Philips, David Markham

Dracula A.D. 1972 (Hammer)
(PC as Lawrence and Lorrimer Van Helsing)
Filmed 27 September – 5 November 1971, at Elstree Studios
Directed by Alan Gibson
with Christopher Lee, Michael Coles, Stephanie Beacham, Christopher Neame

Late Night Extra (BBC Radio 2)
(PC as interviewee)
30 September 1971 live from Broadcasting House
Producer Tony Luke

Be My Guest – Peter Cushing
(BBC Radio 2)
Broadcast 19 November 1971
Recorded 7 October 1971 at Brown's Hotel, Mayfair
Producer John Knight

Man Alive: Comics (BBC 2)
(PC as interviewee)
Recorded 20 – 22 November 1971
Producer James Clark

Fear in the Night (Hammer)
(PC as Michael Carmichael)
Filmed 15 November – 17 December 1971, at Elstree Studios
Directed by Jimmy Sangster
with Judy Geeson, Joan Collins, Ralph Bates

Sounds Natural (BBC Radio 4)
(PC as guest)
Recorded 20 November 1971 at BBC Bristol
Broadcast 10 January 1972

Dr Phibes Rises Again (AIP)
(PC as Captain of the Elsinore Castle*)*
Filmed December 1971, at Elstree Studios

Directed by Robert Fuest
with Robert Quarry, Vincent Price, Terry-Thomas, John Cater

Pánico en el Transiberiano (Horror Express) (Granada /Benmar)
(PC as Dr Wells)
Filmed December 1971 – January 1972, at Studio 70 Complex, Madrid
Directed by Eugenio Martin
With Christopher Lee, Telly Savalas

The Creeping Flesh
(Tigon British/World Film Services)
(PC as Professor Emmanuel Hildern)
Filmed from 31 January 1972, at Shepperton Studios
Directed by Freddie Francis
with Christopher Lee, Lorna Heilbron, George Benson

Asylum (Amicus)
(PC as Mr Smith)
Filmed from 1 April 1972, at Shepperton Studios
PC filming 6, 7 April 1972
Directed by Roy Ward Baker
with Barry Morse, Ann Firbank, John Franklyn-Robbins

Nothing But The Night (Charlemagne)
(PC as Sir Mark Ashley)
Filmed from 18 April 1972, at Pinewood Studios
Directed by Peter Sasdy
with Christopher Lee, Georgia Brown, Diana Dors

Twenty Questions (BBC Radio 4)
(PC as Mystery Voice)
Rehearse/Record 2 June 1972, at the Central Hall, Chatham
Broadcast 5 July 1972
Producer John Cassells

Going for A Song (BBC 1)
Recorded 9 June 1972 at Studio A, BBC Bristol
Producer John King

~~And Now The Screaming Starts!
(Amicus)
(PC as Dr Pope)
Filmed from 17 July 1972, at Shepperton Studios
Directed by Roy Ward Baker
with Stephanie Beacham, Ian Ogilvy

Frankenstein and the Monster From Hell (Hammer)
(PC as Baron Frankenstein)
Filmed from 18 September – 27 October 1972, at Elstree Studios
Directed by Terence Fisher
with Shane Briant, John Stratton, Madeline Smith

The Satanic Rites of Dracula (Hammer)
(PC as Lorrimer Van Helsing)
Filmed from 13 November 1972 – 3 January 1973, at Elstree Studios
Directed by Alan Gibson
with Christopher Lee, Joanna Lumley, Freddie Jones, Michael Coles, William Franklyn

Ask Aspel (BBC 1)
(PC as guest)
Tx: 7 January 1974
Recorded 4 January 1973

Producer Granville Jenkins
with Tony Blackburn

Nationwide (BBC 1)
(PC as guest *'to talk about your latest film,* **Nothing But The Night***')*
Tx: 4 January 1973

The Morecambe and Wise Show (BBC 1)
Tx: 23 March 1973
Recorded 13 February 1973
Rehearse 5 – 11 February 1973
Producer John Ammonds
with Eric Morecambe, Ernie Wise, Georgie Fame, Alan Price, Ann Hamilton

P.M. (BBC Radio 4)
Tx: 18 April 1973
Produced by Helen Wilson
(PC interviewee)

The Zoo Gang: The Counterfeit Trap (ITC)
(PC as Judge Gautier)
Tx 26 April 1974
Filmed April 1973, in France
Directed by John Hough
with John Mills, Barry Morse, Lilli Palmer, Jacqueline Pearce, Philip Madoc

Madhouse (Amicus)
(PC as Herbert Flay)
Filmed from 14 May 1973, at Twickenham Studios
Directed by Jim Clark
with Vincent Price, Adrienne Corri, Linda Hayden

Film 73 (BBC 1)
Featuring filming of **Madhouse**

From Beyond the Grave (Amicus)
(PC as the Proprietor)
Filmed from 4 June 1973
Directed by Kevin Connor
with Ian Carmichael, Ian Bannen, David Warner, Ian Ogilvy

The Amazing World of Kreskin
(Tyne Tees Television)
(PC as guest)
Recorded June 1973
with David Kreskin

The Price of Fear: The Man Who Hated Scenes (BBC World Service)
Recorded 16 June 1973
Producer John Dyas
with Vincent Price

Woman's Hour (BBC Radio 4)
Tx: 20 June 1973
Producer Kay Evans

The Beast Must Die (Amicus)
(PC as Dr Christopher Lundgren)
Filmed from 16 July 1973, at Shepperton Studios
Directed by Paul Annett
with Calvin Lockhart, Charles Gray, Michael Gambon

Orson Welles Great Mysteries:
La Grande Breteche
by Honoré De Balzac, adapted by Martin Worth (Anglia TV)
(PC as Count Gerard De Merret)
Directed by Peter Sasdy

Filmed September 1973
US Tx: 23 November 1973
UK Tx: 27 July 1974
with Susannah York, Michael Gambon

The Legend of the 7 Golden Vampires
(Hammer/Shaw)
(PC as Professor Van Helsing)
Filmed 22 October – 11 December 1973, at
Shaw Studios, Hong Kong
Directed by Roy Ward Baker (and Chang
Cheh, uncredited)
*with Julie Ege, David Chiang, Robin Stewart,
John Forbes-Robertson*

Shatter (Hammer/Shaw)
(PC as Rattwood)
Filmed 17 December 1973 – 15 January 1974
Directed by Michael Carreras (and Monte
Hellman, uncredited)
*with Stuart Whitman, Anton Diffring, Ti Lung,
Lily Li*

La grande trouille (aka Tendre Dracula)
(Vincent Malle-Renn)
(PC as MacGregor)
Filmed January 1974, in France
Directed by Pierre Grunstein
with Alida Valli, Miou-Miou

The Ghoul (Tyburn)
(PC as Dr Lawrence)
Filmed from 4 March 1974,
at Pinewood Studios
Directed by Freddie Francis
*with John Hurt, Don Henderson, Gwen Watford,
Veronica Carlson*

This Is Your Life: Christopher Lee
(Thames Television)
(PC as guest)
Tx: 3 April 1974
*with Vincent Price, Oliver Reed, Veronica
Carlson, Trevor Howard*

What Was He Like?
(PC explains his ideas about the life of Christ)
Recorded Easter 1974

Space: 1999: Missing Link
by Edward Di Lorenzo (ITC/Rai/Group Three)
(PC as Raan)
Filmed May 1974, at Pinewood Studios
Directed by Ray Austin
Tx: 27 February 1976
*with Martin Landau, Barbara Bain, Barry Morse,
Joanna Dunham*

Start The Week (BBC Radio 4)
(PC as guest)
Tx: 15 August 1974 (live)
Producer Hugh Purcell

Legend of the Werewolf (Tyburn)
(PC as Paul Cataflanque)
Directed by Freddie Francis
Filmed from 19 August 1974, at Pinewood
Studios
*with David Rintoul, Ron Moody, Roy Castle,
Hugh Griffith*

Taste for Adventure: Fists of Fire (BBC 1)
Tx: 16 January 1975
Documentary re the boom in kung-fu films,
featuring behind-the-scenes footage of **The
Legend of the 7 Golden Vampires**

Shock Waves (Joseph Brenner/Zopix)
(PC as SS Commander)
Filmed June 1975, on location in Florida
Directed by Ken Wiederhorn
with Brooke Adams, Fred Buch, Jack Davidson

Tomorrow (NBC)
(PC as guest)
with Tom Snyder, Forrest J Ackerman

Trial by Combat (Weintraub/Heller)
(PC as Sir Edward Gifford)
Filmed 1975 on location in London
Directed by Kevin Connor
*with John Mills, Donald Pleasence, Barbara
Hershey*

Horseshoe Theatre Basingstoke
The Heiress by Ruth and Augustus Goetz
21 October – 1 November 1975
(PC as Dr Austin Soper)
Directed by Guy Slater
with Helen Ryan, Jonathan Newth

Haunted – Herstmonceaux Castle
(PC as narrator) 1975
Directed by Paul Annett

The Amazing World of Cinema:
The Mad Scientists (VPS Polymedia)
(PC as narrator/presenter)

Looks Familiar
(PC as guest)
with Denis Norden

The Devil's Men (Getty/Poseidon)
(PC as Baron Corofax)
Directed by Costas Carayiannis
Filmed in November 1975, on location in
Greece
*with Donald Pleasence, Luan Peters,
Nikos Vewrlekis, Costa Skouras*

At the Earth's Core (Amicus)
(PC as Dr Abner Perry)
Filmed from 20 January – March 1976,
at Pinewood Studios
Directed by Kevin Connor
with Doug McClure, Caroline Munro

The New Avengers: The Eagle's Nest
(Mark One)
by Brian Clemens
(PC as Dr Mebach Von Claus)
Tx: 17 October 1976
Filmed April 1976, on location (Skye) and at
Pinewood Studios
Directed by Desmond Davis
*with Patrick Macnee, Joanna Lumley,
Gareth Hunt*

Star Wars (Lucasfilm)
(PC as Grand Moff Tarkin)
Filmed March – June 1976, at Elstree Studios
PC filming from 8 May 1976
Directed by George Lucas
*with Carrie Fisher, David Prowse, Leslie
Schofield, Don Henderson*

The Great Houdinis (US TV)
(PC as Sir Arthur Conan Doyle)
Filmed in Los Angeles, May 1976
(PC filming 12 – 15 May)
Directed by Melville Shavelson
Tx: 8 October 1976 (US)

*with Ruth Gordon, Bill Bixby, Paul Michael
Glaser, Maureen O'Sullivan*

Clapperboard (Thames TV)
Behind-the-scenes on **At the Earth's Core**
Tx: 12 July 1976
with Chris Kelly

Magpie (Thames TV)
Tx: 20 July 1976
Behind the scenes on **At the Earth's Core**
*with Jenny Hanley, Douglas Rae,
Mick Robertson*

Jim'll Fix It: Bank Holiday Special (BBC TV)
('Horror make-up with Peter Cushing')
Tx: 28 August 1976
*with Jimmy Savile, Freddie 'Parrot Face' Davis,
Guys 'n' Dolls*

Aliens in the Mind
(BBC Radio 4 / Radio Scotland)
(PC as Dr John Cornelius)
A six-part serial
1: **Island Genesis** 2 January 1977
2: **Hurried Exodus** 9 January
3: **Unexpected Visitations** 16 January
4: **Official Intercessions** 23 January
5: **Genetic Revelations** 30 January
6: **Final Tribulations** 6 February
Produced by John Dyas
Script by Rene Basilico from an idea by
Robert Holmes
*with Vincent Price, Richard Hurndall, Fraser
Kerr, Irene Sutcliffe, Sandra Clark*

Die Standarte (Battleflag) (Ottokar Runz)
(PC as Major Von Hackenberg)
Filmed October – December 1976 in Spain
and Vienna
Director Ottokar Runz
With Simon Ward, Jon Finch, Viktor Staal

The Uncanny (Cinevideo/Tor)
(PC as Wilbur Gray)
Filmed from 16 November 1976, in
Panavision Studios, Montreal and Pinewood
Studios
Directed by Denis Heroux
with Ray Milland

A Land Looking West (Swan)
(PC as narrator)
Producer John Izzard

Hitler's Son (Naxos)
(PC as Heinrich Haussner)
Filmed in September 1977 – January 1978, at
Arri Studios Munich and on location in Bavaria
Directed by Rod Amateau
with Bud Cort

A Touch of the Sun (Fusetcourt)
(PC as Mr Commissioner Potts)
Filmed 19 June 1978 – 20 August 1978
(PC from 27 July), on location in Zambia
Directed by Peter Curran
*with Oliver Reed, Keenan Wynn, Bruce Boa,
Sylvaine Charlet*

Arabian Adventure (Badger)
(PC as Wazir Al Wuzara)
Filmed September 1978, at Pinewood Studios
Directed by Kevin Connor
*with Christopher Lee, Oliver Tobias,
Milo O'Shea*

The Morecambe and Wise Show
(Thames TV)
(PC as guest)
Tx: 18 October 1978
with Donald Sinden, Judi Dench,
Leonard Sachs

The Detour (short)
(PC as narrator)
Filmed 1978
Directed by Rodney Holland
with John Galdes

Misterio en la isla de los monstruos
(Mystery on Monster Island)
(Fort/Armena)
(PC as William Kolderup)
Directed by Juan Piquer Simon
Filmed 1980, in Puerto Rico, Canary Islands
and Spain
with Terence Stamp, Ian Serra, Paul Naschy

A Tale of Two Cities (Hallmark)
(PC as Dr Alexander Manette)
Filmed 30 July 1980 for six weeks, at
Shepperton Studios and on location in
England and France
Directed by Jim Goddard
with Chris Sarandon, Billie Whitelaw,
Alice Krige, Flora Robson, Kenneth More

Hammer House of Horror:
The Silent Scream
(ITC/Cinema Arts/Hammer)
by Francis Essex
(PC as Martin Blueck)
Tx: 25 October 1980
Shooting of series from 28 June 1980 on
location in Buckinghamshire
Directed by Alan Gibson
with Brian Cox, Elaine Donnelly

The Morecambe and Wise Christmas
Show (Thames TV)
(PC as guest)
Tx: 25 December 1980
Thames Television
with Peter Barkworth, Jill Gascoine,
Alec Guinness, Peter Vaughn, Gemma Craven

Asalto al casino (Black Jack)
(Diffusion SA/Cinespana)
(PC as Sir Thomas Bedford)
Directed by Max H Boulois
Filmed December 1980/January 1981
with Claudine Auger, Hugo Stiglitz, Brian
Murphy

Top Secret! (Abrahams, Zucker, Zucker)
(PC as Bookshop Proprietor)
Filmed 1982
Directed by Jim Abrahams, Jerry Zucker,
David Zucker
with Val Kilmer, Lucy Gutteridge, Michael
Gough, Jeremy Kemp

House of the Long Shadows
(Golan Globus/Cannon)
(PC as Sebastian Grisbane)
Directed by Pete Walker
Filmed August – September 1982,
on location at Rotherfield Park, East Tisted,
Hants
with Vincent Price, Christopher Lee, John
Carradine, Julie Peasgood, Sheila Keith,
Desi Arnaz Jr

Sword of the Valiant
(Golan Globus/Cannon)
(PC as Gaspar, the Seneschal)
Filmed September – October 1982,
in Ireland, Wales and France
Directed by Stephen Weeks
with Miles O'Keeffe, Ronald Lacey, John Rhys
Davies, Cynelle Claire

Tales of the Unexpected: The Vorpal
Blade (Anglia TV)
by Edward D Hoch, adapted by Robin
Chapman
(PC as Karl Von Baden)
Tx: 28 May 1983
Directed by John Jacobs
with John Bailey, Anthony Higgins

Breakfast Time (BBC 1)
Tx: 14 June 1983
PC as guest of the day, including clips from
House of the Long Shadows

Helen Keller: The Miracle Continues
(PC as Professor Copeland)
Filmed 1983
Directed by Alan Gibson
with Blythe Danner, Mare Winningham

The Masks of Death (Tyburn)
(PC as Sherlock Holmes)
Filmed from 21 July 1984
Directed by Roy Ward Baker
with John Mills, Ray Milland, Anton Diffring,
Anne Baxter

Biggles (Compact Yellowbill/Tambarle)
(PC as Air Commodore William Raymond)
Filmed 21 January – March 1985, at
Pinewood Studios
Directed by John Hough
with Neil Dickson, Alex Hyde-White, Fiona
Hutchison

Wogan (BBC 1)
(PC as interviewee, with Nicholas Rowe)
Tx: 10 March 1986 (live)

Jim'll Fix It
(PC as 'fixee' choosing the Helen Cushing Rose)
Producer Roger Ordish
with Christopher Wheatcroft

Pebble Mill at One (BBC 1)
(PC as interviewee)
Tx: 24 March 1986

Look North (BBC 1)
(PC as interviewee)
Tx: 5 June 1986

Everyman: The True Story of
Frankenstein (BBC 1)
(PC as interviewee)
Tx: 19 October 1986

Omnibus: Hammer – The Studio That
Dripped Blood (BBC 2)
(PC as interviewee)
Tx: 26 June 1987
Producers Nick Jones and David Thompson
Narrator Charles Gray

Wogan (BBC 1)
(PC as interviewee)
Tx: 22 May 1987

Terry Wogan hosts first in a two-part
holiday celebration of the golden days of
British cinema
with Christopher Lee, Bryan Forbes, Bernard
Cribbins

Wogan (BBC 1)
(PC as interviewee)
Tx: 19 December 1987

Wogan (BBC 1)
(PC as interviewee)
Tx: 24 February 1988
with Colonel John Blashford-Snell, Joan Chen,
Aztec Camera

Peter Cushing: A One-Way Ticket to
Hollywood (Tyburn)
Tx: 4 June 1989
Directed by Alan Bell
with Dick Vosburgh

This Is Your Life: Peter Cushing
(Thames TV)
Tx: 21 February 1990
with Christopher Lee, Caroline Munro, David
Rintoul, Freddie Jones, Gwen Watford, Peter
Ustinov, Sir James Carreras

The Human Factor: For the Love of
Helen (TVS)
(PC as interviewee)

Newsroom South East (BBC 1)
(PC as interviewee)
Tx: 12 July 1990
with Len Harris

Newsroom South East (BBC 1)
(PC as interviewee)
Tx: 9 August 1990

Human Conflict (BBC Radio Kent)
Broadcast 29 December 1990
Producer Michael Bath
with Alan Dobie

Pebble Mill (BBC 1)
(PC as guest)
Tx: 31 October 1991

Behind the Headlines (BBC 2)
(PC as guest)
Tx: 2 December 1992
with Linda Agran

BBC News (BBC 1)
(PC as interviewee)
Tx: 5 August 1993

Flesh and Blood: The Hammer
Heritage of Horror
(Heidelberg/Bosustow/Hammer)
(PC as narrator)
Part One
Tx: 8 August 1994
Part Two
Tx: 15 August 1994
Recorded 17 May 1994
Directed by Ted Newsom
with Christopher Lee

Addendum

Curtain Up! Presents Stars in Their Choices
Seagulls over Sorrento
by Hugh Hastings
(BBC Light Programme)
(PC as Able Seaman Badger)
Broadcast 4 Jan 1956
Producer Charles LeFaux
with Shaun O'Riordan, Gordon Jackson, Deryck Guyler

The Stars in their Choices
Escape Me Never
by Margaret Kennedy
(BBC Light Programme)
(PC as Sebastian Sanger)
Broadcast 11 Jan 1956
Producer Hugh Stewart
with Mai Zetterling, Brewster Mason

Cushing as the harassed Arthur Grimsdyke in *Tales From the Crypt* (1971)

Source Notes

1 Little Horror
1 *Hammer House of Horror* #18, interview with Alan Frank, March 1978
2 ibid
3 *TV Mirror,* 'The Peter Cushing Story' 3 April 1954
4 Interview with Alan Frank, op cit
5 *An Autobiography* Peter Cushing 1986
6 ibid
7 ibid
8 'The Peter Cushing Story' 3 April 1954, op cit
9 ibid

2 The Madman of Purley
1 Cushing, 1986, op cit
2 ibid
3 'The Peter Cushing Story' 3 April 1954, op cit
4 *TV Times* interview with Katie Ekberg, 3 June 1989
5 'The Peter Cushing Story' 3 April 1954, op cit
6 Cushing, 1986, op cit
7 'The Peter Cushing Story' 3 April 1954, op cit
8 ibid
9 ibid
10 *Past Forgetting* Peter Cushing 1988

3 Hooray For Hollywood
1 *TV Mirror,* 'The Peter Cushing Story' 10 April 1954
2 *Little Shoppe of Horrors* #8, interview with James Kravaal, May 1984
3 'The Peter Cushing Story' 10 April 1954, op cit
4 ibid
5 Cushing, 1986, op cit
6 'The Peter Cushing Story' 10 April 1954, op cit
7 Cushing, 1986, op cit
8 *James Whale* James Curtis 1982
9 Cushing, 1986, op cit
10 'The Peter Cushing Story' 10 April 1954, op cit

4 Take Me Back To Dear Old Blighty
1 Cushing, 1986, op cit
2 *TV Mirror,* 'The Peter Cushing Story' 17 April 1954
3 Interview with the author 1999
4 'The Peter Cushing Story', 17 April 1954, op cit
5 *TV Mirror,* 'Peter is so Patient' 29 October 1955
6 *A One-Way Ticket to Hollywood,* Tyburn, 1989
7 Cushing, 1986, op cit
8 Interview with the author 1999
9 'Peter is so Patient' 29 October 1955, op cit
10 Interview with the author 1999
11 Cushing, 1986, op cit
12 Interview with the author 1999
13 Cushing, 1986, op cit
14 Tyburn documentary, 1988, op cit
15 *Illustrated* Magazine 7 August 1943
16 'The Peter Cushing Story' 17 April 1954, op cit
17 *Times* 7 August 1943
18 Cushing, 1986, op cit
19 *On Q* Kenneth Barrow London 1992

5 French Without Tears
1 Cushing, 1986, op cit
2 *Evening Standard* 10 October 1944
3 Interview with the author 1999
4 Cushing, 1986, op cit
5 *Times* 26 December 1944
6 *Tatler and Bystander* 26 December 1944
7 Quoted in *Peter Cushing,* Donald Fearney, 1995
8 Cushing, 1986, op cit
9 ibid
10 *TV Mirror,* 'The Peter Cushing Story' 24 April 1954
11 *The Life of Laurence Olivier,* Thomas Kiernan, 1981
12 *Laurence Olivier – A Biography,* Donald Spoto 1991
13 Tyburn documentary, 1989, op cit
14 Spoto, op cit

6 Down And Under And Back Again
1 *Darlings of the Gods,* Garry O'Connor, 1984
2 Spoto, op cit
3 Interview with the author 1999
4 Interview with the author 1999
5 Cushing, 1986, op cit
6 Interview with the author 1999
7 Cushing, 1986, op cit
8 Interview with the author 1999
9 *What's On in London* 18 February 1949
10 *Old Vic Yearbook* 1949
11 *Evening Standard* 28 March 1972
12 Interview with the author 1999
13 'The Peter Cushing Story' 24 April 1954, op cit
14 *Tatler* September 1950
15 Cushing, 1986, op cit

7 The Pride of Alexandra Palace
1 Cushing, 1986, op cit
2 *Sight and Sound,* 'Not Quite So Intimate', by Nigel Kneale, Spring 1959
3 *TV Mirror* 'The Peter Cushing Story' 1 May 1954
4 Letter to the author 1999
5 *Radio Times* 1 March 1952
6 'The Peter Cushing Story' 1 May 1954, op cit
7 Cushing, 1986, op cit
8 Interview with the author 1999
9 Letter to the author 1999
10 Interview with Mark A Miller, *Christopher Lee and Peter Cushing,* 1995
11 Letter to the author 1999
12 Cushing, 1986, op cit
13 *Radio Times* 14 March 1953
14 Cushing, 1986, op cit

8 Busy Days and Black Knights
1 *Radio Times* 4 August 1953
2 *Radio Times* 22 August 1953
3 *Radio Times* 23 January 1954
4 ibid
5 *Radio Times* 13 February 1954
6 *Evening Standard* 15 March 1954
7 *Daily Cinema* 9 September 1954

9 Nineteen Eighty-Four And All That
1 Interview with the author 1999

2 Tyburn documentary, 1988, op cit
3 *Daily Worker* 14 December 1954
4 *Daily Express* 14 December 1954
5 *Daily Sketch* 14 December 1954
6 Nigel Kneale, op cit
7 *Times* 31 January 1955
8 *Observer* 6 February 1955
9 *Radio Times* 1955

10 Richard II, Irving Nil
1 *Radio Times* 1955
2 Letter to the author 1999
3 Interview with the author 1999
4 Interview with the author 1999
5 *Radio Times* 29 December 1955
6 *Daily Telegraph* 30 December 1955
7 Quoted in *Hammer Films,* Johnson/Del Vecchio, 1996
8 *Radio Times* 12 August 1956

11 Enter Baron Frankenstein
1 *Tall Dark and Gruesome,* Christopher Lee 1997
2 Interview with the author 1999
3 Interview with the author 1999
4 C A Lejeune, the *Observer* 2 May 1957
5 *Tribune* May 1957
6: *New York Journal* 7 August 1957
7 *Famous Monsters of Filmland* interview with Steve Swires, August 1978
8 *Daily Telegraph* 14 January 1957
9 *Hammer Horror* #7, interviewed with Marcus Hearn, September 1995
10 Interview in *Peter Cushing,* Johnson/Del Vecchio, 1996
11 Interview in *Hammer Films,* Johnson/Del Vecchio, 1996
12 *Times* 3 March 1958

12 A Feast for the Horror-Gobblers
1 *The Films of Peter Cushing* Gary Parfitt 1998
2 Quoted in *A History of Horrors,* Denis Meikle, 1996
3 Tyburn documentary, 1988, op cit
4 Interview with James Kravaal, op cit
5 *Shivers* #22 October 1995
6 *Video Watchdog* #25, interview with Bill Kelley, September 1994
7 *Daily Telegraph* 31 May 1958
8 *Times* May 1958
9 *Variety* 7 May 1958
10 *New York Daily News* 29 May 1958
11 *New York Herald Tribune* 29 May 1958
12 *Daily Cinema*
13 *Kinematograph Weekly* 20 January 1958
14 *Daily Cinema* 2 January 1958
15 Letter to the author 1999
16 Interview with the author 1999
17 *Observer* 31 August 1958
18 *Evening Standard* 28 August 1958
19 *Daily Express* 29 August 1958
20 *Radio Times* 12 March 1958
21 *Times* 14 March 1958
22 *Radio Times* 7 May 1958
23 *Daily Telegraph* 9 May 1958
24 *Evening Standard* 26 May 1958
25 *News of the World* 25 May 1958

13 Elementary Exercises

1 *TV Mirror* 'Toys? They're Not Child's Play' July 1956
2 *Holmes of the Movies,* David Stuart Davies, 1976
3 *Films and Filming* March 1959
4 Quoted in *A History of Horrors* 1996
5 *Daily Cinema* 5 September 1958
6 *Evening Bulletin,* quoted in *Hammer Films,* 1996
7 *Newsweek* quoted in *Shivers #22*
8 *Observer* 29 March 1959
9 *Sunday Times* 29 March 1959

14 That C-r-e-e-p-y Character

1: David Stone *Everybody's* magazine 7 February 1959
2: Cushing, 1986, op cit
3: *Past Forgetting* 1988
4: Steve Swires, *Monsters of Filmland,* August 1978
5: *Christopher Lee and Peter Cushing,* Mark A Miller, 1994
6: *Evening News* 28 September 1959
7 Parfitt, op cit
8 *Little Shoppe of Horrors #4* 1978
9 *Variety* 10 February 1960
10 *Times* 8 February 1960
11 *Daily Telegraph* 6 August 1959
12 *Times* 7 August 1959
13 Vivien Hislop in *Evening News,* 7 November 1959
14 Parfitt, op cit

15 Swashing My Buckle

1 *Times* 7 July 1960
2 *New York Herald Tribune* 6 September 1960
3 *Observer* 10 July 1960
4 *Kinematograph Weekly* 19 November 1963
5 *Variety* 11 January 1961
6 *New York Herald Tribune* 10 October 1963
7 *Kinematograph Weekly,* op cit
8 Cushing, 1988, op cit
9 ibid
10 Letter to the author 1999
11 *Variety* 12 May 1962
12 Interview with the author 1999

16 Abdication, Restoration

1 Patricia Lewis, *Daily Express,* 9 January 1962
2 William Hall, *Evening News* 25 March 1963
3 Cushing, 1988, op cit
4 *TV Times* 3 June 1962
5 ibid
6 *Daily Telegraph* 4 June 1962
7 *Daily Mirror* 24 May 1963
8 *Radio Times* 2 November 1963
9 *A History of Horrors* 1996, op cit
10 ibid
11 Quoted in *The Hammer Story,* Hearn/Barnes, 1997
12 *Times* 16 April 1964
13 Hammer publicity for *The Gorgon*
14 Interview with the author 1999
15 *Films and Filming* December 1963
16 *Daily Telegraph* 8 June 1963
17 *Monthly Film Bulletin* October 1964

17 Men of Steel

1 Cushing, 1988, op cit
2 John Doran *Film Review* March 1965
3 *New York Times* 2 September 1965
4 *Variety* 4 August 1965
5 Interview in *Dalekmania,* Lumiere Pictures, 1995
6 Letter to the author 1999

7 *People* 22 June 1965
8 *Daily Express* 23 June 1965
9 *Variety* 22 March 1967
10 Harold Hobson *Sunday Times* 6 August 1965
11 Cushing, 1988, op cit
12 *Radio Times* 4 November 1965
13 Cushing, 1988, op cit
14 William Hall *Evening News* 25 March 1966
15 *Times* 21 July 1966
16 *Evening Standard* 20 July 1966

18 Back to Baker Street

1 *Variety* 15 March 1967
2 Quoted in Parfitt, op cit
3 *Cinefantastique*
4 Letter to the author
5 Quoted in Parfitt, op cit
6 Interview in *Peter Cushing,* 1994
7 Interview with the author 1999
8 ibid
9 *Daily Mail* 25 September 1968
10 Interview with the author 1999

19 Scientist, Surgeon, Madman, Murderer

1 *Sunday Telegraph* 25 May 1969
2 *Sunday Times* 25 May 1969
3 *Variety* 11 June 1969
4 *Sunday Times* 3 September 1970
5 Interview with the author 1999
6 Interview in *Christopher Lee and Peter Cushing,* 1995
7 *Sunday Times* 28 February 1971

20 Losing Helen

1 Cushing, 1986, op cit
2 ibid
3 Cushing, 1988, op cit
4 Cushing, 1986, op cit
5 ibid
6 ibid
7 *Shivers #44,* interview with Adam Jezard, September 1997
8 Interview with the author 1999
9 Hammer publicity material
10 *Cinefantastique* Vol 2, #3
11 *Sunday Express* 11 July 1971
12 *Sunday Express* 18 July 1971
13 Cushing, 1988, op cit
14 Amicus publicity material
15 Cushing, 1988, op cit
16 *Shivers #22,* op cit
17 Amicus publicity material
18 *Cinefantastique* Vol 2, #3
19 *New York Times* 9 March 1972
20 Interview with Bill Kelley, op cit
21 *The Horror People* John Brosnan 1976
22 Marjorie Bilbow *Cinema TV Today* 7 October 1972
23 *Shivers #35,* interview with Jonathan Rigby and the author, November 1996

21 Can You Cure Unhappiness?

1 Margaret Hinxman *Sunday Telegraph* 23 June 1973
2 *Daily Telegraph* 24 June 1973
3 Mark A Miller interview, op cit
4 Amicus publicity material
5 *Evening Standard* 6 March 1972
6 *Evening Standard* 29 April 1972
7 *Evening Standard* July 1972
8 Interview with the author 1999
9 Interview with Bill Kelley, op cit
10 *The Hammer Story,* 1997, op cit
11 Interview with the author 1999
12 Interview with the author 1999

13 Letter to the author 1999
14 Cushing, 1988, op cit
15 ibid
16 American Peter Cushing Fan Club Journal #16

22 Treading Time

1 *News of the World* 9 June 1972
2 *Shivers #38,* interview with Adam Jezard, February 1997
3 Quoted in *Hammer Horror Collectors' Special,* 1994
4 *The Ghoul* publicity material
5 David Montgomery *Sunday Times* 11 August 1977
6 ibid
7 *Shivers #69,* interview with Mark A Miller, September 1998
8 *Famous Monsters of Filmland #146* August 1978
9 *Fangoria,* quoted in *The Films of John Carradine* 1999
10 Cushing, 1988, op cit
11 Interview with the author 1999
12 *Evening Standard* 15 July 1976
13 *Telegraph* 16 July 176
14 Unpublished interview with Simon Flynn, 2000
15 Parfitt, op cit

23 Still Dancin'

1 Quoted in *Peter Cushing* 1994
2 Tyburn documentary, 1988, op cit
3 *Rolling Stone* 25 August 1977
4 *Films and Filming* October 1977
5 *Evening News* 27 October 1977
6 *American Peter Cushing Club Journal* #13
7 ibid
8 Cushing, 1988, op cit
9 *Touch of the Sun* publicity material
10 *Starburst #27* September 1980
11 Manuel Valencia *Cinefantástico y de terror español 1900-1983* 1999
12 Interview with Mike Hodges 1999
13 Interview with Mike Hodges 1998
14 Letter to the author 1999

24 A Saint in Retirement

1 Cushing, 1988, op cit
2 Afterword in the Midnight Marquee reprint of *An Autobiography* 1999
3 Cushing, 1988, op cit
4 *Sunday Telegraph* 25 June 1983
5 Tyburn documentary, 1988, op cit
6 *Times* 24 December 1984
7 *Times* 23 May 1986
8 Quentin Falk *Guardian* 22 March 1986
9 *Time Out* 12 March 1986
10 *Express* 24 March 1986
11 *Today* 1 June 1987
12 *Scotsman* 23 May 1988
13 *Daily Telegraph* 22 May 1988
14 *TV Times* 3 June 1988
15 *Whitstable Times* 29 March 1989
16 *TV Times* 3 June 1989
17 Interview with the author 1999
18 *Times* 29 December 1990
19 Quoted in *Peter Cushing* 1994
20 Afterword in the Midnight Marquee reprint of *An Autobiography* 1999
21 *Telegraph* 12 August 1994
22 Afterword in the Midnight Marquee reprint of *An Autobiography* 1999
23 *Telegraph* 20 August 1994
24 *Independent* 12 August 1994

Bibliography

The British Film Yearbook 1947-48
Edited by Peter Noble
Skelton Robinson British Yearbooks

The Year That Made The Day
The British Broadcasting Corporation 1953

The Television Annual for 1954
Edited by Kenneth Baily
Odhams Press 1954

The British Film and Television Yearbook 1957-58
Edited by Peter Noble
British and American Press 1957

Three Men and A Gimmick
Including *The Peter Cushing Story* as told to Robert Hirst
The World's Work 1957

The Television Annual 1960
Edited by Kenneth Baily
Odhams Press 1959

The Gary Cooper Story
George Carpozi Jnr
W H Allen 1970

The Horror People
John Brosnan
Macdonald and Jane's 1976

Holmes of the Movies
David Stuart Davies
Bramhall House 1976

Helpmann
Elizabeth Salter
Angus and Robertson 1978

Olivier – The Life of Laurence Olivier
Thomas Kiernan
Sidgwick and Jackson 1981

James Whale
James Curtis
Scarecrow Press 1982

The Avengers
Dave Rogers
ITV Books/Michael Joseph 1983

Darlings of the Gods
A Year in the Lives of Laurence Olivier and Vivien Leigh
Garry O'Connor
Hodder and Stoughton 1984

Coming To You Live!
Behind the Screen: Memories of Forties and Fifties Television
Denis Norden, Sybil Harper and Norma Gilbert
Methuen 1985

The Avengers Anew
Dave Rogers
Michael Joseph 1985

An Autobiography
Peter Cushing
Weidenfeld and Nicholson 1986

Noël Coward: Collected Plays Two
Noël Coward
Methuen Publishing 1986

The Royal Almanac
Paul James
Ravette 1986

Past Forgetting
Peter Cushing
Weidenfeld and Nicholson 1988

Rattigan Plays: One
Terence Rattigan
Methuen 1988

Laurence Olivier – A Biography
Donald Spoto
HarperCollins 1991

On 'Q'
Kenneth Barrow
De Leon Memorial Fund 1992

Peter Cushing: The Gentle Man of Horror and his 91 Films
Deborah Del Vecchio and Tom Johnson
McFarland and Company 1992

British Television: An Illustrated Guide
Compiled for the BFI by Tise Vahimagi
Oxford University Press 1994

Christopher Lee and Peter Cushing and Horror Cinema
A Filmography of their 22 Collaborations
Mark A Miller
McFarland and Company 1995

Peter Cushing
Editor/Publisher Donald Fearney 1995

James Whale: A Biography
Mark Gatiss
Cassell 1995

A History of Horrors
The Rise and Fall of the House of Hammer
Denis Meikle
Scarecrow Press 1996

Hammer Films: An Exhaustive Filmography
Tom Johnson and Deborah Del Vecchio
McFarland and Company 1996

The Hammer Story
Marcus Hearn and Alan Barnes
Titan Books 1997

Tall Dark and Gruesome
Christopher Lee
W H Allen 1977/Victor Gollancz 1997

The British Television Drama Research Guide
Richard Down and Christopher Perry
Kaleidoscope 1997

The Films of Peter Cushing
Editor/Publisher Gary Parfitt 1975/Revised and updated 1998

1956 And All That
The Making of Modern British Drama
Dan Rebellato
Routledge 1999

John Carradine: The Films
Tom Weaver
McFarland and Company 1999

English Gothic: A Century of Horror Cinema
Jonathan Rigby
Reynolds and Hearn 2000

Christopher Lee: The Authorised Screen History
Jonathan Rigby
Reynolds and Hearn 2001

Sherlock Holmes On Screen
Alan Barnes
Reynolds and Hearn 2002

Periodicals
Cinefantastique
Daily Cinema
Doctor Who Magazine
Doctor Who Magazine Spring Special
Famous Monsters of Filmland
Fangoria
Film Review
Films and Filming
Films Illustrated
Hammer Horror
Hammer Horror Collectors' Special
The House of Hammer/Halls of Horror
Kinematograph Weekly
Monthly Film Bulletin
Radio Times
Shivers
Sight and Sound
Starburst
Starlog
The Tatler and Bystander
TV Mirror
TV Times
TV Zone

Fanzines
The American Peter Cushing Club Journal (editor Deborah Bennett)
The Cushing Courier (editor Brian Holland)
Little Shoppe of Horrors (editor Richard Klemensen)

Index

Cushing at home with one of his elaborate model theatres

Peter Cushing, Eunice Gayson and Richard Wordsworth in *The Revenge of Frankenstein* (1958)

Torrence (William Franklyn) consults Lorrimer Van Helsing
in *The Satanic Rites of Dracula* (1972)

The free-spending Frenchman Judge Gautier in *The Zoo Gang: The Counterfeit Trap* (1973)

Principle-Driven Skill Development

Principle-Driven Skill Development

In Traditional Martial Arts

RUSS SMITH

www.TambuliMedia.com
Spring House, PA USA

Disclaimer

The author and publisher of this book DISCLAIM ANY RESPONSIBILITY over any injury as a result of the techniques taught in this book. Readers are advised to consult a physician about their physical condition before undergoing any strenuous training or dangerous physical activity. This book details dangerous techniques that may cause serious physical injury and even death. Practice and training require a fit and healthy student and a qualified instructor.

First Tambuli Media edition: April 30, 2018
©2017 Russ L. Smith

ISBN-13: 978-1-943155-30-9
ISBN-10: 1-943155-30-5
Library of Congress Control Number: 2018942078

Photography by: Fishbone Creative
Edited by Mark V. Wiley
Interior Design by: Summer Bonne
Cover Design by: Alex Do and Summer Bonne

Table of Contents

武林館

Fighting Principles in the Chinese Style

Understand the forms of control, both physical and mental, in all timings: after, during, and before.

In defense, you must utilize the three gates to protect your center and avoid controlling one with two. Move with the strength of your frame to fill the void.

To reach the advanced level, you must stack all the odds in your favor, and overpower the opponent's will with your own.

In offense, you must express short power, utilizing a unified body. The hands are merely the point of contact.

Fill the dead moments, and do not allow hands to chase hands. By remaining relaxed and keeping your weapons online, the closest weapon will find the closest target.

When you master the three joints, you will flow around obstructions, control two with one, press ever forward, and safely create a bridge. Once connected, you can cross, break, stick, transfer, detain, move, and disengage at will.

You must understand the application of strong versus weak as you seek your opponent's center, using the proper hand to open the fourth door.

Always remember that weakening your opponent's structure steals his mind.

© Russ Smith, Burinkan Dojo

Acknowledgments

I would like to acknowledge and thank the following people for their support and encouragement over the years and during the creation of this book:

- My wife, Nicole, who supported my trips overseas and across the country, and my fervent desire to train and study nights and weekends for decades. I would especially like to thank her for opening our home to visitors and making them feel welcome.

- Eric Ling, who helped introduce the depth of quality martial arts in Malaysia and Singapore to the West. I credit him with teaching me what a Chinese teaching model can be, and how it can change our skill development process.

- Mark Wiley, who demonstrated what can be done to effectively transmit a set of traditions by rearranging the contents and using a clearer, more progressive instruction model. Thank you for your friendship, and for freely sharing your knowledge of Eskrima and Ngo Cho Kun with me.

- Marcus Davila, who first shared his insight into Goju-ryu, and helped me reconnect with the art after I drifted away to train in the "cousin arts." I'd also like to acknowledge your coaching and patient teaching ability combined with your tactile sensitivity and expert knowledge of throwing and locking. Lastly, thank you for being an amazing training partner and great friend. Without your openness to explore and pressure-test this material on the dojo floor, aka the "laboratory", we would not have such clarity of understanding. Most of the true, live, skills I have developed are directly attributed to our many hours of touching-hands.

- Kevin Halleran, who did not simply nod at my many early appeals to authority. For challenging me to evaluate and document my assumptions and biases. Thank you for suggesting I use my "Western" mind, and the rational tools of my profession to better understand and teach the art. Thank you for our long friendship and your support.

- Sensei Tony Madamba, who provided me with a strong foundation, and made sure I put in the work…"mo ichi do."

- To Sensei Kimo Wall, who gave me the opportunity to learn the Shodokan methods and provided an example of how to come to terms with tradition.

- To Sensei Gakiya Yoshiaki, who shared the spirit of Okinawa with me. Your evidence-based, pressure- and structure-tested teaching approach is something I value and pass on to my students.

- To Sifu Simon Liu (雷龍春), who freely taught me the once forbidden and rare art of Pak Mei.

- To Sifu Joshua Durham for assisting with the book photos and application examples.

And lastly, but not least, I'd like to thank these fine martial artists for their assistance understanding, and translating Chinese terms into their useful and correct context:

- Sifu Dominic Lim
- Sensei Hing-Poon Chan
- Sifu David Wong
- Tory Ellarson
- Sifu Robert Chu
- Sifu Grant Brown

Forewords

Patrick McCarthy

I am pleased to lend my name to Russ' book because it exemplifies and documents the results of an important journey.

Anyone familiar with my work knows I am passionate about the traditional fighting arts, but prefer functionality over empty ritual. I think Matsuo Basho/松尾芭蕉 [1644-1694] summed up tradition nicely when he wrote, *"Seek not to [blindly] follow in the footsteps of the men of old but rather continue to seek out what they sought."* This book by Russ Smith identifies and describes numerous application principles from all the potentially precursor influences on Goju-ryu. Most importantly, it discusses in extreme detail those closely-guarded secrets known by some, and vigorously sought by early Okinawan Karate pioneers, who were interested in the revered fighting arts of Fuzhou.

Even Miyagi Chojun's perspective on the topic (documented by Nakaima Genkai) of the mysteries of the art handed to him by his teacher, Higashionna Kanryo, point to a lack of understanding in the tradition's transmission:

"Studying karate nowadays is like walking in the dark without a lantern. We have to grope our way in the dark. There are so many things in karate which do not make sense and there are a lot of things I cannot understand. Therefore, while our grand masters are still alive, we have to see them and ask many questions. I think it is still very difficult to find the answers even if we did so."

The author and I have corresponded since the very early 90's. Russ had the good fortune to live in a small town visited periodically by one of my early students and closest, life-long, friends…Coach Ron Beer. I had the opportunity to learn some rare training practices and teach them to Ron. Russ' interests were piqued by the nature of my research, and he began writing to me with questions about the history of Goju-ryu and the progenitor Chinese influences that shaped its practice. Openly sharing with him what I could, Russ continued his journey to better understand the roots of Goju-ryu, both in Okinawa and elsewhere.

In subsequent years, Russ continued to delve deeply in his study of Okinawan Goju-ryu and eventually his pursuits took him to travel throughout the USA, Malaysia, Singapore, the Philippines and Okinawa, all to better understand its fighting concepts and study the art at its source. In addition to the principal tradition, Goju Ryu, his journey also brought him into contact with several southern-based Chinese disciplines [i.e. various schools of White Crane, Five Ancestor Boxing, Grand Ancestor, and White Eyebrow, etc.], which early Okinawan pioneers most likely met.

What Russ has done in this book is to provide dozens of application principles and practices from Southern-based Chinese fighting arts, including ones that most likely influenced Okinawan karate, and Goju Ryu specifically, and not only made them accessible, but most importantly, made them actionable. This work is supported by a theoretical premise I put forward in 1993, in which I suggested that kata were originally never meant to teach anything, but rather culminate the lessons already imparted in two-person drills (Habitual Acts of Physical Violence (HAPV)-Theory). Many of these principles are closely guarded in Fuzhou traditions. They are either overly-summarized as "keywords" or obfuscated in poems. However, in the work which lays before you, they are catalogued and presented in a logical progression with numerous examples.

The principles presented here can help any practitioner enhance their two-person training. They act as a checklist, allowing both the student and instructor to easily determine which principle[s] may be missing in a failed application. In doing so, the opportunity to once again bolster the training practice with the appropriate under-standing and modifications provides a pathway to develop valuable functional skillsets against the most common HAPV.

While explored primarily through the lens of Goju-ryu, such principles, coupled with the unique pathway presented, are essential to both the practitioner and instructor alike as a reminder of the aspects necessary for successful application. The majority of such principles are highly complementary within Goju-ryu, however, they are universal in nature. Like all good ideas, their utility is broad and their application value immeasurable.

I highly recommend this book, not only for its reference value in application principles and practices, but also for its unique structure surrounding teaching models that support the principle-driven skillsets, which are central to Okinawan karate in general, and to Goju Ryu specifically.

In conclusion, I am reminded of something Miyagi Chojun said at the 1936 "Meeting of the Okinawan Masters:" *"They say that karate has two separate sects: Shorin-ryu and Shorei-ryu, however, there is no clear evidence to support or deny this. If forced to distinguish the differences between these sects, then I would have to say that it is only teaching methods that divides them."* I believe the work of this young master most definitely supports such a belief and is destined to become a "go-to" reference for all practitioners of the traditional fighting arts, irrespective of style.

Patrick McCarthy
マカシー　パトリック
Hanshi 9th Dan
範士九段
Australian Black Belt Hall of Fame 2000
Canadian Black Belt Hall of Fame 2012

Marcus Davila

Although we don't know exactly when or where combative arts first began, the history of mankind serves as evidence there has always been a need for a civil and martial means of protection. While the nuances and semantics of each generation's martial traditions may not be fully understood without losing some degree of their original and intended meanings, they serve as an instrumental method from which to record, preserve and convey the wisdoms of discovery and subsistence.

Traditions are known to form and evolve through time from an amalgamation of cultural and cross-cultural origins and sources. The transmission of their essence ultimately becomes dependent on the perceptions, preferences, ability and intent of their promoters. As each generation continues to move farther from the origins of their predecessor's beliefs and methods, it becomes important to investigate the motives for which they were created, and then to substantiate the foundations by which they are followed and passed-on.

The authenticity of martial arts, along with its traditions and lineages will always be subject to speculation and contention due to the vague and fragmented aspects of its pasts. It is important to recognize that the intrinsic nature of customs is to change and adapt through the influences, resources and circumstances of environment, era and technology. If we are to move through the inconsistency of the past, we must consider the true essence and legacy of martial arts, their traditions and lineages are found and manifested through the underlying wisdoms of their teachings, which transcend beyond the attributes or interpretations of any one generation or cause.

Without deliberate means from which to identify, define and develop principle-based methods that effectively demonstrate, apply and evaluate skill progression and prowess, we become dependent on the narratives and experiences of others. The guidance of mentors plays an integral part in the progression of any learning and teaching process. If we are to move beyond learning and teaching through the repetition of imitation, the views of popular consensus, the confines of institutional authority and personal agendas, we must become capable of moving beyond the obstacles of our differences through the merit and fusion of provable pragmatic solutions.

It is with great admiration that I introduce the research and discovery of an avid and adept practitioner of the martial arts. In the following pages, Russ Smith, presents an insightful, intriguing survey of the Okinawan Goju-Ryu Karate style through the perspective of its Chinese influences. Each chapter contains an exceptional index and array of formative concepts for principle-driven teaching and training models, and serves as a beneficial guide from which to align and substantiate methods for the progression of learning and teaching.

I applaud the creation and perspective of this captivating and informative composition and anticipate it will elicit positive and everlasting effects on the future of how precepts of Okinawan Goju-Ryu Karate and their civil and martial strategies and tactics are viewed, regardless of style, lineage or affiliation. I truly believe that the concepts presented in this book will serve as an inspiration that illuminates the path for the

accomplishments of others. In closing I would like to extend my sincere gratitude for the time that Russ and I have spent on the floor sharing the journey as friends, students and teachers. I believe that the best days of our training are yet to come.

Sensei Marcus Davila
Okinawan Goju-Ryu Karate
Dade City, Florida USA

Fred Lohse

I remember a seminar, years ago, in Southern Japan. The sensei had a stellar reputation and excellent pedigree. Training was arduous though and included thousands of repetitions of basics, kata, arm and leg pounding, the works! We ended up tired and sore. Later when asked "What did you learn?" I had to answer honestly, "Nothing. We just worked hard all weekend." Martial arts is hard work so that in itself isn't bad. But that weekend was wasted unless I was just looking for a workout. What we didn't do all weekend was anything that would help us improve on our own after the weekend was over, and anything that clearly demonstrated the principles of our karate and how to develop it in ourselves.

Principles. Ok, another buzzword in martial arts. You hear it a lot these days. Principle-centered practice, principals of combat, principals of movement, and so on. Most systems are indeed based on specific principles. Many good teachers can tell you what they are. However, in Okinawan and Japanese karate circles, principles are often ignored or given lip service. Principles are instead replaced by the idea of revealed knowledge: one should "train the kata until the kata trains you". The idea is that through endless repetition, you will somehow get the system ingrained without realizing it. But, aside from it seeming to take decades to "get it," one major flaw in this model is the introduction of noise. If a teacher misses an important principle of the system in the repetitions, the student will never get it, and not even know it is missing. The repetitions will just ingrain the flaws along with the good material. So, what is one to do about that?

Sensei Russ Smith has taken the principles embedded in his practice and developed a training model that can both error-check the practice and instill the desired principles in the student. This is not simply a personal take on training and teaching. It is based in the use of directly transmitted (i.e., clearly taught) principles found in some Southern Chinese martial arts. It also uses some of the more modern, pedagogical approaches, such as the idea that "the best practitioner must be the best teacher," which many martial arts circles could benefit greatly from. Taken together, these ideas turn out to be complimentary, and challenge anyone who thinks that any change in the martial arts world is a step backwards.

Sensei Russ Smith's ideas seems pretty sound to me. Give the students the tools to self-correct and self-direct. Move from memorization to function. Do it in less time, and with less noise. Sure, repetition and lots of hard work is needed, but instead of waiting for the ideas to reveal themselves in practice, the practice is used to work with the ideas. It makes for a more robust training environment, even if it takes some of the mystique away from the teacher. And, spoiler alert: It is also more fun.

I am glad to see that Russ sensei decided to put this book together. I think both veteran and novice martial artists will enjoy it and find that some experimentation with these ideas will have a positive effect on their art. It represents many hours of hard work and

experimentation, of distilling what he has been taught, and of working on how to best pass that knowledge on. It is extraordinary that he shares it, as not everyone wants to give their best stuff to the public! Enjoy.

Sensei Fred Lohse
Chief Instructor – Boston Kodokan

武林館

1

Introduction

In my experience training, studying, and teaching Okinawan Goju-ryu karate, I've encountered a significant number of students and teachers who have shared many of my same concerns over the teaching model(s) often used to present the content of this tradition.

It is quite common that the curriculum of karate, regardless of specific *style*, is taught in three segments:

- ***Kihon:*** Fundamental motions, both offensive and defensive in nature, and typically practiced solo,

- ***Kata:*** Pre-arranged sequences, both solo and partner-based (as in bunkai-kumite, kiso kumite, sandan gi, and yakusoku kumite), and

- ***Kumite:*** Mock or practice-fighting, which often follows a kickboxing model, where the primary techniques often differed dramatically in shape, execution, and combination than the *kihon* and *kata* motions.

While it is perfectly rational to understand one's training in separate categories, it is unusual that these three forms of training are only *somewhat* overlapping in practice.

In this common model, the analysis and examination of kata (called bunkai / 分解) is an additional activity, resulting in reverse-engineered, self-defense applications

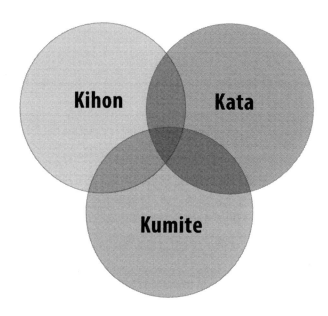

Venn Diagram of Karate's Three Forms of Training

(oyo / 応用 / "one-offs"[1]) or applications "borrowed" from other styles that attempted to explain the original meaning or context of the pre-arranged solo kata.

With this hodgepodge approach, many practitioners are left to assume there must be a list of *rules* for the understanding and application of kata...a "Rosetta stone" of sorts that helps unlock the mystery of the *oyo* contained within.

It has been my experience that this model (*kihon, kata, kumite, oyo*) has left many practitioners of ancient martial traditions in some way frustrated, as they are left with numerous questions:

- Why are the kihon motions not represented well, if at all, in the kumite?

- How will memorized, pre-arranged partner kata lead to live skills?

---

1 "One-off" – a uniquely situational response to a given context and stimulus. For example, "When a person grabs me with grip [X] and his left leg is forward, my right hand starts in [Y] posture and I will perform technique [Z]".

- Does the kickboxing model give me the skills to apply my kihon and kata motions in the appropriate context, and when it's needed the most?

- How will I be able to utilize the more unique motions and combinations only seen in the solo kata in a "live" method consistent with the style's core principles and preferences?

- Why do so many of the "Oyo Bunkai" that I see seem to be irrational, risky, one-offs, or counter to the ideas core to the style?

- Why, under more realistic speed, pressure, and range, do many of the "Oyo Bunkai" I am taught simply fail or leave me dangerously open to counter-attack?

- How will I feel confident that I can learn and then apply the lessons codified in the kata movements?

Because I shared many of these same concerns and questions, and because I was aware of the historical connections between Okinawan karate[2] (Goju-ryu in particular) and the martial arts in and around Fuzhou in the Fujian province of China, I sought out training[3] directly in several of those arts, which have a high likelihood of influencing the formation of the style. I did so, hoping to better understand the teaching methods and training models used by these styles to impact their skill development and application practices.

What I found in many cases was a more clearly defined set of "principles" describing the fighting concepts of the art. I also found that they offered alternative teaching methods to help guide students to apply their art more consistently, to employ their forms in the context in which they were (likely) originally intended, and to help develop "live" skill more quickly.

Chinese arts have long-written poems and books to describe the rationale behind their training methods and fighting theory, even if deeply encoded. The most famous

---

2 Particularly because of the early writings of Patrick McCarthy, Mark Bishop, John Sells, etc.

3 See "About the Author" for more information.

example to have influence in Okinawa is the *General Tian Bubishi*, translated and made widely available by Sensei Patrick McCarthy.

Sensei Patrick McCarthy with a copy of the *General Tian Bubishi*

As we discuss *principles* at length, it's important to first understand that our working definition of the word *principle* is an umbrella term for all of the following words:

- Strategy
- Concept
- Principle
- Theory
- Guideline
- Tactic

- Precept
- Maxim
- Rule
- Preference
- Keyword
- Admonition

A multitude of martial arts have developed, both independently and through innovation across the world and across human history. Unlike weapons, unarmed martial arts (by their nature) have not evolved via an arms and armor "arms race," but instead have developed as variations via a number of *preferences* and *tactics* for the use of the human body as a fighting machine, as well as a tremendous amount of variance in their teaching methods.

The principles discussed in this book, as well as their related examples, rely upon a set of underlying biases and assumptions that speak to the author's understanding and preference around the application of one fighting art, Okinawan Goju-ryu Karate, which is considered by the author to be a clinch-range, standing grappling *and* striking art.

While many of the principles discussed here can support other forms of martial arts at longer ranges, primarily striking *or* grappling art, not all principles will support all arts equally. If you apply Goju-ryu primarily as a striking art, then some of what is presented may not resonate as well with your training paradigm. That is perfectly acceptable, as this model is not the only useful model for understanding this art or all clinch-range arts, grappling arts or striking arts. The real value of this approach is it provides a useful model for outlining a set of goals (principles), suggests their consistent use, and puts focus on ensuring live skill development in its practitioners over the development of pre-determined, memorized routines.

Merely understanding a set of principles alone does not guarantee solutions to all the problems mentioned above; however, having a consistent set of definitions and a clear set of goals and guidelines can assist in developing numerous abilities in the practitioner, such as the following:

- The ability to understand what makes techniques both efficient and effective in application
- The ability to understand what elements of efficacy and effectiveness are missing in a failed application
- The ability to clearly define the skill-development value of a particular training drill

- The ability to utilize proven curriculum-development techniques, such as "backwards-planning"[4], to ensure a curriculum is progressive in its skill-development pedagogy

- The ability to more easily understand unfamiliar techniques and applications from other martial traditions and relate them to commonly understood principles

- The ability to error-correct training curriculum, reshaping it from "memory-based" to "skill-based," and from unnecessarily repetition to progressively skill-building

The highest value of utilizing a principles-first approach in training and teaching is to support the goal of true skill development.

So, HOW Do You Implement a "Principle-Driven" Model?

Even if you don't find yourself personally identifying with the problems discussed or the unanswered questions and concerns many traditional martial artists share, perhaps some of the potential benefits of the principle-driven approach, such as error-detection and correction, still appeal to you. Regardless, the next question to answer is, "If a principle-driven approach is so helpful, how does one make best use of principles in their training and teaching?"

There are several important steps to implement a principle-driven, skills-focused approach in your teaching:

1. It's important to understand that teaching IS communicating, and it represents a class of communication with its own common challenges. As such, terminology is critically important. You must both develop and utilize a consistent lexicon to 1) assist your own thinking and planning processes, and 2) enable clear, concise, and effective communication with students.

---

4 Backwards planning is a method for developing curriculum by clarifying goals before selecting or developing instructional methods and testing methodology.

2. It's important to identify those principles that represent your style's preferences and identify the physical skills that support those principles. Clearly identifying skillsets that support your style's principle-driven approach allows you to create and modify curriculum to support principle-related skill development.

3. It's critical to identify that TEACHING is a profession with a related skillset and goals, distinct from those of a practitioner. It's important as a teacher to be clear that our goals in teaching martial arts must include the idea that developing live skills in our students is a higher priority than training our student's memory. It's also important to keep in mind that students learn to apply information in a progressive process. Students first learn discreet components of information, then understand how that skillset fits into a broader context, and finally learn by applying their knowledge outside of pre-defined drills. Equally important, teachers should have a very clear picture of the goals they are putting forth for their students, and then develop ways of measuring student's progress against those goals. Only when those two activities are complete should the teacher then put effort into developing the drills and lesson plans the students will first encounter. Teachers should utilize this "backwards planning" approach to ensure their teaching methods actually support progressive skill-building.

4. Teachers should work to develop and modify their teaching curriculum, so it supports progressive skill development. First allowing students to gain discreet units of useful "knowledge" necessary to progress. Next, teachers should create training methods to allow students to understand the utility of their discreet skills in a larger context…where and how those methods are useful in self-defense, while also guiding students to combine and link useful skills in that context. Additionally, the teacher must provide an environment and platform that allows the student to both "pressure-test" what they know and also experiment with applying their art in situations not provided for in pre-defined lessons.

Let's discuss this process in a bit more detail.

Step 1 - Understand that teaching *is communicating*.

Shared terminology is the bedrock of effective communication. Teaching is a rather unique form of communication, one in which **the teacher** bears the burden of having to reach the student with their lesson. **The teacher is the only person in the relationship capable of determining whether the message has been** well-and-truly **received.**

This approach may be viewed as counter to the ancient Confucian model that shifts the teacher's burden for success largely to the student; a model that supports primarily the most gifted and/or motivated students.

> 举一隅, 不以三隅反, 则不复也
>
> "Every truth has four corners.
>
> As a teacher I give you one corner, and it is for you to find the other three."
>
> Confucius

The Confucian model has value in that it doesn't support coddling unmotivated students. However, it is perhaps *least appropriate* when applied to teaching martial arts because a student's ability to grasp a lesson quickly and fully may mean the difference between life and death.

With the stakes so high in this form of communication, it's important to communicate well and fully. To be both efficient and effective in communication, terminology must be clear, concise, and consistent, and jargon must be critically examined for usefulness.

Terminology should be clear, concise, and consistent.

Clarity is important because clear communication supports both *effectiveness* and *efficiency*, which are useful goals in any teaching environment.

The most *effective* communication creates an instant, shared understanding between the teacher and student. If communication is clear, the teacher can ascertain the following:

- Have a higher level of immediate confidence that the student received the lesson/message
- Have an easier time detecting and correcting any student errors or misunderstandings

Efficient communication is also *concise.* When communication is not concise, discussion, error-detection, and correction take up a larger portion of training time and is likely to interfere with the student's ability to practice skill-development exercises and then test against the material presented.

In a physical activity, such as martial arts, it's important to maximize physical practice time. Solo practice for beginners and partner-based for all other skill levels allows for true skill development as a primary goal of the student and the teacher. As *efficiency* is gained, teacher and student are able avoid the constant and laborious process of "homing in" on the true meaning of the communication, as well as the error-correction that must be performed after a misunderstanding is encountered.

Consistency also adds tremendous value to the teaching process, because it helps avoid several communication pitfalls. It is, unfortunately, quite natural that people will use one word to mean many things. When teachers make this common mistake, students are left to guess the true meaning of the word, making assumptions based on the context of the word use. This ambiguous use of terminology can lead the student down an ineffective path in their practice, which must be then be identified and corrected, after already being incorrectly ingrained in their bodies.

Likewise, a teacher may use many words to describe one thing. Using multiple terms for the same concept or skill often leaves students wondering if there is information they missed or details unavailable to them each time a new word is used to describe something already known by a different term.

It is very common for adherents of martial arts to use different words to refer to the same thing. Here is an example of using words interchangeably to refer to the same concept: *system, style, method, technique,* and *application.* Lack of a consistent lexicon is one of the causes of a lack of unity among the practitioners in the same martial art. It is further amplified when approaching practitioners of other martial arts.

A seemingly "simple" mistake in word choice could conceivably cost a student an additional year in their training and skill development when incorrect training and re-training efforts are factored and totaled. Consider, for a moment, the training value of a better understanding the Japanese term *uke*, meaning "to receive" when compared to its simplistic English language translation of "block".

Replace jargon with simple English. "Flowery" language can be added (later) to lock in ideas or provide historical context and flavor.

Any specific jargon used should be evaluated to determine if it's absolutely necessary or if simple English terms would be better suited for immediate and initial understanding. Beginning students who are learning martial arts get easily intimidated by learning a physical activity along with a new language. Anything that can be done to streamline a student's learning should be considered by the instructor to facilitate clear and concise communication.

Because teaching is such a critical form of communication, especially when the content may save the student's life, only use flowery language or other jargon when teaching *intermediate and advanced students*.

This more obscure, esoteric or poetic form of communication can be effective in providing additional detail, flavor, and gradation to concepts already understood by students, and can be helpful in explaining useful and subtle refinements of foundational skills.

We owe it to our students to communicate clearly, concisely, and consistently to help them learn efficiently and effectively. Using one word to mean many things or many words to describe one thing will only detract from a student's ability to discern a teacher's meaning the first time. In the realm of martial arts, misunderstandings can easily lead to injuries to one or more students while training or ultimately a hampered ability to apply their skills on the streets, where the stakes are the highest.

Step 2 - Identify the *actionable* principles and their related physical skillsets.

Identifying skillsets that support your style's principle-driven approach allows you to both create and modify curriculum that truly supports the development of those skills. It allows the practitioner to apply the *principles* that support the art's goals and preferences.

It's important to keep in mind that neither *theory* nor *example* are efficiently taught or applied in isolation. Applications can be thoughts of as *examples* of solutions to a problem, while *principles* drive the rationale behind the selection of one potential solution over another. Said differently, applications are *examples* of one or more principles, and *principles* explain the factors likely to make the application successful.

When teaching a principle, a teacher can create a thousand application examples, and when examining applications, the teacher and student need only to look to their list of principles to understand why it succeeded or failed.

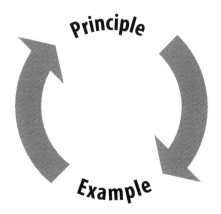

Theory/Example Loop

Because of this relationship between the real (example) and the ideal (principle), it's important to do the following: 1) Know your principles; 2) Be able to articulate and demonstrate them; and 3) Build skillsets that allow those principles to become more widely applicable, so they don't become mere "one-offs" in your toolkit.

Let's take an example common to martial arts: "Moving to the outside." Moving to the outside is often preferential because it represents *flanking*, and flanking is beneficial because it potentially takes the opponent's second arm out of useful position. To make the principle of "moving to the outside" *actionable*, we need to demonstrate what is and isn't flanking, and we need to provide the student several skillsets that support the goal. We need to develop timing drills, footwork drills, and blocking, passing, pushing and pulling drills that support moving ourselves and or our opponent, such that we can navigate "to the outside," when we are not there.

As the instructor, we first need to identify the useful goal (*principle*). Then, we help the student understand the value of that tactic, and, finally, we ensure the student gains the skillsets that allow them to consistently attain the goal.

Step 3 - Teaching is a profession. Approach the process as an educator.

It's important to identify that *teaching* is a profession, with a related skillset and goals, distinct from those of a practitioner. Although some martial traditions support *teaching titles*, it is rare that these titles are the result of obtaining specific education in the skills of the teaching *profession*.

Subsequently, most martial arts practitioners have historically studied under other skilled practitioners, who were not trained educators. This fact may be one of the reasons principle-driven training that is focused on progressive skill-building seems to be the exception, rather than the norm in traditional martial arts.

Skill-building is an important goal.

As martial traditions are often passed down and practiced during times of peace, focus can (perhaps too easily) shift to maintaining the traditions and honoring the memory of the ancestors of the art as one would a relic.

Again, Gustav Mahler reminds us, "Tradition is tending the flame, not worshiping the ashes."

Merely repeating the same memorized sequences handed down to us does not guarantee the transmission of the live skills necessary to protect one's self.

As one of my instructors would say:

> "The form [kata] is not the message. A form is like a story already told.
>
> You have to learn to create your own story."
>
> -Lin Weiguo (林卫国 / Eric Ling)

It is very common that traditional martial training is largely encompassed by the memorization of techniques, combinations, forms (*kata*), or form application. Form application, also called self-defense scenarios, demonstrate "If attacker does A, then I do B" sequences and the repeated reinforcement and practice of those memorized themes. These "one-off" solutions are, unfortunately, not the most efficient ways to develop life skills that transfer to new situations.

What is not common enough among martial traditions is a strong focus on progression from memorization to skill-building. Skill building is the implementation of an *experiential* model that supports trying and failing in a safe environment or an experimental model that provides the student some measure of freedom to "make the system their own."

While these additional forms of skill building rely on memorization, they progress beyond it in the effort to ensure the continued *utility* of the martial tradition.

Understanding is the key to "transferring" (applying) skills.

Again, as an educator, it's also important to keep in mind that students learn to apply information in a progressive process. First, students learn discreet components of information, then understand how that skillset fits into a broader context, and, finally, by applying their knowledge outside of pre-defined drills.

Know ➡ Understand ➡ Transfer (Apply)

In the West, it's well understood that a primary measurement of effective teaching is a student's ability to "transfer" (apply) the skills they learn in classroom drills into new scenarios. The key to transferring skills to new scenarios is the explicit **understanding** of the skills they have learned.

Without understanding, students remain frustrated at learning material they "will never" or "can never" use in the real world. Without understanding, students cannot even determine *when* it's appropriate to apply their specific knowledge, let alone understand *how* to apply their skills in solving a problem. Without the ability to *transfer* their knowledge, a student may realize they are in a circumstance to apply a particular skillset but might not be able to effectively do so because of small variations in circumstance or context.

Clearly, students only able to perform their martial applications in a pre-arranged context have not developed *live* skills they can use in the streets. To truly apply one's knowledge, one must understand the circumstances where that knowledge is valuable, and then be able to transfer that knowledge to a situation completely unlike anything encountered in the learning environment.

Since *transferring* skills to a new situation is analogous to *applying* one's martial training to a new or unfamiliar context, it's critical that students of martial arts learn martial skills *with understanding*. Students' understanding is enabled by useful skill development practices, supporting theory, and clear and consistent terminology.

NOTE: In the rest of this book, we will use "apply" in place of "transfer" to refer to the *application* of martial skills in a live, unscripted environment.

Teaching students *with understanding* is important for numerous reasons:

- It creates *informed practitioners*.
- It keeps inquisitive students mentally *engaged*.
- It provides students who will go on to become teachers with a head-start.
- It gives students the tools they need to continue their learning outside of the classroom.

- It helps students put their training into the correct context when presented with other martial arts.

- Perhaps most importantly, it helps students self-correct when they fail.

Because of this natural process of learning, the instructor must support learning opportunities that support each of these stages.

"Backwards planning" is a valuable process for educators.

Teachers should strongly consider using a "backwards planning" approach when developing or modifying curriculum for their schools. When a teacher's goals are clearly identified, it becomes easier to identify and implement useful testing measures that both teacher and student can rely on to determine if the student is progressing.

When the teacher has both a clear vision of their goals, and an understanding of how they will check their students' progress toward those goals, the teacher can develop lesson plans and supporting drills that are both effective and progressive.

Both the teacher and the student make the educational journey from opposite ends of the spectrum…the teacher solving the maze by starting at the endpoint, and the student following the line drawn by the teacher.

Step 4 - Develop and modify the curriculum to truly support progressive skill-development.

With the understanding that students first learn, then understand, and then apply gained knowledge, the teacher must modify or develop curriculum in multiple forms to support students at each stage of learning. These are further described in Chapter 6 but summarized in the following paragraphs.

First, individual, isolated skill development drills must be developed. These isolated drills may seem very artificial to new students, but they provide an opportunity for both teacher and student to focus on one single, manageable problem/solution set at a time.

Second, once the student has demonstrated proficiency in a handful of useful, related skills, they can be exposed to drills that help them either link skillsets or choose from several related skillsets, depending on the student's desired outcome. These drills give the student the ability to make choices based on their knowledge, goals, and context. Failure in drills of this nature should be encouraged, as the lessons learned from making less effective decisions are likely to be both highly valued and well-remembered by the student. Students learn very well and quickly from making mistakes in a safe environment.

An example of a drill in this category would be one that allows a student to make multiple choices for how to navigate an opponent's blocking arms (inside, outside or below) to continue pressing forward with an attack.

Third, and finally, teachers should provide students training environments and platforms to allow students to both pressure-test and experiment with what they have learned. Pressure-testing provides students the ability to cooperatively navigate variations in speed, angle, and intensity with a partner, while experimentation allows training partners to apply their learning in new and unexpected circumstances as they are given more freedom in how and where to move based on their current level of understanding.

Using this book

I recommend this book be initially read from front to back, however, I fully expect its higher value to be as a continuous reference in which one relevant principle is reviewed at a time, so the reader can analyze their own training paradigm, terminology, and assumptions and then link the information in this book with that already present in their system.

In general, books are a poor medium for passing along non-linear information. Most of principles presented here are non-linear in relationship. Many principles rely upon, support, and assume other principles are in play, and the result is a web of interrelated principles without a singular, correct, path in which to engage.

Principles are interconnected and supportive of one another.

While the highest value obtained from a principle-driven approach has already been outlined as the total is greater than the sum of the parts *when implemented with a progressive teaching methodology*, the individual principles themselves can be incorporated in nearly any order. As discussed in more detail in *Chapter 2: The Foundation – Terminology and Fundamental Assumptions*, principles provide value by being additive in nature.

Any individual principle can help inform one's art; however, principles link, support, and strengthen one another. Of key importance is *consistency*. Once you understand a principle and how to apply it, you should strive to always apply it in the appropriate context.

Caveats

Within these pages, you will undoubtedly come across some, perhaps many, principles you are already familiar with, and you may know them under different terms. You may even come across principles you feel are "universal," particularly if you study a style other than Goju-ryu.

I challenge you to think about principles of application in most cases as more as *preferences* than absolutes or universal truths. After all, *preferences* are one of the reasons so many styles of martial arts exist, and drive many of the reasons practitioners and teachers of the same "style" approach training and application of their art differently. I believe that if you look at the principle-driven model as a series of *preferences*, you can use your own rational analysis to make this model, or any similar model work to your (and your student's) benefit, regardless of the martial tradition(s) you practice and/or teach.

The material presented here is a subset of **one** principle-driven model for Goju-ryu that speaks to my understanding of the art's *preferences* in being a clinch-range, stand-up, striking, locking, breaking, and throwing art. The information presented in the following chapters is a representation of the principle-driven approach now utilized as a portion of the training and teaching at my dojo, the Burinkan.

Consider again that the value of a principle-driven model is greater than the sum of its parts...that individual principles could simply remain in the toolbox of "one-offs," or, when supported with a skills-focused mindset and an intentionally progressive educational framework, could be utilized as a tool to fundamentally change an approach to training, teaching, and application.

Lastly, please remember the photos are merely *examples* intended to help relay the nature of the principles discussed. They are performed in the *aesthetic* of Goju-ryu, however, that does not limit the value of the concepts when applied in other *or against* various shapes or contexts, whether in the dojo of another style of karate, such as a Korean dojang, a Chinese kwoon or on the street.

2

The Foundation: Terminology and Fundamental Assumptions

It may be tempting to skip a chapter titled "terminology", however, it's strongly recommended to not jump ahead without reading this section at least one time.

Later commentary around the actual application principles may not make sense without understanding some of the fundamental preferences and assumptions used to bind this principle-driven model together.

There is also value to noting definitions and documenting our biases and assumptions.

The Reality - What a Martial Art IS

While the term "*martial* art" would be more aptly suited toward fighting systems designed for or purely derived from *battlefield* arts, the term is used through the remainder of this book as a way to describe a systematic practice of civilian self-defense maneuvers.

Typically, a martial art contains fighting principles (goals and preferences) and training components (methods of attaining the skills necessary to reach those goals) to assist in the development of self-preservation & fighting skills. Often, students of the martial arts are also taught the rituals and other trappings of the foreign culture in which the art originated, such as terminology, costumes, uniforms, occasionally philosophy, and, in some rare cases, religion.

It's important to note that many practitioners of historical martial arts consider different components of their art to be "tradition," that is, what is considered sacrosanct and outside the bounds of acceptable innovation, while others are willing and able to segment the content of the art from the delivery model (teaching methods). The latter mindset allows adherents of the tradition to continue to advance the teaching methods, and is the approach this book advocates. As said by Gustav Mahler, "Tradition is not the worship of ashes, but the preservation of fire." As traditions are passed across both cultures and generations, it is important to adjust and enhance the teaching model to allows the tradition the opportunity to survive.

The Myth - What a Martial Art IS NOT

A martial art is not a guaranteed method for the creation of an unstoppable fighter, and it does not ensure that the trained person will succeed against an untrained person. Street fighters have been known to defeat classically trained martial artists due to factors that are described later in this manual. For example, some people are smaller or physically weaker than others and having the disadvantage of these physical attributes, can only attempt to stack the odds in their favor with training that is consistently guided by superior strategy and tactics.

There are no verifiable "magical" or "mystical" energy forces that a teacher can help you unleash to stop your attacker. Empty Force (essentially telekinesis) and Dim Mak (death touch) are tricks to lure people into believing that martial artists are the equivalent of superheroes. These stories are fables. Unfortunately, many students and teachers still believe that these things are possible, which endangers people when they actually need to rely upon their training to protect themselves. While it may seem extreme to say so, I believe that martial arts instructors who teach these esoteric methods of self-defense are directly responsible for the future harm their students will encounter on the street.

I believe all martial arts instructors have a sobering responsibility to their students, to teach them an attainable, de-mystified, and useful skillset as quickly as possible.

The foundational principle of self-defense: "Defend yourself, control your attacker."

Nearly every civilian martial art shares a fundamental philosophy toward "self-defense", which roughly states:

1. Avoid situations that lead to unnecessary fighting.

2. Flee, if possible.

3. If you cannot escape, defend yourself.

While most martial arts schools (and nearly all "self-defense" classes) discuss points #1 and #2, most schools focus mainly on the physical aspects surrounding point #3, which expanded from its typical short-hand (*defend yourself*), becomes our first principle of self-defense:

护身制敌
"Defend yourself, and control your attacker."

-or stated differently-

須先保自已，後著攻他人
"First protect yourself, then attack the other."

This is essentially THE fundamental, even if rarely-stated, principle of all "self-defense"-based martial arts, as the assumption is that the context and purpose of our activity is dictated by an *attacker* attempting to control us…by striking, grabbing, etc.

With that understanding, and clear statement of our foundational principle, it becomes obvious that our primary goal is two-fold:

Defend yourself against attack.[5]

Neutralize the attacker's aggressive action(s). Defending ourselves from whatever form of control the attacker is employing becomes the first identifiable grouping of skillsets.

Control your attacker.

If the martial art practitioner is successful at their initial defense, then they need to immediately be concerned with taking control of the attacker or face being forced to defend again (and again), with the possibility of eventual failure, succumbing to the attacker.

The idea of Controlling the Attacker supports many options: strike, lock, break, choke or throw. The goal of each of these is to remove either the attacker's ability and/or will to do harm. In the Chinese arts, it is often said that *ti, da, shuai, na* (踢打摔拿), meaning "kick, punch, throw, and grab" represent the categories of martial options available to the practitioner. These options represent approaches or techniques toward a goal, but they don't speak well to the goals they support.

Because of this, we first speak of *control* as in any conflict that has progressed beyond words: One party is attempting to exert *physical* control over the other.

The "attacking" party has a goal in mind, and will use one or more forms of *control* to meet that goal:

- "Drag the woman into the car, so I can assault her in private."
- "Knock the man out, so I can escape without being followed."
- "Show the guy who's boss by beating him up in front of everyone."

Not only does the attacker have a goal, but the defender should also have a goal for counter-control, which may be something like the following examples:

---

5 Only in rare circumstances of known, certain, and immediate physical threat does it make sense to use your martial arts training to launch a pre-emptive attack. You should familiarize yourself with local laws regarding both assault and battery and understand that even warranted use of martial arts to defend yourself will cause you to come into direct contact with local law enforcement.

- "Hold the aggressor until authorities arrive."
- "Stop the home invader by any means necessary to ensure my family is safe."
- "Stop my drunk friend from hurting me or himself."
- "Show the attacker I'm not prey, by hitting him back."

From a self-defense perspective, each goal may be achieved using multiple "categories" of application that provide *control* of the attacker in a method most in line within the defender's skillset.

Forms of Control

Rather than follow the Chinese *Ti, Da, Shuai, Na* approach discussed earlier, we find it more helpful to shift our vocabulary to discuss *methods (or forms) of control*.

Control (the attacker's and ours) can take many forms and is categorized here as follows:
- Controlling body posture & balance
- Break structure
- Knockout/Incapacitate
- Pain/Mental

Controlling Posture and Balance is a highly-useful method of control as it provides multiple potential benefits to the controlling party.

When you control your opponent's posture and balance, you are in some way, a "puppet-master," moving the attacker's body against their wishes. Ideally, when you are controlling your opponent's posture, they can no longer step where or when they want, strike or kick with full force, mentally continue to commit to their original plan or easily resist your efforts to maneuver safely.

Methods for controlling posture and balance include, but are not limited to the following actions:
- Twisting

- Sweeping
- Throwing
- Pushing
- Pulling
- Tripping
- Folding (forcing a hinge or sliding joint)
- Entwining
- Striking/Kicking

Breaking Structure[6] is a highly specific form of control, whose goal is to functionally damage a sliding, hinge or ball and socket joint, by tearing the ligaments holding the joint together or by tearing the tendons attaching the surrounding muscles. Dislocation of a ball and socket joint, such as a shoulder separation or dislocation would fall into this category. Potential end-states of truly *breaking* an opponent's structure result in the following: 1) Extreme pain, potentially leading to unconsciousness (or at a minimum, distraction), and 2) Reduced or likely eliminated mobility of the joint.

Methods for breaking structure include, but are not limited to the following:
- Hyper-extension of the joint
- Hyper-flexion of the joint
- Hyper-rotation of the joint

Knockout or incapacitation is a widely sought after goal of civilian conflict. This option leaves the loser completely and dangerously at the mercy of the winner.

Methods for knockout or incapacitation include, but are not limited to the following actions:
- Striking/kicking - typically the head

---

6 Attempted direct break of a long bone (femur, collarbone, humerus) is not included for its lower likelihood for success and its uncommon nature as a fighting goal.

- Choking the throat (using either blood or air chokes)
- Impacting the ground as the result of being thrown, slammed, etc.
- Extreme pain, such as from a broken joint

Taking the opponent's mind can be performed in a myriad of ways and should not be discounted as an important and widely-used form of "control." There are various techniques for intimidating and disorienting opponents; however, it should be noted that striking a person causes pain, potentially leading to surrender by the dominated party.

Methods for inducing pain or other forms of mental control include, but are not limited to the following:

- Threaten/intimidate
- Disorient (i.e. sand to the eyes, spitting in one's face, etc.)
- Striking/kicking vulnerable points, causing pain and doubt
- Locking a joint (forcing it to its maximum range of motion)
- Breaking a joint (forcing it past its maximum range of motion)
- Disrupting one's posture or balance, in effect "taking their mind," as they're forced to focus on moving to retain their position, balance or posture.

We define and categorize "control" in this manner to assist with later training. Doing so allows us to be clear and purposeful in directing our skill driven curriculum to convey the potential benefits and end-states of successful kicking, punching, striking, and locking to meet our self-protection goals according to the situation at hand.

It's highly recommended for both martial practitioners and teachers to study both the force-continuum models utilized by law enforcement as well as local jurisdiction regarding self-defense and use of deadly force. Armed with an understanding of how you will be judged if you have to use self-protection skills, you will be better equipped to make good decisions with your training and teaching time, and enlist the appropriate *form(s) of control* appropriate to the situation.

Use of the word "Advanced"

When it comes to terminology in the martial arts, there is probably no term capable of creating greater misunderstanding, confusion, and lack of focus on true skill development than the word, "advanced." We will spend some time discussing this term, the problems caused by its common use, and recommendations for a more accurate and consistent use of the word as related to both practitioners and principles.

Advanced – connotation

"Advanced" has a set of commonly-held meanings in the martial arts, and to most people *advanced* means something along the following lines:

- "better"
- "more realistic"
- "more complex"
- "more valuable"
- "elite"

Problems that misusing the word "advanced" creates

Misusing the word "advanced" in martial arts can also sound or look like one of these commonly held beliefs or claims:

- Claims to have "advanced" techniques or kata, often withheld from students or held as a "carrot" to maintain the mystery of that not yet learned.

- Considering some techniques or kata to be more advanced than others creates certain problems in the practitioner's mindset and subsequent training. For example, students often discard simple, useful techniques before learning how to properly apply them. Being *simpler* techniques, these MIGHT have the highest likelihood of success, IF properly taught and trained.

- Belief that one form of *control* is more *advanced* than the other (grappling is more valuable than striking or vice versa), when training for various forms of *control* simply provides various options for ending a violent encounter.

We propose that in the context of martial arts, the word *advanced* is better used as a description of an action (application) or person that is *highly efficient* and *highly effective*, and, as a result, **more likely to be successful** in a self-defense scenario.

As a principle-driven model is vital to the efficient development of required skills in practitioners, we find it helpful to be clear on how principles support *advanced* applications and the development of *advanced* practitioners. To do so, we first need to discuss and clarify two common terms in the martial arts, *technique* and *application*, as they are often used interchangeably.

Defining Technique and Application

As *advanced* is often used to describe certain solo techniques (including *rare* solo kata), as well as applications, it's important to examine some recommended definitions for the words *technique* and *application* to then make some suggestions about where the qualitative word *advanced* is truly helpful.

A **technique** is a coordinated, repeatable movement of the practitioner's body. Typically, a technique is codified by a founder of a martial art, who believed a particular movement of the human body supported a specific fighting goal in such a manner that the movement is worth repeating and refining for fast, reliable, and explosive use to suit the art's primary control method(s).

Techniques answer the following questions:

- "How should I plan to deal with different violent situations I think I might be presented with in my environment?"
- "What movements do I think are useful enough to practice repeatedly in order to build speed and power?"
- "What can I practice in isolation to prepare for violence?"

A technique must be combined with sufficient power, proper range, timing, speed (attributes) in a situation (context) that supports a particular goal (strategy) against an opponent to create an *application*.

An *application* is the usage of a technique, in a suitable situation, relative to an opponent. It is a means of moving or otherwise affecting the **opponent's** body, for a predetermined purpose or effect, leading to *control*.

Applications answer the questions:

- "What exactly can or should I do relative to an attacker to achieve a useful form of defense or counter-control?"

- "How can I succeed against a resisting opponent who may have the initiative, and might be bigger and stronger than me?"

In short, a *technique* is a movement without clear, immediate context, while a technique applied in any useful context is an *application*.

We propose that a technique must be *applied*, in context, to be able to be qualitatively judged as useful, appropriate, successful or *advanced*. After all, techniques are simply movements of the practitioner's body. How can one solo movement without context be judged against any other?

For example, it is often taught in some martial arts that closed-fisted blocks are *basic*, while open-handed blocks are more *advanced*. However, taking just a moment to consider, it is clear that a closed-fisted block has the ability to strike with the fist during or after the block, while an "open-handed" block has the alternative ability to easily rake the eyes or grab rather than hit. Both options can defend against an attack and provide a means for quickly counter-controlling the attacker. How can we easily say one is more advanced than the other, since both meet the fundamental goals of a martial art?

We propose that using the term *advanced* in reference to a *technique*, singular or in combination, creates more problems than it solves, but calling a particular application *advanced* is possible, given the definitions just provided for *advanced*, *technique*, and *application*.

Ok, so then what makes an application advanced?

Given those definitions of technique and application, how can we then qualitatively judge an *application* to determine if it's truly *advanced*?

By a practitioner's success at achieving the application's intended goals in *controlling the attacker.*

A successfully applied application is one that is correct for the situation, the energy applied, the postures, positions, relative strength and size of both attacker and defender, foot and hand placement, range, timing, and dozens of other factors.

Those *factors* can be described by **principles**, and the more principles appropriately applied during an application, the higher the chance of that application being successful at achieving its intended goal(s).

Thus, with those definitions for *technique* and *application*, and the specific understanding of what contributes to an *advanced* application, we suggest the following:

1. An *advanced* application is an application which employs all relevant, useful principles to provide the highest chances of success to the defender in achieving his intended outcome in controlling the attacker, and

2. An *advanced* practitioner (rather than *beginning* or *intermediate*) can apply all relevant principles simultaneously to ensure that his applications have the highest chance of success against an attacker.

There is good reason to suggest there are no advanced *techniques*, only properly or improperly applied ones. It's ***how well*** techniques are applied that makes the difference, and principles help practitioners discuss, understand, and ultimately train to execute applications well enough to be considered, qualitatively *advanced*.

Another way of thinking about *advanced* applications is that they **"stack the odds"** in favor of the practitioner by enlisting multiple factors for success even in a single, otherwise simple movement.

Discussing principles can be quite challenging as they form a conceptual "web" of context, with some principles assisting and informing others and some principles relying upon others. It's actually easier to apply multiple principles than to discuss them, because applying principles to your training is simply an additive process. Each principle incorporated into your training, and ultimately your applications, will help to *stack the odds* in favor of your success against your opponent.

With very few exceptions, principles can be added to your training and teaching in nearly any order, as demonstrated in the associative property of addition.

The associative property of addition:

Step 1	3 + 4 + 1	=	3 + 4 + 1
Step 2	(3 + 4) + 1	=	3 + (4 + 1)
Step 3	(7) + 1	=	3 + (5)
Step 4	8	=	8

Ultimately, regardless of the order principles are introduced, the eventual outcome will be the same…*an increased chance of success.*

Although few people have taken the time to write out their reasoning for believing that no *technique* is advanced, many have intuited that some other <u>factors</u> (principles) of application are truly responsible for *advanced* application, rather than the shape of the fingers or the rarity of a particular kata.

It may be helpful to be reminded of several things often said in traditional martial arts that demonstrate the value of this recommended treatment of the word *advanced*:

- "The real secret is just hard work."
- "Everything is in Sanchin."
- "I can defeat you, using only a [fundamental technique]."
- "One style's secrets are another style's basics."
- "X is the most basic technique, and, at the same time, the most advanced."
- "The more I learn, the more I realize that the basics are the most important."

- "Any technique, properly learned and applied, can be the technique that saves your life."
- "Person A's skill is so high, he can beat Person B, even with the most basic technique."

So, given some clarification around the word *advanced*, some consistent definitions of *technique* and *application*, and an understanding of how *advanced applications* can be executed by equally *advanced practitioners* to "stack the odds" in favor of their success, we are able to use principles as tools to both error-correct our training, and demystify martial traditions in the goal of supporting their ongoing utility.

Fa/Xing/Gong – A Simple Framework Example

Fujian Feeding Crane Boxing (Shihequan / 食鶴拳) contains within its style, a simple model for understanding of its art, the ***three abilities*** (san cai / 三才). Essentially, this framework provides a quick "litmus-test" for the determination of whether the practitioner is likely to be successful in applying their skills. In short, this combination of ***principles*** (fa / 法), ***applications*** (xing / 形), and *physical **attributes*** (gong / 功) forms a simplified checklist for the practitioner and teacher. The practitioner's ability (or lack thereof) to appropriately manifest all three simultaneously is a direct indicator of the practitioner's "advancement" or growth in the art of Shihequan.

Principles answer the following questions:
- "What" to do, in terms of preference for Defense and Control.
- "When" is each approach or technique appropriate?
- "Where" to apply the technique for maximum effectiveness?
- "Why" to apply each approach to fighting?

Applications answer the following question:
- "How" to create examples that manifest the fighting principles, while still enlisting supporting principles of defense, movement, structure, etc.?

Attributes answer the following question:

- "How well" – in terms of *speed, power, flexibility, etc.*

Think of attributes as the "engine" that delivers the maneuvers of the art.

NOTE: When people say, "it's not about the art or style, it's about the practitioner," they are often talking about **both** the *attributes* of the person, **and** that person's *advancement* in the art.

Like a three-legged stool, all legs must be present to provide the needed platform for proper execution of the art. For example, if any one of the following are missing, a certain outcome can be predicted:

Lacking principles (fa):

- If you use both of your hands to remove an attacker's grab, you won't have anything available to block the incoming punch.
- If you use your hands to block low kicks, you may get punched in the face.

Lacking useful applications (xing):

- If you don't know how to defend low kicks, you'll take damage to the legs or you'll use your hands, pulling them out of their preferred "zone".
- If you don't know how to grapple, a grappler will be able to dominate you.

Lacking relevant physical attributes (gong):

- Any application lacking the power to cause damage or at least distraction is useless.

While principles can be categorized in many ways (structure, movement, application, power, training, teaching, etc.), Chapters 3-5 focus on various application principles, and are grouped roughly according to the Shihequan san cai:

- Chapter 3 – Generalized/Fundamental Principles (Fa)
- Chapter 4 – Application principles focused on using our anatomical "tools" effectively (Xing)
- Chapter 5 – Power and Energy-related principles (Gong)

Chapter Summary

So far, we've clarified the definition of *martial art*, discussed the underlying (and often unstated) *fundamental principle* of all self-defense-based martial arts, and then further discussed what it means to *control* an attacker.

We've also defined both *technique* and *application* to better understand *advanced* as a qualitative term to avoid problems arising from its misuse, and to make it clearer that consistent application of multiple underlying success *factors* or **principles** are what lead some **applications** and **practitioners** to be considered truly *advanced*.

About the photo examples that appear in this book:

As we move forward into Chapters 3 and beyond, numerous application *examples* have been provided in the goal of assisting with the understanding of each principle, tactic, concept or keyword. Unless otherwise noted, the "**defender**" in each sequence is wearing the **black top**, regardless of whether the *defender* is demonstrating a defensive or offensive movement in the photos provided.

Also, while we discuss specific principles that recommend to NOT needlessly pull the hand back to a "chambered" position, many photo examples make use of the chambered position for clarity of photography by removing the non-dominant (for sake of principle discussed) hand from obstructing photographic details.

武林館

3

Fa (General Methods)

In Chapter 3, we review several generalized principles, many of which are relatively universal in nature across fighting arts.

Timing, aggression, and position are key themes in the principles of Chapter 3.

Timing – Understand the "Game"

Understanding timing is the key to *mastering* timing, and mastering timing is the key to successful counter-control.

As we know from the foundational principle of self-defense -- *defend yourself, control your attacker* – we are primarily training to *respond* to an attempt of control from an assailant. *Responding* is synonymous with *reacting*, and it is also widely understood that action is faster than reaction.

Since our attacker is *acting*, and we are *reacting*, are we therefore **slower**? *Slower* may not be the most accurate term to use, so let's dive into what is really happening when we are *reacting*.

There is a widely-published model for the thinking process called the OODA loop:

In the OODA loop, we:

- Observe a situation
- Orient ourselves within the situation
- Decide what to do about the situation
- Act to influence the outcome

In a self-defense scenario, by the time a defender has gotten to step #1 of the OODA loop (observing an incoming attack), the attacker is already in step #4 (acting). The defender is often at least three steps behind in the thinking process, and the attacker is going to be acting again, quickly, leaving the defender in a perpetual state of reacting.

Because the attacker may be relentless in continuing their attacks, it can be extraordinarily difficult to progress from part one of a response (*defend yourself*) to part two (*control your attacker*).

Typical scenario:

1. Attacker attempts to control defender
2. Defender succeeds at defending
3. Attacker again attempts to control defender
4. Defender succeeds at defending

Left in a state of perpetual defense, it is likely that the defender will eventually fail in their defense, and ultimately succumb to the attacker's control, unless the defender can somehow do more than simply defend to stop the attacker's continued advance.

Given that example, let's discuss a few important terms related to timing that can assist analyzing and modify training and application options:

After, During, and Before

We are typically assuming in a self-defense scenario, that the defender is first acting *in the after*, as the attacker is the one initiating the action, acting *before* the defender.

If we liken a fight to a dance, the attacker is leading the dance, and the defender is following…acting in the *after*, responding to the leader, merely reacting. The leader acts according to their whim, unimpeded, the follower has the difficult task of keeping up. The leader of the dance is acting *in the before*. The leader is deciding where on the floor the dance moves will take both dancers. The follower is merely along for the ride, with no control, and no say, as they are acting *in the after*.

Next, let's move away from the dance analogy, back to the self-defense scenario. We've discussed how important it is to move as the defender as quickly as possible from *defend yourself*, which we defined as an *after* activity, to *control the attacker*, which is most successful when performed *in the before*, because of the inherent difficulty in reacting efficiently.

But, with the assumption that we are starting in the *after*, how can a defender change the situation, such that they move from the *after* to the *before*?

The defender can do so by acting both efficiently and effectively in the *during*, and the following are the two primary methods that can be used:

1. Counter-attacking *while* we block/receive or otherwise defend against the attacker, or
2. Attaining some *additional* form of control WITH our defensive motion. (breaking the attacker's balance, inflict pain, etc.)

Option 1: Counter-attacking while blocking/receiving an attack

Given the first principle of self-defense, *defend yourself, control your attacker*, is in two parts, the most efficient thing to do is perform both parts at the same time.

If we do so, we can change the situation to something like the following:

1. Attacker attempts to control defender

2. Defender succeeds at defending, while at the same time applying a form of counter-control

3. Attacker foregoes their second attack and switches to defending the incoming control

4. Defender continues counter-control

5. Attacker continues defending

Until which point the attacker fails to defend…leading to the defender's success at counter-controlling. As you see, the key to moving from the **after** (Step 1), through the **during** (Step 2), into the **before** (Step 4) requires that we enlist some form of aggressive counter-control as early as possible, and simultaneous to our defense.

The following example demonstrates all three timings, acting in defense only while in the *after*, counter-attacking (while blocking) in the *during*, and striking again in the *before*. As you can see in the example, we start with the assumption that the defender is in the *after*, perhaps caught unaware, only able to defend ourselves…which does little to change the defender's situation. At this point, the defender is merely blocking, still stuck in the first half of *defend yourself, control your attacker*.

The defender has blocked upward, creating an opening to the middle and lower levels, and (as executed) the defender's block has **only** served to keep the defender safe a moment longer…it has not interrupted, or otherwise *controlled* the attacker. The attacker continues, planning to exploit the defender's opening with a second punch. The defender blocks downward to defend the exposed area, but simultaneously counter-punches, stealing the initiative from the attacker by both blocking and striking in the *during*.

Landing a punch, the defender has now taken the attacker's mind, albeit temporarily,

by slowing down and interrupting the attacker's OODA loop, which had been planning to throw a 3rd punch. Since the defender's right hand is already in position for a second attack (mere inches from the target), he throws the punch, now acting in the *before*.

Note that this example, in its mid and final stages, also enlists several principles, such as *closest weapon / closest target*, and *keep weapons on-line,* which will be further described in this chapter and in chapter 4.

Other options

Other examples of applications that work under this approach to counter-attacking efficiently *in the during*, include:

- Using body motion, such as dodging, angling, or ducking (in lieu of blocking/receiving), while counter-striking from the safe position.

- Using the arm(s) to block/receive while simultaneously kicking or otherwise disrupting the attacker's legs.

Option 2: Attaining some *additional* form of control WITH our defensive motion.

The prior method is an example of how to *in the during* enlist both sides of the body simultaneously, each working in a different role…one hand working defensively, while the other hand works offensively.

This alternative option for acting efficiently *in the during* is to perform a singular initial motion that is multi-purpose, yet not complex and time-consuming. This *defense as offense* requires the defender perform a more *advanced* defensive maneuver that "stacks" principles (all discussed in great detail in this chapter as well as in chapters 4 and 5), such as the following:

- *Stretching techniques,*
- *Closest weapon/closest target,*
- *Three gates/three segments,*
- *Keep weapons on-line,*
- *Unified body,*
- *Strong vs weak,*
- *Attack the opponent's posture and balance,* and
- *Seek the center*

A simple example of this is a singular blocking/receiving motion that disrupts the attacker's balance, which also disrupts the attacker's second punch and allows for a counter-punch that is less likely to be blocked by the attacker.

As attacker punches to the middle level, the defender receives the attack with a middle-level "block." Defender immediately shifts from the *middle block* shape as he lifts with the elbow and disrupts the attacker's balance. The defender then counters.

A middle crossing block can, with a change in range and angle, disrupt an attacker's posture and balance.

Allowing a counter-punch while attacker is destabilized.

Other options

Other examples of applications that work to act efficiently *in the during*, include the following:

- Immediately striking with the blocking hand (*closest weapon, closest target*)
- Using a blocking/receiving motion to sink, pull, or rotate the attacker, disrupt his balance, posture or position, similar to the above example (*attack the opponent's posture or balance*)
- Striking the attacker's attacking limb and causing significant pain.
- Note: It's quite difficult to cause a level of pain that is sufficiently distracting during an adrenaline-fueled altercation.
- Breaking the attacker's attacking limb, causing structural damage AND causing significant pain (*bridging* principle – *break*).

Summary

Understanding timing may be **the** most important concept in understanding and managing any conflict, as nearly anything done *in the before* has a higher chance of success, as it has a lower chance of being countered successfully by the party *in the after*. This poses a challenge in a self-defense scenario when the odds are stacked against the defender. The defender must enlist every possible success factor (principle of application) to act both efficiently and effectively "*in the during*" to survive.

It is often said in Southern Chinese martial traditions:

> "It doesn't matter who began first, the one who reaches the destination earliest is the winner."
>
> -or, simply-
>
> 後人發，先人至
> "Start later, but arrive sooner."

Aggression is required; passivity will ultimately lose

An overly-defensive martial strategy is bound to eventually fail, when the attacker is not counter-controlled into submission quickly and efficiently. Even if our desire in a given self-defense situation is to be kind to our attacker, we must immediately move from *defend yourself* to *control your attacker* without reservation or hesitation. **In this context, to be *aggressive*, regardless of your intended method(s) of control is to speak of effort, intensity, and efficiency, not anger or adrenaline.** Quite to the contrary, we want to remain as relaxed and high-functioning as possible during an altercation.

Once we have identified the signs of an aggressor attempting to assert physical control, we must immediately act to defend ourself from harm, and, furthermore, act until we shut down the attacker's will and/or ability to continue.

Should we not be fully committed to stop the attacker's continued threat, we take the risk that every additional second the conflict continues we risk making a mistake and succumbing to our attacker. Only by moving immediately to the counter-control, will we stop the attacker and end the fight.

It's important to be aware of the self-defense laws we are subject to at home, work, and in public. We should train to have various less-than-lethal options available to us, and ensure they are highly-functioning by applying our principles and tactics to their application.

Regardless of whether we believe at the onset of an altercation that we need to apply lethal or less-than lethal force to an attacker, there is no downside to treating every actual situation with the full mental commitment (the aggressive pressure) necessary to see it through to its successful outcome with you safe, and your attacker controlled.

This level of commitment is fundamental to a martial tradition seeking to maintain its utility, and most of the principles presented represent various options of increasing the *aggressive* quality of martial movements of all types, including so-called *blocks*.

Stretch your techniques as necessary

It's helpful to remember that martial *techniques* practiced solo are the equivalent of a Platonic *ideal.* They often are executed with the expectation of an attacker that is the same height as the practitioner, positioned directly to the practitioner's front.

However, when *applied* against an opponent or partner, those movements must *stretch* to take a shape affected by various factors, including: purpose, physical context, and starting point.

Purpose

As already mentioned, when blocking/receiving an attack, the defender may seek to strike or unbalance the attacker with the blocking arm to apply the block more effectively to escape being stuck *in the after*. This may change the timing, trajectory or energy (rebounding, sticky, etc.) to support the block's secondary goals.

The same can be true for a punch. The defender may be counter-punching the attacker with the goal of simultaneously deflecting the attacker's punch with the same arm, which may require changing the trajectory or target of a "typical" punch.

Physical Context

As techniques are typically practiced solo in accordance with an imaginary attacker of the same height as the practitioner, any height disparity between the defender and the attacker will require immediate adjustments to the placement and typical self-reference points for the applied technique.

Likewise, adjustments must be made for techniques applied at angles that are off-center due to the relative positions of defender and attacker, as well as for the force applied by both parties.

Starting point

Likewise, when truly applying a martial tradition, not all techniques start from the artifices of the training environment. Not all blocks or punches start from a chamber or middle-block or down-block preparatory posture. Techniques must eventually flow from one position to another without engaging an artificial staging point.

In addition to practicing for the situations above, a thorough study of combinations can greatly assist the smoothing out of transitions from one technique to another to support live skill development.

It's highly recommended that practitioners examine the transition of all major movements in combination and by category, study how standard techniques *stretch* from one position to another:

- Attack to Attack
- Attack to Defense
- Defense to Defense
- Defense to Attack

Defender's punch is blocked by the attacker, who counters. Defender performs a high block directly from the punch position.

Defender's middle block becomes an appropriate starting position for a shuto (chop) to the neck.

Keep in mind it is possible to *stretch* a technique so far it becomes ineffective at its intended task, because it loses leverage or fails to cover the defender's vulnerable area(s). In those cases, it is often helpful to enlist modifications to range, footwork, and angulation to allow the techniques to stay in a useful range and position to avoid this problem.

Regardless of the reason you may need to *stretch* your technique to adapt to either a situation or goal, it's important to remember that (in a progressive, skills-development model) the solo version of a technique is best thought of as an *ideal*, meant to ingrain consistent and powerful movement habits **so that** the student can safely move on to partner training where the movement is then *applied* in various contexts that will require adjustment from the solo form.

Applying the technique *appropriately* for the circumstance should be a driving goal for both teacher and student.

Face the front – Bring all the "guns" to the front

Because they typically specialize in sophisticated hand-movements, Southern Chinese styles of the Hakka and Fuzhou varieties favor front-facing postures that bring the practitioner's arms into close range with the attacker, and "baits" attacks to the position inside the "frame" of the arms, such as the following:

- "Beggar asks for rice" (hat yi lo mai / 乞兒攞米) posture of Southern Mantis,

- "Facing the sun" (zhao yang / 招陽) posture of Yong Chun White Crane,

- "Sinking the joints" (che chat / 坐節) posture of Grand Ancestor boxing/Taizuquan,

- "Vibrating hands" (chun chiu / 駿手) of Five Ancestor boxing/Ngo Cho Kun, or

- "Double pulling" (shuang chou / 雙抽) from White Eyebrow/Pak Mei

Southern Mantis's "Beggar Asks for Rice" (乞兒攞米) posture, demonstrated by Sifu Alex Do

Yong Chun White Crane's "Facing the sun" posture (招陽), demonstrated by Sifu Pan Cheng Miao, photo courtesy of Haki Celikkol

Taizuquan's "sinking the joints" (坐節)
performed by Sifu Zhou Kun Min

Ngo Cho Kun's "vibrating hands" (駿手)
performed by Sifu Alexander L Co

The fighting postures and theories of these "cousin arts" illuminate the value of postures like the Sanchin "frame" as a fighting guard, supportive of numerous application principles. The shapes of these postures not only bring the arms closer to the attacker, but they protect the armpits, ribs, liver, and spleen, while "baiting" the attacker to attack the defender's centerline and then be enveloped by the defender's arms, much as someone might breach a castle's outer gate, only to be surrounded and cut down from all sides in the bailey. While this position does bring additional exposure to the defender's groin, most of these related arts rely on leg maneuvers to defend the lower body, while the arms defend and attack in their upper-body "zone".

As mentioned in the section on *stretching techniques*, even training devices such as the "chambered" hand, previously thought of as a *home* position, should be modified and re-evaluated in a progressive training model. One of numerous benefits of the Sanchin

Pak Mei's "double pulling" hands (雙抽), demonstrated by Sifu Cheung Lai Chuen

Goju-ryu's Sanchin "frame" or "double middle block posture", demonstrated by the author

frame is that it becomes the new, more *aggressive, home* position in skill-development practices, particularly when other principles such as *continue forward, flow around obstructions*, and *closest weapon/closest target* (covered in the next section) are studied and incorporated.

Side-facing compromise

While keeping "all guns to the front" suggests the use of the Sanchin frame as the preferred engagement posture, Goju-ryu demonstrates another common fighting position, particularly when in a low side-facing stance (such as shiko-dachi), that suggests in-close grappling scenarios. This alternative has the far/rear hand over the sternum, and is visible in kata like Saifa, Seiunchin, Shisochin, Seipai, and Kururunfa. This posture is a good reminder to keep all hands as close as possible to the attacker, allowing the practitioner to utilize many bridging principles (found in chapter 4) to apply preferred counter-control measures.

Some examples from Goju-ryu kata:

Saifa (backfist/sternum)

Saifa (hammerfist/sternum)

Seiunchin (uppercut/sternum)

Seipai (opening posture)

Shisochin (elbow/sternum)   Kururunfa (elbow/sternum)

Guarding the centerline

The last example of this principle in action relates primarily to arts that opt to protect the centerline, rather than "invite" it. The arts that prefer to immediately cover the centerline, typically rely on the fighting strategy described in Southern Taizuquan as follows:

> "Lead hand attacks like a lance, rear hand defends like a shield."
>
> 前手取人如矛, 後手防己如盾
>
> While both hands are not fully extended, one rests at the elbow, reminiscent of the "reinforced block" found in some Okinawan Karate styles.

Various martial traditions prefer this option, including:

Motobu Kenpo's Meotote (夫婦手)
Photo courtesy of Patrick McCarthy

Wing Chun's "asking hands" (man sau / 問手) Demonstrated by Sifu Robert Chu

Some of the styles that utilize an inviting centerline also reserve the option to cover the centerline depending upon preference or situation.

Regardless of the option(s) you prefer, or your art focuses on, it's important to consider the following points:

- Your art's techniques will ultimately *stretch* from these most typical starting points, and

- *Home*, from an application perspective, will rarely be a fist chambered at the ribs or hip

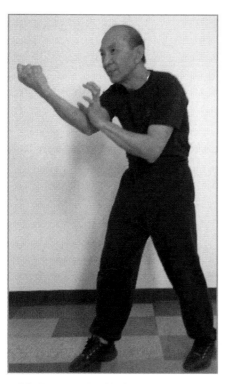

Sifu Simon Lui (雷龍春) demonstrating
Pak Mei's "fierce tiger guarding gate"
(猛虎看門)

Sifu Mark Wiley demonstrating Ngo Cho
Kun's Centerline Posture (子午中肢)

Closest Weapon, Closest Target – You're already mostly there

Closest weapon, closest target may initially sound like a principle that is so obvious that it doesn't need to be mentioned; however, like a lot of other seemingly common-sense principles, if you don't consistently look for opportunities to incorporate the principle in your training, and teach and practice it regularly, it will be missed or forgotten, leading to lost opportunities, inefficient practice, and lack of potential efficiency in your martial applications.

One of the primary training methods that can support this principle of *closest weapon, closest target* is the study of transitions from blocking motions to immediate, same-hand, counter-strikes. Tensho kata provides Goju-Ryu practitioners with several examples; however, there are a great many more to discover, incorporate and practice.

Below are some simple examples from common blocking positions, which are excellent options to explore in fundamental kumi-waza (partner training) practices, such as sandan gi (high, middle, low blocking/punching training). Additional examples will be found in the section on *three segments* in chapter 4.

Examples

A high block on the inside lends itself to an immediate uraken (backfist) to the face.

A middle cross block from the outside is already 90% of the way to a viable target.

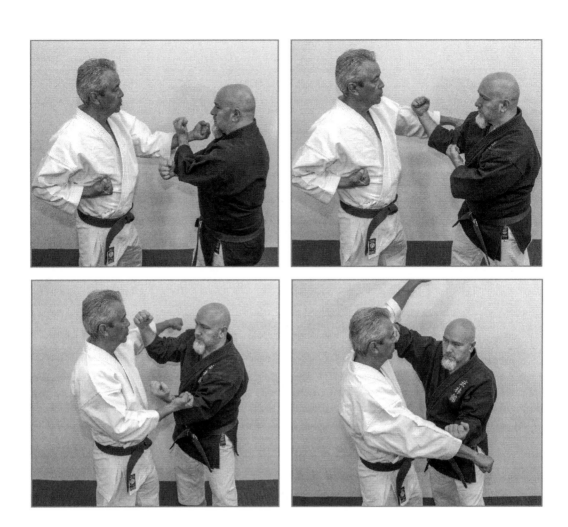

A middle block on the inside can "ride" upward pressure and strike with a round punch, instead (example from Seipai kata).

A cross block on the outside can also follow the line of the arm to shuto (chop) the neck (from Gekisai kata)

A low block can both attack the face during it's early phase, and punch directly to the liver, once in final position.

Continue forward, clearing obstructions – Press the attack

While we already discussed (in *face the front*) the value of keeping the hands forward, we should keep in mind that training practices can too easily carry over into application scenarios, and a common example of this is the "chambered" hand in many martial traditions.

Because of this training device, often one of the most difficult progressions for traditional martial artists to implement in their training is *closest weapon, closest target*...since training provides abundant practice in bringing the hand *home* to the "chambered" position to begin a new technique.

Because fighting at a clinch-range often relies more on feeling and pressure than visual clues, it is highly likely that an opponent will feel a backwards motion on the defender's part, and rush in to fill that void created by the defender. Much like a battle line, a retreat on the defender's side easily opens up an advance on the attacker's side. An *aggressive* mindset (again, effort and intensity, not anger) coupled with tactics supporting moving *continually forward*, rather than backward, can help the defender move more quickly from **the after**, through **the during**, to **the before** where they will be more effective.

While pressing the attack in the forward direction is useful for the reasons mentioned, any counter-attack posed by the defender is likely to be blocked or otherwise thwarted by the attacker. Because of this, our training should also support the delivery of continuous attacks that assume obstructions will be placed in the way, only to be flowed around or removed, ultimately allowing the defender's counter-control measures to be fully exerted. When we meet an obstruction, we must push, pull, attack high and low, changing our angle, pressure, speed, and timing to find our target and implement our will over the attacker's.

Some Chinese arts describe this as the principle of "leaking" (漏) or "flowing" (流), as it describes how a droplet of water finds its way:

> "Water does not resist. Water flows. When you plunge your hand into it, all you feel is a caress. Water is not a solid wall, it will not stop you. But water always goes where it wants to go, and nothing in the end can stand against it. Water is patient. Dripping water wears away a stone. Remember that, my child. Remember you are half water. If you can't go through an obstacle, go around it. Water does."
>
> -Margaret Atwood, *The Penelopiad*

In White Crane, they discuss this principle using the phrase:

"when the hand extends, it hits three times"

一出三打

The intention is not to focus on the number three, but that when coupled with other principles like *closest weapon, closest target* and the *three segments* (Chapter 4), the arm should be able to hit, or otherwise *control* in multiple ways before returning "home".

The following are some examples of pressing forward the attack while clearing obstructions:

When the defender is blocked "below" the elbow, rolling over and continuing with a backfist is an option.

When blocked deeply and/or directly into the crease of the elbow, the middle block opens the center for an uppercut to the chin (from Sanchin kata) while deflecting the attacker's punch to the outside.

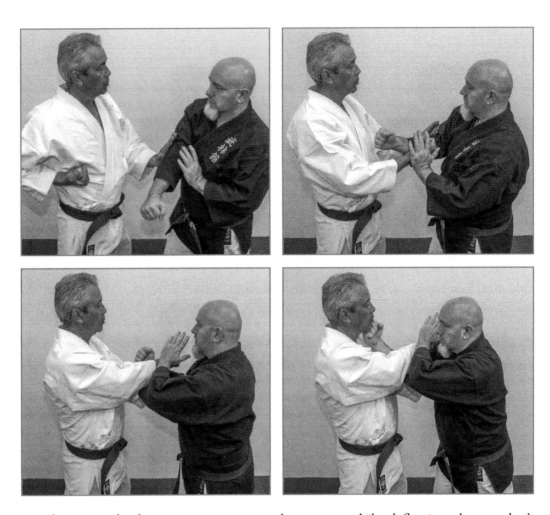

Another example demonstrates opening the center, while deflecting the attacker's punch to the inside.

The defender's punch is deflected upward, so the defender uses that point of contact to pull the attacker's obstruction down, allowing an uppercut to the side of the jaw.

When the defender's punch is pressed downward, it continues in a circular direction to strike the attacker in the temple (another example of Seipai kata).

As we discussed earlier, principles are typically interrelated. Some principles describe a strategy, while others describe a tactic that supports that strategy.

Continue forward, clearing obstructions is a principle that is enabled by *facing the front*, and endeavoring to always utilize the *closest weapon* against the *closest target*. It is an example of an *aggressive* option to any self-defense scenario.

Fill the Dead Space (Optimizing timing)

One thing we clearly don't want to do is perform a three-part combination (block, transfer, strike) against a single-count attack. This is unrealistic, and potentially dangerous training, as cursory analysis demonstrates that in the time the defender performs three movements, one cannot assume or guarantee the attacker won't punch twice more. Variances in reaction time among humans don't support the idea that some people are at least three times faster than others.

This example, and ones very similar, are common-place in traditional martial arts:

A common three-count response: Receive/Transfer/Counter-strike

To avoid falling into inefficient or ineffective training practices that might carry over into our application scenarios, and instead stay focused on what makes applications *advanced*, we can consider and implement the lessons of principles already discussed such as those listed below:

- *Timing*
- *Stretch your techniques*
- *Aggression*
- *Closest weapon, closest target*

One application method is to continuously engage both sides of your body, weaving together techniques from both the left and right sides of the body in a fluid transition from defense to offense, and in a manner that supports the goals of moving from the *after* through the *during* and into the *before* or simply maintaining control of the *before*.

One **teaching method** for developing an efficient set of interleaved options that helps ensure you have the option of striking (or otherwise *controlling*) on each "beat", follows this training progression:

1. Practice one-handed blocking motion (block on "beat" #1).

2. Practice one-handed blocking motion with immediate transition to counter-attack with the *same* hand (block on beat #1, counter-attack on beat #2).

3. Practice one-handed blocking motion, while simultaneously striking with the *opposite* hand (block and counter-strike both on beat #1).

4. Combine Progressions 2 & 3: Practice one-handed blocking motion, while simultaneously striking with the opposite hand. Immediately counterattack with the blocking hand (block and counterstrike both on beat #1, and perform additional strike on beat #2).

We'll discuss and demonstrate this progression below.

Progression 1 – One-handed Blocking

At this stage, the student is practicing a blocking/receiving technique solo, moving, and with a partner to gain the skills related to effective receiving: Range, timing, placement, pressure, angle, structure, etc.

Progression 2 – One-handed Blocking with immediate counterattack

In the second progression, the student practices transitioning quickly and efficiently from the receiving technique to a counterstrike. This mode of training is exemplified in the Goju-ryu kata, Tensho, and it expresses the concept of chaining motions in series.

Note: Several examples of "progression #2" were also presented in the previous section on *closest weapon, closest target.*

Progression 3 – Block with one hand and simultaneous attack with opposite hand.

The third progression requires that the student coordinate both sides of the body to execute two disparate motions simultaneously. This style of motion is pivotal to acting effectively *in the during*.

Progression 4 – Combine Progressions #3 and #2

Progression 4 – Combine Progressions #3 and #2 (opposite side)

The fourth progression combines progressions #3 and #2 to ensure that both arms are adequately involved on the first beat, allowing for a strike on the first beat, and then transitioning the blocking/receiving hand immediately to a secondary strike from *the closest weapon* to *the closest target*. In this scenario, the defender acts **in the during** on the first beat (attributed to progression #3), and transitions immediately from defense to counter-strike with the blocking hand (progression #2) to secure the defender's position **in the before**.

These methods require the practitioner to *stretch* techniques beyond the ideal/solo form to transition to locations other than the "chamber" between motions, and continue from the current position directly to the *closest target*. Regardless of which training progressions you utilize in your training and teaching, it's important to remember that speed alone is often not the primary solution to a problem, given that martial artists are not able to ensure they will be 2-3 times as fast as an attacker. It is recommended for instructors to introduce other principles used to support teaching and training methodologies that avoid reliance on fast-twitch muscle alone.

Flanking, Positioning and the *Proper* Hand

One of the most common principles shared among martial arts is to "move to the outside." To discuss the relative merits of this common principle, we will begin by reviewing a few common positions one may seek or find oneself in during an encounter. While not exhaustive, they are helpful when discussing training assumptions and the concept of *proper hand*.

The following major positions are described by the position of the *defender*, relative to the *attacker*:

1. Double Inside
2. Double Outside
3. Overlapping (head inside or outside)
4. Outside
5. Flanking (what people typically mean when they say "move to the outside")
6. Flanked

Double Inside Position

In the *double inside* position, the defender is "surrounded" by the attacker, which can feel unnerving. Fortunately, this negative aspect is offset by the benefit of relatively unimpeded access to the most vulnerable points of the attacker's anatomy (throat, groin, eyes, xiphoid, spleen, liver, etc.).

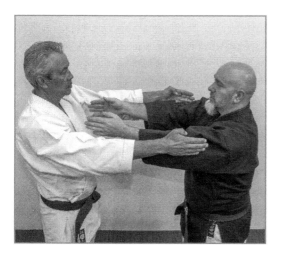
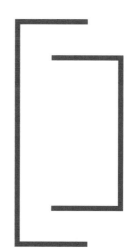

Double Inside Position

Double Outside Position

Inversely, the *double outside* position feels like a dominant position, as we surround the attacker; however, the attacker has easier access to our most vulnerable points so we must be careful to protect them in this position.

Double Outside Position

Overlapping (head either inside or outside)

In the "overlapping" position, one of our arms is *inside* the attacker's arms, while the other is *outside*. This position well supports applications that trap one of the attacker's arms between both of ours. The position of the head inside or outside of the attacker's arms should be explored for both defensive and offensive possibilities.

 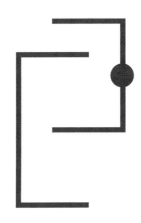

Overlapping position (head inside)

 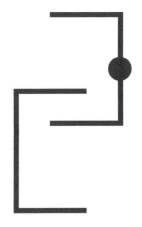

Overlapping position (head outside)

A point of caution is that the overlapping position is largely the same for both people, because it has relatively equal, positional benefits to both the attacker and defender in much the same way a common throw, O soto gari (outer reaping throw) is a "mirrored" posture for both the participants. What ultimately makes O soto gari successful, as well as difficult to counter, are the other principles that support its success such as: kuzushi (breaking balance), tsukuri (complementary body positioning), and kake (execution of correct energy to complete the throw).

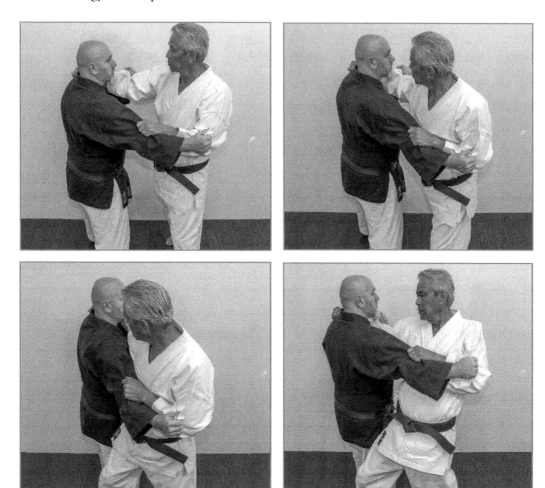

Attacker attempts to throw defender with O-soto-gari. Positions are mirrored. Defender has an opportunity to counter with exactly the same technique if other factors are not present to ensure its success.

Outside

Outside is the position most typically engaged in traditional karate training. Many fundamental kumite are typically performed in this position, as is *kakie* (Goju-ryu's fundamental sticky-hands exercise). In this position, we are typically engaged with our attacker's arm, *right-on-right*, or *left-on-left*, and both the defender's and attacker's *far hands* are essentially out of useful position.

Outside position (right hands engaged)

Flanking

Flanking is a special case of the "outside" position, where the *flanking* person is in the *outside* position, but rotated toward the *flanked* person's center.

From here, we are typically out of useful range of the attacker's *far hand*, and our flanking hand can:

- Reach around the head/neck
- Grab the opposite shoulder from the rear
- Push or disrupt the attacker's balance

Flanking (defender on the outside)

Flanked (and "self-flanked")

When a defender is *flanked*, the attacker has all the same *flanking* benefits described above, but with the defender at the disadvantage. While this may seem obvious; what is not so obvious is the defender's actions can easily lead to a situation where the defender puts themselves in a flanked situation, which we define as *self-flanked*.

In the example below, the defender (in the bottom of the image) has engaged the attacker's right arm with their own right arm from the inside position. In this scenario, it wasn't the attacker's action that caused the defender to be flanked, it was the defender's choice of applying their right arm to the attacker's right arm from the inside position. We dub this a "wrong hand" engagement.

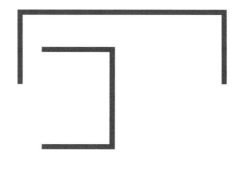

Self-Flanked ("Wrong" hand engagement) – Defender on bottom

A *self-flanked* situation, forcing the engagement of the defender's "wrong" hand, can also occur when the attacker has pinned or otherwise *detained* one of the defender's arms. In such cases, a *wrong-hand* engagement may not be avoidable.

Attacker grabs and pulls us across with "same" hand, then punches. Defender reacts with "wrong" hand.

Analysis

When reviewing the major positional options between attacker and defender, it should become clear that *flanked* or *self-flanked* is potentially the worst position for the defender to be in as it largely removes the defender's "rear" hand from the fight.

For similar reasoning, *flanking* is tactically a superior position because it largely removes the attacker's *far hand* from effective reach, which efficiently halves the attacker's available tools. It's important to understand that flanking is one of the few truly superior positions as it changes the tools the other party has in the fight, similar to disarming someone holding a weapon.

It's also important to consider that *flanking*, and moving to the outside in general is a highly defensive maneuver. How so? Because it's effects serve to perform the following results:

1. Avoid engagement with the attacker's other hand, and
2. Move away from the most vulnerable targets (eyes, throat, xiphpoid, liver, spleen, bladder, and groin) in favor of the safety of flanking.

While the other major positions (*double inside*, *double outside*, *overlapping*, and *outside*) all have specific tactical strengths, weaknesses, and options, their applications are beyond the scope of this book so we will move on to a concept that helps support a practitioner's ability to consistently flank an opponent: "Proper" hand.

The *proper hand* is the hand that is engaged when an opponent attacks so the defender does not create a *self-flanking* situation.

The proper hand is the left hand against an attacker's right punch. Had the defender engaged the attacker's right hand with their own right hand (dubbed *wrong hand* in comparison), they would be particularly vulnerable to the opponent's left hand follow-up.

Since the *proper hand* concept helps a practitioner not only avoid self-flanking, but also sets up a potential flanking position relative to the attacker, developing the skill of engaging with attacks using the *proper hand* provides the practitioner multiple positional opportunities through the acquisition of a single skillset.

The following is an example of a drill that supports the placement of the proper hand, the avoidance of self-flanking scenarios, and ultimately one of the common bridging options that supports fully flanking, that of *transfer* (see *bridging-transfer* in Chapter 5).

"Proper" hand Drill

Step 1 – Feeder (in black) and receiver (in white) establish center frames. Step 2 – Feeder reaches quickly out to touch receiver's solar plexus. Step 3 – Receiver blocks with the "proper" (same-side) hand.

Step 4 (optional progression) – Receiver "transfers" feeder's hand, moving to the *outside* position.

Some Important Points regarding this drill, depending on the role:

Feeder: Don't telegraph. Practice using a *twitch*-like motion to reach forward from a relaxed state, and do not immediately retract.

Receiver: Don't push downward, press toward the attacker's *center*. The fundamental technique here is similar to *chudan-uchi-uke* (mid-level inward block), not *osae-uke* (pressing downward block).

About Step 4 - Transfer: When ready, add the secondary motion of a typical two-hand block to *transfer* contact from the *proper* hand to the secondary hand. That frees the *proper* hand to fully flank the opponent.

Note: If we don't transfer our *proper* hand when flanking, we stay in the *outside* or *overlapping* position rather than the flanking position, because our initial *proper* hand cannot reach behind the person.

Once the drill has built in the appropriate upper-body skills, the *proper hand* practice should be coupled with stepping and footwork to move the defender to the flank position, rotated appropriately to bring their *far* hand into position.

Forcing the "4th door" (四門)

In some Chinese martial arts, the area outside of the both arms, and behind the body (posterior/dorsal) is called the *4th door*. This is the location where the defender positions his or herself when flanking.

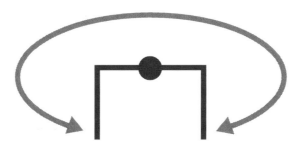

However, there are two primary methods to accomplish the flanking position. One is described above, which is to "move to" the 4th door by applying footwork to the *proper hand* practice and *transferring* the *bridge* from the *proper* hand to the secondary hand, combining the upper and lower-body skillsets to flank an attacker.

The other is to "force" the 4th door. When *forcing the 4th door*, you utilize one or both arms to rotate the attacker such that the attacker's 4th door *moves*, in effect, placing the defender inside.

Some examples:

Example 1 - From the outside position

Defender receives the attacker's punch and rotates attacker by applying pressure to the elbow. Defender applies choke from rear (from Saifa kata).

Example 2 - From the overlapping position

Defender receives attacker's double push, passing attacker's left arm under and rotating him so that the defender now flanks the attacker. Defender breaks the attacker's elbow (application of sukui uke/scooping block from saifa, seiunchin, seisan, kururunfa, and suparinpei kata).

Combining options

There are two main options for flanking: 1) *Moving to the flank*, and 2) *Forcing the 4th door*. Each of these should be explored and trained. There is also a third option to explore as well, and that is combining the two.

To be equally effective, the defender need only *move* half as far as well as *rotate* the attacker one-half the typically required amount. Depending on the situation, moving less while in contact with the attacker may be safer, and rotating the attacker half as far may be easier to accomplish.

Summary

Regardless of your (or your art's) preference(s) for position, in a live altercation, a defender has limited ability to force the context and positions available. Because of the chaos of combat, it's valuable to understand and train for a number of scenarios and options while understanding the relative strengths and weaknesses of each.

Described above are a few "hands up" scenarios. Training should also include scenarios where the defender is completely surprised with hands down, pushed against a wall, starting in a choke-hold, etc. As the variations are infinite, we recommend developing core training around several common scenarios and then relying on a more free-form *platform* to give students the experience of applying and *transferring* (Chapter 1) their art in various positions difficult to foresee. An example *platform* with a progressive teaching method is presented in Chapter 6.

Chapter Summary

In Chapter 3, we've discussed timing…defined *after*, *during*, and *before*, and discussed the unique challenge of moving from the *after*, through the *during* to the *before*. *Aggression* was defined, not as an emotional attribute, but as a "pressure" or an imperative to move as efficiently as possible from *defense* to *counter-control*.

We described several reasons that an art's foundational movements must *stretch* to support its utility, as well as why there are numerous reasons for, and postures that support the goal of, keeping the hands as close as possible to the attacker (*face the front*), where they can find easy targets (*closest weapon, closest target*).

In similar context, we analyzed why moving *continuously forward*, rather than back *home*, helps support efficient and effective control, while knowing that *obstructions* will be placed in the way, only to *be flowed around or removed*.

We discussed a progression of training that supports the defender weaving defense and attack in such a way as to *fill both space and time*, and help the defender steal the initiative, and leave little opportunity for the attacker to regain it.

Lastly, we reviewed a number of major positions the defender and attacker may find themselves in and took a deep dive into how to both flank an attacker and avoid self-flanking by training the *proper* hand response.

4

Xing (The Tools)

Chapter 4 discusses some specific details about anatomical tools. In Goju-ryu, like many Southern Chinese martial arts, there is a focus on upper body techniques over kicking, so most of these representative principles focus on the bridges (arms).

These principles tend to suggest creative ways to ensure your upper-body techniques are safe, efficient and multi-purpose.

Three gates and Three segments

As mentioned in the section on *Flanking, Positioning and the Proper Hand* in the previous chapter, the majority of vital points are on the inside of the body. Beyond that, the "center" of the body is represented approximately by the line of the spine and represents the rotational center and center of mass.

Strikes directed at our center of mass are particularly damaging…their energy fully impacts our physiology and posture, and the energy isn't easily dissipated in rotation. Likewise pushes or pulls that connect with our center have the greatest effect. Deeper analysis of the use of rotation for its defensive and offensive value is beyond the scope of this book; however, rotational energy and rotational positioning of an opponent are valuable tools and worthy of in-depth study.

In an empty-handed martial art, the "tools" we have relate to the human body, with the primary tools to interact with the world being our arms. Our arms are very important because they are delivery vehicles for our nerve-dense hands, which we use to manipulate our environment. Given the close proximity of our arms to the majority of our vital organs, including the brain, they are our primary tool to defend against attack.

Nerve-density Drawing of the Human Body
Image source: https://www.art.com/products/p22105168571-sa-i7527371/peter-gardiner-motor-and-sensory-homunculi.htm

Because our hands are so densely-packed with nerves, it is common to emphasize hand-related details and applications, while we underutilize the rest of our arm. Our arms consist of three primary parts: the hand, forearm, and upper arm, which is separated by the wrist and the elbow joints, and connected to the body by the shoulder joint.

The three primary components of the arm

- Hand/Wrist
- Forearm/Elbow
- Upper Arm/Shoulder

This is important to realize since part of the value of systematic martial arts is the

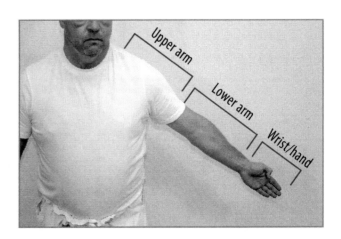

attempt to leverage underutilized aspects of human physiology wherever possible. The arm could be compared to a spear. Use only the tip, and you lose the utility of also blocking with the shaft or striking with the butt end of the weapon.

It is very common to utilize **less than** the full potential of our anatomy, and several principles can help us gain the advantage of its full use, both *defensively* and *offensively*, by considering further the capabilities of our multipart arms.

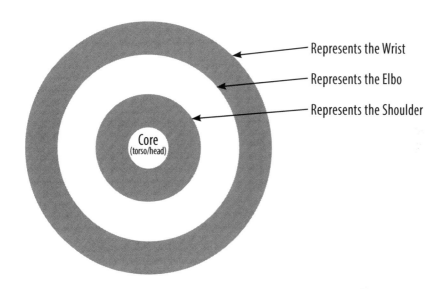

Three Gates and Three Segments

Defensively – Three Gates (san men / 三門)

As a general rule, one is likely to be attacked toward the center as these attacks are likely to penetrate deeply, rather than deflecting due to rotation of the torso on its vertical axis.

From a defensive perspective, the three "gates" of arm could be thought of as the concentric castle gates with our spine/center playing the role of the castle to be guarded.

The Concentric Castle Gates Surrounding the Castle

Image source: http://primaryfacts.com/1049/different-types-of-castles-facts-and-information/

So, in this analogy:

- Castle = Spine/center

- Inner Gate = Shoulder/Upper Arm

- Middle Gate = Elbow/Forearm

- Outer Gate = Wrist/Hand

As we move forward to discuss examples of utilizing the defensive nature of the three sections of the arms, we'll use this shorthand method to describe the gates:

- 1st gate – wrist/hand

- 2nd gate – forearm/elbow

- 3rd gate – upper-arm/shoulder

Defender performs *wrong-hand* cross block (2nd gate) against a face punch, requiring a defense with kuri-uke (back of elbow block/3rd gate) against the second punch (from kururunfa/seiunchin kata)

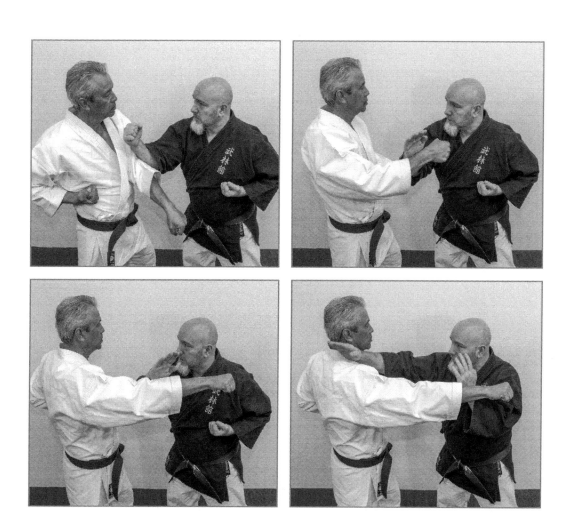

Defender block's attacker's first punch with 2nd gate (forearm) and block's attacker's second punch with 1st gate (wrist) before counter-attacking.

Defender receives attacker's right-hand punch with *wrong hand* nagashi-uke (flowing block/1st gate), and defends against attacker's left-hand punch with his right forearm/ elbow (2nd gate) (an application of seiunchin kata "archer's posture")

Should we utilize our palm or wrist to block a punch and the opponent immediately punches with the other hand, we might either raise or lower our elbow to block the second punch. The opponent might then utilize his first hand to press our elbow and punch us once more. If we still cannot utilize our free hand (due to range/position), then our only remaining option may be to rotate our body and block with our shoulder.

Since the shoulder is not highly mobile it has limited defensive capability, so it's recommended to consider the roles of both the 1st and 2nd gates for their defensive value against an attacker's multiple attacks. Likewise, it's highly recommended that defensive motions make the best possible use of the 2nd gate to keep the hand free for immediate or simultaneous counter-attack (see Chapter 4, Hands don't chase hands).

Offensively – Three Segments (san jie / 三節):

Earlier, a comparison was made between the human arm and a spear; a better example would consider that an arm is essentially a "flexible" weapon. The arm is much more like a flail, a three section staff, nunchaku or chain, weapons that were typically developed or deployed for the purpose of attacking "around" obstacles, typically acting as a shield. In essence, a flexible weapon is one that is meant to strike *around obstructions*.

In the empty hand context, the arm's flexibility and multiple joints can be utilized to continuously attack or to attack around the opponent's blocks.

For instance, I may punch my opponent, who then blocks my arm. If their blocking contacts my arm between my wrist and elbow, I can move in, fold my elbow, and attack with it. Should my elbow then be blocked by my opponent's other hand, I can sink my elbow, move in, and attack with my shoulder.

This concept should be thoroughly investigated and practiced, resulting in the ability to continue striking through and around blocks with a variety of "non-typical" striking surfaces.

Examples (Attack ⇨ Attack)

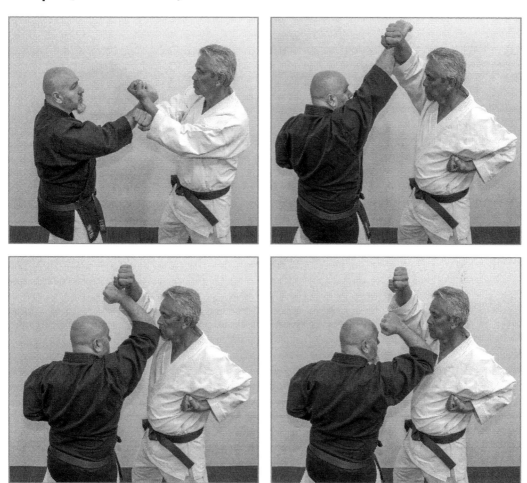

Defender's high punch (1st segment) is blocked, so he immediately transitions to elbow (2nd segment) to face or sternum.

Defender strikes low (1st segment), and is blocked. Defender immediately "folds," continuing with an elbow (2nd segment) that targets the liver.

Defender punches (1st segment) and is blocked, then rolls down and behind the attacker's elbow, grabbing with his left hand and using the upper arm (2nd segment) or shoulder (3rd segment), depending on the angle, to break the attacker's elbow.

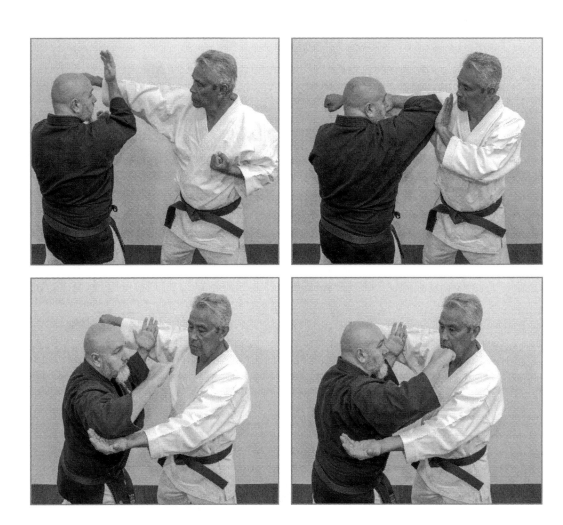

Defender engages the punch with *wrong-hand*, but aggressively switches to a lead-elbow attack (2nd segment) to the face. Attacker blocks the elbow, so defender rotates by pulling back his right hip, opening the attacker's center. Now unobstructed, the defender punches (1st segment) to the face.

Examples of Mixed Defense/Offense

Defense ⇨ Attack:

Defender engages with left wrist (1st gate), grabs with the right hand, and then transfers pressure to the left shoulder (3rd segment), while striking with a rear elbow to the liver (2nd segment) (from kururunfa kata).

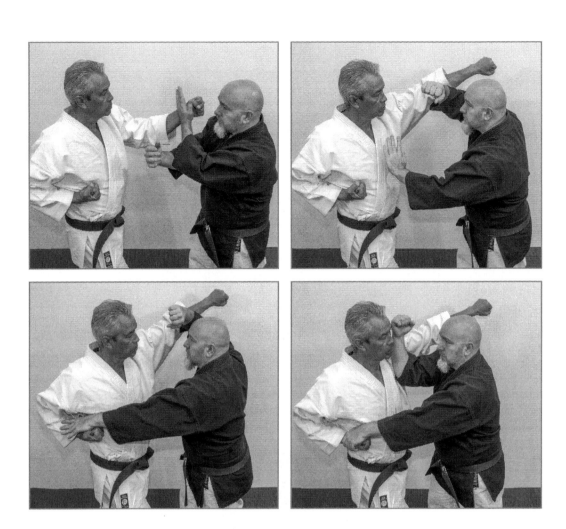

Defender performs high block (2nd gate) on the inside, and transitions into a dropping tettsui-uchi (hammerfist/1st segment) to face, while detaining the attacker's other hand.

Defender performs a *wrong-hand* cross block (1st gate), and chop to neck (1st segment). He then has to defend against body hook using his right forearm (2nd gate), finishing by punching the attacker in the spleen (1st segment).

Defender blocks a liver punch with right elbow (2nd gate), and immediately counter punches (1st segment) to face. Defender then uses a lift of the right elbow (2nd segment), pull of the left arm, and rotation of the waist to throw the attacker.

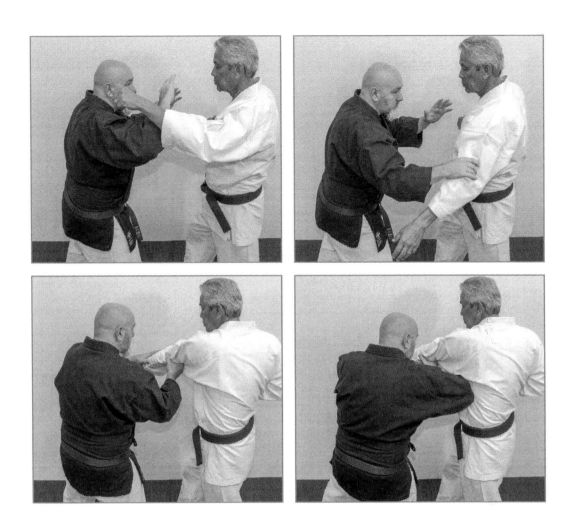

Defender uses sukui uke (scooping block/1st segment) to pass the attacker's punch under, and then elbow strikes (2nd segment) the attacker's floating ribs.

Defender's high punch is blocked, and the attacker takes advantage of the opening. The defender executes a dropping elbow tip defense (2nd gate) against the punch, transitioning immediately into an uppercut (1st segment).

Defender blocks the attacker's punch and immediately uppercuts. Defender then utilizes the position of the upper arm to pull the attacker off-balance, while punching to the chin (from seisan kata). Defender then switches to an arm throw, similar to *kaiten nage (wheel throw/aikido)* or *puter kepala (turn the head/silat)*.

Since the empty hand equivalent of an "arms-race" is the understanding and implementation of principles that support both efficiency and effectiveness, a primary method of advancing one's abilities is to better utilize the tools already available. While difficult because of the extreme hand-focus humans develop, a thorough study and practice of the use of **all** portions of the arm, both for offensive and defensive purposes can allow the practitioner to accomplish more, with the same tools.

Hands Don't Chase Hands

As mentioned in relation to the *three gates* and *three segments*, it's very common to remain hand-focused in martial arts training. Our hands have an extremely high density of nerves per square inch, and therefore easily become a focus of our training, and ultimately our applications. The hands themselves are given the primary role for nearly all applications involving the arms…striking, grabbing, pushing, pulling, etc.

Normally, principles tell you what to do or what goals to strive for, but there are exceptions, particularly when there a common mistakes people make in their training, despite having principles that tell them otherwise.

The admonition *"Hands don't chase hands"* is a reminder to the practitioner to use the forearms (2nd gate/segment in substitution for the hands in most circumstances, and also serves to remind us that controlling the opponent's hands is rarely the primary goal of an application.

Self

As mentioned, the arms have many surface areas that are potentially striking surfaces. The arms have three primary joints (wrist, elbow, shoulder), which allows for a great many offense, defense, and simultaneous defense/offense options.

For instance, one could block an opponent's punch, and then while pressing and pinning the opponent's attacking arm at the elbow with one's own elbow immediately counter-attack with an uppercut from the punching hand.

This cannot occur if one is overly focused on the hand/fist. The entire arm is a both a weapon and a shield. At any given moment, it can fulfill the role of one, the other or both.

All the joints of the arm must be engaged, and all the surfaces utilized for both offensive and defensive purposes. Don't use the hand or palm if the forearm or elbow can do the same job.

From the perspective of the practitioner's tools, you could say, "*Hands don't chase hands* **if the forearm could do the same job.**"

Opponent

Also remember that the opponent has more than just hands, and most of our *controlling* methods relate to other parts of the attacker's anatomy.

If, as a practitioner, you engage the attacker at the hand or wrist only, keep the following in mind:

- It's difficult to control their body or shut down their ability to continue fighting by engaging at the wrist. Engaging at the elbow has an enhanced benefit for breaking the attacker's balance.

- The attacker's elbow is potentially far more powerful and dangerous than their hand or fist, if left uncontrolled.

- Hands move faster than the elbows, and are harder to track at realistic speeds.

- Many common goals for control typically have a lot to do with vital points, balance, and structure of the body. The arms can often be treated as a temporary obstacle for us to overcome.

Control Two with One

Since we all share the same anatomy, we must look to tactical advantages to help ensure our success and safety. There are methods that allow the attacker to utilize one hand to cover or trap two hands (yi fu er / 一伏二). This should be fully explored, as utilizing one limb to temporarily disable two typically allows the practitioner to utilize his or her free hand without further obstruction, similar to the benefit gained by flanking.

The principle of the *three gates* and *three segments* can assist with the development of this skill. A primary method to control two with one is to control one hand with our hand, and using the forearm or elbow of the same arm pin, block or otherwise detain the other arm.

Defender detains the attacker's right arm with his right wrist (1st segment) and the attacker's left arm with his right elbow (2nd segment).

Inversely, the defender first defends against the attacker's left punch with his right elbow (2nd segment) and then detains the attacker's right arm with his right osae uke (from seipai and suparinpei kata).

In this example, the defender applies ura uke (back of hand block), and slides in deeply to control the far hand, controlling the attacker's left hand with the 1st segment while trapping the attacker's right arm between his ribs and elbow (2nd segment) (from kururunfa kata).

This example from seisan kata has the defender sinking into the attacker from the outside and then barraging him with punches and forearm strikes.

In this example, the defender envelopes both of the attacker's arms with one arm, allowing the defender's other arm to execute a takedown (from seiunchin kata).

Beware Two on One

The defender controlling two of the attacker's arms with one of their own is an optimal scenario in that it clearly stacks the odds *two-to-one* in the defender's favor. There remains a number of *applications* in martial traditions that require the inverse…the use of both of the defender's arms against the attacker's one, the majority of which are forms of *control* aimed at throwing the attacker, or locking or breaking their joints.

Likewise, it is not completely uncommon for an attacker to attempt the same *two-on-one* maneuvers against the defender. Let's discuss both scenarios briefly.

Defender Applying Two-on-one Maneuver

The most important thing to remember when applying techniques requiring two points of contact is that they don't all require that those points of contact use both hands. Given that reminder, coupled with the principle of *three segments*, *two-on-one* applications should be reviewed, modified, and trained to utilize one of the following options, whenever possible:

1. **One hand and one forearm** – leaving one hand free to defend or strike
2. **Two forearms** – leaving both hands free to defend or strike
3. **One hand or forearm and one point of contact on the torso, neck, hip or thigh** – leaving at least one hand free to defend or strike

The "arm bar" technique in the Goju-ryu Shisochin kata provides an overt example of option #1. Rather than engaging both *hands*, Shisochin makes use of applying the 2nd segment, rather than the 1st:

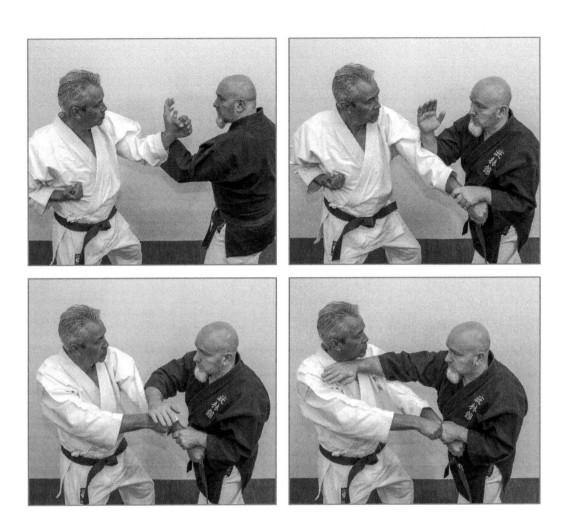

Defender's arm-bar method leaves one hand free to deal with a secondary attack.

Should the attacker resist the defender's arm bar by pulling the defender's arm (1st segment) out of position, the defender then breaks the attacker's arm across his chest, and then elbows (2nd segment) the attacker in the chin.

In addition to using the "outside" of the elbow to apply pressure, the inside of the elbow joint can be used to "grab" or *detain* the opponent, leaving the defender's hands free.

Dealing with Attacker's Two on One

There exist scenarios where your opponent may engage both of their arms against one of yours, in an attempt to hold, lock or break the limb, to throw you to the ground, or to otherwise compromise your structure, balance or posture.

Should the opponent present such a situation, there are two major options available to the defender: **Strike** or **strip**.

Option A - Strike

In this case, it's extremely important to immediately strike the attacker, preferably in the face or head. If done quickly, this has a high degree of success as your opponent's hands are engaged and cannot block. Likewise, if done in the correct timing, the opponent's attempt to endanger your 'trapped' arm will be thwarted.

If both attacker's hands are occupied, they are likely open to a direct strike.

As soon as the defender realizes the attacker is engaging both arms to apply a lock, break or throw, he can defend his elbow joint by bending it, ram the attacker with an elbow or shoulder, and then strike the attacker's face.

Option B - Strip

If the attacker has two hands on your one arm, use both points of contact to push, move or otherwise control your balance, and then use your free hand to strip one of his hands having the effect of "splitting" their force, removing their ability to triangulate their pressure.

Defender realizes the attacker is setting up a lock or break, so he strips the attacker's hand furthest from the shoulder of his own grabbed arm. Defender immediately counter-attacks with a strike and throw (another application of the "arm-bar" from shisochin kata, applied to the head).

Defender should avoid attempting to strip the attacker's hand closest to his shoulder, as that can allow the attacker the opportunity to provide additional pressure and trap the once-free limb.

Keep Weapons On-line

Similar to how a billiards player executes each shot to set up his next shot, in martial arts, one should attempt to always lead the engagement so that every action sets up some form of useful follow-up.

One of the simplest examples of this concept relates to fundamental blocking and receiving motions.

For example, Chudan Soto Uke, applied to the outside position could end up in the same *ideal* place that a practitioner would perform it in solo practice. The practitioner could also utilize the principles of *stretching techniques*, and *keep the weapon on-line*, ending with the forearm aimed at the face of the opponent with the fist poised to uppercut, mere inches from its intended target, and then prepare to enlist the principle of *closest weapon, closest target*.

See below for several common examples:

 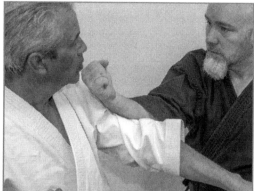

The middle inward block (chudan uchi uke) can be aimed to remain on target for uppercut…

…as can the middle outward block.

Gedan harai (low, sweeping block) works similarly…using the body to rotate the opponent, one brings the forearm and fist in line with the opponent's ribs, enabling a smooth transition from the "block" to a counter-punch directly from the blocking position, without "chambering" the punch.

Gedan Uchi Uke (low inward block) can be aimed at the opponent's center for a quick counterattack to the spleen, liver or ribs in the same way.

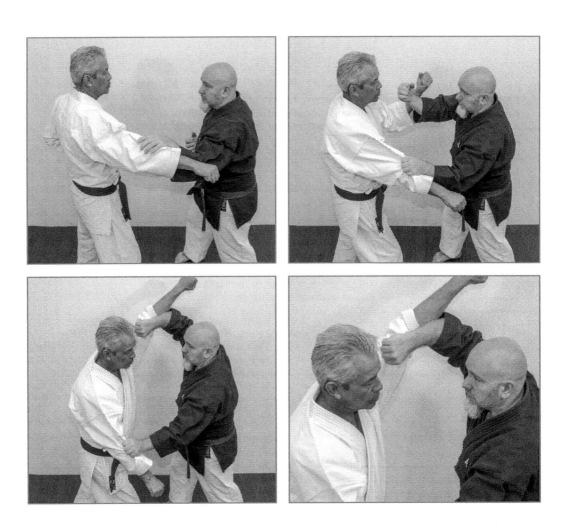

On the inside position, the high block can be aimed directly at the attacker's head or face for a quick counter-attack (as per seipai kata or seiunchin kata's "archer's posture").

As discussed in the section on *stretching techniques*, there is a useful limit for each technique to stretch. Beyond that, the motion or anatomical shape may no longer support the intended application. In those scenarios, consider changing the stepping, stance height, rotation or other positional factors to support a useful application that still benefits from the *"Keep the weapon on-line"* principle.

Bridging Principles/Keywords

Like Goju-ryu, Southern Chinese styles of martial arts are well known for their so-phisticated arm movements, such that a saying developed in China to describe the specialties of gong-fu (*kung-fu*) styles, "Southern Fists and Northern Kicks" (南拳北腿). In southern styles, the forearms are referred to as "bridges" (橋), and the act of applying techniques with the arms against the opponent's arms is called be "bridging", as they (in effect) connect our torso with our attacker's.

Arms meeting create a "bridge" between defender and attacker.

Because these Southern Chinese styles specialized in techniques of the *bridges*, they also developed numerous **bridging principles**, keywords used to describe options or tactics for dealing with bridge-on-bridge applications. Since the defender typically comes to the fight with the same human anatomy as the attacker, it must be our *advanced* application of principles in coordination with our anatomical tools that allows us to stack the odds in our favor. A clear understanding of bridging methods and options helps us to be very purposeful when both teaching and training those applications.

Five Ancestor Boxing (Ngo Cho Kun / 五祖拳) has a four-part poem on bridging methods, which is shown below:

橋法四訣	**Bridge Method, Four Formulas** (Translation)
過、有橋橋上過	**Cross** – If a bridge exists, cross it
添、無橋添作橋	**Create** – If you are without a bridge, create one
斷、見橋即斷橋	**Break** – When you meet a bridge, break it
粘、粘橋不離橋	**Stick** – When you stick to a bridge, don't separate from it

This poem describes a set of four bridging principles favored by the style. Below, we discuss these four in detail, along with four additional bridging principles that are helpful in codifying nearly all bridging movements to guide both training and application in skill building drills.

Create (添)

We start with "create," because one assumption of a close-range, standup fighting art is the preference to fight at a range that allows us to bring all our tools to the fight, including elbows, shoulders, headbutts, etc. Because of this, we need to "close the gap," and move safely from out-of-range to our preferred range.

One strategy to assist with closing the gap is to create a bridge with the opponent's arm. This bridge allows us to "monitor" the arm while we enter short range. In this respect, we are using our arm much like an insect would use their antennae...to reach out and touch, to feel, and monitor.

It's important to keep in mind that *creating* a bridge does no more than that. It does not move, hinder, or hurt the attacker, it simply creates a point of contact, allowing the defender to feel, rather than see what is happening at the clinch-range with the engaged limb. Other bridging principles are enlisted when doing more than monitoring the attacker's bridge.

Note that a bridge is created any time limbs come into contact, regardless of the intention or label attached to that motion. Two common scenarios typically *create a bridge*. The first is when the practitioner attacks which causes the defender to *block*. The second involves the practitioner *blocking* an opponent's attack.

Again, *creating* a bridge is not the same as *blocking*; it's merely *creating a bridge*. The "blocking" action follows the *creation* of the bridge, and is represented by another bridging principle (*move*), which we'll discuss in detail shortly.

Common reasons to Create a Bridge:

1. To negotiate the gap while entering, to monitor the attacker's bridge(s)

2. To set up the majority of bridging options, requiring contact (*disengage* below being the exception)

3. To "feint" the attacker's arm to move into a desired location, where it's not covering a desired target

Defensively, a bridge is *created* any time the defender blocks/receives an attack.

Offensively, a bridge is *created* any time the defender's attack is intercepted by the attacker.

Disengage (脫)

The bridging principle that most clearly represents the opposite of *create* is *disengage*. *Disengage* supports tactics that require us to free our arm from contact with our attacker's.

Common reasons to Disengage from a Bridge:

1. To move from one contact point to another on the attacker's body (such as: arm to body)

2. As a component of the *transfer* principle that allows our arms to "swap roles" and allow a flanking attack

3. To allow our "power side" to shift from a defensive to offensive role

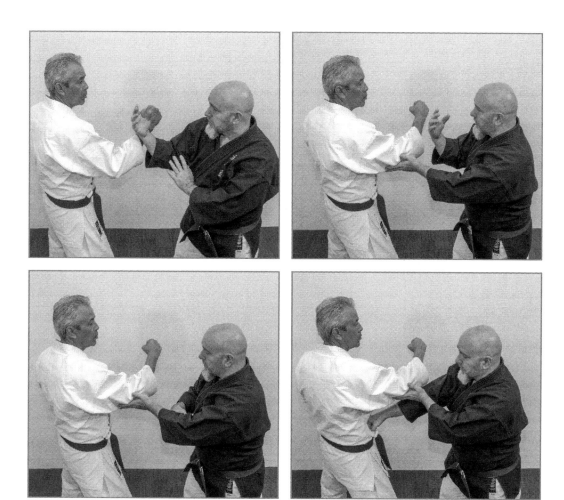

Defender lifts and *detains* the attacker's elbow with his left hand, *disengaging* his right hand to strike to the attacker's liver (from seisan/suparinpei kata).

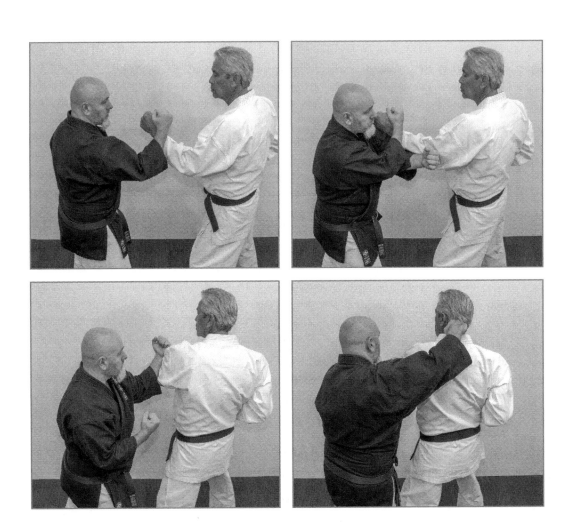

Defender first receives the attacker's punch with his right hand, and then transfers to the left hand, *disengages* his right hand to allow for a flanking, circular punch to the attacker's occipital region.

The same can be done while disengaging by transferring to a "bicep grab" of the attacker's arm.

Move (行)

With our arms connected, we can push and pull the attacker's limbs, to simply defend an attack, to support tactical maneuvers specifically regarding re-positioning the limbs, or to indirectly maneuver the torso, given the arm's connection to the torso.

Common reasons to Move a Bridge:

1. To deflect an attack from its intended target ("block", deflect, parry, redirect)

2. To open a target for a striking maneuver

3. To set up a throw or counter a set up for a throw

4. To set up a lock or break or to counter the same

5. As a connection to the torso that allows movement of the attacker's torso

   a. Push/Pull/Rotate

All deflections/parries/redirections that keep an attack from finding a target exemplify the keyword *move*.

"Blocks" can be utilized to open areas of the attacker's anatomy for attack. In this case, a cross block transitions to a low block to open center and move the defender to the inside position, where the spleen becomes a viable target.

Sukui uke (scooping block) acts to *move* the attacker's arm down and to the front of the defender, where it then becomes safe to engage both arms on the attacker's one and break his elbow.

In this example, the defender uses downward pressure on the attacker's punching arm to open the chin to a counterattack.

Detain (拘 / 扣)

Similar to "move," detain seeks to affect the attacker by taking control of what their limb is "allowed" to do. By pinning, holding or otherwise obstructing the attacker's arm in a particular location, the attacker is disallowed the opportunity to reposition it, making it possible to attack a particular target without being impeded by or counter-attacked with that limb.

Common reasons to Detain a Bridge:

1. To keep the attacker's bridge from defending a target

2. To keep the attacker's bridge from attacking or moving to a position advantageous to them

Kake uke (hooking block) can be utilized to hold the elbow in position to keep the attacker from pivoting to defend against a flanking attack.

In this example, kake uke leads to a wrist grab and downward pull that keeps the attacker from defending the face attack with his right elbow.

The defender's combination of cross block and ura tsuki (undercut punch) creates a "frame" that leads to a trap of the attacker's left arm.

In some circumstances, the ribs and elbow can be used to *detain* an attacker's arm, making it possible to counterattack more easily, grapple, throw or break the arm.

Reminder: *Hands don't chase hands* is also extremely relevant for implementing *detain*, as the elbow can be a useful tool in detaining the opponent's limb, while the hand remains free to counter or defend.

Cross (過)

From a *bridging* perspective, "Cross" does not refer to a cross *shape* (+), but to follow the line of the limb to the torso, as one *crosses* a bridge to travel from one riverbank to the other.

When the limbs meet at their outer extremities, wrist to wrist, we can use the attacker's limb itself as a guide. This method of going "across" the bridge allows us to find a known target (typically neck, armpit, ribs, spleen or liver) without relying on eyesight, as well as maintain contact with that limb while moving in.

Aggressively *crossing* the bridge to attack the head or body in the hopes of pre-empting the attacker's secondary attack is a valuable skillset to train for when a practitioner finds themselves in a *wrong-hand, self-flanked* situation, regardless of the cause.

Common reasons to Cross a Bridge:

1. To safely navigate the "gap" into an area difficult to defend, while maintaining contact

2. To find the targets, without sight

   a. Neck is at the base of the arm (above)

   b. Armpit is at the base of the arm (below)

From the inside high-block position, following the line of the attacker's arm will lead to the neck.

Defender *crosses* the bridge from the inside with a punch of his own (from kata seisan/ suparinpei).

Crossing the bridge from the low position leads to the armpit, ribs, spleen or liver.

In this example, the defender crosses the high bridge to the face, and the low bridge to the liver (from sanseiru/ suparinpei kata).

Break (斷)

There are significant strategic benefits to removing one or more of the opponent's limbs from the fight, since a literal *disarm* nearly ensures a defender's ability to then counter-control an attacker.

Breaking demonstrates the strategy:

舍本逐末

"Ignore the root to go after the branches."

However, many breaks, particularly of the elbow, require multiple points of contact and often have the defender *chasing hands*. Therefore, a thorough study of breaking options that don't require the defender engaging both hands on a single of the attacker's arms should be performed.

The use of a *hands forward* posture like the Sanchin frame, along with *stretching techniques*, and extensive use of the *three gates* and *three segments* will help the practitioner circumvent some of these dangers, particularly when coupled with movement strategies that utilize *the overlapping position* (see *flanking and proper hand*).

When breaking the bridge, consider all these options as targets: fingers, wrist, elbow, and shoulder.

Common reasons to Break a Bridge:
1. To disable one of the attacker's limbs
2. To take the attacker's mind, through pain (by interrupting the OODA loop)
3. To make it possible to close the gap to close range safely

Kake-uke applied as a finger grab and break

The upward elbow and pressing block combination can aggressively meet an incoming punch (from shisochin kata).

An outside low block can transition into an elbow break (another expression of the "sanchin" frame).

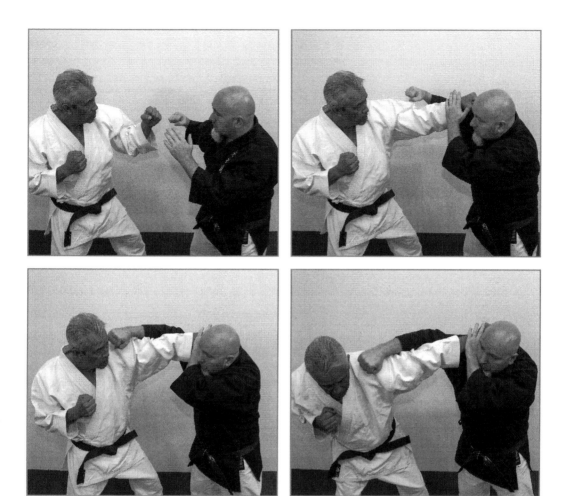

An incoming straight punch can be engaged from the "head inside, overlapping" position to break the elbow (another expression of kata seisan/suparinpei)

If an outside elbow break fails because the attacker's elbow drops, the defender can change the angle to attack and separate the shoulder (an expression of the upward elbow from shisochin or kururunfa kata).

Stick (粘)

Sticking to an opponent's bridges is a specialty of some Southern Chinese martial arts like Southern Mantis and Wing Chun. *Sticking* could be thought of as the passive version of *move*…whereas *moving a bridge* is an active (*aggressive*) action on the part of the defender. *Sticking to a bridge* is passive, merely following the attacker's motion. Because of the passivity of *stick*, compared to the aggressive nature of *move*, *stick* is rarely used for any significant length of time. *Stick* is most often used in conjunction with *move*.

Common reasons to Stick to a Bridge:

1. To actively monitor at close range what's happening with an attacker's body without having to "see"

2. To wait briefly for a better opportunity or better position…for instance, an angle of the attacker's elbow to exploit

Defender shuffles back and engages the attacker's body punch. Defender *sticks* to attacker's arm as attacker then re-punches to head, ducking under while *sticking* to maintain contact. Once on the outside, in the flank position, the defender elbows the attacker. Alternatively, or in addition, the defender can perform a takedown from the flank position.

Defender receives attacker's punch with his right arm, and while receiving the attacker's second punch, he *sticks* to the retreating arm until the defender can *detain* the attacker's arm against the attacker's body, unbalancing him and allowing the defender's palm to the face to find the target.

Transfer (換)

There are times when we first engage an attacker using an arm that we subsequently need to then free up to perform another maneuver; however, we don't feel comfortable simply breaking contact and *disengaging* because we may then be attacked by the limb we lose contact with.

In that case, we may want to maintain overall contact by *transferring* contact from one of our bridges to the other by *creating* a bridge with a new arm and *disengaging* with the original arm. This combination of *create* and *disengage* by two arms is then defined as an exchange or *transfer*.

In many styles, including Goju-ryu, many so called "blocking" or receiving maneuvers are performed with both hands, and this is referred to in various way by practitioners:

- "Block, Check"
- "Block, Trap"
- "Parry, Pass"
- "Minor hand, Major Hand"
- "Block, Control"

Using the full understanding of bridging principles, it's clear that the act of two-handed "blocking" is a four-part compound activity that includes a *transfer* action:

1. Primary Hand – **Create** bridge to meet the attacking limb.
2. Primary Hand – **Move** bridge to ensure the defender's safety (the actual "block" or "redirect").
3. Secondary Hand – **Create** bridge to take the place of the primary hand.
4. Primary Hand – **Disengage** from attacking limb to re-position for next maneuver.

In this example, the transfer action is the combination of steps #3 and #4, and it's also worth highlighting here that transfer alone **does not imply** any specific addition form of control.

Given that understanding, it can be helpful to review the prior list of descriptions for the two-part blocking maneuver from a bridging principles perspective, and to consider what they might imply:

- "Block, Check" and "Block, Trap" both seem to speak to the bridging principle of *detain*, which is an optional form of control that can be applied after the *transfer* is complete. However, since *detain* is an optional form of control, it's not present in every blocking scenario.

- "Parry, Pass" seems to imply *moving* the bridge after the transfer or simply describes the *move* action of the "primary" hand. (see step #2 above).

- "Major hand, Minor hand" seems to speak of the arm's *role* in the act of blocking (the *move* component of the action), where the primary/first (*major*) hand engaged defends against the attack, whereas the secondary (*minor*) hand has a role unrelated to defense.

- "Block, control" is accurate only if the new bridge hand ("secondary" in the example) subsequently does something else to **control** the attacker, such as *move* or *detain*.

Again, since *transfer*, alone, is a form of repositioning, and NOT a form of control, transfer is often followed by an action that would enlist an additional bridging principle, typically *move* (to break balance), *move* (to pass over/under to change positions) or *detain* (to keep it from interrupting our next movement with the now free primary hand).

Common reasons to Transfer a Bridge:

1. To allow an arm to fully "flank" the attacker
2. To move from the inside to outside gate or vice versa
3. To free up your "power" arm for a finishing blow

The following pictures illustrate typical two-handed blocking/receiving use for flanking purposes:

1) Create bridge (left hand).

2) Move Bridge (left hand).

3) Create Bridge (right hand).

4) Disengage Bridge (left hand).

Defender receives the attacker's hook punch, passing it over his head and transfers it to his left hand to allow for a flanking counter-strike.

Defender's punch is blocked and he frees his right arm by transferring the attacker's block to his left hand. This frees the defender's right hand to deal with the attacker's left punch and counter.

Summary

It's helpful to keep in mind that bridging principles are typically of the "keyword" variety, in that they don't typically further explain exactly "how" to perform the task, just that the option is available, and should be understood and studied further.

A cursory examination of the eight bridging keywords helps to clarify both if and how each option supports various methods of control:

Keyword	Control Method
Create	(none)
Disengage	(none)
Move	YES *(controlling posture and balance)*
Detain	YES *(controlling posture and balance)*
Cross	(none)
Break	YES *(breaking structure)*
Stick	(none)
Transfer	(none)

Chapter Summary

In Chapter 4, we've discussed several principles that relate to a person's primary tools, their arms (or "bridges"). First, we discussed how additional defensive (*three gates*) and offensive options (*three segments*) are enabled by better utilizing the full capabilities of the arms and then we enlisted a rare admonition against "*Hands chasing hands*" as a reminder that the forearm or elbow can often take on the role previously occupied by our nerve-dense hands.

We also covered one of the many tactics supported by this approach: The ability to stack the odds in the defender's favor by controlling two of the attacker's limbs with one of their arms. In addition, we covered how to more safely apply our two arms against one of our attacker's, and how to best take advantage of an attacker that does the same.

Likewise, we demonstrated how *stretching* techniques keep our tools aimed at a target (*keep weapons on-line*), and supports several foundational principles, such as *closest weapon/closest target, continue forward,* etc.

Lastly, we identified and demonstrated the *eight major bridging* principles: *Create, disengage, move, detain, cross, break, stick,* and the compound principle with many confusing nicknames…*transfer.*

5

Gong (The Power)

Chapter 5 discusses principles related to *power, leverage, body structure,* and *energetics.*

Techniques, even when combined with strategy, will not ensure success if the practitioner does not have the sensitivity to understand the forces applied on them, and if they don't have the ability to utilize their body to generate the applied martial power necessary for the situation.

出手用四面之力，急去速來，猶猛虎搶豬之勢，或擒或送，無異靈貓捕鼠之形、偵其舉動，奪其氣力。

Hand techniques require the use of the body. The body generates the power and the hands serve as the instruments of contact.

Like a cat catching a rat, a tiger pulls down a wild boar with its body; the claws serve as the means of contact.

— *General Tian Bubishi* (琉球武備志)

Translation by Hanshi Patrick McCarthy.

Fight with the Unified Body

As both defender and attacker come to the fight with the same human anatomical tools, it must be our brains, our usage, our *advanced* application of these tools that makes the difference and helps us prevail. Another way of *stacking the odds* in our favor is to ensure, whenever possible, we apply much of our body, our unified structure, against the weakest and most isolated components of the attacker's body.

Consider the problem of a person pushing something heavy, like a car. A car is remarkably heavy, and the human body is poorly-suited to the task. Simply standing naturally and pushing with the arms is insufficient for several reasons:

1. Standing straight doesn't align the human structure in the direction of necessary force, and

2. Arm-strength is significantly less than the force needed to push a stationary car.

However, when a low stance is employed that redirects force at an angle, and the arms are locked to the body, then the strength of the larger leg muscles are engaged, and it becomes possible to accomplish what was not prior to applying knowledge of the additional *principles* of geometry and leverage.

Now consider that punching an attacker, pushing an attacker or simply dealing with the raw force of an attack is a remarkably similar problem. In self-defense scenarios, it's reasonable to assume that (on average) an attacker will only prey on what are perceived as *weaker* victims. *Stacking the odds* in the defender's favor is what makes it possible for a person with less impressive physical attributes to have a chance at succeeding against a stronger opponent.

Many martial traditions speak about this goal of combining, unifying and coordinating the power of the human body in reference to the development of explosive striking power:

- Coordinated joint forces (chinkuchi / チンクチ) from Okinawan karate

- Five Parts Power (ngo ki lat / 五肢力) from Ngo Cho Kun

- Six Powers (luk ging / 六勁) of Pak Mei

- Eight hard and Twelve Soft (ba gang, shi er rou / 八剛十二柔) of White Crane

- Six Harmonies (liu he / 六合), found in many styles of Chinese martial arts

While it's quite common to discuss, train, and apply this unification of power in a ballistic manner for striking purposes, less common is a study of how to utilize this unification of power for both grappling and blocking/receiving/bridging actions, where it is equally useful.

Applying *unified* body power can assist in pushing, pulling, and rotating opponents for grappling and throwing maneuvers, as well as generating power necessary to tear tendons and ligaments in order to dislocate the wrists, elbows, and shoulders of stronger opponents.

Grappling

In grappling, one attaches the attacker's limbs to our body and moves his or her body to control the opponent. Grappling should not simply pit arm-strength against arm-strength.

An arm bar disconnected from the defender's body provides little control.

When the defender pulls the arms close while locking down the musculature of the latissimus dorsi, and then rotates the body, a more powerful lock or break can be applied.

When the defender's body power is unified against the attacker's isolated arm, the difference in power and leverage favors the defender.

The same situations can occur on the low-line (from kata saifa, seisan, kururunfa or suparinpei).

To gain maximum leverage, the defender may need to "lock" the arm down and use body motion to *move* the attacker from a strong position.

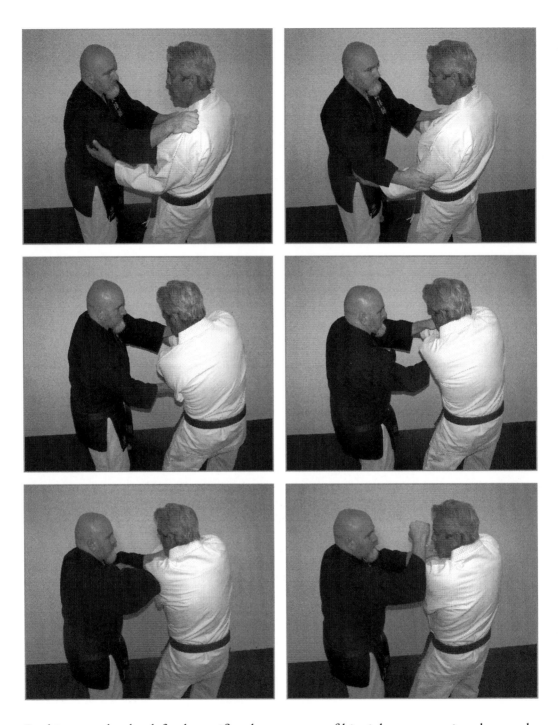

In this example, the defender unifies the structure of his right arm, passing the attacker's arm down and in front using his core muscles. The defender then passes control of the attacker's shoulder to his right elbow (2nd segment) to allow an attack to the face with the 1st segment.

Blocking/Receiving/Bridging Actions

Bridging actions that incorporate *move* also benefit from unifying the arms with the body and moving the attacker's bridge with the strength of the larger muscle groups of the back and legs enlisted.

Attempting to push by merely utilizing the extension of the triceps muscle is likely to fail in *moving* the attacker.

When the defender "locks" the arm in place and pushes with a unified body, the attacker's posture and balance can be compromised.

When pulling or rotating the attacker, the concept is the same…the hands create the connection, but the body unifies to rotate or pull.

Strong vs Weak

Given a detailed study of *bridging*, we can examine the structure of the arm and see that the upper arm is stronger, but less mobile, while the lower arm has more mobility, but less strength.

The upper arm is "stronger" because the arm functions as a ***class-three lever***, a classic machine. The upper arm is closer to the fulcrum (the joint), and therefore can sustain a heavier load. The lower arm, by contrast, is further from the fulcrum and therefore unable to sustain an equivalent load, unaided.

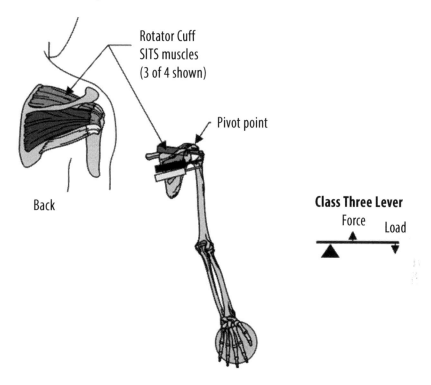

Class Three Lever

The shoulder is a *class 3* lever, as is the elbow.

It is important to remember the portion of our arm (or our opponent's arm) closer to the shoulder joint is *strong*, while the portions of the arm further from the shoulder joint is *weak*. We can refer to the principle of *strong vs weak* as a reminder of how to ensure our bridging applications take advantage of the best possible leverage.

When bridging, it's important to understand (and ultimately, *feel*) whether you're in either a *weak* or *strong* position that's beneficial to your intended application based on factors of both strength and mobility.

Remember when bridging, any number of combinations of contact are possible:

1. Defender's *weak* to attacker's *weak*

2. Defender's *weak* to attacker's *strong*

3. Defender's *strong* to attacker's *weak*

4. Defender's strong to attacker's *strong*

Recall that *strong* typically also equates to *less mobile* and weak typically equates to *more mobile*. When analyzing applications in terms of *weak vs strong, mobility* should also be taken into consideration.

Some general rules of thumb include the following:

1. When engaging strong on weak, apply your strength quickly before they disengage or move to a better location.

2. When you've engaged weak on strong, you'll likely lose in applying strength and leverage, so *disengage, cross* or *move* quickly.

To discuss some specific examples of *strong vs weak*, consider further that the upper arm has a section that is closer to the shoulder. This could be considered the *strong of the strong*. The upper arm also has a section further from the shoulder, near the elbow. This can be considered the *weak of the strong*.

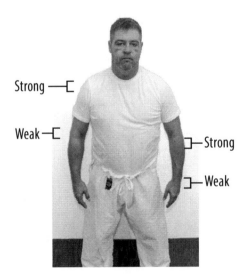

The same consideration can be applied to the lower arm…the area of the forearm near the elbow could be called the *strong of the weak*, and the wrist area, the *weak of the weak*.

Four primary contact points: 1) Strong of the strong: 2) Weak of the strong; 3) Strong of the weak; and 4) Weak of the weak.

If we create a relative scale of leverage (1 to 100) for the four major contact points, it may look something like the following picture:

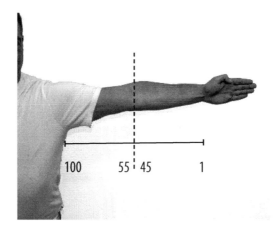

1. Leverage 100 – Strong of the Strong (shoulder)
2. Leverage 55 – Weak of the Strong (just above the elbow)
3. Leverage 45 – Strong of the Weak (just below the elbow)
4. Leverage 1 – Weak of the Weak (wrist)

Notice the relative closeness in location, and therefore leverage, of the *strong of the weak* and the *weak of the strong* contact points. While the location just above the elbow is slightly stronger than the location below the elbow, the location below the elbow is significantly more *mobile* due to close proximity to the elbow joint. The *strong of the weak* is nearly as strong as the location above the elbow, but is also able to change direction/angle of energy much more quickly and with less need to move the entire body.

Typically, application of *strong on weak* involves the defender applying their more mobile *strong of the weak* (leverage of 45) against the attacker's *weak of the strong* (leverage of 55).

This may initially sound like a losing strategy; however, the defender can continue to stack the odds in their favor by applying a *unified body* and the *three segments* in addition to leverage, which can easily bolster against the small, relative difference in leverage alone.

The high block, when applied to "strong of the weak" against "weak of the strong" typically has sufficient leverage to be effective.

This position also allows shifting higher or lower, depending on the specific height, angle, and energy of the attacker.

Applying the high block, wrist ("weak of the weak") against the elbow ("weak of strong"), with a relative leverage of 1 vs 55, typically results in the attacker overpowering the defender.

The same is true for receiving attacks in the midline. When "strong of the weak" is applied against "weak of the strong," there is typically sufficient leverage to be effective and mobility necessary to adapt to normal changes in height, angle, and pressure.

Like the high block, the middle block applied without regard to "strong vs weak" (1 vs 55) can easily be overpowered by an attacker.

When *strong vs weak* is applied, the defender can more easily apply additional control by unbalancing an opponent or smothering his continued attacks.

A defender applying low block with *strong vs weak* in mind has a higher chance of success in rotating the attacker and bringing his punch *on-line*.

Likewise, a defender, who does not apply appropriate leverage can be more easily countered by an attacker.

Attack the Opponent's Posture and/or Balance

As briefly discussed in the section on "Forms of Control" in Chapter 2, disrupting your opponent's posture and balance can be a highly beneficial *form of control*, for several reasons:

1. It can disrupt the attacker's OODA loop (see Chapter 3's "Timing" section).

2. It can disrupt their ability to launch additional attacks with power on target.

3. It can create openings the defender can exploit.

4. It begins the process of unbalancing an opponent, which cannot be as easily ignored as pain.

While many of the forms of control can be thought of as a singular preference to end an altercation, *attacking the opponent's posture/balance* could instead be thought of as analogous to "salt," in that while salt generally makes most foods taste "better," *attacking the opponent's posture/balance* is something that can add to the effectiveness of **nearly every motion** performed by the defender and connected to the attacker, be it blocking receiving, grapping or striking.

There are two primary approaches common in effectively *attacking the opponent's posture/balance*: 1) Seeking the attacker's center, and 2) Applying one or more of the four primary directional energies from Southern Chinese Martial arts (*sink, float, spit, swallow*).

Seek the Center

Whether attacking with a strike or any form of a pushing or pulling action, it's important to seek the opponent's center of mass, typically represented by their spine.

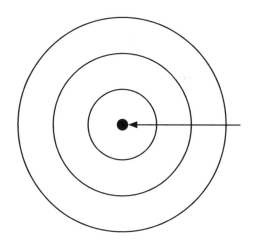

A strike or push aimed directly at the attacker's center is more likely to deliver maximum energy into the target.

 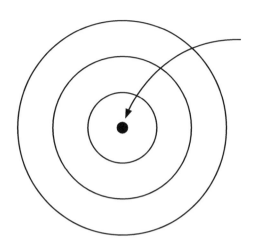

A circular or indirect attack can still deliver maximum penetration into the target, if the point of aim is at the attacker's center of mass.

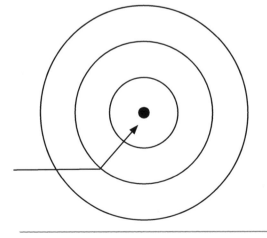

The attacker's arms connect to the attacker's center, and, as a result, can be used by the defender to transfer energy into the attacker.

A strike or push whose force or angle is not aimed at the center of mass will likely deliver less energy directly into the target as both intentional and unintentional rotation caused by either the attacker or defender reduces the effects of that power on the attacker. Energy lost typically causes the attacker to rotate, with valuable penetrative energy skipping off like a stone skipped across the surface of a pond, and, in a worst-case scenario, actually lends power to the attacker's incoming attack.

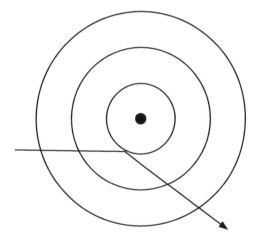

Penetrative energy is lost as a portion of the energy rotates the attacker.

Much like strikes, blocks that also seek to disrupt an attacker's posture or balance have a higher chance of success when aimed at the attacker's center.

If the attacker rotates while the defender is attempting to apply pressure to their center, the defender can use the elbow (2nd segment) to reacquire and disrupt the center.

When this pressure is not aimed at the center, the attacker can rotate and counterattack more easily, as shown in this example:

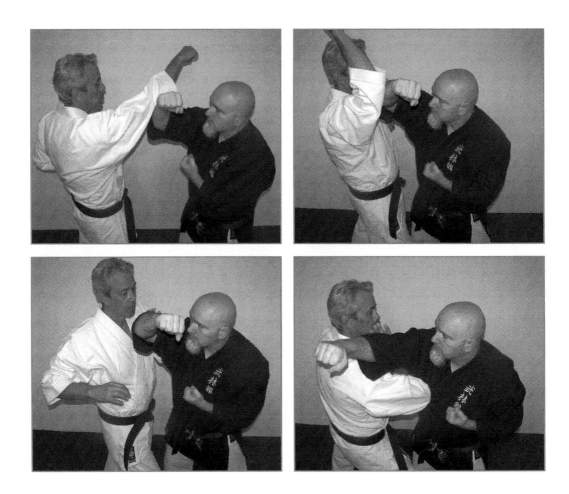

When the defender applies the pressure in the vertical direction, the attacker can rotate, pull back, and counterattack from underneath.

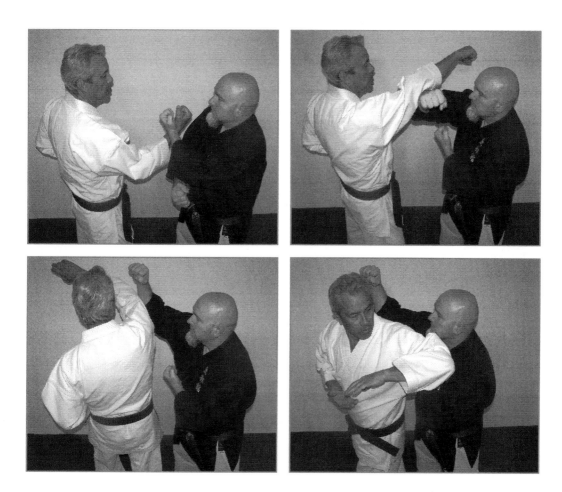

If the defender's pressure is applied horizontally, the attacker can rotate and strike the defender with a rearward elbow.

Utilizing Two Points of Pressure

If you are utilizing only one arm to provide pressure toward the opponent's center, the opponent may be able to react quickly enough to rotate and deflect that force away from their center.

However, utilizing two arms, you can "triangulate" pressure to affect your opponent's center. This achieves two things: 1) More easily directs the force toward the center; and 2) Assists in keeping the opponent from rotating away from your pressure.

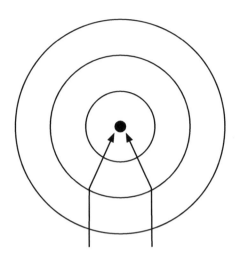

Triangulation of force

Two points of contact on the attacker make it possible for the defender to more easily disrupt their posture and balance.

The defender can utilize two arms to lock the attacker's arm, and use the arm to off-balance the attacker, as the arm is connected directly to the attacker's center.

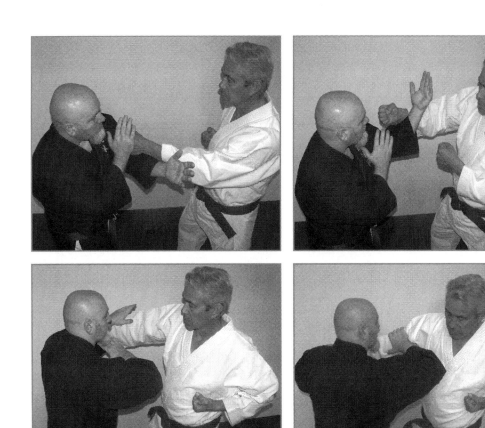

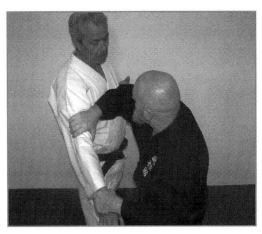

(opposite side)

In the example on page 186, the defender utilizes the two motions of a "typical" middle block to receive two punches from the attacker. Detaining the attacker's right arm with his left hand, he uses his right hand (1st segment) to hook the triceps and the right elbow (2nd gate) to first strike and then affect a throw. (This is an example of the shisochin kata arm bar from the inside position.)

Defending Against Two Points of Pressure

A primary defense against two points of pressure triangulating against your center is to "strip" one of the attacker's arms from its location, which then forces the attacker to either: 1) Attempt to re-engage the stripped arm to continue; 2) Change the direction of energy with their remaining attachment point and attempt to continue with only one contact point; or 3) Abandon the tactic altogether.

Typically, this stripping or splitting motion is done with an energy moving in two directions.

In this example, the splitting of the attacker's energy occurs just before the attacker contacts the defender (an expression of chu/ge uke from seiunchin kata).

This similar example shows where the defender's splitting energy brings his right hand lower. In this circumstance, the defender uses *closest weapon, closest target* to strike the groin with 1st segment and the chin with 2nd segment.

In this example, the attacker has full contact with the defender's clothing. Defender strikes to the face on the way to splitting the attacker's energy, opens the center for a knee strike to the spleen (from saifa kata).

In this situation, the attacker is pinning the defender's arm against his body. Defender rotates to the right, and then strips one arm with osae (pressing), countering with a backfist to the attacker's face. (An example from seiunchin kata)

Again, the defender should avoid attempting to strip a point of contact close to the shoulder, as chances of becoming *detained* by the attacker are increased.

Apply the Four Movement Concepts

The four primary movement concepts (sei noi biu ging / 四內標勁) of Southern Chinese boxing describe several primary options for *disrupting an attacker's posture and balance*, and are most easily applied to an opponent once his *center* is available for exploitation:

   5. **Sink** (chaam / 沉)– This heaviness can restrict the attacker's lower and upper body movements

沉：如泰山壓頂

Sink: Like Mount Tai Pressing Down

6. **Float** (fau / 浮) – Lifting a portion of their body connected to their core can cause the attacker to become highly concerned about their own ability to maintain balance

浮：如飛鳶定地

Float: Like a Kite Flies

7. **Spit** (tou / 吐) – Projecting power into the attacker can shift their balance, causing them to take a step or projecting off-center, and result in a rotation of their body.

吐：如猛虎出林

Spit: Like a Fierce Tiger Exits the Forest

8. **Swallow** (tun / 吞) – Pulling the attacker can disrupt or rotate their structure in the same manner as spit.

吞：如貓兒戲鼠

Swallow: Like a Young Cat Plays with a Mouse

Middle block – The standard shape of the outward middle block is a downward wedge.

This shape most easily applies a downward, ***sinking*** energy.

The same is true for the inward middle block.

Shifting either to an upward elbow redirects force upward, *floating* the opponent.

The outward high block is a shape perfectly suited to *floating* an opponent.

The defender demonstrates an example of *spit* that can assist in rotating the attacker in preparation for a throw or simply jamming the shoulder to prevent a punch. A pull to the neck demonstrates *swallow*.

Every punch, push or direct strike is an example of *spit*.

Using the sanchin pulling motion to open the attacker's center is an example of *swallow*.

A cross block transferring a low-line strike to a pulling low block/elbow combination demonstrates **swallow** (from kururunfa kata).

Deflecting punches can demonstrate a combination of *spit* and *sink*...

…or *spit* and *float*.

Short Power

In order to deliver powerful strikes in the clinch range, and to take full advantage of principles that enable *aggressive* forward pressure, such as *closest weapon/closest target, keep the weapon on-line, continue forward/clearing obstructions*, it's helpful to develop what is typically called either "**short power**" (duan jin / 短勁) or "**inch power**" (cun jin / 寸勁) in Southern Chinese martial traditions.

By design, striking with *short power* doesn't require a large "wind-up," or pull-back, which could be exploited by the attacker.

When a defender retreats to "wind up" for a punch, the attacker exploits the retreat.

While striking with a well-coordinated and *unified body* helps to support the delivery of power from short range, there are a few other considerations when attempting to both train and deliver *short power*.

Engaging the Whole Body, and then "Pop the Clutch"

Since our power often stems from rotations of the hips and torso via contact from the ground in a coordinated chain up the body, the power can be expressed through the body and then, at the last moment, "connected" to the arms in the same way a car with a manual transmission can have the engine accelerated while in neutral, and then "pop the clutch" to link the engine to the wheels via the transmission for a fast start.

With this approach, power can be added to a stiff arm or thrusting elbow strike without first pulling back.

Stiff arm, powered by the lower body and core (from shisochin kata).

The same form of stiff-arm transfer of power from the core can be utilized from the low-block position.

At closer range, in the clinch, the tip of the elbow can be driven into the sternum... again driven by the legs and rotation of the core and torso.

Training – stiff arm against pad or heavy bag. Utilize the same rotational power used in fundamental punching training.

Alternatively, relax the arm and then lock or extend it at any point during the forward rotation/thrust.

Coordinated Relaxation and Whipping

Strikes benefit from quick acceleration. Sufficient speed to create devastating strikes can only be achieved if antagonistic muscle groups are as relaxed as possible to avoid muscle pairs working against one another.

The style Goju-ryu is said to be named from one of the lines of the so called "Eight Laws of the Fist" (拳法之大要八句), an eight-line poem from the Okinawan Bubishi. However, the concept of gang-rou ("goju"/"hard & soft") is fundamental to all Fuzhou and Hakka martial arts, and is a concept that is critical to the development of explosive power. Poems like the one below from Five Ancestor Boxing are found in most Southern Chinese martial traditions:

全刚易折、全柔易缠，刚柔相济、操胜在手

All hard…easy to break, all soft…easily entangled
Hard and soft working together, victory is at hand

The idea that hard and soft both have a place in martial arts and are to be coordinated is the key to many methods of expressing explosive power (fajin / 發勁). While many styles like Goju-ryu have oral teachings such as "remain relaxed until the moment of impact and then tighten down," it can be remarkably difficult to do so.

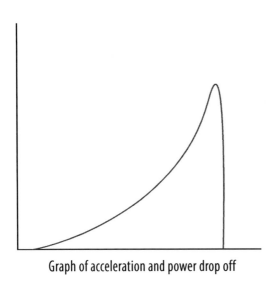

Graph of acceleration and power drop off

One method of practice that can assist in development of relaxation both before **and after** a strike comes from Shouting Crane's (minghequan/鳴鶴拳) fundamental punching practice. This punching method has a "whipping" body mechanic, similar to an upward "uraken" (back-knuckle strike), and it's training method helps identify and focus on relaxation.

Starting from a completely relaxed posture, the hips rotate and the energy is expressed upward through the body to the shoulder, elbow, and wrist, where there is a momentary "squeeze." Then body tension is dropped as quickly as possible, and 100% of the tension is released from the arm, which then drops and naturally slaps the practitioner on the thigh.

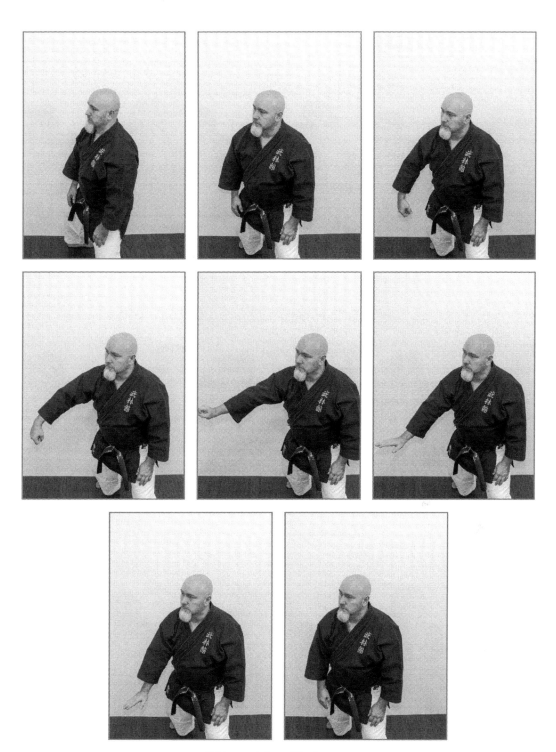

Whip punch from Minghequan

This style of training is beneficial because it assists in relaxing before striking to reduce or completely remove the muscle tension of the non-primary muscle in each muscle pair involved in the strike, which aids in acceleration.

An additional benefit from this training is the ability to willfully relax again after a strike in order to be prepared for the next strike. This ability to relax after striking can decrease the "reload" time between effective strikes.

Twitch, Don't Push

An important aspect to striking with *short power* in a manner that is effective in clinch-style situations is to enlist a "twitching" action of the muscles, similar to the hypnagogic jerk that sometimes occurs as you start to fall asleep. In contrast, using slow acceleration enables the attacker to feel and anticipate the next move, and allows him or her to adjust to the defender's movement.

In White Eyebrow (白眉) this is described as "shock power" (驚勁):

驚勁: 如受火燒或針刺突然反應發出的勁

"Shock power – like the strength sent out suddenly when you are burned or get pricked by a needle."

Sanchin frame – punch without retracting, using a twitching action

Practice the same "twitching" motions from blocking positions

Consider Enlisting the Shoulder

Some Southern Chinese traditions, such as White Eyebrow (白眉) and Feeding Crane (食鶴拳) enlist additional acceleration and penetration by training to increase the range of motion and power of the shoulder carriage, which can be expressed in isolation, or in combination with hip torque.

Fundamental practice for range of motion in the shoulder carriage: With arms straight, flex shoulders backward and forward.

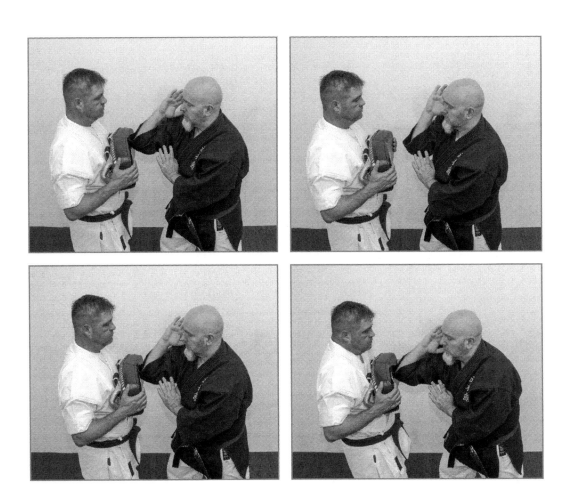

Partner pad exercise with forward elbow, using shoulder motion only

While the exercises demonstrated here relate specifically to forward motion of the shoulder, there are numerous methods for training the shoulder up, down, back, and in diagonal directions, which are beyond the scope of this work.

Be first to Change the Energy

In Chinese martial arts, the keyword *hua* (化) is often used to describe situations of **change** or **transformation**. From a martial perspective, *change* is an important reminder to not be overly attached to the idea of a specific technique so we can, when opposed, quickly change our tactics to meet the changing situation we are confronted with.

Resisting in a single direction is relatively simple…we realign our posture and engage additional supporting muscles in order to provide resistance to a singular pressure. However, resisting *changing* pressure is remarkably difficult for the reasons discussed earlier that are related to *timing*. Resisting a change in pressure puts the resisting person in the *after*, which is clearly a non-desirable situation.

Humans have a hard time providing concerted and coordinated resistance in multiple directions. An extended arm might easily resist a push down, but not the addition of a sudden and unexpected push sideways, for instance.

This strategy is exemplified by the Chinese saying:

四两拨千斤

"Use four ounces to topple a thousand pounds."

Being *first to change the energy* is a refinement and expansions of the timing concept surrounding seeking to master *the before*, but applied to situations where sustained contact exists and pressure between the attacker and defender have neutralized one another.

Stagnant Situations

When an attacker and defender meet/match force, both angle and pressure, it's important to be the first to change the angle and pressure of the energy.

Being first, obviously, puts that person *in the before*, forcing the opponent to react *in the after*.

Attacker and defender are at a stalemate of pressure on the outside position. Defender peels the bridge away to the outside and slips into the center with an elbow (an expression of seiunchin kata).

Defender throws a circular punch at the attacker, which the attacker defends against. Defender sinks his elbow, changing his punching energy downwards, which pulls the attacker's arm down, opening the attacker's face for a second punch.

Defender meets the attacker's punching energy with a *wrong-hand* inside block, but then immediately changes the blocking energy downward, rotating the attacker, and moving the defender away from the attacker's second punching hand. Defender counters to the jaw.

While *be first to change the energy* could be thought of as "simply" a restatement of our understanding of timing, there are two main reasons to isolate this principle from *timing*.

First, it is not always immediately apparent that a situation has led to stagnant (matched/opposed/neutralized) pressures. A natural human instinct is often to continue to attempt to "finish" the technique that is being opposed, while the more valuable trained response is to quickly abandon the first approach, *change the energy*, and *continue forward/clearing obstructions*.

Second, understanding this principle can help to "train your eyes" to better understand application examples you may see others perform, even in styles very unlike the one(s) in which you train. Many applications you may see others perform are successful largely because they have taken control *of the before* by identifying a pressure-related stalemate and being the first to *change*. This situation may not be as obvious, from a timing perspective, as a striking maneuver, and it's very helpful to have the understanding and vocabulary to identify why a particular application is highly successful.

Chapter Summary

Chapter 5 focused on concepts surrounding power, leverage, and pressure.

We covered some of the benefits of *unifying* the body, to best engage larger muscle groups, and then discussed the leverage concept of *strong vs weak*, identifying contact points on the defender and attacker that maximize utility of movement while engaging the best available leverage.

One of the primary forms of *control* discussed in Chapter 2 is how to attack *the opponent's posture and balance*. This technique was further discussed in the context of providing continuous, added control during nearly any sustained circumstance of physical contact.

We identified a foundational concept, *seeking the center*, and then discussed how to enhance this approach by enlisting one or more of the four primary movement principles of Fujian martial traditions: *sink, float, spit,* and *swallow*.

Short power, and its critical nature in supporting other related principles in a clinch-range martial art was covered, along with application examples and a few training methods.

Lastly, we discussed a principle that fuses pressure and timing with a reminder to be quick to identify situations of equalized pressure between defender and attacker, and to *be first to change the energy* in those circumstances, also referred to as taking command *of the before*.

6

A Teaching Model for
Progressive Skill Development

As briefly discussed in Chapter 1 ("So, HOW do you implement a "principle-driven" model?"), the full value of a principle-driven model can only be leveraged when the principles are supported by a mindset that values skills over memorization *and* is coupled with a teaching model that progressively allows the student to navigate in sequence all three stages of learning. Without these prerequisites, principles remain merely a checklist with which one can correct "one-off," memorized applications.

From the perspective of curriculum development for martial arts, the stages of skills-driven learning roughly map in this manner:

#	Stages of learning	Skills development models
1	*Knowledge*	Multiple individual, discreet drills for isolated skill development, each supporting one or more of the art's principles or goals.
2	*Understanding*	Drills should allow for the following: 1. Link and combine isolated skills 2. Put skills into useful context 3. Highlight similarities and differences among isolated skillsets

3	*Transference/ Application*	A safe platform, paradigm or training method that allows students to transfer and apply what they have learned:
		1. Explore the limits of their understanding,
		2. Test assumptions,
		3. Pressure-test techniques, concepts, and applications, and
		4. Experiment with alternatives to those provided by their instructor(s)

Step 1 - Individual Skill Development (Knowledge)

So far, we've discussed over thirty principles handed down to us from various martial traditions that support the application practices of a clinch-range, standing grappling and striking system. In a few cases, we demonstrated specific, isolated drills that can help inform and teach skills related to those discreet principles.

Unfortunately, the development of an individual skill to support a principle-driven goal does not guarantee the appropriate skill will manifest at the right moment to support the form of control needed at the critical time.

At this stage, individual skills are really still "one-offs," in the way many pre-arranged applications are…they demonstrate a pre-defined response to a particular situation. Several things are still missing…the assurance the skill will be applied from a sense of "feeling" (or simply with very little conscious thought) and that it will be applied correctly, given the many options available to the practitioner.

For instance, one particular reference point, "lead arm low," requires contacting the inside of the opponent's same-side arm. In this skill, there are many potential variables that lead to the "best" response: Which leg we each have forward, the style of pressure (heavy, light, retracted/disengaged), how far our bodies leaned forward, exactly where we are contacting our "bridges," given what we know about the *three gates* and *strong vs. weak* technique, etc.

Knowing how to deal with that simple scenario and apply the correct principles using their related skills is complex, and must be executed largely without the luxury of conscious thought. There is no time to "do the math," or look up the right answer … we need to have "felt" and experienced this situation or one very similar, and "fought" our way out of it before, if we are to resolve the situation quickly, and in our favor. Individual, isolated drills help the student gain components of that experience.

And let's be clear, as a teacher, you will not create a drill for every permutation to help every student develop the "feeling" necessary to select between two "options" for every given reference point. You will most likely provide a level of isolated training that is effective in a certain situation, and then move the students forward to learn other individual skills to be linked and combined in later lessons.

For a student's advancement through the stages of learning, it is critical that the teacher not occupy student's training time with continue practice of skills already acquired. Once a skill has been developed by a student, they should be progressed to drills that expand on that skill, link that skill to other skills, use that skill in alternative situations or simply move on to learning other skills.

It is also very helpful to the teacher to clearly articulate the intended goal(s) of each drill and drill option…which skill(s) the drill is intended to develop, and which principle(s) are supported with those skills. This knowledge allows the student to "study" the tradition, rather than merely "train" or "practice". As every drill has value in a particular direction and deficits in all others, it can help student and teacher alike to be clear about the intended value(s) of every training activity, allowing constant error-detection and correction as related to both short and long-term training goals.

While the purpose of this book is to discuss a set of conceptual premises with examples for clarity and not lay out a codified or complete curriculum, it is the author's hope that the information provided can be used by the reader to modify or create isolated skill-development drills that support the principles identified and valued in the reader's own martial tradition.

The majority of the principles (and related examples) selected for inclusion can be incorporated into any art's training regarding the receiving, parrying or blocking portion of the curriculum…the portion of the curriculum most concerned with moving from *the after*, efficiently and effectively through *the during* to allow the defender to become the person in control of *the before*, where nearly anything becomes possible.

Step 2 - Combined Skills with "Selection" (Understanding)

To help prepare the student for a truly free-form platform, it's important to help students work through applying their skills in ways that deal with variations from pressure, to timing, to physical reference points.

For each skill development drill, it's helpful to add more than one scenario as a "trigger" to understand the varying options in a *similar* scenario so the defender can react to aggression with some set of available options such as the following:

- Lethal or less-than-lethal options against an attacker,

- Deciding to move from the outside position to the inside, or vice versa,

- Responding with a grappling maneuver or repeatedly disengaging to focus on kicking

To give an example, we present an "obstruction-clearing" drill, the intended purpose of which is to provide the defender a set of skills in dealing with being obstructed/ blocked, given some specific and common variations in that situation. Specifically, this obstruction clearing drill helps us practice the principle of *continue forward, flow around obstructions*.

In this drill, the *feeder* is much like a boxing coach holding mitts. The feeder will randomly vary their method of blocking, allowing the defender the opportunity to *feel* the stimulus that points to the "contextually-correct" follow-up response, allowing them to *flow around the obstruction*, and into their next attack.

Feeder's blocking method	Defender's "flow" response
Block "shallow," between elbow and wrist	Hinge elbow, advance and backfist or uppercut.
Block deeply into elbow and center	Pull back to middle block (a la Sanchin) to open the attacker's center to a secondary attack.

| Block with excessive downward pressure | Let arm drop out the bottom and circle up/around for a round punch to the temple. |

The defender punches the feeder, and is blocked. Depending on *how* the feeder blocks, the defender will select one of three following possible options for dealing with the obstruction.

Option 1: When the feeder blocks lower than the elbow or across the center line. The defender "rolls" to a backfist or uppercut.

Option 2: When the feeder blocks into the defender's elbow with pressure *seeking the center*, the defender pulls the center open and strikes with the pulling hand.

Option 3: When the feeder blocks and pushes too far down, the defender drops out the bottom and punches from the outside.

Step 3 - Free-form platform/Laboratory (Transference)

Nearly all forms of Chinese martial traditions include some form of two-person experimentation and pressure-testing "platform" which assists students in *transferring/applying* their *understanding* into new situations.

These *platform* drills are described in many ways:

- Pushing hands (推手)
- Sticking hands (黐手)
- Rolling hands (輾手)
- Coiling hands (盤手)
- Crossing hands (過手)
- Listening hands (聽手)
- Kneading hands (搓手)
- Loose hands (散手)
- Bridge hands (橋手)
- Bridge-building (搭橋)
- Negotiating with hands (講手)
- Lifting limbs (舉技)

Regardless of the tradition's naming convention for the training platform, the purpose is typically similar…it provide the student with a training environment that has boundaries or limitations for safety. This environment allows them to test out the material they have learned, push the boundaries of their skills and understanding, and allow them to "transfer" their skills to situations and positions not otherwise present in predetermined drills.

The remainder of this chapter is a systematic, five-level progression for a "sticking-hands" platform. This platform is intended for further refining and linking the skills developed in prior, isolated drills. Some of the values of this platform include:

- The addition of many new reference points to start application practice

- Increased randomness of responses by attacker and defender
- The opportunity to utilize additional parts of the body in new ways
- The opportunity to utilize an art's foundational movements in new ways

Summary of the Training Progression

The five levels of progression through the platform guide the student through a set of skills by identifying particular skills to be focused on by role and level. The role that appears in **bold** in the table below is the one that is working on the "Primary Skills Developed." Most levels (1-4) require the switching of roles to allow all students the opportunity to exercise all of the skills at level.

Level	"Primary" Skill(s) Developed	Role A**	Role B**
1*	Sticking, Matching, "Listening"	Leader	*Follower*
2*	Target Selection, Position, Entries	*Attacker*	Follower
3*	Redirection, Neutralization, Awareness	Attacker	*Neutralize*
4*	Flowing Around Obstructions, Alternatives	*Attacker (Combinations)*	Neutralize
5	Varying "Forms of Control"	*Attacker (All forms of Control)*	*Neutralize and Counter*

*Levels 1-4 require a formal switch in roles during practice. Level 5 introduces a cooperative, fluid switch in intention/role.

** Bold/Italics indicates which person in each level and role is receiving the primary skill-development benefits from the drill.

Note: this training method specifically isolates "power" and its related speed and acceleration. Other training methods exist that isolate other skill components, such as timing or flow in order to allow for the analysis of power as a solution to application problems.

During this training, it is very important that the instructor guides the exercise by giving the following pointers and asking questions:

- "What was that? Can you do that again?"
- "Can you let me try that again? Please do X."
- "Would you mind slowing down a bit?"
- "It's OK with me, if you want to speed up a little"
- "I feel like you're a little too far away, just playing at the wrists…can you get a bit closer?"
- "Don't forget to try X"
- "Don't forget, we're not supposed to do X, that's something we do in level Y."
- "Don't forget, *winning* isn't important, there's more to be learned by getting into and out of bad situations and weird positions"
- "Invest in loss."

Level 1 – Sticking, Matching, "Listening"

The leader moves his or her arms along the student's full range of movement at a constant slow-to-moderate pace, while the follower attempts to simply *stick* to the leaders arms.

At this level, the student seeks to learn how to harmonize their movement with that of the opponent, and feel, rather than simply see, how the leader is moving.

The follower should allow themselves to stick with varying surfaces, not just the hand/wrist. It's partly a study in anatomy for the follower.

The leader (in black) moving through full range of motion. The follower (in white) *sticking to the leader's arms.*

Typical Mistakes:

Made by the Leader:

- Skipping forward to aggressive movements
- Varying speed or speeding up
- Staying "too tight," meaning limiting range of motion to the typical body box. Use this as an opportunity to open up to the full range of motion.

- "Threading" the arms, forcing the transfer of the follower's second arm to attach to only one of the leader's arms. This essentially disengages the follower from one arm, forcing them to find and reengage, rather than having both arms stuck to only one of the leader's arms.

Made by the Follower:

- Skipping forward to neutralization motions that block or otherwise "defend" against the Leader's motions

- Engaging only the hands and wrists. All surfaces of the arm and shoulder should be engaged, as necessary.

Made by Both:

- Staying in a stationary stance

- Staying too "hand-focused.". Utilize all surfaces of the arms.

- Loosing contact with one hand (switching to single-handed play)

- Adding strength or power

Level 2 - Target Selection, Position, Entries

In Level 2, the "leader" develops and expresses aggressive intention, becoming the "attacker". The attacker will aim strikes at vulnerable targets, and/or move in such a manner as to set up (but not fully execute) potential grabs, throws, wrenches, etc. This level is a study in multiple potential reference points from which to apply techniques.

The follower should continue to "ignore" the aggressive actions of the attacker, and stick to the attacker's arms. This is difficult, but important to allow the attacker the ability to explore target selection while *connected* to an opponent, as the follower's arms are not neutralized, but act to create natural barriers and force the attacker to create and expose openings.

The follower should, however, be training their "eyes" and concentrating on feeling to better understand the exact moment when the leader has opened a line of potential attack by opening the center, adjusting the arms to take a dominant position, moving into a proper striking range, etc.

It will be VERY difficult for the follower to not move into a "defender" role at this point. The intention is to not stay at this level so long that the follower develops bad habits (not reacting when threatened).

Attacker (in black), clears a path for a right punch to the spleen. Follower (in white) merely *sticks* to the attacker at this stage.

Typical Mistakes:

Made by the Attacker:

- Finishing the attacks. The attacks should be lined up and positioned and near the target, but should not be completely executed. The follower should know that the attacks would have been successful.

- Limiting their attacks to standard weapons only. Use all parts of the body to attack. Be creative.

- Limiting their attacks to standard targets. Attack all parts of the body. Be creative.

- Using speed to attempt to "beat" the stickiness and break free.

Made by the Follower:

- Neutralizing the attacker's advances

- Failing to notice the attack opportunities aimed at them

Made by Both:

- Adding strength, trying to "win" or changing speed dramatically.

Level 3 - Redirection, Neutralization, Awareness

At this level, the defender is now allowed to neutralize the attacks against them. With the constant change in reference points, the defender becomes more aware of the potential lines of attack.

Attacker (in black) attempts a palm strike to the face, and the defender (in white) redirects.

Typical Mistakes:

Made by the Attacker:

- Starting an attack and not committing to it. Commitment creates useful exaggeration for the drill, and gives the defender the opportunity to focus on better methods of neutralization.

Made by the Defender:

- Over-neutralizing – defending in motions larger than one's "body box."

- Neutralizing too early – waiting until the attack is close to complete sets up a situation more like that will be encountered at realistic speed, when the defender's OODA (observe, orient, decide, act) loop would be required to process the situation *before* being able to neutralize.

- Counterattacking: The desire to counter-attack has to be suppressed at this level, in order to focus more specifically on the "minimum-required-neutralization."

Made by Both:

- Increasing speed to "win" the drill

- Moving too quickly from one technique to the next

Level 4 - Flowing Around Obstructions, Alternatives

At this point the attacker begins to deal with the fact that their initial attacks will likely be neutralized. The defender's neutralization should be seen as only an *inconvenience,* an *obstruction* that must be either removed or flowed around, so the attacker should attack, deal with the obstruction, and launch a secondary attack from the new position.

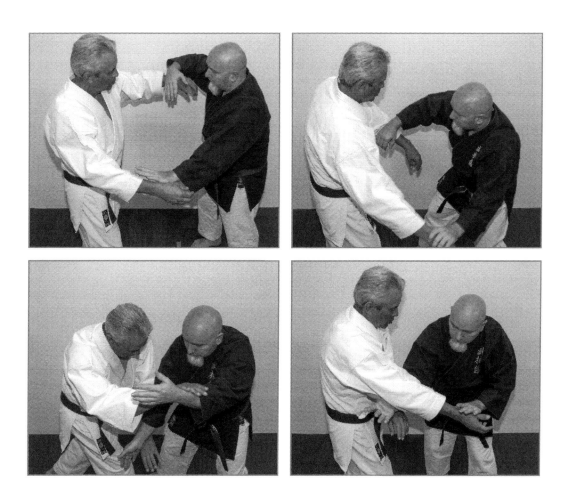

Attacker (in black) attempts the same spleen punch. Now neutralized by the defender (in white), the attacker switches to an arm break.

Typical Mistakes:

Made by the Attacker:

- Launching too many linked attacks too early. Initially, one attack, repositioning, and one secondary attack should be initiated, and then a pause before another volley is introduced.

Made by the Defender:

- Applying too much resistance to the attacker's repositioning efforts (build a gradual resistance)
- Applying too much resistance to the attacker's secondary attack

Both:

- Level of power/strength should be decided on verbally BEFORE starting the drill so everyone knows what they are training on.

NOTES: Timing should become more staccato. Attack, then neutralize. If either attacker or defender don't think the neutralization was effective, then discuss, repeat, and work through alternatives.

This is an opportunity to explore continuing the attack from a neutralized position, flowing around obstacles.

Level 5 - Varying "Forms of Control"

Level 5 opens the training paradigm to allow for not only all forms of control, but more fluid definitions of "attacker" and "defender." Strikes, unbalancing, kicks, throws are all interspersed, and the partners continuously determine who is given the "right of way" to perform a fully committed technique.

Typical Mistakes:

- Being "competitive." In this platform, much more is learned/gained by "losing." This should be a safe platform for experimentation of many kinds.
- Trying to "win" instead of trying new approaches and experimenting; not investing in loss.

- Staying too tightly in one's own body box does not allow the practitioner to get into the very unusual places this drill can support. Coming up with methods for recovering from "bad" positions can be one of the best takeaways from this method of training.

- Sticking to "standard" techniques. The entire body is a tool that can be utilized at close range. Try to think "out of the box" in this safe environment. Bump with the legs. Press with the head. Pull with the chin.

- Only trying things "once." If it doesn't work the first time, have a dialogue with your training partner. Try to set up the situation and try again.

- Not fully experimenting with one's full range of tools or the full range of targets.

- Attempting to force certain scenarios/actions, rather than waiting for opportunities to present themselves.

- Changing speeds to "win." If both parties are working at certain speeds and intensity (hopefully mutually determined before starting), suddenly shifting to a higher level of speed or power in the middle of a technique can give an illusion of success where there is none. For example, if I am moving at relatively slow speed x and you defend with a fast block that means to make the block actually work, you would have to be able to move at 2-to-3x when x is my full speed as opposed to a decided on training speed.

The very worst thing that can be done is to treat this platform as a "competition," rather than a "laboratory."

Use this progression and platform to experiment in a safe environment, and to push your skill development in directions that are hard to describe in other forms of training.

武林館

Afterword

I sought out training in several precursor arts (White Crane, Five Ancestors, White Eyebrow, etc.) for the light they might shed on Goju-ryu. I found these arts have fascinating preferences, teaching methods, and training methods…some of which were supportive of Okinawan Goju-ryu and some not. The subset selected for inclusion in this book align with my understanding of the core application concepts and preferences of the Goju-ryu style, based on my experiences and the information shared with me by my Goju-ryu teachers and mentors. Any faults in the approach presented or understanding reflected within are mine alone. I take full responsibility for the contents of this book, as it reflects my study, journey, and conclusions, not those of my teachers. Lastly, it reflects a portion of the teaching model exercised and taught in my Burinkan (martial forest hall / 武林館) school.

The in-depth explanation of the over two dozen principles presented in this book, would, to some traditionalists, constitute a blasphemous act. Ancient quanpu (boxing manuals / 拳譜) such as the Ryukyu Bubishi that contain such specific information are historically guarded in martial traditions. A trope long used in Wuxia novels and Kung Fu movies is a school's *quanpu* is stolen, giving the rival school access to the martial secrets of the hero's clan.

I have noticed a recent interest in "principles" across the traditional Okinawan martial arts community, yet have seen scant reference to written *actionable* principles. It is my primary hope that this book helps fill a gap in the martial community, much of which seem to be yearning for meaning and understanding of our shared, ancient traditions. If this book sparks meaningful discussion and helps teachers and practitioners increase live skills in applying these martial traditions, my efforts to learn, codify, and document this material will be rewarded.

At the very least, I hope that the concepts in this book can assist practitioner and teacher alike in performing any necessary error-detection or correction in their application practices.

I also foster the much broader hope that it allows traditionalists to "come to terms with tradition" and consider that changing the teaching model is an acceptable way to honor tradition, while both allowing *and requiring* us to become better teachers, maintaining and strengthening the value of the martial traditions in our custody.

In my opinion, far too many teachers and practitioners of traditional martial arts focus heavily on memory based practices to the exclusion of other teaching methods (utilized by other martial arts and martial sports) that are heavily "skills-focused." I believe one powerful way traditional martial arts can regain their respect in society is by focusing on their originally intended utility. These useful skills require supportive teaching methods that are not overly focused on memorized practices.

I am also hopeful this principle-driven model help restores kata (kyung, forms, taolu) to their prior place in martial traditions: That of a summarized reminder of lessons already learned by students prior to memorizing the kata. The lessons of kata in earlier times were likely the lessons of the "kihon waza" (the "foundational" movements of the style) applied to the additional combinations and variations found in the forms. There would have been no need for additional rules to *decipher* the forms.

While this book focuses primarily on application-related principles and discusses very few actual teaching and training methods, its overriding theme is the demonstration of a core Burinkan teaching principle: To "teach with understanding." Like applications, teaching, coaching, and training are all guided by principles if they are to be repeatable and progressive. If this book sparks interest in such, a book may be forthcoming on the principles of teaching.

Lastly, I would like to extend a welcome from the Burinkan. If you found this book helpful to your way of training, you would likely enjoy a visit to the Burinkan to touch-hands with other like-minded teachers and explore this approach to training and teaching traditional martial arts.

Russ Smith
Chief Instructor, Burinkan Martial Arts
Burinkan.org

About the Author

Born in Michigan, Russ Smith expressed an interest in martial arts as a young teenager, and began learning karate basics with a family friend. It wasn't until Russ was on an extended visit to the Philippines in the late 1980's that he began his formal training in Japanese Goju-Ryu.

Upon his return to the USA, Russ's interest in the origins of Goju-Ryu were piqued by authors such as Patrick McCarthy, John Sells, and Mark Bishop, which led him to seek out instruction in the Okinawan version of the style.

At this point, Russ has made numerous trips overseas to train Goju-Ryu and Matayoshi Kobudo in Okinawa, and several styles of Fujian Gung Fu in Malaysia, Singapore, and the Philippines. Russ has instructor-level certifications in Goju-ryu, Matayoshi Kobudo, Five Ancestor Boxing, White Eyebrow, and Integrated Eskrima.

Russ's focus is preserving, promoting, and researching the martial traditions of Okinawa, Southern China, and the Philippines. Russ lives in Central Florida and works in the IT industry. Russ is happily married to his wife, Nicole, and has a son, Dane. Russ is honored to have many wonderful friends, mentors and teachers throughout the martial arts world.

6th generation Instructor - Goju-ryu Karate

4th generation Instructor - Matayoshi Kobudo

8th generation Instructor - Pak Mei (White Eyebrow)

6th generation Instructor - Ngo Cho Kun (Five Ancestor Boxing)

武林館

Interview with Dr. Mark Wiley

Q: **Many people know you primarily as a writer, editor, and the owner of Tambuli Media. For those that don't know about your long and extensive background in the martial arts, can you tell our readers about your background both in training and teaching martial arts?**

A: As a kid, I was beaten up walking home from school in 1979. As a result, my mother signed me up for Taekwondo lessons. I loved it and became instantly hooked. I started watching "Kung-Fu Theater" every weekend and became mesmerized by classic Kung Fu films like "Kid with the Golden Arms" and "Master Killer (The 36th Chamber of Shaolin)," and of course TV shows like "Kung-Fu" and "The Wild, Wild West." The movies and tv shows combined with subscriptions to magazines like "Kick Illustrated" and "Black Belt" and "Inside Kung-Fu," made me dream about having a life in the martial arts.

My parents also had books on their shelves about acupuncture, Chinese zodiac, Buddhism and the I-Ching. In every martial arts movie or show I saw and the books I read, the martial art master was also a healer, and there was always a "hidden manual" that held the secrets of the art. Life was clear to me: I must master martial arts, the healing arts, and write books. I started cross training in different arts as a teen and when my parents ordered Chinese food I was in heaven! Beginning in my twenties, I started traveling around the U.S. and throughout Asia to study directly under the masters of many arts that I had read about.

Over the years, I've narrowed my focus in the arts to three tracks. The first is Filipino Eskrima, which I love dearly. I have traveled around the U.S. and Philippines dozens of times to locate, train under, and interview the world's greatest Filipino masters; there are about three dozen of them. The ones who had the greatest influence on me — as in how I later shaped my own expression of the art — include, Remy Presas, Angel Cabales, Herminio Binas, Florendo Visitavion, Ramiro Estalilla, Benjamin Luna Lema, and Antonio Ilustrisimo.

The second art of deep study for me is Fukien Five Ancestor Fist (Ngo Cho Kun, Wuzuquan), under the tutelage of Sigong Alex Co of the Beng Kiam Athletic Club. There is little known in the West about Fukien Five Ancestor Fist, although it is very popular in South China and Southeast Asia. I am the only Westerner to become a lineage holder in this line of the art!

The third track is the study of self-cultivation through various methods of Qigong (energy development), Neigong (internal development), Weigong (external development), and meditation. Along with this is doctoral studies in alternative medicine, traditional Chinese medicine, and bodywork therapies. As such, this training has immersed me into the theory of body structure, balance, movement, and breath and energy receiving and expanding. This has greatly influenced my empty hand training and also broadened the mechanics of my weapons training in FMA.

Q: Can you tell us a bit about the most important principles in Fukien Five Ancestor Fist, and how these principles affect the teaching and training of the art?

A: Fukien Five Ancestor Fist is a deep system of martial movements based in concepts and principles of five other styles: Emperor Boxing, Monk Boxing, Crane Boxing, Monkey Boxing, and Do Mo's body structure methods.

There are several sets of principles or movement concepts that inform the application of the lose Ngo Cho Kun techniques found in the forms. Without these principles, their application will not be effective against a resisting (non-compliant) opponent.

1. Body Structure Development. One of the key components is how to develop a strong body structure that can receive and deploy (or issue) force. Every empty-hand form within Ngo Cho begins with the Qi Kun or "commencement fist." This short set contains a series of root movements that form the basis of every technique in the system. It also contains the method of holding the body in stance and posture while static, turning, raising, and lowering and sinking energy into the Dan Tien (elixir field), which moves energy up the spine, down through the legs into the floor, out through the arms, and through the chest. We utilize a series of "pressure tests" to train and test the strength of the body structure and root while employing the

movement concepts of "Float, Sink, Swallow, Spit" during the hand movements. When all are combined with a technique, it is referred to as Ngo Ki Lat or the unity of "Five Parts Power."

2. Four Directional Displacements. These include Float, Sink, Swallow and Spit and refer to methods of displacing your opponent's body structure to destroy balance by lifting his limbs or base (floating); lowering his limbs or body (sink); pulling him off balance (swallow); and pushing his limb or trunk backward (spit). Usually, two of these are combined for a solid technique application. For example, one might employ swallow and sink when applying a straight arm lock. This directional-displacement concept must be applied to all hand techniques to effectively counter an opponent.

3. Single and Double Hand Techniques. The hand techniques in Ngo Cho are not taught ad hoc, but related through the five categories of "single short hand," "single long hand," "double short hand," "double long hand," and "combined short and long hand" combinations. Thinking of the hands in this way, applications become informed by limb position. Double-long hand techniques, for example, could be applied when both hands simultaneously strike or push the opponent. However, they can also be applied when one hand strikes the attacking limb while the other hand strikes the body. The combined short/long hand informs techniques where there is a grab and pull along with a strike (e.g., Kao Ta).

4. Bridge Arm Theory. This is a theory that informs principles for engaging the opponent. It refers to methods of "making a bridge," "moving a bridge," "breaking a bridge," and "avoiding a bridge," among others. The principle is to use the bridge (arm contact) and apply the other principles above to employ an effective technique. This theory tells us what to do when the opponent strikes and we engage or when he blocks our counter and when our arms are crossed, etc. It is also important for knowing when to kick in Ngo Cho, as "there is no kick without a bridge."

Of course, the most effective application principle is to combine all the above in each technique. When you are attacked, you would utilize a hand technique, maintain your structure to receive force, issue force to break your opponent's structure, utilize a bridge method, and displace the opponent in one of the four directions. The solo forms and two man sets comprise the words of the style, while these four principles teach its language in conversation.

Q: Can you tell us how you reformulated your learning in the Filipino Martial Arts into a heavily principles-driven model, and why you felt it was helpful?

A: My experiences with the many masters I trained with was that some were easily able to strike me at certain times while others were not; even with the same set up and technique. Some of the masters were able to do specific disarms easily on me, while others struggled with the very same disarm technique. How could this be so if a technique was a "technique" and, thus, shouldn't it be made effective by anyone? Understanding this puzzle ("When is a technique good and when/why does it fail?") set me on a path of insight and discovery into FMA that eventually led to the development of Integrated Eskrima.

Integrated Eskrima is not a new style of FMA. It is a different way of understanding, seeing, and training the art. Every technique is compartmentalized into several areas: Mode, Range, Gate, Timing, Footwork, Angle. Once I understood each of these areas, and I categorized each segment of a technique, it became easy for me to identify why the techniques worked well sometimes and not at other times. The Integrated Eskrima curriculum is structured around developing the understanding and skills that come forth through this compartmentalized approach combined with the concepts of "Leak" and "Flow" and "Gap Filling" and others.

The basic training includes talking while doing. For example, when we practice a footwork we say, "This moves me from medium range to long range and back again, while also changing my gate from inside to outside." In this way, students learn the principles for applying the footwork (and strikes and defenses) while practicing them. Every technique has a range, footwork, striking energy, and method. By focusing and developing across many areas, students truly gain deep insight into applying FMA broadly in a short amount of time.

Sources / References

Chen, Huoyu. *Nan Shao Lin Wu Zu Quan*. Taibei Shi: Da Zhan Chu Ban She You Xian Gong Si, 2012. Print.

Cheng, Thomas. *Pak Mei Kung-fu Developed by Master Thomas Cheng*. Tin Wo Press & Publishing Co., Ltd., 2009

Choi, Sam. *Master Sam Choi Pak Mei Kung-fu & Chinese Culture*. Tin Wo Press & Publishing Co., Ltd., 2011

Co, Alexander L. *The Way of Ngo Cho Kun Kung Fu*. Jafaha Publications, 1983

Co, Alexander L. *Five Ancestor Fist Kung-fu: The Way of Ngo Cho Kun*. Rutland, VT: Charles E. Tuttle, 1997. Print.

Gang, Li. *He Quan Shu Zhen*. Tai Bei: Yi Wen Wu Zhu Wen Hua You Xian Gong Si, 2011. Print.

Han, Jin Yuan. *Fundamentals of Nan Shaolin Wuzuquan*, Vols 1-8, First Edition. Print.

Hiroshi, Takamiyagi. *Gosoku Kenpo*. 2013. Print.

Kinjō, Akio.*Karateden Shinroku: Genryūgata to Denrai No Nazo O Toku*. Tōkyō: Chanpu, 2005. Print.

Kinjō, Akio. *Karateden Shinroku: Genryūgata to Denrai No Nazo O Toku 2*. Tōkyō: Chanpu, 2005. Print.

Kōchi, Yūji. *Shōrin Zenji Den Seitō Hakkakuken*. Tōkyō: Fukush ōdō, 2004. Print.

Li, Zailuan. *Fu Jian He Quan Mi Yao*. Xin Bei Shi: Wu Zhou, 2011. Print.

Liang, Weiming. *Zhongguo Wu Gong Tu Dian = Iconographic Dictionary of Chinese Traditional Kung-fu*. Xianggang: Tian He Chuan Bo Chu Ban You Xian Gong Si, 2010. Print.

Liu, Yin Shan. *(Chinese) White Crane Gate. Feeding Crane Boxing.* 1973. Print.

Liu, Yin Shan. *(Chinese) Feeding Crane Secrets.* Print.

Liu, Gu, and Yu-zhang Su. *Bai He Men Shi He Quan.* Tai Bei Xian Zhong He Shi: Wu Zhou, 2005. Print.

McCarthy, Patrick. *The Bible of Karate. Bubishi.* Tokyo: Charles E. Tuttle, 1997. Print.

Nisan, David S. *The General Tian Wubeizhi: the Bubishi in Chinese Martial Arts History.* Lionbooks Martial Arts Co, 2016. Print.

Pan, Changan. *White Crane Sacred Hand.* 2008. Print.

Pang, Williy. *Pak Mei Kung Fu: Martial Concepts & Training Methods.* New York: TNP Multimedia, 2011. Print.

Su, Yinghan. *Yong Chun White Crane Boxing Overview.* Xiamen University Press, 2016. Print.

Wang, Yi Ying. *Minghe Quanpu (Shouting Crane Boxing Manual).* Print.

Watts, Martin. *Yong Chun White Crane Kung Fu.* Lulu Press. 2017. Print.

Wiggins, Grant P., and Jay McTighe. *Understanding by Design.* Alexandria, VA: Association for Supervision and Curriculum Development, 2008. Print.

Wiley, Mark V. *Mastering Eskrima Disarms.* Spring House, PA: Tambuli Media, 2013. Print.

Wong, Yiu Kai. *Bai Mei Martial Arts Series No. 1: Zhi Bu Biao Zhi.* Twin Age Ltd., 2012

Wong, Yiu Kai. *Bai Mei Martial Arts Series No. 2: Jiu Bu Tiu.* Twin Age Ltd., 2012

Wu, Feng. *South Family Crane Boxing Applications and Drills.* 2015. *Print.*

Xin, Chaoshe. *Fu Jian Shao Lin Quan.* Tai Bei Shi: Xin Chao She Chu Ban, 1994. Print.

Xu, Jindong, and Ye, Qinghai. *Wuzuquan Illustrated* 五祖拳圖說. Print.

Yang, Jwing-Ming, and Shou-Yu Liang. *The Essence of Shaolin White Crane - Martial Power and Qigong.* Jamaica Plain (Mass.): YMAA Publication Center, 1996. Print.

You, Fengbiao. *Zhong Hua Rou Shu Da Quan.* Tai Bei Shi: Yi Wen Wu Shu Wen Hua Chu Ban, 2008. Print.

Yu, Chiok Sam. *Chinese Gentle Art Complete: The Bible of Ngo Cho Kun.* Tambuli Media, 2014

Zheng, Weiru, and Jieping He. *Zheng Weiru Bai Mei Gong Fu.* Xianggang: Tian He Chuan Bo Chu Ban You Xian Gong Si, 2009. Print.

Zhou, Kunmin. *Quanzhou Tai Zu Quan.* Xianggang: Tian Di Tu Shu You Xian Gong Si, 2007. Print.

Zhou, Kun Min. *Quanzhou Taizuquan: The Art of Fujian Emperor Fist Kung-Fu.* Tambuli Media, 2017. Print.

Zhou, Mengyuan. *Wu Zu Quan Zhi Sheng Qi Zhao.* Beijing: Beijing Ti Yu Da Xue Chu Ban She, 1996. Print.

Zhou, Mingyuan, and Zhiqiang Zhou. *Nan Shao Lin Wu Zu Quan.* Fuzhou: Fujian Ren Min Chu Ban She, 1998. Print.

Links and errata

See Burinkan.org for links to examples and errata as well as wall charts suitable for display in your school.

Appendix A – Keyword Examples

In addition to principles, keywords are very common in martial arts, particularly the Chinese martial arts. Below is a collection of keyword "sets" found in many of the martial arts. Each set is worth considering and exploring.

Warmup Practice Study/Experiment Cool Down	Practitioners Coaches Teachers Innovators/Developers/ Adapters	Relax (Soft) Explode (Hard)
Punch Kick Throw/Sweep/Unbalance Lock/Break/Strangle	Learn Master Transcend (Shu-Ha-Ri)	High Middle Low
Train Teach Learn Exercise	Principles - Fa Attributes - Gong Techniques - Xing	High (Middle) Low
Observe Orient Decide Act	Basic Intermediate Advanced	Hands Up Hands Down
Preserve Promote Research	Kihon Kata Kumite	Float Sink
Defense Offense	Solo Partner	Swallow Spit
Singular/Isolation Combination	Inside Outside	Receive Send
Stationary Moving	Circular Straight	Realism Safety

Printed in Great
Britain
by Amazon